Lecture Notes in Computer Science 11277

Commenced Publication in 1973
Founding and Former Series Editors:
Gerhard Goos, Juris Hartmanis, and Jan van Leeuwen

Editorial Board

More information about this series at http://www.springer.com/series/7411

Noureddine Boudriga · Mohamed-Slim Alouini
Slim Rekhis · Essaid Sabir
Sofie Pollin (Eds.)

Ubiquitous Networking

4th International Symposium, UNet 2018
Hammamet, Tunisia, May 2–5, 2018
Revised Selected Papers

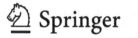 Springer

Editors
Noureddine Boudriga ⓘ
University of Carthage
Carthage, Tunisia

Mohamed-Slim Alouini ⓘ
King Abdullah University of Science
and Technology
Thuwal, Saudi Arabia

Slim Rekhis ⓘ
University of Carthage
Carthage, Tunisia

Essaid Sabir ⓘ
Hassan II University
Casablanca, Morocco

Sofie Pollin ⓘ
KU Leuven
Leuven, Belgium

ISSN 0302-9743   ISSN 1611-3349   (electronic)
Lecture Notes in Computer Science
ISBN 978-3-030-02848-0   ISBN 978-3-030-02849-7   (eBook)
https://doi.org/10.1007/978-3-030-02849-7

Library of Congress Control Number: 2018958462

LNCS Sublibrary: SL5 – Computer Communication Networks and Telecommunications

This Springer imprint is published by the registered company Springer Nature Switzerland AG
The registered company address is: Gewerbestrasse 11, 6330 Cham, Switzerland

About UNet Conference Series

UNet is an international scientific event that highlights new trends and findings in hot topics related to ubiquitous computing/networking. This fourth edition was held during May 2–5, 2018, in the fascinating city of Hammamet, Tunisia.

Ubiquitous networks sustain the development of numerous paradigms and technologies such as distributed ambient intelligence, context-awareness, cloud computing, wearable devices, and future mobile networking (e.g., B4G and 5G). Various domains are then impacted by such a system, such as security and monitoring, energy efficiency and environment protection, e-health, precision agriculture, intelligent transportation, home-care (e.g., for elderly and disabled people), etc. Communication in such a system has to cope with many constraints (e.g., limited capacity resources, energy depletion, strong fluctuations of traffic, real-time constraints, dynamic network topology, radio link breakage, interferences, etc.) and has to meet the new application requirements. Ubiquitous systems offer many promising paradigms aiming to deliver significantly higher capacity to meet the huge growth of mobile data traffic and to accommodate efficiently dense and ultra-dense systems. A crucial challenge is that ubiquitous networks should be engineered to better support existing and emerging applications including broadband multimedia, machine-to-machine applications, Internet of Things, sensor networks, and RFID technologies. Many of these systems require stringent quality-of-service constraints including better latency, reliability, higher spectral and energy efficiency, but also some quality-of-experience and quality-of-context constraints.

The main purpose of UNet Conference Series is to serve as a forum that brings together researchers and practitioners from academia and industry to discuss recent developments in pervasive and ubiquitous networks. This conference provides a forum for exchanging ideas, discussing solutions, debating the challenges identified, and sharing experiences among researchers and professionals. UNet also aims to promote adoption of new methodologies and to provide the participants with advanced and innovative tools able to catch the fundamental dynamics of the underlying complex interactions (e.g., game theory, mechanism design theory, learning theory, SDR platforms, etc.).

Welcome Message from the UNet 2018 Chairs

It is our pleasure to welcome you to the proceedings of the 2018 edition of the International Symposium on Ubiquitous Networking, UNet 2018. The conference was held in the city of Hammamet, Tunisia, during May 2–5, following up on the success of past editions. Tunisia has a growing and active community of networking researchers and the choice of Hammamet for UNet 2018 allowed its attendees, coming from all parts of the globe, to interact in a fascinating environment.

The growth of pervasive and ubiquitous networking in the past few years has been unprecedented. Today, a significant portion of the world's population is connected to the Internet most of the time through smart phones, and the Internet of Things promises to broaden the impact of the Internet to encompass devices ranging from electric appliances and medical devices to unmanned vehicles. The goal of UNet is to be a premier forum for discussing technical challenges and solutions related to such a widespread adoption of networking technologies, including broadband multimedia, machine-to-machine applications, Internet of Things, security and privacy, data engineering, sensor networks, and RFID technologies. Toward this aim, we had four main technical tracks of papers covering all the aspects of ubiquitous networks.

The UNet 2018 program featured four invited talks addressed by distinguished keynote speakers: Prof. Michele Zorzi from University of Padua (Italy), Prof. Robert Schober from Friedrich Alexander University (Germany), Prof. Moncef Gabbouj from Tampere University of Technology (Finland), and Prof. Mounir Ghogho from the International University of Rabat (Morocco)/University of Leeds (UK). This year, UNet was co-located with the IEEE 5G-IoT Summit Hammamet led by Professors Mohamed-Slim Alouini (KAUST University, Saudi Arabia), Noureddine Boudriga (University of Carthage, Tunisia), Slim Rekhis (University of Carthage, Tunisia), Fethi Tlili (University of Carthage, Tunisia), Essaid Sabir Hassan II University of Casablanca, Mustapha Benjillali (INPT, Morocco), Latif Ladid (University of Luxembourg, Luxembourg), Ashutosh Dutta (Columbia University, USA), Mounir Ghogho (International University of Rabat-Morocco/University of Leeds, UK), Walid Abdallah (Aviation School of Borj El Amri, Tunisia), and Yacine Djemaiel (Higher Institute of Technological Studies in Communications, Tunisia).

With a rich program that reflects the most recent advances in ubiquitous computing, involving a broad range of theoretical tools (e.g., game theory, mechanism design theory, learning theory, machine learning, etc.) and practical methodologies (e.g., SDR/SDN platforms, embedded systems, privacy and security by design, etc.) to study modern technologies (e.g., LTE-A, LTE-B, 5G, IoT), we were very pleased to welcome our attendees to this new edition of the UNet conference series.

We are very thankful to the Communication Networks and Security Research Lab (CN&S) from the University of Carthage, and the Tunisian Association for Research and Innovation in Telecommunication and Security (@RITS) for co-organizing this exciting event. We are grateful to our technical sponsors, without whom UNet 2018 would not have been possible. We would like to thank Springer Science+Business Media the and IPv6 Forum. We are also very thankful to all our sponsors and patrons (SUP'COM, University of Sfax, University of Tunis, TBS, ENSEM, MOBITIC).

Enjoy the proceedings!

September 2018   Noureddine Boudriga
                                                                Mohamed-Slim Alouini

Welcome Message from the UNet 2018 TPC Chairs

It is with great pleasure that we welcome you to the proceedings of the 2018 International Symposium on Ubiquitous Networking (UNet 2018), which was held in Hammamet, Tunisia. The conference featured an interesting technical program of five technical tracks reporting on recent advances in ubiquitous communication technologies and networking, ubiquitous Internet of Things: emerging technologies and breakthroughs, mobile edge networking and fog-cloud computing, data engineering for ubiquitous environments, and cyber-security for ubiquitous communication. UNet 2018 also featured four keynote speeches by world-class experts, and one invited paper session.

We received 87 paper submissions from 19 countries and four continents. From these, 30 regular papers and five short papers were accepted after a careful review process to be included in the UNet 2018 proceedings. The regular-paper acceptance rate was 34% whereas the overall acceptance rate in UNet 2018 was 40%.

The preparation of this excellent program would not have been possible without the dedication and the hard work of the different chairs, the keynote speakers, and all the Technical Program Committee members and reviewers. We take this the opportunity to acknowledge their valuable work, and sincerely thank them for their help in ensuring that UNet 2018 will be remembered as a high-quality event.

We hope that you will enjoy this edition's proceedings.

September 2018

Slim Rekhis
Essaid Sabir
Sofie Pollin

Organization

Organizing Committee

General Chairs

Noureddine Boudriga   University of Carthage, Tunisia
Mohamed-Slim Alouini   King Abdullah University of Science and Technology, Saudi Arabia

Technical Program Chairs

Slim Rekhis   University of Carthage, Tunisia
Essaid Sabir   ENSEM, Hassan II University of Casablanca, Morocco
Sofie Pollin   KU Leuven, Leuven, Belgium

Main Tracks Chairs

Mustapha Benjillali   INPT, Morocco
Adel Ghazel   University of Carthage, Tunisia
Halima ELbiaze   University of Quebec at Montreal (UQAM), Canada
Mounir Ghogho   International University of Rabat-Morocco/University of Leeds, UK
Sabrina De Capitani di Vimercati   University of Milan, Italy

Publication Chairs

Bruno Miguel Silva   University of Beira Interior, Portugal
Mohamed Sadik   ENSEM, Hassan II University of Casablanca, Morocco

Workshops and Special Sessions Chairs

Rachid EL-Azouzi   University of Avignon, France
Tembine Hamidou   New York University of Abu Dhabi, Abu Dhabi, UAE

Tutorial Chairs

Fethi Tlili   University of Carthage, Tunisia
Mohamed El Kamili   Sidi Mohammed Ben Abdellah University of Fez, Morocco

Local Arrangements and Registration Chairs

Walid Abdallah   Aviation School of Borj El Amri, Tunisia
Yacine Djemaiel   Higher Institute of Technological Studies in Communications, Tunisia

Publicity Chairs

Lamia Chaari	University of Sfax, Tunisia
Tania Jiménez	University of Avignon, France
Abdellatif Kobbane	ENSIAS, Mohammed V University of Rabat, Morocco
Wessam Ajib	University of Quebec at Montreal (UQAM), Canada
Dario Bauso	University of Palermo, Italy
Jong-Hoon Kim	Kent State University, USA
Sami J. Habib	Kuwait University, Kuwait

Technical Program Committee

Abdelhamid Belmekki	INPT, Morocco
Abdellatif Kobbane	Mohammed V University of Rabat, Morocco
Abdelmajid Badri	Hassan II University of Casablanca, Morocco
Abdelmajid Khelil	Landshut University of Applied Sciences, Germany
Abdulkadir Celik	King Abdullah University of Science and Technology, Saudi Arabia
Abdulrahman Alabbasi	KTH Royal Institute of Technology, Sweden
Adel Ghazel	University of Carthage, Tunisia
Ahmed El Maliani Drissi	Sidi Mohammed Ben Abdellah University, Morocco
Alessandro Chiumento	KU Leuven, Belgium
Alonso Silva	Nokia Bell Labs, France
Al-Sakib Khan Pathan	Southeast University, Bangladesh
Amal Hyadi	McGill University, Canada
Antoine Bagula	University of the Western Cape, South Africa
Asma Ben Letaifa	University of Carthage, Tunisia
Basem Shihada	King Abdullah University of Science and Technology, Saudi Arabia
Bruno Miguel Silva	University of Beira Interior, Portugal
Bruno Tuffin	Inria, Rennes, France
Carlos Alberto Kamienski	Federal University of ABC, Brazil
Dhananjay Singh	Hankuk University of Foreign Studies, South Korea
Dhouha Krichen	University of Carthage, Tunisia
Dieter Fiems	Ghent University, Belgium
Dimosthenis Ioannidis	Centre for Research and Technology Hellas, Greece
Donghyun Kim	Kennesaw State University, USA
Elarbi Badidi	United Arab Emirates University, UAE
Emna Zedini	King Abdullah University of Science and Technology, Saudi Arabia
Faissal El Bouanani	Mohammed V University in Rabat, Morocco
Fatma Benkhelifa	King Abdullah University of Science and Technology, Saudi Arabia
Fethi Tlili	University of Carthage, Tunisia
Francisco Javier Lopez-Martinez	University of Malaga, Spain

Gabriele Anderst-Kotsis   Johannes Kepler University Linz, Austria
Giampaolo Bella   Catania University, Italy
Gianluigi Ferrari   University of Parma, Italy
Giuseppe Ruggeri   Mediterranea University, Italy
Gyu Myoung Lee   Liverpool John Moores University, UK
Habib Fathallah   University of Carthage, Tunisia
Haijun Zhang   University of Science and Technology Beijing, China
Hakim Ghazzai   Qatar Mobility Innovations Center, Qatar
Halima ELbiaze   University of Quebec at Montreal, Canada
Hamza Dahmouni   INPT, Morocco
Hongjiang Lei   Chongqing University of Posts and
   Telecommunications, China
Houbing Song   Embry-Riddle Aeronautical University, USA
Houria Rezig   El Manar University, Tunisia
Hyunbum Kim   University of North Carolina at Wilmington, USA
Imran Ansari   Texas A&M University at Qatar, Qatar
Ismail Berrada   Sidi Mohamed Ben Abdellah University, Morocco
Jean-Pierre Cances   University of Limoges, France
Joel Rodrigues   National Institute of Telecommunications (Inatel),
   Brazil
Jong-Hoon Kim   Kent State University, USA
José Luis Hernandez Ramos   University of Murcia, Spain
Krzysztof Szczypiorski   Warsaw University of Technology (WUT), Poland
Kumar Yelamarthi   Central Michigan University, USA
Lamia Chaari   University of Sfax, Tunisia
Leila Boulahia   University of Technology of Troyes, France
Liang Yang   Guangdong University of Technology, China
Lin Cai   Illinois Institute of Technology, USA
Loubna Echabbi   INPT, Morocco
Luis Quesada   University College Cork, Ireland
Maha Sliti   University of Carthage, Tunisia
Mahdi Ben Ghorbel   University of British Columbia, Canada
Majed Haddad   University of Avignon, France
Md Zakirul Alam Bhuiyan   Fordham University, USA
Megumi Kaneko   National Institute of Informatics, Japan
Michael Losavio   University of Louisville, USA
Miguel Franklin de Castro   Federal University of Ceará, Brazil
Mohamed El Kamili   Sidi Mohammed Ben Abdellah University of Fez,
   Morocco
Mohamed Koubaa   University of Tunis El Manar, Tunisia
Mohamed Raiss El Fenni   INPT, Morocco
Mohamed Sadik   Hassan II University of Casablanca, Morocco
Mohammed Erradi   Mohammed V University, Morocco
Mojtaba Aajami   Yonsei University, South Korea
Mort Naraghi-Pour   Louisiana State University, USA
Mouna Garai   DGET, Tunisia

Mounir Ghogho	International University of Rabat-Morocco/University of Leeds, UK
Mourad El Yadari	Moulay Ismail University, Morocco
Mudassir Masood	King Fahd University of Petroleum and Minerals, Saudi Arabia
Muhammad Ali Imran	University of Glasgow, UK
Murat Uysal	Ozyegin University, Turkey
Mustapha Benjillali	INPT, Morocco
Nabil Benamar	Moulay Ismail University, Morocco
Nasir Saeed	King Abdullah University of Science and Technology, Saudi Arabia
Neji Youssef	University of Carthage, Tunisia
Nik Bessis	Edge Hill University, UK
Nourhene Ellouze	University of Jendouba, Tunisia
Olivier Brun	LAAS-CNRS, France
Oussama Elissati	INPT, Morocco
Oussama Habachi	University of Limoges, France
Paolo Bellavista	University of Bologna, Italy
Parul Garg	University of Delhi, India
Paulvanna Nayaki Marimuthu	Kuwait University, Kuwait
Ping Zhou	Qualcomm, USA
Rabah Attia	University of Carthage, Tunisia
Rachid EL-Azouzi	University of Avignon, France
Rachid Saadane	EHTP, Morocco
Razvan Stanica	INSA Lyon, France
Rick McGeer	University of California, USA
Ridha Hamila	Qatar University, Qatar
Rosa Figueiredo	University of Avignon, France
Sabrina De Capitani di Vimercati	University of Milan, Italy
Said Andaloussi	University of Hassan II, Morocco
Salah Benabdallah	University of Tunis, Tunisia
Salvatore Distefano	University of Kazan, Russia
Sami Faiez	Manouba University, Tunisia
Sami Habib	Kuwait University, Kuwait
Sarra Berrahal	University of Carthage, Tunisia
Satish Chikkagoudar	Pacific Northwest National Laboratory, USA
Sergio Saponara	University of Pisa, Italy
Seyeong Choi	Wonkwang University, South Korea
Sherali Zeadally	University of Kentucky, USA
Sofiane Cherif	University of Carthage, Tunisia
Stefano Chessa	University of Pisa, Italy
Stefanos Gritzalis	University of the Aegean, Greece
Stylianos Basagiannis	United Technologies Research Centre, Ireland
Sung Sik Nam	Korea University, South Korea

UNᴇᴛ'18 Keynote Speakers

UNIT 18 Network Operators

Overview of Artificial Intelligence, Machine Learning and Big Data Analytics with Applications in Various Decision-Making Environments

Moncef Gabbouj

Tampere University of Technology, Finland

Abstract. Artificial Intelligence (AI) can be defined in many ways, but one thing all experts agree upon is the key role machine learning plays in AI. This keynote will adopt a tutorial style to first provide a quick overview of the current state of AI and reviews in some details the main approaches followed in machine learning, with a special focus on the more recent advances in deep learning and neural networks. We will also present a hierarchical layered approach that exploits many types of sensor and non-sensor signals and data, and proposes suitable representations, as well as processing and analysis algorithms in order to apply machine learning, including deep and shallow learning. The framework can be explored in various decision-making environments, including healthcare and wellbeing, surveillance, and media and entertainment to mention a few fields.

Biography

Moncef Gabbouj received his BS degree in electrical engineering in 1985 from Oklahoma State University, Stillwater, and his MS and PhD degrees in electrical engineering from Purdue University, West Lafayette, Indiana, in 1986 and 1989, respectively.

Dr. Gabbouj is a Professor of Signal Processing at the Department of Signal Processing, Tampere University of Technology, Tampere, Finland, where he leads the Multimedia Research Group. Dr. Gabbouj held the prestigious post of Academy Professor with the Academy of Finland 2011–2015. He held several visiting professorships at different universities, including The Hong Kong University of Science and Technology, Hong Kong (2012–2013), Purdue University, West Lafayette, Indiana, USA (August–December 2011), the University of Southern California (January–June 2012), and the American University of

Sharjah, UAE, (2007–2008). He was Head of the Department during 2002–2007, and served as Senior Research Fellow of the Academy of Finland in 1997–1998 and 2007–2008. His research interests include multimedia content-based analysis, indexing and retrieval, machine learning, nonlinear signal and image processing and analysis, voice conversion, and video processing and coding.

Dr. Gabbouj is a Fellow of the IEEE, a member of the European Academy and the Finnish Academy of Science and Letters. He is the past Chairman of the DSP Technical Committee of the IEEE Circuits and Systems Society and member of the IEEE Fourier Award for Signal Processing Committee. He was Honorary Guest Professor of Jilin University, China (2005–2010). He served as associate editor of the IEEE Transactions on Image Processing, and was guest editor of Multimedia Tools and Applications, the European journal Applied Signal Processing. He is the past chairman of the IEEE Finland Section, the IEEE Circuits and Systems Society, Technical Committee on Digital Signal Processing, and the IEEE SP/CAS Finland Chapter. He was also (co-)Chairman of BigDataSE 2015, EUVIP 2014, CBMI 2005, and WIAMIS 2001.

Robotic Communication: When Communication Theory Meets Control Theory

Mounir Ghogho

International University of Rabat-Morocco/University of Leeds, UK

Abstract. Mobile robots (terrestrial and aerial) are gaining importance in an increasing number of applications. They often require wireless communication capabilities to complete their tasks, and in some applications the main task of the robot is communication/relaying of information. The conventional approach to adding communications capabilities to mobile robots does not leverage the fact that the robot can control its position and can hence move in such a way as to improve the communication performance through spatial/mobility diversity. Since the energy consumption due to mobility is tightly linked to the robot's state vector transitions (kinematics and dynamics) over time, communication-aware path/trajectory planning requires a good knowledge of both control theory and communication theory. Therefore, designing efficient communication systems for mobile robots calls for a new paradigm where control theory plays a pivotal role. In this talk, this paradigm will be described and illustrated through examples, and new research opportunities will be presented.

Biography

Mounir Ghogho received his PhD degree in 1997 from the National Polytechnic Institute of Toulouse, France. He was an EPSRC Research Fellow with the University of Strathclyde (Scotland), from Sept 1997 to Nov 2001. In December 2001, he joined the University of Leeds where he was promoted to full Professor in 2008. While still affiliated with the University of Leeds, he joined the International University of Rabat (UIR) in January 2010, where he is currently the Director of TICLab (ICT Research Laboratory) and Scientific Advisor to the President. He is a Fellow of IEEE, a recipient of the 2013 IBM Faculty Award, and a recipient of the 2000 UK Royal Academy of Engineering Research Fellowship. He is currently an associate editor of the IEEE Signal Processing Magazine and a member of the steering committee of the Transactions of Signal and Information Processing. In the past, he served as an Associate Editor of the IEEE Transactions on Signal Processing and IEEE Signal Processing

Letters, a member of the IEEE Signal Processing Society SPCOM, SPTM and SAM Technical Committee. He chaired many conferences and workshops including the European SIgnal Processing conference Eusipco2013 and the IEEE workshop on Signal Processing for Advanced Wireless Communications SPAWC'2010. He is the Eurasip Liaison in Morocco.

Spectrum Sharing and Networking Issues in 5G mmWave Cellular Networks

Michele Zorzi

University of Padova, Italy

Abstract. This talk will discuss some relevant networking issues for 5G mmWave cellular systems. First, we will give an extensive discussion on the potential benefits and technical challenges of spectrum sharing in a mmWave context. We will show that from this points of view this scenario is much more promising than traditional cellular systems in sub-6 GHz bands. We will also discuss the role of coordination between different operators for the purpose of managing the inter- and intra-system interference, which is shown to be the ultimate limiting factor in spectrum sharing. Second, we will discuss how directionality makes it more difficult to implement and operate network management functionalities, with specific reference to Initial Access and Cell Search, where the energy/latency/detection tradeoff is of particular interest. Finally, we will briefly describe our full-stack 5G mmWave cellular simulator, which includes the whole protocol suite as well as detailed mmWave channel models, and present some examples of system-level results it can provide.

Biography

Michele Zorzi was born in Venice, Italy, on December 6th, 1966. He received the Laurea Degree and the Ph.D. in Electrical Engineering from the University of Padova, Italy, in 1990 and 1994, respectively. During the Academic Year 1992/93, he was on leave at the University of California, San Diego (UCSD), attending graduate courses and doing research on multiple access in mobile radio networks. In 1993, he joined the faculty of the Dipartimento di Elettronica e Informazione, Politecnico di Milano, Italy. After spending three years with the Center for Wireless Communications at UCSD, in 1998 he joined the School of Engineering of the University of Ferrara, Italy, where he became a Professor in 2000. Since November 2003, he has been on the faculty at the Information Engineering Department of the University of Padova. His present research interests include performance evaluation in mobile communications systems, random access in mobile radio networks, ad hoc and sensor networks, energy constrained communications protocols, and broadband wireless access.

Dr. Zorzi was the Editor-In-Chief of the IEEE Wireless Communications Magazine in 2003–2005, is currently the Editor-In-Chief of the IEEE Transactions on Communications, and serves on the Editorial Boards of the IEEE Transactions on Wireless Communications, the Wiley Journal of Wireless Communications and Mobile Computing and the ACM/URSI/Kluwer Journal of Wireless Networks. He was also guest editor for special issues in the IEEE Personal Communications Magazine ("Energy Management in Personal Communications Systems," Jun. 1998) and the IEEE Journal on Selected Areas in Communications ("Multi-media Network Radios," May 1999, and "Underwater Wireless Communications and Networks," to be published in 2008). He is a Fellow of the IEEE.

Synthetic Molecular Communication for Future Nano-Communication Networks

Robert Schober

Friedrich Alexander University (FAU), Erlangen, Germany

Abstract. Synthetic molecular communication is an emerging research area offering many interesting and challenging new research problems for communication engineers, biologists, chemists, and physicists. Synthetic molecular communication is widely considered to be an attractive option for communication between nano-devices such as (possibly artificial) cells and nano-sensors. Possible applications of nano-communication networks include targeted drug delivery, health monitoring, environmental monitoring, and bottom-up^2 manufacturing. The IEEE and ACM have recently founded several new conferences and journals dedicated to this exciting new and fast growing research area.

In this keynote, we will give first a general overview of the areas of synthetic molecular communication and nano-networking. Components of synthetic molecular communication networks, possible applications, and the evolution of the field will be reviewed. Subsequently, we will give an introduction to various synthetic molecular communication strategies such as gap junctions, molecular motors, and diffusion based molecular communication. Thereby, we will focus particularly on diffusion based synthetic molecular communication, identify the relevant basic laws of physics and discuss their implications for communication system design. One particular challenge in the design of diffusive synthetic molecular communication systems is intersymbol interference. We will discuss corresponding mitigation techniques and provide some results. Furthermore, we will present several receiver design options for diffusive synthetic molecular communication, discuss their respective advantages and disadvantages, and elaborate on the impact of external phenomena such as molecule degradation and flow. In the last part of the talk, we will discuss some research challenges in synthetic molecular communication from a communication and networking point of view.

Biography

Robert Schober received the Diplom (Univ.) and the Ph. D. degrees in electrical engineering from Friedrich-Alexander University Erlangen-Nuremberg (FAU), Germany, in 1997 and 2000, respectively. From May 2001 to April 2002 he was a Postdoctoral Fellow at the University of Toronto, Canada, sponsored by the German Academic Exchange Service (DAAD). From 2002 to 2011, he was a Professor and Canada Research Chair at the University of British Columbia (UBC), Vancouver, Canada. Since January 2012 he is an Alexander von Humboldt Professor and the Chair for Digital Communication at FAU. His research interests fall into the broad areas of Communication Theory, Wireless Communications, and Statistical Signal Processing.

Robert received several awards for his work including the 2007 Wilhelm Friedrich Bessel Research Award of the Alexander von Humboldt Foundation, the 2008 Charles McDowell Award for Excellence in Research from UBC, a 2011 Alexander von Humboldt Professorship, a 2012 NSERC E.W.R. Stacie Fellowship, and the 2017 Wireless Communication Technical Committee Recognition Award. In addition, he has received several best paper awards for his research and is listed as a 2017 Highly Cited Researcher by the Web of Science. Robert is a Fellow of the Canadian Academy of Engineering, a Fellow of the Engineering Institute of Canada, and a Fellow of the IEEE. From 2012 to 2015, he served as Editor-in-Chief of the IEEE Transactions on Communications. Currently, he is the Chair of the Steering Committee of the IEEE Transactions on Molecular, Biological and Multiscale Communication and serves on the Editorial Board of the Proceedings of the IEEE. Furthermore, he is a Member at Large of the Board of Governors and a Distinguished Lecturer of the IEEE Communications Society.

Contents

Mobile Edge Networking and Fog-Cloud Computing

Ubiquitous Internet of Things: Emerging Technologies and Breakthroughs

Cyber Security for Ubiquitous Communications

Special Session on Wireless Networking, Applications and Enabling Technologies for Unmanned Aerial Vehicles

Ubiquitous Communication
Technologies and Networking

Comparative Study of Estimation Algorithms for Predistorter Coefficients of GaN Power Amplifier

Haithem Rezgui[✉], Fatma Rouissi[✉], and Adel Ghazel[✉]

GRESCOM Lab, SUP'COM, University of Carthage,
Cité Technologique des Communications, El Ghazala, Ariana, Tunisia
{haithem.rezgui, fatma.rouissi, adel.ghazel}@supcom.tn

Abstract. The purpose of this paper is to compare two estimation methods when identifying the coefficients of the Simplified Volterra Series (SVS) model, in order to linearize a class AB GaN Power Amplifier (PA) driven by a 20-MHz LTE-A signal. First, a Digital Predistorter (DPD) design using the cholesky decomposition based inversion method and the Least Square QR (LSQR) algorithm is carried out, and next the performances of each method are analyzed in terms of computational complexity and suppressing distortions capability. The co-simulation test results show that the LSQR performs better than Cholesky decomposition in terms of Adjacent Channel Power Ratio (ACPR) and Normalized Mean Square Error (NMSE) by a margin of 3 dB and 4 dB, receptively.

Keywords: RF power amplifier · Digital predistortion · Volterra series
Estimation algorithms · Look-up table (LUT)

1 Introduction

To compensate the Power Amplifier (PA) nonlinearity, Baseband Digital Predistortion (DPD) has been widely used as one of the most advantageous linearization techniques [1–7]. The DPD technique is based on the PA behavior characterization in order to produce its mathematical inverse function. This mathematical model is then placed before the PA stage to correct its nonlinearity and the final output signal will be linear according to the original input signal [2].

Recently, the bandwidth employed in modern wireless communication systems continues to increase to satisfy the consumers' requirements in term of data rates. Long Term Evolution (LTE) and LTE advanced (LTE-A) systems are characterized by a wide signal bandwidth that can achieve 100 MHz, and this disturbs the design of the RF transmitter, such as the characterization of the PA behavior which becomes highly nonlinear when the bandwidth increases [1, 4].

Commonly, memory polynomial models functions have been used in the literature, essentially, the widely known Memory Polynomial (MP) model [2] and the Wiener and the Hammerstein models [3]. Recently, Volterra Series (VS) models and its reduced forms have gained a considerable attention because of its high efficiency compared to

© Springer Nature Switzerland AG 2018
N. Boudriga et al. (Eds.): UNet 2018, LNCS 11277, pp. 3–13, 2018.
https://doi.org/10.1007/978-3-030-02849-7_1

the other models [4]. However, estimation algorithms used to identify the models coefficients need to be focused on. In [4], the Compressed Sampling Matching Pursuit (CoSaMP) technique is applied for an assortment of well-known models as the MP and the Simplified Volterra Series (SVS) models to extract their coefficients and to reduce the DPD implementation complexity. The test results given for a Doherty PA using a 100-MHz LTE-A signal show an Adjacent Channel Power Ratio (ACPR) improvement of 12 dB. One drawback of CoSaMP based DPD is that such algorithms are typically slow. Sparse Bayesian Learning (SBL) approach is used in [5] to identify the parameters of the PA behavioral model and the coefficients of the predistorter inverse function. The experimental results show that with this technique, the ACPR can achieve the communication standard obligation.

The objective of the present work is to compare two different mathematics algorithms to estimate the SVS model coefficients [4]: an iterative method based on the Least Square QR (LSQR) theory [8] and a direct method based on the cholesky decomposition [9, 10]. Then a proposed DPD architecture is implemented and tested using measured data from a highly nonlinear class AB GaN PA driven by a 20-MHz LTE-A signal. The Normalized Mean Square Error (NMSE), and the ACPR metrics are used to compare the performances of the two methods.

2 SVS Model Overview

2.1 VS Model

The modeled complex output $y_{vs}(n)$ at a time instant n is mathematically related to the complex input sample $x(n)$ and the precedent sames $x(n - q_K)$ through [4]:

$$
\begin{aligned}
y_{VS}(n) = & \sum_{q_1=0}^{Q-1} w_1(q_1) \times (n - q_1) \\
& + \sum_{q_1=0}^{Q-1} \sum_{q_2=q_1}^{Q-1} w_2(q_1, q_2) \times (n - q_1) \times (n - q_2) \\
& + \sum_{q_1=0}^{Q-1} \sum_{q_2=q_1}^{Q-1} \sum_{q_3=q_2}^{Q-1} w_3(q_1, q_2, q_3) \times (n - q_1) \times (n - q_2) \times (n - q_3) + \ldots \\
& + \sum_{q_1=0}^{Q-1} \sum_{q_2=q_1}^{Q-1} \ldots \sum_{q_K=q_{K-1}}^{Q-1} w_k(q_1, q_2 \ldots q_k) \times (n - q_1) \times (n - q_2) \ldots \times (n - q_K)
\end{aligned}
\tag{1}
$$

Where K and Q are the nonlinearity order and the memory depth, respectively, $w_k(q_1, q_2 \ldots q_k)$ is named the discrete-time coefficient of the Kth Volterra kernel order.

Checking Eq. (1), the number of terms to be extracted rises exponentially with the order of nonlinearity and memory depth. That's why, simplified variants of the VS models are used to model the highly nonlinear PAs and to establish the predistorter inverse function.

2.2   SVS Model

A new pruned VS model that combines three simplification aspects was developed in [4]. The SVS model takes advantage of an additional complex branch which allows to suppress the IQ-imbalance drawbacks as presented in [11]. In order to reduce the overall number of coefficients, the model employs the magnitude $|x(n)|$ of the input samples as reported in [12]. Also, another simplification is based on the use of the Dynamic Deviation Reduction (DDR) approach [13] so each sample $x(n)$ is factored into the input entries with n to $n - D$ indices, where D represents the DDR order. Thus, the equation that defines the SVS model can be given as [4]:

$$y_{SVS}(n) = y_A(n) + y_B(n) \tag{2}$$

$$
y_A(n) = \sum_{q_1=0}^{Q-1} w_{a1}(q_1)x(n - q_1)
$$

$$
+ \sum_{q_1=0}^{Q-1} \sum_{q_2=q_1-D}^{q_1} w_{a2}(q_1, q_2)x(n - q_1)|x(n - q_2)|
$$

$$
+ \sum_{q_1=0}^{Q-1} \sum_{q_2=q_1-D}^{q_1} \sum_{q_3=q_2-D}^{q_2} w_{a3}(q_1, q_2, q_3)x(n - q_1)|x(n - q_2)||x(n - q_3)| + \ldots
$$

$$
+ \sum_{q_1=0}^{Q-1} \sum_{q_2=q_1-D}^{q_1} \cdots \sum_{q_k=q_{k-1}-D}^{q_k-1} wa_k(q_1, q_2 \ldots q_k)x(n - q_1)|x(n - q_2)| \ldots |x(n - q_k)|
$$

$$\tag{3}$$

$$
y_B(n) = \sum_{q_1=0}^{Q-1} w_{b1}(q_1)x(n - q_1)^*
$$

$$
+ \sum_{q_1=0}^{Q-1} \sum_{q_2=q_1-D}^{q_1} w_{b2}(q_1, q_2)x(n - q_1)^*|x(n - q_2)|
$$

$$
+ \sum_{q_1=0}^{Q-1} \sum_{q_2=q_1-D}^{q_1} \sum_{q_3=q_2-D}^{q_2} w_{b3}(q_1, q_2, q_3)x(n - q_1)^*|x(n - q_2)||x(n - q_3)| + \cdots
$$

$$
+ \sum_{q_1=0}^{Q-1} \sum_{q_2=q_1-D}^{q_1} \cdots \sum_{q_k=q_{k-1}-D}^{q_{k-1}} w_{bk}(q_1, q_2 \ldots q_k)x(n - q_1)^*|x(n - q_2)| \ldots |x(n - q_k)|
$$

$$\tag{4}$$

Where $y_{SVS}(n)$ and $x(n)$ are the complex output and input of the model, respectively, w_a and w_b are the coefficients of the SVS model.

3   Estimation Algorithms Overview

Various types of least square algorithms have been used to extract the models coefficients. The straightforward method is to formulate the SVS model function in (2), (3) and (4) using the generic linear system expressed as [14]:

$$\tilde{\mathbf{y}} = \mathbf{\Phi}_x \cdot \mathbf{W}_x \tag{5}$$

The output vector $\tilde{\mathbf{y}}$ of dimension $M \times 1$, is an estimate of the measured output waveform $\mathbf{y}$, where M is the entire number of samples. Each output signal $\tilde{y}(n)$ at an instant n corresponds to a $M \times 1$ vector $\mathbf{\Phi}_x(n)$ created with the input signal as depicted in [15]. $\mathbf{\Phi}_x$ is $M \times N$ matrix that assembly all the $\mathbf{\Phi}_x(n)$ vectors where N is the total number of the model coefficients. $\mathbf{W}_x$ is a $N \times 1$ vector including the model coefficients. We pursue a similar method to establish the predistorter coefficients as:

$$\tilde{\mathbf{x}} = \mathbf{\Phi}_y \cdot \mathbf{W}_y \tag{6}$$

And the estimation error is written as:

$$e(n) = x(n) - \tilde{x}(n) \tag{7}$$

The estimated input vector $\tilde{x}$ is generated from the output vector $\mathbf{y}$ as demonstrated in Fig. 1, so, $\mathbf{\Phi}_y$ is established similar to $\mathbf{\Phi}_x$ with $y(n)$ instead of $x(n)$. To estimate the predistorter coefficients, the Least Square (LS) method based on the minimization of the square of the residual function $\|e\|_2$, where $\|\cdot\|_2$ stands for the Euclidean norm [16] is applied in this work. Thus, the predistorter coefficients are defined as [15]:

$$\mathbf{W}_y = \left(\mathbf{\Phi}_y^H \mathbf{\Phi}_y \right)^{-1} \mathbf{\Phi}_y^H \cdot \mathbf{x} \tag{8}$$

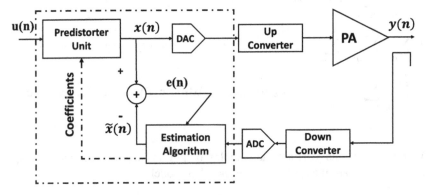

Fig. 1. Simplified block diagram of the proposed DPD architecture

W_y is the estimated LS solution of (8) where $\mathbf{\Phi}_y^H$ denotes the complex conjugate transpose of matrix $\mathbf{\Phi}_y$. The Eq. (8) requires a complex inversion of the covariance matrix $(\mathbf{\Phi}_y^H \mathbf{\Phi}_y)$ of dimension $N \times N$.

For large dimension matrices, matrix inversion becomes very difficult, the cholesky decomposition method and the LSQR algorithm are used in this work to deal with this issue.

3.1 Matrix Inversion Based on the Cholesky Decomposition

The cholesky decomposition method allows to obtain easily the inverse matrix $\left(\mathbf{\Phi}_y^H \mathbf{\Phi}_y\right)^{-1}$, due to its efficiency to deal with linear equation [9].

Let our target matrix:

$$U = \mathbf{\Phi}_y^H \mathbf{\Phi}_y \tag{9}$$

First, cholesky approach decomposes U as the product of an upper triangular matrix S and its transpose conjugate such that:

$$U = S^H S \tag{10}$$

Where s_{ij} are the elements of S $(1 \leq i \leq j \leq N)$ given by [9, 10]:

Diagonal part: $s_{ii} = \sqrt{u_{ii} - \sum_{K=1}^{i-1} s_{ki}^* s_{ki}}$

Upper terms: $s_{ij} = \frac{1}{s_{ii}} \left(u_{ij} - \sum_{k=1}^{i-1} s_{ki}^* s_{kj}\right)$

Where u_{ij} are the elements of U $(1 \leq i \leq N, 1 \leq j \leq N)$ and s_{ki}^* is the conjugate value of s_{ki}.

This implies:

$$U^{-1} = S^{-1} S^{H^{-1}} \tag{11}$$

Let's define $P = S^{-1}$, where $P = (p_1, p_2 \ldots p_N)$ is computed as follows:

$$S \times \mathbf{p_i} = \mathbf{id_i} \tag{12}$$

Where $\mathbf{id_i}$ are the columns of the identity matrix
Once P is computed, we can easily calculate U^{-1} as:

$$U^{-1} = PP^H \tag{13}$$

3.2 Coefficients Estimation Based on the LSQR Algorithm

In this case, the Eq. (8) can be solved by obtaining W_y as:

$$\mathbf{\Phi}_y^H \mathbf{\Phi}_y . \mathbf{W}_y = \mathbf{\Phi}_y^H . \mathbf{x} \tag{14}$$

Let $\mathbf{Z} = \mathbf{\Phi}_y^H . \mathbf{x}$, Eq. (13) can be rewritten as:

$$\mathbf{U} . \mathbf{W}_y = \mathbf{Z} \tag{15}$$

LSQR is an iterative algorithm which was proposed in [8] for solving least square linear problem. This approach is equivalent to the conjugate gradient least square (CGLS) but requires fewer iterations to obtain similar results [17]. Based on the bi-diagonalization method, LSQR uses a regularization parameter β_{LSQR} and solves (15) as [17]:

$$\min_{\mathbf{W}_y}(\|\mathbf{Z} - \mathbf{U}\mathbf{W}_y\|_2^2 + \beta_{LSQR}^2 \|\mathbf{W}_y\|_2^2) \tag{16}$$

For each iteration LSQR generates an estimated solution $\mathbf{W}_{y_i}$ in order to minimize the residual norm $\|\mathbf{Z} - \mathbf{U}\mathbf{W}_y\|_2$.

4   Implementation and Test Results

Figure 1 presents the bloc diagram of the DPD stage where $u(n)$ is the input signal to the predistorter unit, whose output $x(n)$ feeds the PA to produce output $y(n)$.

In this work, we have employed the measured input/output data from a class AB GaN PA using a 20-MHz LTE-A signal with a one-carrier configuration. The input signal has a peak-to-average power ratio (PARP) of 7.5 dB and was sampled at 92.16 MHz. The proposed DPD is based on the SVS model with $K = 7$, $Q = 4$ and $D = 2$. Also, the predistorter coefficients were extracted from a training data of 8000 samples which implies that $M = 8000$ and $N = 616$.

The co-simulation test set-up has been developed to compare the performances of the cholesky decomposition method and the LSQR algorithm in identifying the coefficients of the proposed DPD solution. Hence, the test set-up is performed using:

- A Matlab-based model of a class AB GaN PA using a 20-MHz LTE-A signal.
- A Matlab-based processing of the estimation algorithms.
- An FPGA-based implementation of the Predistorter unit.

4.1   FPGA Implementation

The estimated coefficients obtained from the estimation algorithm block are copied to the predistorter unit to predistort the input signal as shown in Fig. 1. In this work, 616 coefficients are used to construct the SVS model polynomial function. That's why a large number of multipliers and adders are needed to implement the predistorter unit. For this reason, the Look Up Table (LUT) solution [18] is used to implement the predistorter function in FPGA as detailed in Fig. 2.

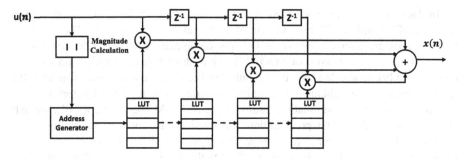

Fig. 2. LUT-based predistorter unit

The proposed DPD design has been implemented in VHDL, on the target Xilinx FPGA Zynq-7000SoC XC7Z020-CLG4841. The FPGA used resources for the designed predistorter are reported in Table 1.

Table 1. FPGA used resources.

Resources	Used	Available	Percentage
Slice LUTs	3299	78600	4.19%
Slice registers	709	157200	0.45%
Block RAM	56	285	19.64%
DSP48E1	220	400	55%

Obtained results show that the proposed predistorter takes up a little portion of the Slice LUTs and Slice Registers available resources however, it occupies 55% of the total DSP48E1 cores. To counteract this, mathematical methods to simplify the predistorter models are required.

4.2   Test Results

The linearization performances of the proposed DPD in terms of ACPR and the NMSE between the output signal and the original input signal for each method are summarized in Table 2.

Table 2. ACPR and NMSE comparison

Configuration	Cholesky decomposition			LSQR algorithm		
	ACPR		NMSE	ACPR		NMSE
	Upper	Lower		Upper	Lower	
No DPD	−36.19	−36.81	–	−36.19	−36.81	–
With DPD	−38.94	−40.39	−32.43	−43.12	−43.56	−36.86

In Table 2 we notice that LSQR performs better than cholesky decomposition in terms of ACPR and NMSE by a margin of 3 dB and 4 dB, receptively. The enhanced performances are also confirmed by the low complexity of the LSQR, because its running time is on the order of $O(N)$ [17], while the Cholesky requires time on the order $O(N^3)$ [9], where N is the total number of the model coefficients. Note that, the results seen above are obtained after only 188 iterations of the LSQR algorithm.

Figure 3 reports the simulation results of the AM–AM characteristics of class AB GaN PA with and without predistortion. Obtained results approve the ability of the proposed DPD architecture to suppress the nonlinear distortion (static nonlinearity + memory effect). It can be seen that the LSQR algorithm based DPD allows for a better linear behavior which confirms the obtained linearization performances given in Table 2.

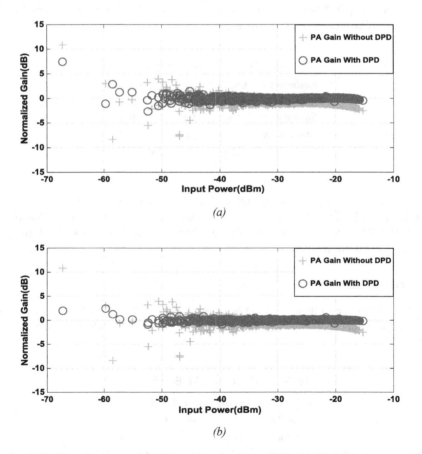

Fig. 3. AM/AM performance of the PA with and without DPD. (a) Cholesky decomposition. (b) LSQR Algorithm.

Also, the output power spectrum after applying the proposed DPD using each of the estimation approach is given in Fig. 4. An improvement in spectral regrowth reduction in the adjacent bands is noticed, the proposed DPD is able to remove the out-of-band emission. The out of band component can be reduced by around 4 dB when the cholesky decomposition is applied to identify the predistorter unit coefficients and by 7 dB for the LSQR algorithm which corroborates the advantage of the LSQR algorithm in term of achieving better linearization performance.

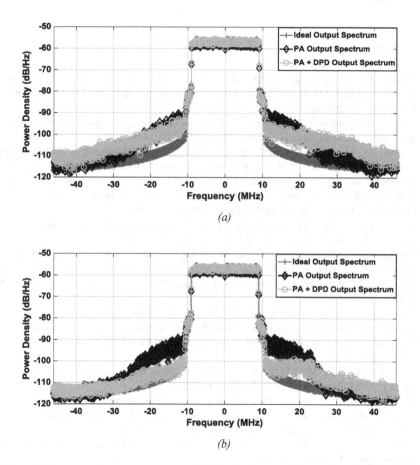

Fig. 4. PA measured output spectrum. (a) Cholesky decomposition. (b) LSQR Algorithm.

5   Conclusion

Two estimation methods, LSQR and cholesky decomposition have been applied in order to identify the PA nonlinear behavioral and the predistorter inverse function coefficients. Tests results shown for a class AB GaN PA using a 20-MHz- LTE-A signal confirm the advantage of the LSQR algorithm compared to the cholesky decomposition method in terms of achieving better performances and lower complexity while reducing by 7 dB the ACPR metric. However, FPGA implementation of the predistorter unit shows that 55% of the total DSPs cores must be used because of the large number of coefficients required by the SVS model. A further work will investigate a simpler form of the predistorter model.

Acknowledgment. The authors wish to thank Prof. Fadhel Ghannouchi and Dr. Ramzi. Darraji from the iRadio Lab, University of Calgary, AB, Canada for providing the power amplifier measurements.

References

1. Younes, M., Kwan, A., Rawat, M., Ghannouchi, F.: Linearization of concurrent tri-band transmitters using 3-D phase-aligned pruned Volterra model. IEEE Trans. Microw. Theory Techn. **61**(12), 4569–4578 (2013)
2. Kim, J., Konstantinou, K.: Digital predistortion of wideband signals based on power amplifier model with memory. Electron. Lett. **37**, 1417–1418 (2001)
3. Gilabert, P., Montoro, G., Bertran, E.: On the Wiener and Hammerstein models for PA predistortion. In: APMC 2005 Asia-Pacific Microwave Conference Proceedings (2005)
4. Abdelhafiz, A., Kwan, A., Hammi, O., Ghannouchi, F.: Digital predistortion of LTE-A power amplifiers using compressed-sampling-based unstructured pruning of volterra series. IEEE Trans. Microw. Theory Techn. **62**(11), 2583–2593 (2014)
5. Peng, J., He, S., Wang, B., Dai, Z., Pang, J.: Digital predistortion for power amplifier based on sparse Bayesian learning. IEEE Trans. Circ. Syst. II Exp. Briefs **63**, 828–832 (2016)
6. Benchahed, A., Ghazel, A., Mabrouk, M., Rebai, C., Ghannouchi, F., et al.: RF digital predistorter for power amplifiers of 3G base stations. In: IEEE Proceedings of 13 International Conference on Electronics, Circuits and Systems, Nice, France, pp. 999–1002 (2006)
7. Rezgui, H., Rouissi, F., Ghazel, A.: FPGA implementation of the predistorter stage for memory polynomial-based DPD for LDMOS power amplifier in DVB-T transmitter. In: 2017 International Conference on Advanced Systems and Electric Technologies (IC_ASET), pp. 356–359. IEEE (2017)
8. Paige, C., Saunders, M.: LSQR: an algorithm for sparse linear equations and sparse least squares. ACM Trans. Math. Soft. **8**, 43–71 (1982)
9. Burian, A., Takala, J., Ylinen, M.: A fixed-point implementation of matrix inversion using Cholesky decomposition. In: Proceedings of the 46th IEEE International Midwest Symposium on Circuits and Systems, vol. 3, pp. 1431–1434 (2003)
10. Krishnamoorthy, A., Menon, D.: Matrix inversion using Cholesky decomposition. In: Proceedings of SPA, pp. 1–3 (2013)
11. Ghannouchi, F., Younes, M., Rawat, M.: Distortion and impairments mitigation and compensation of single-and multi-band wireless transmitters. IET Microw. Antennas Propag. **7**(7), 518–534 (2013)
12. Zhu, A., Brazil, T.: Behavioral modeling of RF power amplifiers based on pruned Volterra series. IEEE Microw. Wirel. Compon. Lett. **14**(12), 563–565 (2004)
13. Zhu, A., Pedro, J., Brazil, T.: Dynamic deviation reduction-based behavioral modeling of RF power amplifiers. IEEE Trans. Microw. Theory Tech. **54**(12), 4323–4332 (2006)
14. Ghannouchi, F., Hammi, O., Helaoui, M.: "Behavioral Modeling and Predistortion of Wideband Wireless Transmitters", Technology & Engineering (2015)

15. Morgan, D., Zhenngxiang, M., Kim, L., Zierdt, M., Pastalan, I.: A generalized memory polynomial model for digital predistortion of RF power amplifiers. IEEE Trans. Sig. Process. **54**(10), 3852–3860 (2006)
16. Reichel, L., Ye, Q.: A generalized LSQR algorithm. Numer. Linear Algebra **15**, 643–660 (2008)
17. Zelinski, A., et al.: Comparison of three algorithms for solving linearized systems of parallel excitation RF waveform design equations: experiments on an eight-channel system at 3 Tesla. Concepts Magn Reson. Part B: Magn. Reson. Eng. **31B**(3), 176–190 (2007)
18. Muhonenm, K., Kavehrad, K.: Look-up table techniques for adaptive digital predistortion: a development and comparison. IEEE Trans. Veh. R Technol. **49**(5), 1995–2002 (2000)

Approximating Sweep Coverage Delay

Gokarna Sharma$^{(\boxtimes)}$ and Jong-Hoon Kim

Department of Computer Science, Kent State University, Kent, OH 44242, USA
sharma@cs.kent.edu, jkim72@kent.edu

Abstract. We consider the following fundamental sweep coverage problem that arises in mobile wireless sensor networks: Given a set of k mobile sensors and a set of m points of interests (POIs) in the Euclidean plane, how to schedule the mobile sensors such that the maximum delay between two subsequent visits to a POI by any sensor is minimized. We study two scenarios of this problem: (i) start positions of the sensors are fixed such that they must return to their start positions between subsequent traversals to POIs that fall in their trajectories, and (ii) sensor positions are not fixed and they are not required to return to their start positions between subsequent traversals. Scenario (i) models battery-constrained sensors which need to be recharged frequently, whereas scenario (ii) models sensors that have no constraint on battery and hence frequent recharging is not necessary. We present two constant factor approximation algorithms for each scenario. The problem we consider is NP-hard and, to the best of our knowledge, these are the first algorithms with guaranteed approximation bounds for this problem.

1 Introduction

Tremendous work in the literature of wireless sensor networks (WSNs) has established that one of the major applications of sensor networks is on surveillance problems [1,3,4,12,15,16,20,21,23–29,31]. These surveillance problems require specific coverage requirements for different proposes. The vast majority of work on surveillance problems using static and mobile WNSs focused on providing two kinds of coverage: *full coverage* and *barrier coverage*. In full coverage, sensors deployed over the given field continuously monitor the entire area. Any point within the area is ensured to be covered by at least one sensor. A full coverage is usually required when users need to fully monitor the entire environment. In barrier coverage, sensors are deployed to form a barrier for detecting any intruders crossing the given barrier area, which is generally a line segment or a strip. The sensors then guard the barrier by guarding the crossing paths. The κ-full coverage and κ-barrier coverage variations of these problems were also studied [1,12,16,20,26,28,29,31].

Both the full and barrier coverage problems can be classified as the *static* coverage problems since the given area (or barrier) needs to be covered at all times by the sensors. In contrast, some applications may require that coverage be provided for the specific given points periodically, i.e., the points do not need

© Springer Nature Switzerland AG 2018
N. Boudriga et al. (Eds.): UNet 2018, LNCS 11277, pp. 14–27, 2018.
https://doi.org/10.1007/978-3-030-02849-7_2

to be covered at all times and they only need to be visited within a specific period. One immediate application of such setting is in patrolling where certain points of interests (POIs) are visited within a specific time period. This problem is called *sweep coverage* and it differs from the static coverage problems as POIs do not need to be covered at all times and only the specific time requirement for inspecting the POI needs to be satisfied. Li *et al.* [18] were the first to study this problem from the objective of minimizing the number of sensors given the sweep period. We denote this problem as MinSensorSweep – given a set of m POIs and the (global) sweep period t, the goal is to schedule sensors such that the sweep coverage requirement is satisfied with the minimum number of sensors.

Contributions. In this paper, we consider the sweep coverage problem with the objective of minimizing the coverage delay. That is, given a set of m POIs and a set of k mobile sensors, the goal is to schedule the given sensors such that the sweep period t is minimized. We denote this problem as MinDelaySweep. MinDelaySweep is different than MinSensorSweep since we deal with the problem of minimizing the time period between two subsequent visits of the POIs. The only previous work that studies this problem is due to Chen *et al.* [5] where they provided several algorithms to minimize the coverage delay. However, their algorithms were evaluated only through experimentally and no approximation bounds were given. Therefore, we focus on designing algorithms and proving achievable approximation bounds for MinDelaySweep.

We consider two different scenarios of MinDelaySweep. The first scenario, called Predefined-Start, covers the case in which start positions of sensors are fixed and after every traversal of the POIs in their trajectories, the sensors go back to their start positions. This scenario is useful when sweep coverage is provided by the battery-constrained mobile sensors which need to be recharged quite frequently at their base stations. The second scenario, called Not-Predefined-Start, covers the case in which sensor positions are not fixed and they do not need to go back to their base stations after every traversal of the POIs as they are assumed of having sufficient energy (i.e., they are not battery-constrained) to provide the sweep coverage for a very long time.

Someone may say that existing techniques and algorithms for MinSensorSweep can be used to solve MinDelaySweep. The idea is to take a solution of MinSensorSweep and see which value of t minimizes the sweeping period for all the POIs. However, this process needs to be repeated at least $\mathcal{O}(\log t)$ times to figure out the right value of t (since the values starting from 1 upto the right value t need to be checked and at least a binary search is needed). Moreover, the solution depends on the solution of MinSensorSweep used. Furthermore, it is worth to note that MinDelaySweep is a NP-Hard problem. Therefore, we focus on the algorithms that provide good approximation of the exact solution and run in polynomial time. We give two algorithms each for Not-Predefined-Start and Predefined-Start scenarios of MinDelaySweep.

- We provide a 2δ-approximation algorithm for the Not-Predefined-Start scenario of MinDelaySweep and a $(\delta + 2 - \frac{1}{k})$-approximation algorithm for the Predefined-Start scenario of MINDELAYSWEEP, where δ is the approximation ratio of an algorithm for the *traveling salesman* problem (TSP).

- We provide a 2γ-approximation algorithm each for both the Not-Predefined-Start and Predefined-Start scenarios of MINDELAYSWEEP, where γ is the approximation ratio of an algorithm for the *tree cover* problem (TC).

Using Christofides's algorithm [6] to compute the solution for TSP tour, we obtain 3-approximation for the Not-Predefined-Start scenario of MINDE-LAYSWEEP and $(\frac{7}{2} - \frac{1}{k})$-approximation for the Predefined-Start scenario of MIN-DELAYSWEEP (Christofides's algorithm has the approximation ratio of 1.5 for the TSP tour). Using the algorithms of Even *et al.* [8] to compute the solution for TC tours in both Not-Predefined-Start and Predefined-Start scenarios of MINDELAYSWEEP, we obtain 8-approximation for both of our algorithms (Even *et al.*'s algorithm has the approximation ratio of 4 for both the rooted and unrooted versions of TC tours). These bounds can be improved if we have better approximation factors for both δ and γ. From recent work on tree and cycle cover problems [14,19], we can obtain 6-approximations for our algorithms based on TC tours. To our best knowledge, these bounds are the first approximation bounds for the NP-hard MINDELAYSWEEP.

Although our solutions look like direct extensions of the existing results on TSP and TC, no such approximation bounds were known in the literature for MINDELAYSWEEP (except experimental study with no approximation bounds in [5]). Our study is interesting since it shows that MINDELAYSWEEP is related to the problem of finding k TSP and TC tours of equal lengths in graphs. Given a solution with k equal length tours, a solution for MINDELAYSWEEP is no more than the factor of 2 times more than the k equal length tour solution used to solve MINDELAYSWEEP.

For the TSP based solution for Not-Predefined-Start scenario, we take a TSP tour and divide that tour into k-subtours in such a way that the approximation obtained from the division is no more than 2 times the approximation of the one single tour. For the Predefined-Start scenario, we use the k-splitour concept of Frederickson *et al.* [9] (details later) and obtain k trajectories such that the claimed approximation bound is still satisfied after the trajectories are modified to include the start positions of sensors. For the TC based solution for both Not-Predefined-Start and Predefined-Start scenarios, we use the concept of Even *et al.* [8] to build k trees such that the approximation obtained is no more than 2 times the approximation of each tree.

Related Work. There is a vast literature on coverage problems in mobile WSNs, which can be divided into three main categories: full coverage, barrier coverage, and sweep coverage. The full and barrier coverage problems are static coverage problems, whereas the sweep coverage problem is a dynamic coverage problem. The full coverage problem is heavily studied under *area* and *point* coverage [3,25,27,28]. Several papers studied how mobile sensors can be used to assist static coverage under a hybrid setting of mobile and static sensors. The k-coverage problem through mobile sensors is also studied in both mobile WSNs and in hybrid setting in [1,12,16,20,26,28,29,31]. Howard *et al.* [13] proposed a potential-field based algorithm and ensured that the initial configuration of the nodes quickly spreads out to maximize coverage area. A virtual-force-based sensor movement strategy to enhance network coverage is considered in [32].

Kumar *et al.* [15,16] studied barrier coverage where the sensors need to form a barrier to prevent intruders from crossing the barrier. They contributed significantly on theoretical foundations and provided several local algorithms that work based on limited neighborhood information. They also studied density requirements for achieving barrier coverage preserving connectivity requirements. These papers [4,21,23,24] studied several different aspects of barrier coverage. *Target coverage* problem is considered in [3,7,17] for tracking both static and moving targets.

As we mentioned above, most of the existing works focus on static coverage (full and barrier) with stationary configurations of sensors. Even with mobile sensors, they focus mostly on achieving an optimized deployment through their mobility without exploring dynamic coverage [18]. The concept of this kind of coverage was originally studied in the context of robotics, e.g. [2], focusing mainly on the coverage frequency. Li *et al.* [18] were the first to study sweep coverage which necessitates the dynamic coverage in the context of mobile WSNs. They studied sweep coverage with the objective of minimizing the number of mobile sensors (i.e., MINSENSORSWEEP) for required sweep coverage time period. The sweep time period is given for any POI and the objective was to fulfill that timing requirement minimizing the number of sensors. MINSENSORSWEEP is further studied by [10,11,18,22,30].

Roadmap. We discuss model and preliminaries in Sect. 2. We then present and analyze two approximation algorithms for Not-Predefined-Start scenario of MINDELAYSWEEP in Sect. 3. We repeat this process for Predefined-Start scenario in Sect. 4. We conclude in Sect. 5 with a short discussion.

2 Model and Preliminaries

We consider a set $\mathcal{M} = \{s_1, s_2, \ldots, s_k\}$ of k mobile sensors and a set $\mathcal{P} = \{p_1, p_2, \ldots, p_m\}$ of m static POIs in the Euclidean plane $\mathbb{R}^2$. We denote by c_i the position of the POI $p_i \in \mathcal{P}$ in $\mathbb{R}^2$, which is fixed. Each POI $p_i \in \mathcal{P}$ has a unique identifier (UID). We denote by $\mathsf{dist}(p_i, p_j)$ the Euclidean distance between two POIs p_i and p_j. We assume that mobile sensors $s_i \in \mathcal{M}$ move at a constant speed v in $\mathbb{R}^2$. If speed is not the same, then the speed can be taken as a ratio to compute the length of the trajectory that the mobile sensor should traverse. Each sensor s_i has the limited sensing range and the POIs are said to be *covered* (i.e., visited or scanned) only when the mobile sensors *pass through* the positions of the POIs. We assume that the time is divided into time units and the unit distance corresponds to one time unit.

We consider two scenarios of the problem. In the first scenario, called Predefined-Start, all the mobile sensors $s_i \in \mathcal{M}$ start from the predefined positions to scan specific POIs along their trajectories and they go back to their predefined start positions after one complete traversal of their trajectories. They then recharge their battery and start their next traversal. We ignore the time to recharge mobile sensors assuming that it is negligible; if it is not the case then, the recharging delay can also be taken into account while computing trajectories. This represents a large class of mobile WSN applications where sensors are highly power-constrained. In the second scenario, called Not-Predefined-Start, the mobile sensors $s_i \in \mathcal{M}$ have no constraint on (battery) power and can scan POIs in their trajectories for a quite long time without recharging. Therefore, the mobile sensors do not need to go back to the predefined positions.

We study the sweep coverage problem with the objective of minimizing the coverage delay, which we denote by MINDELAYSWEEP. More precisely, we aim to schedule k mobile sensors in $\mathcal{M}$ to scan the m POIs in $\mathcal{P}$ such that they delay between subsequent visits to POIs by sensors is minimized and each POI is scanned at least once in one traversal of any sensor. We have the following definitions for MINDELAYSWEEP.

Definition 1 ([18]). *A POI is said to be t-sweep covered by a sweep algorithm $\mathcal{F}$ if and only if it is covered at least once every t time units by the sensors scheduled by $\mathcal{F}$.*

Definition 2 ([18]). *A set of POIs are said to be globally sweep covered by a sweep algorithm $\mathcal{F}$ if and only if every POI p_i is t_i-sweep covered under $\mathcal{F}$.*

Definition 3. *The sweep coverage delay is the maximum t_i among POIs under $\mathcal{F}$.*

Definition 4. *Given a set of k mobile sensors and a set of m POIs, the sweep coverage delay minimization problem, MINDELAYSWEEP, is to schedule k mobile sensors to globally sweep cover the POIs such that the sweep coverage delay is minimized.*

Given $\mathcal{M}$ and $\mathcal{P}$ in the Euclidean plane $\mathbb{R}^2$ and Not-Predefined-Start scenario, the deployment of the POIs in $\mathcal{P}$ can be represented by an undirected weighted complete graph $G = (V, E, \mathfrak{w})$, where V is the set of all POIs in $\mathcal{P}$ and, for any two POIs p_i and p_j, there is an edge between them, i.e., $(p_i, p_j) \in E$. Moreover, there is a weight function $\mathfrak{w} : E \to \mathbb{R}^+$ such that $\mathfrak{w}(e) = \text{dist}(p_i, p_j)$ for an edge $e = (p_i, p_j) \in E$. We denote by $c_{\max} := \max_{e \in E} \mathfrak{w}(e)$, the maximum weight edge in E.

In Predefined-Start scenario, the deployment of the POIs in $\mathcal{P}$ and the sensors in $\mathcal{M}$ can be represented by an undirected weighed graph $G' = (V, V', E', \mathfrak{w})$, where V is the set of all POIs in $\mathcal{P}$, V' is the set of predefined start positions of the mobile sensors in $\mathcal{M}$, for any two POIs p_i and p_j, there is an edge $e = (p_i, p_j) \in E'$, and $\mathfrak{w}(e) = \text{dist}(p_i, p_j)$. Furthermore, for any start position s_i and any POI p_j, there is an edge (s_i, p_j) between them such that $e' = (s_i, p_j) \in E$ and $\mathfrak{w}(e') = \text{dist}(s_i, p_j)$.

Given G or G' and k mobile sensors in $\mathcal{M}$, the goal in MINDELAYSWEEP is to find a set of k trajectories to scan all m POIs in $\mathcal{P}$ such that the maximum length among k trajectories in minimized. MINDELAYSWEEP is NP-hard. Take the Not-Predefined-Start scenario and $|\mathcal{M}| = 1$ (there is only one sensor in $\mathcal{M}$ such that $k = 1$). This setting is equivalent to finding the minimum length Hamiltonian path that passes through all POIs in $\mathcal{P}$ which is a well-known NP-hard problem. Therefore,

Theorem 1. MINDELAYSWEEP *problem is NP-hard.*

Since MINDELAYSWEEP is NP-Hard, we look for approximation algorithms. We use the existing literature on traveling salesman problem (TSP) and tree cover problem (TC) and derive four approximation algorithms. Two approximation algorithms are for Not-Predefined-Start scenario and the rest two are for Predefined-Start scenario.

We now provide several definitions which are useful later in the algorithms. A *tour* is a path that visits all the POIs starting from some initial vertex (POI) v_1 and ends at the same vertex v_1 in G after visiting all the nodes of G exactly once, i.e., $R = \{v_1, v_2, \ldots, v_m, v_1\}$. Note that two subsequent nodes in R are connected by an edge. A *subtour* is a tour that is obtained by dividing the tour R into more than one segments such that a segment contains all the vertexes in the tour R in the same order starting from some initial vertex of the subtour to the ending vertex of that subtour. For example, if R is divided into two tours R_1 and R_2 starting from v_1, then $R_1 = \{v_1, \ldots, v_t, v_1\}$ and $R_2 = \{v_{t+1}, \ldots, v_m, v_{t+1}\}$.

A tree cover of a graph G is a set of trees $\mathcal{T} = \{T_1, \ldots, T_k\}$ such that $V = \bigcup_{i=1}^{k} V(T_i)$. The cost of the tree T_i is defined by $\mathsf{Cost}(T_i) = \sum_{e \in T_i} \mathfrak{w}(e)$. The cost of a tree cover $\mathcal{T}$ is $\max_{T_i \in \mathcal{T}} \mathsf{Cost}(T_i)$. An r-rooted tree cover of a graph G is a tree cover $\mathcal{T}$, where each tree $T_i \in \mathcal{T}$ has a distinct root $r \in \mathcal{Z}$, where $\mathcal{Z} \subset V$ denotes a set of root nodes. Note that the roots of T_i and T_j for $i \neq j$ must be distinct. However, trees may share some nodes and edges to other trees.

3   TSP Tour Based MINDELAYSWEEP Algorithms

We present two algorithms, Not-Predefined-Start-TSP and Predefined-Start-TSP. Not-Predefined-Start-TSP is suitable for Not-Predefined-Start scenario of MIN-DELAYSWEEP and Predefined-Start-TSP is suitable for Predefined-Start scenario.

Not-Predefined-Start-TSP Algorithm. The pseudocode of Not-Predefined-Start-TSP is given in Algorithm 1. The basic idea behind Not-Predefined-Start-TSP is to find a trajectory for each sensor and ask that sensor to cover (scan) the POIs that are in that trajectory. To find the trajectories, we use the the well-known ideas on constructing a TSP tour and dividing the tour to obtain k trajectories. For the TSP tour construction in G, Not-Predefined-Start-TSP selects a node, say v_1, among the POIs as a starting vertex and uses a known algorithm for TSP (say Christofides [6]).

Denote the TSP tour obtained through this construction by $R := \{v_1, v_2, \ldots, v_m, v_1\}$ and let $\mathsf{Cost}(R) = L$. R is then divided into k-subtours (or

---

Algorithm 1. Not-Predefined-Start-TSP

---

1 Pick a POI v_1;

2 Use an algorithm for TSP and find a TSP tour $R = (v_1, v_2, v_3, \ldots, v_n, v_1)$ with $Cost(R) = L$;

3 Let $c_{\max}$ be the longest edge in R. Remove $c_{\max}$ from R such that $L = L - c_{\max}$;

4 **For** $j \leq 1$ to $j < k$ **do**

5   Find the last POI $v_{l(j)}$ such that the cost of the path from v_1 to $v_{l(j)}$ along R is not greater than $\frac{j}{k}L$;

6 Obtain k subtours as

7 $R_1 = (v_1, \ldots, v_{l(1)}), R_2 = (v_{l(1)+1}, \ldots, v_{l(2)}), \ldots, R_k = (v_{l(k-1)+1}, \ldots, v_n),$

8 Add an edge from the last node in each subtour to its first node such that

9 $R_1 = (v_1, \ldots, v_{l(1)}, v_1), R_2 = (v_{l(1)+1}, \ldots, v_{l(2)}, v_{l(1)+1}), \ldots,$
     $R_k = (v_{l(k-1)+1}, \ldots, v_n, v_{l(k-1)+1}),$

10 Assign one sensor to each $R_j, 1 \leq j \leq k$;

---

trajectories), say $R_j, 1 \leq j \leq k$, of almost equal length starting from v_1. The division process works as follows. Let $c_{\max}$ be the longest edge in R. Then, $c_{\max}$ is removed from R such that $L = L - c_{\max}$. Now, starting from v_1, the POIs that fall in R upto length L/k are assigned to R_1 such that $R_1 = \{v_1, \ldots, v_{l(1)}\}$, where $v_{l(1)}$ the last vertex in R_1. Similarly, starting from v_1, the POIs that fall in R upto length $2L/k$ except the POIs that are already in R_1 are assigned to R_2 such that $R_2 = \{v_{l(1)+1}, \ldots, v_{l(2)}\}$, where $v_{l(2)}$ is the last vertex in R_2. According to this division, $R_k = \{v_{l(k-1)+1}, \ldots, v_n\}$ and we have k sub-tours. Moreover, we have that $\mathsf{Cost}(R_i)$ and $\mathsf{Cost}(R_j)$, $1 \leq i, j \leq k, i \neq j$ are at most the factor of 2 from each other. The reasoning is that R is divided in to equal fragments and the length of the edge between the last POI of one sub-tour and the first POI of next subtour changes the length of each fragment only by the factor of 2. These k subtours are updated by adding the starting vertex of each subtour at the end of that tour to obtain one trajectory such that $R_1 = \{v_1, \ldots, v_{l(1)}, v_1\}, R_2 = \{v_{l(1)+1}, \ldots, v_{l(2)}, v_{l(1)+1}\}$, and so on. As sensors do not have predefined start positions and there are k sensors, these sensors are randomly assigned to traverse k trajectories computed. We prove the following theorem for the approximation ratio of Not-Predefined-Start-TSP.

Theorem 2. *The approximation ratio of* Not-Predefined-Start-TSP *is at most* 2δ, *where* δ *is the approximation ratio of an algorithm for TSP.*

Proof. Let L_{OPT} be the length of the optimal tour for TSP in G. Moreover, let L be the length of the TSP tour obtained using an algorithm for TSP. We have that $L = \delta \cdot L_{OPT}$, where δ be the approximation ratio of an algorithm used to compute the TSP tour. Since the tour R is divided into k subtours, we have that the time t_{TSP} required to sweep each subtour R_j is such that $t_{TSP} \leq \frac{2\delta \cdot L_{OPT}}{v}$. This is because the lengths of the subtours are within the factor of 2 from each other. Let t_{OPT} be the time period in the optimal solution. In other words, there is a sweep algorithm $\mathcal{A}$ in which if we use k sensors moving at constant speed

---

Algorithm 2. Predefined-Start-TSP

---

1 Pick a POI v_1;
2 Use an algorithm for TSP and find a TSP tour $R = (v_1, v_2, v_3, \ldots, v_n, v_1)$ with $Cost(R) = L$;
3 **For** $j \leq 1$ to $j < k$ **do**
4   Find the last POI $v_{l(j)}$ such that the cost of the path from v_1 to $v_{l(j)}$ along R is not greater than $\frac{j}{k}(L - 2c_{\max}) + c_{\max}$;
5 Obtain k-tour by forming k subtours as
6      $R'_1 = (v_1, \ldots, v_{l(1)})$, $R'_2 = (v_{l(1)+1}, \ldots, v_{l(2)}), \ldots, R'_k = (v_{l(k-1)+1}, \ldots, v_n)$,
7 Assign each subtour R'_j to mobile sensors $s_i \in \mathcal{M}$ such that $c(s_i, R'_j) \leq c(s_m, R'_j), s_i \neq s_m$;
8 **For** $j = 1$ to $j = k$ **do**
9   Update the subtour R'_j by adding sensor s_j assigned to it in its beginning and end and denote it by R_j;

---

v each sensor will be visited in minimum time units. As L_{OPT} is the length of the shortest route for the corresponding TSP, we get $t_{OPT} \geq \frac{L_{OPT}}{v}$ for one mobile sensor. Therefore, the approximation ratio of Not-Predefined-Start-TSP is bounded by $\frac{t_{TSP}}{t_{OPT}} \leq \frac{\frac{2\delta \cdot L_{OPT}}{v}}{\frac{L}{v}} \leq 2\delta$. □

Since Christofides's algorithm [6] has approximation 1.5, we obtain:

Corollary 1. *Using Christofides's algorithm [6] for TSP tour,* Not-Predefined-Start-TSP *achieves the approximation ratio of at most* 3 *for* MinDelaySweep.

Predefined-Start-TSP Algorithm. The pseudocode of Predefined-Start-TSP algorithm is given in Algorithm 2. The main idea of this algorithm is to find a TSP tour R similar to Not-Predefined-Start-TSP. However, due to the predefined start positions of the sensors, R need to be carefully split into k subtours and also the sensors needs to be carefully assigned to cover the POIs in those subtours. We use the approach of Frederickson et al. [9] to divide the tour R into k-subtours. Moreover, after the tour is divided into k-subtours, the mobile sensors that minimizes the cost $Cost(s_i, R_j)$ is assigned to R_j to provide the coverage for the POIs in R_j, where $Cost(s_i, R_j)$ is the minimum distance from the position of any sensor $s_i \in \mathcal{M}$ to any node in subtour R_j.

The k-SPLITOUR algorithm of Frederickson et al. [9] starts from some vertex, say v_1, and finds the last POI $v_{l(j)}$ in R such that the cost of the path from v_1 to $v_{l(j)}$ is not greater than $\frac{j}{k}(L - 2c_{\max}) + c_{\max}$, where $c_{\max}$ is the maximum weight of an edge in E. Then it forms k subtours as $R'_1 = \{v_1, \ldots, v_{l(1)}\}, R'_2 = \{v_{l(1)+1}, \ldots, v_{l(2)}\}, \ldots, R'_k = \{v_{l(k-1)+1}, \ldots, v_n\}$. Each subtour R'_j is assigned to a sensor $s_i \in \mathcal{M}$ which minimizes the cost $Cost(s_i, R'_j)$. Finally, each subtour R'_j is updated by adding the sensor that assigned to cover it in the beginning and end to get R_j, i.e., if a sensor s_i is assigned to R'_j, then we have that $R_j = \{s_i, v_{l(j-1)+1}, \ldots, v_{l(j)}, s_i\}$. That is, R_j is the trajectory for sensor s_i. We prove the following results for the approximation ratio achieved by Predefined-Start-TSP.

Lemma 1. *Let C_k be the cost of the largest of the k-subtours generated by Algorithm 2. Algorithm 2 guarantees that $C_k \leq \frac{L}{k} + 2c_{\max}(2 - \frac{1}{k})$.*

Proof. We have that $\mathsf{Cost}(R_1') \leq \frac{1}{k}(L - 2c_{\max}) + c_{\max}$. Similarly, $\mathsf{Cost}(R_k') \leq \frac{1}{k}(L - 2c_{\max}) + c_{\max}$. For each j, $1 \leq j \leq k - 2$, $\mathsf{Cost}(R_j') \leq \frac{1}{k}(L - 2c_{\max})$.

Now, while updating the tours by adding the sensors that are assigned to the subtour, we have that $\mathsf{Cost}(R_1) \leq \mathsf{Cost}(R_1') + \mathsf{Cost}(v_1, s_1) + \mathsf{Cost}(v_{l(1)}, s_1)$. We have that $\mathsf{Cost}(s_1, v_1) + \mathsf{Cost}(v_{l(1)}, s_1) \leq 3c_{\max}$ due to triangle equality, since $\mathsf{Cost}(v_1, v_{l(1)}) \leq c_{\max}$. Therefore, $\mathsf{Cost}(R_1) \leq \frac{1}{k}(L - 2c_{\max}) + 4c_{\max}$. Similarly, $\mathsf{Cost}(R_k) \leq \frac{1}{k}(L - 2c_{\max}) + 4c_{\max}$. For each $j, 1 \leq j \leq k - 2$, $\mathsf{Cost}(R_j) \leq \mathsf{Cost}(R_j') + \mathsf{Cost}(s_j, v_{l(j)+1}) + \mathsf{Cost}(v_{l(j+1)}, s_j)$. Moreover, we have that $\mathsf{Cost}(s_j, v_{l(j)+1}) + \mathsf{Cost}(v_{l(j+1)}, s_j) \leq 4c_{\max}$.

Thus, $C_k = \max_j \mathsf{Cost}(R_j) \leq \frac{1}{k}(L - 2c_{\max}) + 4c_{\max} \leq \frac{L}{k} + 2c_{\max}(2 - \frac{1}{k})$. □

We immediately have the following lemma for the optimal cost.

Lemma 2 ([9]). *Let C_k^* be the cost of the largest subtour in an optimal solution for the k-subtours. We have that $C_k^* \geq \frac{1}{k}C^*$, where C^* is the cost of an optimal TSP tour.*

Theorem 3. Predefined-Start-TSP *achieves the approximation ratio of at most $\delta + 2 - \frac{1}{k}$, where δ is the approximation ratio of an algorithm for TSP.*

Proof. We have that $L \leq \delta C^*$, where C^* is the cost of the optimal solution for TSP. Moreover, we have that $C_k^* \geq \frac{1}{k}C^*$, and due to traingle inequality, $c_{\max} \leq \frac{1}{2}C_k^*$ [9]. Therefore, combining Lemmas 1 and 2, and substituting L, $c_{\max}$, and C_k^* by their values, the theorem follows. □

Corollary 2. *Using Christofides's algorithm [6] for TSP tour,* Predefined-Start-TSP *achieves the approximation ratio of at most $\frac{7}{2} - \frac{1}{k}$ for* MINDELAYSWEEP.

4   Tree Cover Based MINDELAYSWEEP Algorithms

We present two algorithms, Not-Predefined-Start-TC and Predefined-Start-TC. Not-Predefined-Start-TC is suitable for Not-Predefined-Start scenario of MINDELAYSWEEP and Predefined-Start-TC is suitable for Predefined-Start scenario of MINDELAYSWEEP.

Not-Predefined-Start-TC Algorithm. The pseudocode of Not-Predefined-Start-TC is given in Algorithm 3. Not-Predefined-Start-TC uses an unrooted tree cover construction algorithm Unrooted-TC(G, k, B) to compute a set of k trees $\mathcal{T} = \{T_1, \ldots, T_k\}$. These k trees are then converted to k tours and assign one sensor in each tree to scan the POIs that belong to those trees.

We discuss here the Unrooted-TC(G, k, B) algorithm of Even *et al.* [8] to compute a set $\mathcal{T}$ of k trees given as input these three parameters: the graph G, the number of trees k (which is equal to the number of mobile sensors in $\mathcal{M}$),

---

Algorithm 3. Not-Predefined-Start-TC

---

1 Use an algorithm Unrooted-TC(G, k, B) for the unrooted version of TC problem and find a set of k trees $\mathcal{T} = \{T_1, \ldots, T_k\}$;
2 Transform each tree $T_i \in \mathcal{T}$ into a tour P_i using an appropriate tour construction algorithm given a tree;
3 Assign a mobile sensor to each tour P_i to cover the POIs that are in that tour;

---

and a bound on the cost of each tree B. Unrooted-TC(G, k, B) then either returns that the bound B chosen for the cost of the tree is too small or finds a tree cover $\mathcal{T} = \{T_1, T_2, \ldots, T_k\}$ of cost at most $4B$ for each $T_i, 1 \leq i \leq k$.

Unrooted-TC(G, k, B) of Even et al. [8] works as follows. It first removes the edges of G with weight larger than B. This may divide G into a set of connected components which are denoted by $\{G_i\}$. Then a minimum spanning tree MST_i is computed for each G_i. After that $\text{Cost}(MST_i)$ is computed and this cost is divided by $2B$ to determine the number of trees k_i required to cover the vertices in G_i. If $\sum_i (k_i + 1) > k$ for k_i determined for every G_i, then it gives more than k trees which means that the estimate of B is small and Unrooted-TC(G, k, B) has to repeat this process with larger B such that $\sum_i (k_i + 1)$ is equal to k. We need exactly k trees since we have k sensors in $\mathcal{M}$. When $\sum_i (k_i + 1) = k$, then each MST_i is decomposed to $k_i + 1$ trees T_i^j such that $\text{Cost}(T_i^j) \in [2B, 4B)$, where $1 \leq j \leq k_i$. The leftover of MST_i after constructing k_i trees is assigned to L_i which is called the leftover tree. Therefore, Unrooted-TC(G, k, B) returns in total k trees and Even et al. [8] showed that the cost of each tree is at most $4B$.

Not-Predefined-Start-TC then transforms the k trees obtained using Unrooted-TC(G, k, B) into k tours as follows. For each edge $(i, j) \in T$, we ask Not-Predefined-Start-TC to add another edge between i and j with the same weight $w(ij)$. Note that the subgraph consisting only of the edges in T and these new duplicate edges provides an Euler cycle. Note also that the total cost of the Euler cycle is 2 times $\text{Cost}(T)$. Let P be that cycle. Then the tour is obtained as follows. If P has a sequence like $i, j, l, \ldots, o, i, p$, then we replace it by $i, j, l, \ldots, o, p$ (removing the second i in the sequence). The difference here in the total cost of P is only due to the deletion of the second i. As the edge weights in G satisfy triangle inequality, we have that $w(op) \leq w(oi) + w(ip)$. Therefore, this shortcut process does not increase the cost of P and it is within 2 times the cost of T.

Even et al. [8] proved the correctness of Unrooted-TC(G, k, B) in the sense that it returns a set of k trees with desired properties if proper cost bound B is provided as an input. Our discussion of the Unrooted-TC(G, k, B) algorithm of [8] for $\mathcal{T}$ construction is for an illustration purpose and other available algorithms for the unrooted tree cover problem can also be used in Line 1 of Algorithm 3 to compute $\mathcal{T}$. Therefore, we focus here on the general approximation ratio achieved by Not-Predefined-Start-TC.

Theorem 4. *The approximation ratio of* Not-Predefined-Start-TC *is at most* 2γ, *where* γ *is the approximation ratio of an algorithm for the unrooted version of* TC.

Proof. Let γ be the approximation ratio of the algorithm used to compute the solution for the unrooted version of TC. In the tour construction process, we increased the cost of each tree by a factor of at most 2. Therefore, the approximation of Not-Predefined-Start-TC is at most 2γ.   □

Since Even *et al.*'s algorithm [8] has the approximation ratio of 4 for the unrooted version of TC, we obtain the following corollary.

Corollary 3. *Using the Even et al.'s algorithm [8]* Unrooted-TC(G, k, B), Not-Predefined-Start-TC *achieves the approximation ratio of* 8 *for* MINDELAYSWEEP.

Predefined-Start-TC Algorithm. The pseudocode of Predefined-Start-TC is given in Algorithm 4. Predefined-Start-TC uses a rooted tree cover construction algorithm Rooted-TC(G, k, B) to compute a set of k trees $T = \{T_1, T_2, \ldots, T_k\}$ such that each tree T_i is rooted at a start position of a sensor. These k trees are then converted to k tours using an appropriate tour construction algorithm and the sensor that is in the start position (i.e., the root of the tree) is asked to to scan the POIs that fall in those trees.

We discuss here the Rooted-TC(G, k, B) algorithm of [8] which takes as input the same three parameters as in Unrooted-TC(G, k, B). Rooted-TC(G, k, B) then either returns that the bound B chosen for the cost of the tree is too small or finds a tree cover $T = \{T_1, T_2, \ldots, T_k\}$ of cost at most $4B$ for each $T_i, 1 \leq i \leq k$.

Rooted-TC(G, k, B) removes edges with weights greater than B and compute k different minimum spanning trees T_i with k different roots as the starting positions of the sensors. Some of the trees in T_i can be empty in the sense that they may contain only the root node. Rooted-TC(G, k, B) then decomposes each tree T_i into j trees such that $\mathsf{Cost}(T_i^j) \in [B, 2B)$, for every j, and assign the leftover of the tree T_i after dividing it into j trees to the leftover tree L_i. According to the construction $\mathsf{Cost}(L_i) < B$. Each tree $\mathsf{Cost}(T_i^j)$ is then matched to the roots that are at distance at most B from it. If not all tree are matched, then it is the case that the bound B chosen is too small and Rooted-TC(G, k, B) repeats this k tree construction and matching by choosing a larger value of B. If all trees are matched then Rooted-TC(G, k, B) returns k trees rooted at the start positions of k sensors.

The Predefined-Start-TC algorithm then transforms the k trees obtained using Rooted-TC(G, k, B) into k tours similar to the technique we discussed in Not-Predefined-Start-TC. Each tour P_i constructed for the tree T_i has the cost that is at most 2 times the cost of T_i.

Even *et al.* [8] proved the correctness of Rooted-TC(G, k, B) in the sense that it returns a set of k tree with desired properties of proper cost B is provided as an input. Similar to Not-Predefined-Start-TC, our discussion of the Rooted-TC(G, k, B) algorithm of [8] for T construction is for an illustration purpose and other available algorithms for the rooted tree cover problem can also be used in Line 1 of Algorithm 3 to compute T. Therefore, we prove the following theorem.

Algorithm 4. Predefined-Start-TC

---

1 Use an algorithm Rooted-TC(G, k, B) for the rooted version of TC problem and
   find a set of k trees $\mathcal{T} = \{T_1, \ldots, T_k\}$ rooted at the start positions of k sensors
   (the roots are different for each tree);
2 Transform each tree $T_i \in \mathcal{T}$ into a tour P_i using an appropriate tour
   construction algorithm given a tree;
3 Ask the mobile sensor in the start position that is in that tour P_i to cover the
   POIs that are in P_i;

Theorem 5. *The approximation ratio of* Predefined-Start-TC *is at most* 2γ, *where* γ *is the approximation ratio of an algorithm for the rooted version of* TC.

Proof. Let γ be the approximation ratio of the algorithm used to compute the solution for the rooted version of TC. Predefined-Start-TC modifies the tree cover that is obtained by Rooted-TC(G, k, B) to form a tour in the expense of factor 2 increase in the cost of each tree. Therefore, the approximation of Predefined-Start-TC is 2γ. □

Since Even *et al.*'s algorithm [8] has the approximation ratio of 4 for the rooted version of TC, we obtain the following corollary.

Corollary 4. *Using the Even et al.'s algorithm [8]* Rooted-TC(G, k, B) Predefined-Start-TC *achieves the approximation ratio of 8 for* MinDelaySweep.

5   Concluding Remarks

We considered the fundamental problem of sweep coverage in mobile WSNs. We studied this problem with the objective of minimizing the coverage delay given the limited set of k sensors to cover a set of m POIs in the Euclidean plane. For the future work, it is interesting to improve the approximation ratios of our algorithms. For the practical aspect, it is interesting to experimentally evaluate our algorithms, especially the tree cover based algorithms, on the performance they achieve in real world scenarios.

References

1. Bai, X., Xuan, D., Yun, Z., Lai, T.H., Jia, W.: Complete optimal deployment patterns for full-coverage and k-connectivity in wireless sensor networks. In: MobiHoc, pp. 401–410 (2008)
2. Batalin, M.A., Sukhatme, G.S.: Multi-robot dynamic coverage of a planar bounded environment. Technical report (2002)
3. Cardei, M., Thai, M.T., Li, Y., Wu, W.: Energy-efficient target coverage in wireless sensor networks. In: INFOCOM, pp. 1976–1984 (2005)
4. Chen, A., Kumar, S., Lai, T.H.: Designing localized algorithms for barrier coverage. In: MobiCom, pp. 63–74 (2007)

5. Chen, W., Chen, S., Li, D.: Minimum-delay pois coverage in mobile wireless sensor networks. EURASIP J. Wirel. Commun. Netw. **2013**, 262 (2013)
6. Christofides, N.: Worst-case analysis of a new heuristic for the travelling salesman problem. Technical report (1976)
7. Ding, L., Wu, W., Willson, J., Wu, L., Lu, Z., Lee, W.: Constant-approximation for target coverage problem in wireless sensor networks. In: INFOCOM, pp. 1584–1592, March 2012
8. Even, G., Garg, N., KöNemann, J., Ravi, R., Sinha, A.: Min-max tree covers of graphs. Oper. Res. Lett. **32**(4), 309–315 (2004)
9. Frederickson, G.N., Hecht, M.S., Kim, C.E.: Approximation algorithms for some routing problems. In: FOCS, pp. 216–227 (1976)
10. Gorain, B., Mandal, P.S.: Approximation algorithms for sweep coverage in wireless sensor networks. J. Parallel Distrib. Comput. **74**(8), 2699–2707 (2014)
11. Gorain, B., Mandal, P.S.: Line sweep coverage in wireless sensor networks. In: COMSNETS, pp. 1–6 (2014)
12. Hefeeda, M., Bagheri, M.: Randomized k-coverage algorithms for dense sensor networks. In: INFOCOM, pp. 2376–2380 (2007)
13. Howard, A., Mataric, M.J., Sukhatme, G.S.: Mobile sensor network deployment using potential fields: a distributed, scalable solution to the area coverage problem. In: Asama, H., Arai, T., Fukuda, T., Hasegawa, T. (eds.) Distributed Autonomic Robotic Systems 5, pp. 299–308. Springer, Tokyo (2002). https://doi.org/10.1007/978-4-431-65941-9_30
14. Khani, M.R., Salavatipour, M.R.: Improved approximation algorithms for the min-max tree cover and bounded tree cover problems. In: Goldberg, L.A., Jansen, K., Ravi, R., Rolim, J.D.P. (eds.) APPROX/RANDOM -2011. LNCS, vol. 6845, pp. 302–314. Springer, Heidelberg (2011). https://doi.org/10.1007/978-3-642-22935-0_26
15. Kumar, S., Lai, T.H., Arora, A.: Barrier coverage with wireless sensors. In: MobiCom, pp. 284–298 (2005)
16. Kumar, S., Lai, T.H., Balogh, J.: On k-coverage in a mostly sleeping sensor network. In: MobiCom, pp. 144–158 (2004)
17. Li, D., Cao, J., Liu, M., Zheng, Y.: K-connected target coverage problem in wireless sensor networks. In: Dress, A., Xu, Y., Zhu, B. (eds.) COCOA 2007. LNCS, vol. 4616, pp. 20–31. Springer, Heidelberg (2007). https://doi.org/10.1007/978-3-540-73556-4_5
18. Li, M., Cheng, W., Liu, K., He, Y., Li, X.Y., Liao, X.: Sweep coverage with mobile sensors. IEEE Trans. Mob. Comput. **10**(11), 1534–1545 (2011)
19. Liang, W., Lin, X.: Approximation algorithms for min-max cycle cover problems. IEEE Trans. Comput. **64**(3), 600–613 (2014)
20. Liu, B., Brass, P., Dousse, O., Nain, P., Towsley, D.: Mobility improves coverage of sensor networks. In: MobiHoc, pp. 300–308 (2005)
21. Liu, B., Dousse, O., Wang, J., Saipulla, A.: Strong barrier coverage of wireless sensor networks. In: MobiHoc, pp. 411–420 (2008)
22. Lu, X., Chen, S., Chen, W., Li, D.: Sweep coverage with mobile sensors on two-way road. In: Wang, R., Xiao, F. (eds.) CWSN 2012. CCIS, vol. 334, pp. 335–345. Springer, Heidelberg (2013). https://doi.org/10.1007/978-3-642-36252-1_31
23. Saipulla, A., Westphal, C., Liu, B., Wang, J.: Barrier coverage with line-based deployed mobile sensors. Ad Hoc Netw. **11**(4), 1381–1391 (2013)
24. Wan, P.J., Yi, C.W.: Coverage by randomly deployed wireless sensor networks. IEEE/ACM Trans. Netw. **14**(SI), 2658–2669 (2006)

25. Wang, B.: Coverage problems in sensor networks: a survey. ACM Comput. Surv. **43**(4), 32:1–32:53 (2011)
26. Wang, D., Liu, J., Zhang, Q.: Probabilistic field coverage using a hybrid network of static and mobile sensors. In: IWQoS, pp. 56–64 (2007)
27. Wang, J.: Efficient point coverage in wireless sensor networks. J. Comb. Optim. **11**, 291–304 (2006)
28. Wang, W., Srinivasan, V., Chua, K.-C.: Trade-offs between mobility and density for coverage in wireless sensor networks. In: MobiCom, pp. 39–50 (2007)
29. Wang, X., Xing, G., Zhang, Y., Lu, C., Pless, R., Gill, C.: Integrated coverage and connectivity configuration in wireless sensor networks. In: SenSys, pp. 28–39 (2003)
30. Xi, M., Wu, K., Qi, Y., Zhao, J., Liu, Y., Li, M.: Run to potential: sweep coverage in wireless sensor networks. In: ICPP, pp. 50–57 (2009)
31. Zhou, Z., Das, S., Gupta, H.: Connected k-coverage problem in sensor networks. In: ICCCN, pp. 373–378 (2004)
32. Zou, Y., Chakrabarty, K.: Sensor deployment and target localization based on virtual forces. In: INFOCOM (2003)

Cell Selection Game in 5G Heterogeneous Networks

Maroua Gharam[(✉)] and Noureddine Boudriga

Communication Networks and Security Research Lab,
University of Carthage, Tunis, Tunisia
`maroua.gharam@supcom.tn`

Abstract. Recently, the deployment of small-cell with overlay coverage has emerged as a reliable solution for 5G heterogeneous network (HetNets). While they provide useful properties, these architectures bring several challenges in network management, including interference alignment, extensive back-hauling, and cell selection within HetNets. In this work, we model the cell selection paradigm in 5G HetNets using a non-cooperative game-theoretic framework, and we show that it admits an equilibrium using mixed strategy Nash Equilibrium (NE) method.

Keywords: Game theory · 5G heterogeneous networks · Cell selection

1 Introduction

Over the last decade, anywhere and anytime wireless connectivity has become a reality and has resulted in the increase of data traffic. 5G networks are anticipated to form a new generation of cooperative ubiquitous mobile networks meeting the demand of mobile users. The noticeable growth of the resulting data traffic is assumed to pose enormous loads on the radio spectrum resources in future 5G networks.

Therefore, network densification using small-cells is considered to be a key solution in the emerging networks. The deployment of small-cell in a given area permit to provide a huge capacity gain and bring small base stations closer to users' devices. Nevertheless, the great deployment of small-cells presents several challenges in network management, including interference alignment, extensive back-hauling, and cell selection within HetNets.

Indeed, since the cell selection procedure is generally based on the received signal strength, the heterogeneity of transmission power in the HetNets raises the complexity of the network planning. However, such criterion is no longer applicable due to the disproportion of transmission power. In addition, the maximum Signal to Interference plus Noise Ratio (SINR) based cell selection in the case of HetNets affects the load balancing and does not guarantee the intended performance in terms of spectral efficiency. For these reasons, we use game theory to study the cell selection issue while maintaining the quality of service (QoS) level required by users and maximizing the spectral efficiency.

© Springer Nature Switzerland AG 2018
N. Boudriga et al. (Eds.): UNet 2018, LNCS 11277, pp. 28–39, 2018.
https://doi.org/10.1007/978-3-030-02849-7_3

Consequently, the main contributions of this paper are as follows:

- We propose a non-cooperative game theoretic model describing the cell selection in 5G HetNets composed of small and macro-cells belonging to two different tiers. The proposed model considers two players User Equipment (UE) and Base Station (BS) with different utility functions.
- We prove the convergence of the proposed game using a mixed strategy NE.
- We design a cell selection method for 5G HetNets where we consider simultaneously the UEs' strategies and the BSs' strategies. We show through simulation the effectiveness of the proposed game in reducing the users' blocking rate and enhancing the network performances in 5G HetNets.

This paper is organized as follows. Section 2 gives a brief profile about related work. In Sect. 3, we describe the network architecture and we present the cell selection game model. In Sect. 4, we present the equilibrium determination in the cell selection game model. Section 5, we evaluate the performance of the proposed game through simulation work. Finally, Sect. 6 concludes the paper.

2 Related Work

Game theory is a part of applied mathematics which is concerned with the decision made in a conflict situation. It provides a large set of mathematical tools modeling and analyzing interactions among the rational entities based on the gain perceived by these entities. In addition to the economic domains, game theory is also employed in communication engineering to solve several kinds of problems concerning power control, resource allocation, radio access technology (RAT) selection, and node participation. It has been widely used to analyze the cooperative and non-cooperative behaviors of mobile nodes in the cell selection issue within a HetNet. In this context, many studies have been conducted toward the application of game theory in cell selection issue within the HetNets.

Authors in [5] proved the convergence to the NE for a wireless interface selection with three main broadband technologies. Authors in [1] studied the dynamics of RAT selection games in HetNets where users selfishly select the best RAT while maximizing their throughput. Through simulation results they noticed that the proposed game converge to NE within a small number of switching. However, in these works, the throughput is considered as the only objective function without considering the pricing scheme.

In [8], authors proposed a non-cooperative game for RAT selection where they considered a throughput function and a pricing function. However, through simulation results, they concluded that the convergence time and the pertinence are improved when users have sufficient information about each other and about the network, which is not the case in the real world applications.

Moreover, the aforementioned papers consider that the HetNet belongs to the same network operator. In [2], authors investigated cell selection issue in a HetNet composed of small and macro-cells belonging to two different tiers. They proposed a non-cooperative game getting the best distribution of UEs among small and macro BSs and they proved the convergence to a NE. However, since each BS is able to serve a limited number of users, the users' blocking rate could increase when the users' number is growing, which may decrease the system QoS.

Therefore, this work consider a non-cooperative cell selection game in 5G HetNets composed of small and macro-cells belonging to two different tiers. The proposed game takes into consideration a capacity and a pricing functions. In this game the users' blocking rate is improved by contributing several BSs of different network operators in the communication. Such network operators must have build a prior agreement between them (as referred to as communication agreement [4]) allowing a free movement over the cells of different operators (Table 1).

Table 1. Comparison between existing works

Reference	Cells belonging to different tiers	No need for other users' information	No need for network's information	Cross-tiers interference protection	Users' blockage protection
Naghavi [8]		×			
Dhifallah [2]	×	×	×	×	
Our proposal	×	×	×	×	×

3   Network Architecture and Model Description

3.1   Network Architecture

We consider a HetNet, depicted in Fig. 1, consisting of small-cell base stations $(S-BSs)$ added in the area of macro-cell base station $(M-BS)$ improving the system throughput and enhancing the flexibility to offload data traffic from $M-BSs$. $M-BSs$ and $S-BSs$ are deployed by different operators and they interact according to communication agreements. The coverage area of $M-BSs$ may be overlapped to deal with the coverage hole problem. Moreover, we assume that the entire spectrum is divided into sub-bands, where each sub-band is assigned to a specific BS to reduce the cross-tiers interference. We also assume that users are in mobility and may request a service from a $M-BS$ or a $S-BS$.

Indeed, when a mobile user selects a $S-BS$, this latter accepts to serve it only when its maximum capacity is not reached yet, otherwise, it can redirect the request to the closest $M-BS$ of the same operator, or to a $M-BS$ of an other operator according to the communication agreement established between the operators. However, when the user selects a $M-BS$ to serve it, this latter may accepts the request whenever its maximum capacity is not yet reached, or forward the request to the closest BS belonging to the same or different operator.

Therefore, the $BS's$ decision depends on its own capacity and on the neighboring node's capacity, which represents the maximum number of users that can serve. The capacity of each BS is limited in order to guarantee the required QoS. Hence, the income of each BS depends on the total number of UE that it serves and on the total number of UE served by the whole network. Once the $UE's$ request is accepted by a given BS, the latter must pay the service fees. These fees are shared between the BSs involved in the communication.

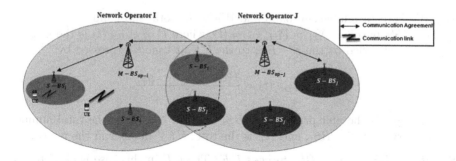

Fig. 1. Heterogeneous network architecture

3.2 Cell Selection Game Model

This sub-section is devoted to present the theoretical model that we proposed in order to find an appropriate cell selection scheme in a HetNet. To this end, we consider that, at the time t, a UE is near to a $S-BS$ and receives a high SINR from the close $M-BS$, as well. We assume that there is a QoS threshold defined in advance permitting the $S-BS$ to delegate the UE to the best closest $M-BS$ even if that decreases its revenue. Therefore, we propose a non-cooperative game with two players (UE and BS). Each player has different set of pure strategies, Table 2, where it selfishly selects the strategy that ensures him the greater payoff. Thus, the $UE's$ utility function is based on the link capacity with the selected BS. However, the $BS's$ utility function depends on the service price of a served user at a time t. Therefore, we propose the following strategy combinations:

Select $S-BS_i$ **&** $S-BS_i$ **Serves** UE**:** In this strategy combination, the UE is very close to the $S-BS_i$ and its signal is stronger than its $M-BS_i$. At the same time, the $S-BS_i$ strategy is to serve this UE because the maximum number of UEs that it can serve is not reached. In this case the UE and the BS have the same strategy. Therefore, the $UE's$ payoff is:

$$X_{11} = C_{S-BS_i}(t) + G_{UE,S-BS_i}(t)$$

where $C_{S-BS_i}(t)$ is the normalized link capacity when the UE is associated to the $S-BS_i$, expressed by:

$$C_{S-BS_i}(t) = \frac{W_{S-BS_i}(t)log_2(1 + SINR_{S-BS_i})}{max(C_{S-BS_i}(t))}$$

With $W_{S-BS_i}(t)$ is the used bandwidth and $SINR_{S-BS_i}$ is the signal to interference plus noise ratio of the $S-BS_i$.

$G_{UE,S-BS_i}(t)$ is the $UE's$ gain when it selects the $S - BS_i$, expressed by:

$$G_{UE,S-BS_i}(t) = \frac{W_A}{W_T} + C_{S-BS_i}(t)$$

with W_A is the available sub-band and W_T is the total sub-band.

The $BS's$ payoff is: $Y_{11} = P_{UE,S-BS_i}(t)$, where $P_{UE,S-BS_i}(t)$ is the price of the service provided by the $S - BS_i$ to the UE at time t, expressed by:

$$P_{UE,S-BS_i}(t) = \frac{P_{S-BS_i} \times N_{S-BS_i}}{N_T}$$

With P_{S-BS_i} is the unit price of $S - BS_i$' service, N_{S-BS_i} is the total number of UEs served by $S - BS_i$, and N_T is the total UEs' number in the network.

Select $S - BS_i$ & $M - BS_i$ Serves UE: The UE in this case is close to the $S - BS_i$, but this latter can not serve it because the maximum number of UEs that it can serve is reached. The $S - BS_i$ receives the request of the UE and redirects it to its $M - BS_i$. In this case, the UE payoff is:

$$X_{21} = C_{M-BS_i}(t)$$

Where $C_{M-BS_i}(t)$ is the normalized link capacity when the UE is associated to the $M - BS_i$, expressed by:

$$C_{M-BS_i}(t) = \frac{W_{M-BS_i}(t)log_2(1 + SINR_{M-BS_i})}{max(C_{M-BS_i}(t))}$$

with $W_{M-BS_i}(t)$ is the used bandwidth and $SINR_{M-BS_i}$ is the signal to interference plus noise ratio of the $M - BS_i$. The $BS's$ payoff is:

$$Y_{21} = \frac{P_{UE,M-BS_i}}{2}$$

where $P_{UE,M-BS_i}(t)$ is the price of the service provided by the $M - BS_i$ to the UE at time t, expressed by:

$$P_{UE,M-BS_i}(t) = \frac{P_{M-BS_i} \times N_{M-BS_i}}{N_T}$$

With P_{M-BS_i} is the unit price fixed for the $M - BS_i$, N_{M-BS_i} is the total number of users served by $M - BS_i$, and N_T is the total number of users in the whole network. $P_{UE,M-BS_i}(t)$ is divided by 2 because the request of the UE is firstly sent to the $S - BS_i$ then it is redirected to the $M - BS_i$. In this case, the price of the service is shared between $S - BS_i$ and $M - BS_i$.

Select $S - BS_i$ & $M - BS_j$ Serves UE: The UE in this case is close to the $S - BS_i$, but this latter can not serve it because the maximum number of UEs that it can serve is reached. The $S - BS_i$ receives the request of the UE and redirects it according to a communication agreement to the closest $M - BS_j$ through the $M - BS_i$. Therefore, $UE's$ payoff is:

$$X_{31} = C_{M-BS_j}(t)$$

where $C_{M-BS_j}(t)$ is the normalized link capacity when the UE is associated to the $M - BS_j$ belonging to an other operator, expressed by:

$$C_{M-BS_j}(t) = \frac{W_{M-BS_j}(t)log_2(1 + SINR_{M-BS_j})}{max(C_{M-BS_j}(t))}$$

With $W_{M-BS_j}(t)$ is the used bandwidth and $SINR_{M-BS_j}$ is the signal to interference plus noise ratio of the $M - BS_j$. The $BS's$ payoff is:

$$Y_{31} = \frac{P_{UE,M-BS_j}(t)}{3}$$

Where $P_{UE,M-BS_j}(t)$ is the price of the service provided by the $M - BS_j$ to the UE at time t, expressed by:

$$P_{UE,M-BS_j}(t) = \frac{P_{M-BS_j} \times N_{M-BS_j}}{N_T}$$

With P_{M-BS_j} is the unit price fixed for the $M - BS_j$, N_{M-BS_j} is the total number of users served by $M - BS_j$, and N_T is the total number of users in the whole network. $P_{UE,M-BS_j}(t)$ is divided by 3 because the communication includes three entities ($S - BS_i$, $M - BS_i$, and $M - BS_j$). In this case, these entities will share the price of the service paid by the UE.

Select $M-BS_i$ & $S-BS_i$ Serves UE: In this case the UE selects the $M-BS_i$ as it provides the best signal strength, but this latter cannot serve it because the maximum number of UEs that it can serve is reached. So, the $M - BS_i$ redirects it to the closest $S - BS_i$ in order to balance the load and provides a better QoS to the served UEs.

Therefore, the $UE's$ payoff is: $X_{12} = C_{S-BS_i}(t)$.

And, the $BS's$ payoff is: $Y_{12} = \frac{P_{UE,S-BS_i}(t)}{2}$, where $P_{UE,S-BS_i}(t)$ is divided by 2 because the request is firstly sent to the $M - BS_i$ then it is redirected to the $S - BS_i$ belonging to it. Therefore, $M - BS_i$ and $S - BS_i$ will share the service price paid by the UE.

Select $M - BS_i$ & $M - BS_i$ Serves UE: In this strategy combination, the UE selects the $M - BS_i$ while the $M - BS_i$ strategy is to serve the UE because in this instant it is off-loaded. In this case the UE and the BS have the same strategy. Therefore, $UE's$ payoff is:

$$X_{22} = C_{M-BS_i}(t) + G_{UE,M-BS_i}(t)$$

$G_{UE,M-BS_i}(t)$ is the $UE's$ gain when it selects the $M - BS_i$, expressed by:

$$G_{UE,M-BS_i}(t) = \frac{W_A}{W_T} + C_{M-BS_i}(t)$$

The $BS's$ payoff is: $Y_{22} = P_{UE,M-BS_i}(t)$.

Select $M - BS_i$ *&* $M - BS_j$ *Serves* UE: The UE in this case is close to the $M - BS_i$, but this latter can not serve it because the maximum number of UEs that it can serve is reached. In this case, the $M - BS_i$ redirects the request of the UE to the closest $M - BS_j$ that offers the best QoS according to a communication agreement.

Therefore, $UE's$ payoff is: $X_{23} = C_{M-BS_j}(t)$.

The $BS's$ payoff is: $Y_{23} = \frac{P_{UE,M-BS_j}(t)}{2}$,

$P_{UE,M-BS_j}(t)$ is divided by 2 because the request is firstly sent to the $M - BS_i$ then it is redirected to the $M - BS_j$ which has a communication agreement with. Therefore, $M - BS_i$ and $M - BS_j$ will share the service price paid by the UE.

Table 2. Matrix game

UE BS	select $S - BS_i$	select $M - BS_i$	$q - mix$
$S - BS_i$ serves UE	(X_{11}, Y_{11})	(X_{12}, Y_{12})	$qY_{11} + (1-q)Y_{12}$
$M - BS_i$ serves UE	(X_{21}, Y_{21})	(X_{22}, Y_{22})	$qY_{21} + (1-q)Y_{22}$
$M - BS_j$ serves UE	(X_{31}, Y_{31})	(X_{23}, Y_{23})	$qY_{31} + (1-q)Y_{23}$
$p - mix$	$p_1X_{11} + p_2X_{21} + (1-p_1-p_2)X_{31}$	$p_1X_{12} + p_2X_{22} + (1-p_1-p_2)X_{23}$	

4 Equilibrium Determination in Cell Selection Game

The NE represents the solution for players in non-cooperative games. One of the essential objectives in this work is to prove the existence of NE. There are two main types of NE defined in non-cooperative game [7], the pure strategy and the mixed strategy. In a pure strategy, each player's strategy is the best response to the strategies of other players. However, it is not suitable for the cell selection game because it leads to the non-causal problem even if the game processes a pure strategy [3]. Thus we introduce the concept of mixed strategy NE.

A mixed strategy for player i is a probability distribution over his set of available actions. In other words, if player i has K_i actions, a mixed strategy is K_i dimensional vector $p = (p_1, p_2, ..., p_K)$ where $0 \le p_k \le 1$ and $\sum_{k=1}^{K} p_k = 1$.

In our situation, we consider that each UE has 2 possible actions consisting of $K_{UE} = \{select\ S - BS_i,\ select\ M - BS_i\}$, and each BS has 3 possible actions consisting of $K_{BS} = \{S - BS_i\ serves\ UE,\ M - BS_i\ serves\ UE,\ M - BS_j\ serves\ UE\}$. According to the NE theory, there is a mixed strategy NE where $player_1$ playing $(action_1, p_1^*, p_2^*)$ and $player_2$ playing $(action_1, q^*)$ do not have interest to change their actions. Our objective is finding p_1^*, p_2^*, and q^*.

Theorem

Let $p_1^* \in [0,\ \frac{G_{UE,MBS_i}(t)}{G_{UE,MBS_i}(t)+G_{UE,SBS_i}(t)}]$ and $p_2^* = \frac{p_1^* \times G_{UE,SBS_i}(t)}{G_{UE,MBS_i}(t)}$, be the optimal probabilities of the UE when it decides to select $S - BS_i$ and let $q^* = \frac{2P_{UE,MBS_i}(t)-P_{UE,SBS_i}(t)}{2(P_{UE,SBS_i}(t)+P_{UE,MBS_i}(t))} + \frac{P_{UE,MBS_i}(t)-P_{UE,SBS_i}(t)}{2P_{UE,SBS_i}(t)+\frac{2}{3}P_{UE,MBS_i}(t))}$, be the optimal probabilities of the BS when it decides that the $S - BS_i$ serves the UE.

There is a mixed strategy NE, UE (select $S - BS_i$, p_1^*, p_2^*), BS ($S - BS_i$ serves the UE, q^*) where the UE selects the $S - BS_i$ if the probability $p_1 > p_1^*$ and $p_2 > p_2^*$ and the $BS's$ action is $S - BS_i$ serves the UE if $q > q^*$.

Proof

- We consider the UE strategies:
  - If the UE plays (select $S - BS_i$), its expected payoff is:

$$E(select \quad S - BS_i) = p_1 X_{11} + p_2 X_{21} + (1 - p_1 - p_2)X_{31}$$

  - If the UE plays (select $M - BS_i$), its expected payoff is:

$$E(select \quad M - BS_i) = p_1 X_{12} + p_2 X_{22} + (1 - p_1 - p_2)X_{23}$$

After all calculation made, the UE will select the $S-BS_i$ when $E(select \quad S-BS_i)$ is greater than $E(select \quad M - BS_i) \Longrightarrow p_1 > p_1^*$ and $p_2 > p_2^*$, where:

$$p_1^* \in [0, \ \frac{G_{UE,MBS_i}(t)}{G_{UE,MBS_i}(t) + G_{UE,SBS_i}(t)}] \ and \quad p_2^* = \frac{p_1^* \times G_{UE,SBS_i}(t)}{G_{UE,MBS_i}(t)}$$

with $0 < p_1^* \leq 1$; $0 < p_2^* \leq 1$.

- We consider the BS strategies:
  - If the BS plays ($S - BS_i$ serves the UE), its expected payoff is:

$$E(S - BS_i \ serves \ the \ UE) = qY_{11} + (1 - q)Y_{12}$$

  - If the BS plays ($M - BS_i$ serves the UE), its expected payoff is:

$$E(M - BS_i \ serves \ the \ UE) = qY_{21} + (1 - q)Y_{22}$$

  - If the BS plays ($M - BS_j$ serves the UE), its expected payoff is:

$$E(M - BS_j \ serves \ the \ UE) = qY_{31} + (1 - q)Y_{32}$$

After all calculation made, the BS will choose the strategy $S - BS_i$ serves the UE when $E(S - BS_i \ serves \ the \ UE)$ is greater than $E(M - BS_i \ serves \ the \ UE)$ and greater than $E(M - BS_j \ serves \ the \ UE) \Longrightarrow q > q^*$, where:

$$q^* = \frac{2P_{UE,MBS_i}(t) - P_{UE,SBS_i}(t)}{2\left(P_{UE,SBS_i}(t) + P_{UE,MBS_i}(t)\right)} + \frac{P_{UE,MBS_i}(t) - P_{UE,SBS_i}(t)}{2P_{UE,SBS_i}(t) + \frac{2}{3}P_{UE,MBS_i}(t))}$$

4.1   System Features

In this game, the two set of players have different requirements, the UEs' need is to select the cell that provides the required QoS during mobility, whereas, the BSs' aim is to distribute the users between different cells in order to balance the load. These requirements are affected by the variation of the number of users served in the whole network. Moreover, the players' strategies are based on the probability value that depends principally on their requirements.

As indicated before, p_1^* and p_2^*, represent the optimal probabilities of the UE when it decides to select $S - BS_i$. Their expressions depend on the $UE's$ gain. These probabilities are affected by the increased number of users in the network. Therefore, p_1^* and p_2^* will decrease when the number of users served by the cell is increasing, because more the cell becomes charged, more the QoS is deteriorated.

On the other hand, q^* represents the optimal probability of the BS when it decides that the $S - BS_i$ serves the UE. Its expression depends on the service price, which is firstly affected by the number of users in the whole network. Indeed, when the number of users in the whole network is increasing, q^* will increase because in load time, the BS player decides that the $S - BS_i$ serves the users in order to balance the load. However, when the network is few charged, the $M - BS_i$ accepts most of users' request as the required QoS is respected.

Also the expression of q^* depends on the number of BS involved in the communication, which is denote by α and can take three possible values ($\alpha = 1$, 2, or 3). Indeed, in the case of $\alpha = 1$, the UE and the BS select the same strategy, then the service price is given to the cell that serves the UE. In the case of $\alpha = 2$, the UE selects $S - BS_i$ or $M - BS_i$ and the BS redirects the request to an other one belonging to the same operator, or, the UE selects $M - BS_i$ and the BS redirects the request to $M - BS_j$ belonging to an other operator, then the service price is divided between the selected cell and the serving cell. Finally, in the case of $\alpha = 3$, the UE selects $S - BS_i$ and the BS redirects the request to $M - BS_j$ belonging to an other operator, then the service price is divided between $S - BS_i$, $M - BS_i$ and $M - BS_j$.

5   Performance Evaluation

In this section, we evaluate the performances of the proposed non-cooperative cell selection game within 5G HetNets using MATLAB software. As depicted in Fig. 2(a), we consider an urban zone implementing two macro-cell BSs with radius of 800 m for each one. We assume that the coverage areas of the $M - BSs$ are overlapped. In addition, we consider that each $M - BS$ is overlaid by 5 $S - BSs$ where each $S - BS$ radius is equal to 100 m. We also assume that the network is full charged when each $M - BS$ serves 30 $users$ and each $S - BS$ serves 10 $users$ simultaneously. The main parameters of this simulation are based on works presented in [2] and in [6] and they are listed in Fig. 2(b).

In Fig. 3, we present the best response function of each player when the network is half charged (55 UEs). As indicated in the previous section, q represents the probability of the BS to decide that $S - BS_i$, $M - BS_i$, or $M - BS_j$ serves the UE. However, $p_2 = \frac{p_1 \times G_{UE,SBS_i}(t)}{G_{UE,MBS_i}(t)}$ represents the probability that the UE selects $S - BS_i$ or $M - BS_i$ during mobility. Indeed, when the BS decides that the $S - BS_i$ serves the users with less than 50% of probability q, the UE should choose to select $S - BS_i$ with 0% of probability p_2. And whenever BS chooses

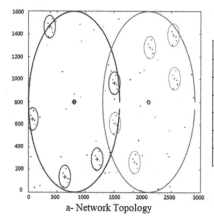

Parameters	Values
M-BS transmission Power	40W
S-BS transmission Power	2W
Frequency band	2,6GHz
5G bandwidth	60GHz
$SINR_{M-BS}$	5dB
$SINR_{S-BS}$	30dB

b- Simulation Parameters

a- Network Topology

Fig. 2. Communication environment

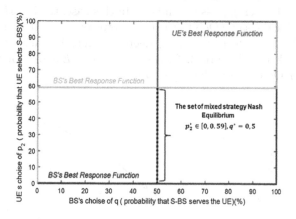

Fig. 3. Combined best response functions

that the $S - BS_i$ serves the users with more than 50% of probability q, the UE should choose to select $S - BS$ with 100% of probability p_2.

The same thing for UEs' strategies. When the UE selects $S - BS_i$ with a rate lower than the range between [0%, 59%] of probability p_2, the BS should choose that $S - BS_i$ serves the UE with 0% of probability q. And whenever the UE selects $S - BS_i$ with a rate more than the range [0%, 59%] of probability p_2, the BS should decide that $S - BS_i$ serves the UE with 100% of probability q. Since p_2 varies according to the variation of p_1 between p_{1-min} and p_{1-max}, a set of p_2 optimal probability are detected. Therefore, the mixed strategy NE is the set of values ($p_2^* \in [0, 0.59]$ and $q^* = 0.5$) representing the intersection of the $BS's$ best response functions with the $UE's$ best response function.

Now, we study the evolution of (p_1^*, q^*) according to the variation of the UEs number. p_1^* represents the optimal probability of the UE when it decides to select $S - BS_i$ strategy. Figure 4(a), shows the behavior of p_1^* with the growth

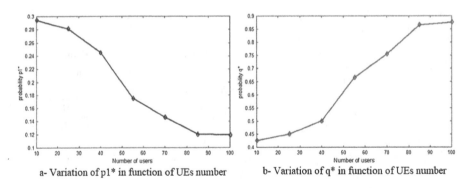

a- Variation of p1* in function of UEs number   b- Variation of q* in function of UEs number

Fig. 4. Evolution of p_1^*, q^* in function of UEs number

of the UEs' request on the network. Indeed, when the network is half charged (UEs number ≤ 40 users), p_1^* is around 0.3. In this case, the $S - BS_i$, $M - BS_i$, and $M - BS_j$ offer the same QoS to the UE. However, when the number of UEs associated to the $S - BS_i$ increases, p_1^* decreases until it reaches the minimum when the network is full charged. In this case, the UE looks for the cell that provide a better QoS than its best $S - BS_i$.

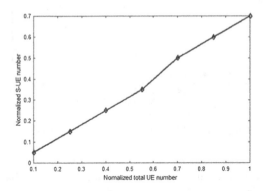

Fig. 5. The rate of $S - UE$ from the total UE number

Figure 4(b), shows the evolution of q^* with the increase of the total number of UEs associated to the whole network. q^* represents the optimal probability of the BS when the $S - BS_i$ serves the UE. We notice that q^* increases slightly until the network becomes half loaded. When the UEs number exceeds the half of the network capacity, q^* increases significantly until reaching its maximum when the network is full loaded. In the beginning of the load time, the BS decides that the $S - BS_i$ serves a few number of UEs' request since the $M - BS_i$ is low loaded. However, in load-off time, $S - BS_i$ accepts most of the received requests, as long as the required QoS is respected, in order to balance the load.

Figure 5 presents the load of the $S - BS$ network compared to the overall load. In the loaded time, the global network strategy tends to associate UEs to the $S-BSs$ in order to balance the load between macro and small-cells. However, in the load-off time, the selection strategy tends to distribute the UEs.

6   Conclusion

In this paper, we focused on the cell selection issue during mobility in 5G Het-Nets. To this end, we proposed a non-cooperative cell selection game with two players (UE and BS). This game realizes an equilibrium in the UEs distribution while respecting the required QoS and maximizing the network's gain. Simulation results are provided to show the performance of the proposed game.

References

1. Aryafar, E., Keshavarz-Haddad, A., Wang, M.: RAT selection games in HetNets. In: Proceedings of IEEE INFOCOM, July 2013
2. Dhifallah, K., Gourhant, Y., Senouci, S.-M.: Cell selection game in heterogeneous macro-small cell networks. In: Proceedings of IEEE International Conference on Communications (ICC), July 2017
3. Gao, L., Wang, X., Sun, G.: A game approach for cell selection and resource allocation in heterogeneous wireless networks. In: Proceedings of the 8th Annual IEEE Communications Society Conference on Sensor, Mesh and Ad Hoc Communications and Networks (SECON), August 2011
4. Gharam, M., Boudriga, N.: An agreement graph-based-authentication scheme for 5G networks. In: Sabir, E., García Armada, A., Ghogho, M., Debbah, M. (eds.) UNet 2017. LNCS, vol. 10542, pp. 509–520. Springer, Cham (2017). https://doi.org/10.1007/978-3-319-68179-5_44
5. Ibrahim, M., Khawam, K., Tohme, S.: Congestion games for distributed radio access selection in broadband networks. In: Proceedings of the IEEE Global Telecommunications Conference (GLOBECOM), January 2011
6. Kelif, J.-M., Senecal, S., Coupechoux, M.: Impact of small cells location on performance and QoS of heterogeneous cellular networks. In: Proceedings of the IEEE 24th International Symposium on Personal Indoor and Mobile Radio Communications (PIMRC), November 2017
7. Lin, J.-S., Feng, K.-T.: Femtocell access strategies in heterogeneous networks using a game theoretical framework. J. IEEE Trans. Wirel. Commun. **13**(3), 1208–1221 (2014)
8. Naghavi, P., Rastegar, S.H., Shah-Mansouri, V.: Learning RAT selection game in 5G heterogeneous networks. J. IEEE Wirel. Commun. Lett. **5**(1), 52–55 (2016)

Prospects and Challenges of Free Space Optical Communications

Abir Touati[1(✉)], Farid Touati[2], Abderrazak Abdaoui[2], Amith Khandakar[2], and Ammar Bouallegue[1]

[1] National Engineering School of Tunis, SYSCOM Laboratory,
University of Tunis El Manar, Tunis, Tunisia
abirtouati@qu.edu.qa, ammarbouallegue.syscom@gmail.com
[2] Department of Electrical Engineering, Qatar University, Doha, Qatar
{touatif,abderrazak.abdaoui,amitk}@qu.edu.qa

Abstract. Free space optical (FSO) transmission is a technology which uses a narrow laser beam to transmit the signal from the source to the destination through the free space. Although it has various advantages, a laser beam propagating through the atmosphere is subjected to different kind of disturbances causing the attenuation of the signal and, in some extreme conditions, leading to the link outage. In fact, the atmospheric turbulences and the chemical nature of the medium is the main source of link attenuation. In this paper, we present the different challenges of FSO communications: absorption, pointing errors, atmospheric turbulence and scattering phenomenon. Moreover, based on the strength of turbulences, we will detail the FSO channel modeling. Then, we introduce some techniques to overcome the weakness presented by FSO link under different strength of atmospheric turbulences.

Keywords: Absorption · Atmospheric turbulence · Misalignment · RF

1 Introduction

Free space optical communications (FSO) have witnessed a growing interest in the last few decades due to its various advantages. In fact, FSO communications ensure secure communications using straight line to transmit data. Thus, the whole communication channel is in the visible area and any tapping activity will be detected [1]. In addition, the cost of FSO installation is low compared to the optical fiber and RF systems [2]. The FSO systems use a laser beam with a frequency in the range of Terahertz (THz). This frequency makes it able to support a large bandwidth which in turn ensures a high data rate compared to the conventional RF systems (10 to 100 Mbps) [3]. The FSO technology can be used for indoor or outdoor transmissions. Despite its various advantages, FSO communications have several limitations. FSO systems suffer from being highly sensitive to atmospheric and weather conditions. In the nature, fog is the biggest

© Springer Nature Switzerland AG 2018
N. Boudriga et al. (Eds.): UNet 2018, LNCS 11277, pp. 40–48, 2018.
https://doi.org/10.1007/978-3-030-02849-7_4

challenge for FSO communications [4,5,8]. In addition, fog affects the transmission where the waves are in the visible and the infrared ranges. This is due to the fact that, in these ranges, the fog's particles and the wavelength of laser beam have the same order of magnitude. Several experimental tests were made to study the influence of fog on FSO. These studies serve to characterize and measure the attenuation of the laser beam. In [6], the authors have presented several empirical models to predict the fog attenuation, then they identify the most rigorous model. They have found that the attenuation depends on the wavelength of FSO transceiver and on the visibility. On the other hand, link performances depend also on the nature and on the chemical composition of the propagation medium. The transmitted light can react with the particles presented in the atmosphere causing beam spreading, known as aerosols [7]. Hence, an interaction with the particles leads to several phenomenon that affect the link, e.g., absorption, scattering and atmospheric turbulences. Atmospheric turbulence is due to the unequal distribution of humidity and temperature in different parts of the atmosphere [8]. Several research works were conducted to investigate the effect of atmospheric turbulences on communications performances. Their studies supported by experimental tests show the effects of weather conditions and factors on the refractive index known also as the strength of atmospheric turbulences. In [9], Augustine et al. have used an experimental indoor test in order to evaluate the effects of thermal turbulence on the laser beam in term of refractive index. They have studied the fluctuation of the refractive index using the experimental data and Andrews and Phillips model. They have found that the refractive index is depending on the temperature. In [10], an experimental test of beam wander variance induced by the atmospheric turbulence has been studied. The test was made using an optical turbulence generator chamber. They confirmed that the increase of temperature gradient can cause serious impairment of FSO link. In [11], the authors made an experimental test to show the effects of harsh climate on FSO communications. They found that the temperature has the strongest effect on the link performance.

The remainder of this paper is organized as follows: In Sect. 2, we present an overview of the different source of impairments affecting the FSO communications. Then, we present the FSO channel model in Sect. 3. In Sect. 4, we introduce the different techniques used to overcome the weakness of FSO link under different strength of atmospheric conditions. Finally, Sect. 5 concludes this paper.

2   FSO Challenges

In FSO communications, laser beam is spread through the atmosphere from the transmitter to the receiver. This beam is subject of many sources of attenuation. In fact, the laser reacts with the atmosphere particles causing the attenuation of the signal. The total atmospheric attenuation is due to the scattering and to the absorption phenomena. In fact these phenomenon result from the interactions between the laser beam and the molecules of the gas and the aerosols present in the atmosphere. As given by [4,12], the aerosol is a set of particles of different forms: such as spherical or irregular. In the following, we will present the different challenges for the FSO transmissions.

2.1 Absorption

Absorption of the laser beam is caused by the interaction of the emitted photons and the molecules/atoms existing in the atmosphere (i.e., N_2, CO_2, H_2O, O_2, etc.). This interaction leads to the disappearance of some photons and their energies will be converted to heat causing an elevation of the temperature. The absorption is considered as "selective wavelength" phenomenon due to its dependence on the type of gas and its concentration in the atmosphere. The wavelength range is divided into two principal zones: Transparent and opaque zones. For, the wavelengths at the first zone, the absorption is considered minimal and it can be neglected. However, in the blocking zone, the absorption is maximal [12]. In order to overcome the effects of atmospheric absorption on laser beam propagation and taken into account that it is too difficult to control the chemical composition of the atmosphere, the FSO systems are made with wavelengths falling in the transparent zone. Thus, in the experimental work, the absorption phenomenon is neglected and the atmospheric attenuation is depending only on the scattering coefficient.

2.2 Scattering Phenomenon

Scattering phenomenon is depending on the size of aerosols and molecules present in the atmosphere. Based on the size of these particles, the scattering can be classified into Rayleigh and Mie scattering. The Rayleigh scattering appears when the particle size (r) is relatively small compared to the wavelength λ of incident beam (i.e., $r < \lambda/10$). However, the Mie scattering appears when the aerosols size are comparable to the wavelength of the transmitted light (i.e., $\lambda/10 < r < 10\lambda$). In the nature, the most known phenomenon causing scattering are fog and haze. In fact, the fog's particles and wavelength of the incident light have the same order of magnitude, reacting together leads to the apparition of Mie scattering phenomenon. In the nature, the fog appears as clouds touching the ground formed from the water vapor. In fact, when the water vapor present in the atmosphere becomes in excess, the surplus of vapor condenses. Hence, when warm and moist air flows over a colder surface the fog appears. As a result, the fog particles reduce the atmospheric visibility. The visibility is defined as the greatest distance at which an object can be clearly seen by a human observer. It is measured by the Runway Visual Range (RVP) which refers to the path length crossed by a luminous flow until its intensity is reduced to 5% of its original value.

2.3 Pointing Errors

The laser beam, transmitted by the source to the destination, is travelling in a straight line. Thus, any misalignment between the transmitter and the receiver causes pointing errors that affect the link performances. These pointing errors are mainly caused by building sways, mechanical vibrations, dynamic wind loads and thermal expansion. The effects of pointing errors on FSO transmission are considered as critical issues because these errors would increase the outage probability and bit-error rate and consequently decrease the channel capacity [13, 14]. In order to mitigate the misalignment fading many techniques can be used. In fact, complex tracking mechanism can be employed to align the laser beam between the transmitter and the receiver by using a feedback channel. However, the FSO systems based on this mechanism are expensive [15]. On the other hand, for short distance, a laser beam with an increase in the power budget is considered as a suitable solution [16].

2.4 Atmospheric Turbulence

The large amount of solar irradiance absorbed by the earth surface causes an important increase of the ambient temperature and leads to the formation of warm air around the ground. This warm air passes over the surrounding air and leads to the inhomogeneity of the ambient atmosphere. This inhomogeneity is manifested by the formation of cells and eddies with different sizes and temperatures and with different refractive index [8, 17, 18]. The refractive index is the key factor of scintillation phenomenon caused by the atmospheric turbulence and characterizes the strength of atmospheric turbulence. In general, refractive index depends on altitude and weather factors such as temperature, solar irradiance and humidity [17, 19]. The eddies react with the transmitted laser beam and cause random phase and amplitude variations of the received signal inducing distortion in the optical wave front. This phenomenon is called "scintillation" and it is responsible of the signal degradation and of the fading of the received power [20, 21].

3   Channel Model

The atmospheric turbulences are random fluctuations of the intensity and the phase of the received signal. In the literature, several models are employed to explore the intensity of these fluctuations. The most used models are Log-Normal and Gamma- Gamma. In fact, for low to moderate turbulences, the fading can be modeled by Log-Normal distribution, while for moderate to strong turbulence; the fading is modeled by Gamma-Gamma distribution [13, 14].

3.1   Log Normal Model

The density probability function (PDF) of Log-Normal distribution is given as follow

$$f_h\left(h\right) = \frac{1}{\sqrt{8\pi}h\sigma}\exp\left\{-\frac{\left(\ln(h)+2\sigma^2\right)^2}{8\sigma^2}\right\} \qquad (1)$$

where h is the normalized channel fading, σ is the scintillation index characterizing the strength of atmospheric turbulence.

3.2   Gamma-Gamma Model

The density probability function (PDF) of Gamma-Gamma distribution is given as follow

$$f_h(h) = \frac{2(\alpha\beta)^{(\alpha+\beta)/2}}{\Gamma(\alpha)\Gamma(\beta)} h^{\frac{(\alpha+\beta)}{2}-1} K_{\alpha-\beta}\left(2\sqrt{(\alpha\beta h)}\right), \tag{2}$$

where the parameters α and β are related to the atmospheric conditions and represent, respectively, the effective number of large and small scale eddies of the scattering process. $K_n(.)$ is the modified Bessel function of the second kind of order n and $\Gamma(.)$ denotes the Gamma function. The parameters α and β are given by [22] and denote the effective number of large and small scale eddies.

4   Techniques to Mitigate the Effect of FSO's Challenges

To bridge this gap and overcome the weakness of FSO link under strong atmospheric turbulence, several techniques are used. In the following, we will present some techniques already existed and have been tested.

4.1   Hybrid FSO/RF System

This technique consists of adding an RF link to the FSO link. This setup can exist into two configurations.

(1) *Hard switching configuration:* For the hard switching configuration, at any time only one link is active while the other link is idle. In fact, while the atmospheric conditions are favorable, the FSO is active. Otherwise, the RF will be activated and FSO goes into idle state, Fig. 1. However, the disadvantage of this approach is that the RF link can be selected for a large period and the channel capacity of FSO link is wasted.

(2) *Soft switching configuration:* In the soft switching, the two links are activated simultaneously, Fig. 2. In this configuration, the use of channel coding (i.e., Raptor codes,...) is mandatory. In fact, the data is encoded then sent through the two links. At the receiver side, the data is collected from the two links and it is stored, then decoded and interpreted.

The performances of the soft and hard switching configurations, under foggy weather, is presented in [23]. They have found that the encoded system (i.e. soft switching approach) can provide significantly higher throughput particularly in adverse weather condition than the hard switching configuration. On the other hand, the performance of soft switching configuration under harsh climate has been studied in [24]. The authors have found that the soft switching configuration under harsh and desert climate with high temperature ensures a high level of quality of service compared to the individual FSO link.

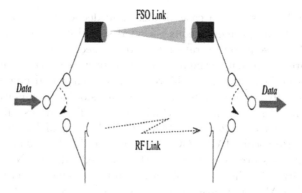

Fig. 1. Hybrid FSO/RF hard switching configuration.

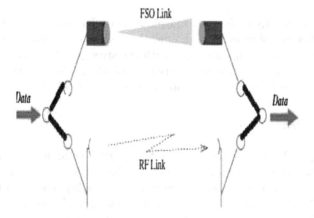

Fig. 2. Hybrid FSO/RF soft switching configuration.

4.2 Hybrid Automatic Repeat Request

In most of the recent related works, the HARQ (automatic repeat request) protocols are used on FSO communications. These protocols are used to overcome the
loss of data presented under atmospheric turbulences. The main idea of HARQ is
based on the acknowledgment (ACK) received from the receiver [14]. If a positive
ACK is received that means that the transmitted packet was received without
error. Thus, the sender will move to the next packet. However, when a negative
ACK (NACK) is received, which means that an error affected the transmitted
packet, a re-transmission is then required. The re-transmission process continues
until a positive ACK is received or a maximum number of rounds M is achieved.
Note that, the process of re-transmission depends on the type of HARQ used.
In the following we will present two types of HARQ.

(1) *HARQ with incremental redundancy (HARQ-IR):* For the HARQ-IR, for
each packet generated by the transmitter, a number of parity bits are added.

A positive ACK is sent in case of successful decoding. In contrary, in case of decoding failure, the erroneous packet is stored in a buffer at the receiver and a NACK is sent to the transmitter. In the second round, new parity bits are generated then sent to the receiver. This process continues until an ACK is received or M rounds are achieved. Thus, each round contains different parity bits. After each rounds, at the receiver side, a combination of all the stored parity bits is carried out which ensure a high successful decoding.

(2) *HARQ with chase combining (HARQ-CC):* In case of HARQ with Chase Combining Protocol (HARQ-CC), when a decoding failure occurs, the erroneous packet is stored in a buffer at the received side and NACK is sent to the transmitter [30]. The transmitter re-sends the same packet until an ACK is received or M rounds are achieved. At the receiver side, for each round, maximal ratio combining (MRC) is carried out to all the previous received packets.

Note that for low to moderate atmospheric turbulences, the HARQ technique can be an efficient solution to overcome the loss of data. However for strong turbulences, the loss of data increases with the strength of turbulences and the re-transmission technique becomes a useless solution. Thus, in this case using the hard or soft switching configuration can be a great solution.

5   Conclusion

In this paper, we have presented an overview of FSO communications. We have introduced the different challenges faced by a laser beam propagating through the atmosphere. These sources of attenuation can highly affect the link performances and in the worst case cause the link outage. Moreover, we have presented the FSO channel modeling for different strength of atmospheric turbulence. Then, we have presented some techniques that can be used to overcome the weakness of FSO link under different strength of atmospheric turbulence.

References

1. Gupta, A., Anand, P., Khajuria, R., Bhagat, S., Jha, R.K.: A survey of free space optical communication network channel over optical fiber cable communication. Int. J. Comput. Appl. **105**(10), 32–36 (2014)
2. Mahdy, A., Deogun, J.S.: Wireless optical communications: a survey. In: 2004 IEEE Wireless Communications and Networking Conference. WCNC 2004, vol. 4, pp. 2399–2404. IEEE (2004)
3. Kaushal, H., Kaddoum, G.: Optical communication in space: challenges and mitigation techniques. IEEE Commun. Surv. Tutor. **19**, 57–96 (2016)
4. Naboulsi, M., Sizun, H., Fornel, F.: Propagation of optical and infrared waves in the atmosphere. In: Proceedings of the Union Radio Scientifique Internationale (2005)
5. Touati, A., Abdaoui, A., Touati, F., Khandakar, A., Bouallegue, A.: Indoor test of the fog's effect on FSO link. In: Proceedings of SPIE, vol. 10096, p. 1009619-1 (2017)

6. Ijaz, M., Ghassemlooy, Z., Pesek, J., Fiser, O., Le Minh, H., Bentley, E.: Modeling of fog and smoke attenuation in free space optical communications link under controlled laboratory conditions. J. Light. Technol. **31**(11), 1720–1726 (2013)

7. Nazari, Z., Gholami, A., Vali, Z., Sedghi, M., Ghassemlooy, Z.: Experimental investigation of scintillation effect on FSO channel, Newcastle Upon Tyne, UK (2016)

8. Bendersky, S., Lilos, E., Kopeika, N.S., Blaunstein, N.: Modeling and measurements of near-ground atmospheric optical turbulence according to weather for middle east environments. In: European Symposium on Optics and Photonics for Defence and Security, pp. 350–361. International Society for Optics and Photonics (2004)

9. Augustine, S.M., Chetty, N.: Experimental verification of the turbulent effects on laser beam propagation in space. Atmósfera **27**(4), 385–401 (2014)

10. Yuksel, H.: Studies of the effects of atmospheric turbulence on free space optical communications (2005)

11. Touati, A., Abdaoui, A., Touati, F., Uysal, M., Bouallegue, A.: On the effects of temperature on the performances of FSO transmission under qatar's climate

12. Ghassemlooy, Z., Popoola, W., Rajbhandari, S.: Optical wireless communications: system and channel modelling with Matlab®. CRC Press (2012)

13. Farid, A.A., Hranilovic, S.: Outage capacity optimization for free-space optical links with pointing errors. J. Light. Technol. **25**(7), 1702–1710 (2007)

14. Trung, H.D., Pham, A.T., et al.: Pointing error effects on performance of free-space optical communication systems using SC-QAM signals over atmospheric turbulence channels. AEU-Int. J. Electron. Commun. **68**(9), 869–876 (2014)

15. Petkovic, M.I., Dordevic, G.T.: Effects of pointing errors on average capacity of FSO links over gamma-gamma turbulence channel. In: 2013 11th International Conference on Telecommunications in Modern Satellite, Cable and Broadcasting Services (TELSIKS) (2013)

16. Sandalidis, H.G., Tsiftsis, T.A., Karagiannidis, G.K.: Optical wireless communications with heterodyne detection over turbulence channels with pointing errors. J. Light. Technol. **27**(20), 4440–4445 (2009)

17. Leclerc, T.T., Phillips, R.L., Andrews, L.C., Wayne, D.T., Sauer, P., Crabbs, R.: Prediction of the ground-level refractive index structure parameter from the measurement of atmospheric conditions. In: SPIE Defense, Security, and Sensing, p. 76850A. International Society for Optics and Photonics (2010)

18. Sadot, D., Kopeika, N.S.: Forecasting optical turbulence strength on the basis of macroscale meteorology and aerosols: models and validation. Opt. Eng. **31**(2), 200–212 (1992)

19. Pesek, J., Fiser, O.: Research of refractive index impact on dual wavelenght FSO link attenuation. In: 2011 International Conference on Applied Electronics (AE), pp. 1–3, IEEE (2011)

20. Bendall, C.S., Frederickson, P.A., Davidson, K.L., Zeisse, C.R.: Estimating the refractive index structure parameter (Cn2) over the ocean using Bulk methods. J. Appl. Meteorol. **39**, 1770–1783 (2000)

21. Xie, G., Dang, A., Guo, H.: Effects of atmosphere dominated phase fluctuation and intensity scintillation to DPSK system. In: 2011 IEEE International Conference on Communications (ICC), pp. 1–6. IEEE (2011)

22. Lee, I.E., Ghassemlooy, Z., Ng, W.P., Uysal, M.: Performance analysis of free space optical links over turbulence and misalignment induced fading channels. In: 2012 8th International Symposium on Communication Systems, Networks and Digital Signal Processing (CSNDSP), pp. 1–6. IEEE (2012)

23. Zhang, W., Hranilovic, S., Shi, C.: Soft-switching hybrid FSO/RF links using short-length raptor codes: design and implementation. IEEE J. Sel. Areas Commun. **27**(9), 1–11 (2009)
24. Touati, A., Hussain, S.J., Touati, F., Bouallegue, A.: Effect of atmospheric turbulence on hybrid FSO/RF link availability under Qatar harsh climate. Int. J. Electr. Comput. Energ. Electron. Commun. Eng. **9**(8) (2015)
25. Chatzidiamantis, N.D., Georgiadis, L., Sandalidis, H.G., Karagiannidis, G.K.: Throughput-optimal link-layer design in power constrained hybrid OW/RF systems. IEEE J. Sel. Areas Commun. **33**(9), 1972–1984 (2015)

Switching Between Diversity and Spatial Multiplexing in Massive MIMO Systems

Halima Bergaoui$^{(\boxtimes)}$, Yosra Mlayah$^{(\boxtimes)}$, Fethi Tlili$^{(\boxtimes)}$,
and Fatma Rouissi$^{(\boxtimes)}$

Higher school of communication of Tunis (SUP'COM), Tunis, Tunisia
{halima.bergaoui,fethi.tlili,rouissi.fatma}@supcom.tn,
yousra.mlayeh@supcom.rnu.tn

Abstract. In this paper, a new scalable and adaptable STBC (space time bloc coding) architecture is proposed. This architecture is based on switching between diversity and spatial multiplexing depending on the instantaneous channel state and offers an improvement of bit error rate performances comparing to conventional STBCs.

Keywords: Massive-MIMO · Diversity · Spatial multiplexing
Post-processing SNR · Switching algorithm · Adaptation

1 Introduction

With the continuous growth of wireless systems, new demands are required, such as more connected devices, larger data traffics volume and better quality of services at a reduced cost [1], which leads to a huge need of improvements.

Large-scale Multiple-Input Multiple-Output (Large-scale MIMO) is based on the use of a large number of service antennas at the base station to help focusing signal's energy into smaller regions of space [2]. It helps improving throughput and energy efficiency [3]. Furthermore, increasing antennas' number is beneficial even for low Signal to Noise Ratio (SNR) [4].

The most known MIMO techniques are diversity and Spatial Multiplexing. Diversity uses multiple antennas to send many copies of the data stream. It aims to enhance wireless link quality [5, 6]. Spatial multiplexing consists on sending different data streams independently in order to offer higher peak throughput [7].

Several works studied adaptation techniques in order to enhance bit error rate (BER) performances in MIMO systems [8–12]. Particularly, they studied adaptation of MIMO techniques to the instantaneous channel state by switching between diversity and spatial multiplexing.

With the growing number of antennas, implementation of switching techniques and even diversity techniques is becoming more and more complex and less performing.

In this paper, we resolve the problem of switching techniques' implementation in large-scale MIMO system by proposing an embedded architecture.

This paper is organized as follows: Section two describes the system's structure and the role of each component. Then, section three details the switching techniques'

© Springer Nature Switzerland AG 2018
N. Boudriga et al. (Eds.): UNet 2018, LNCS 11277, pp. 49–57, 2018.
https://doi.org/10.1007/978-3-030-02849-7_5

implementation's problem in large-scale MIMO and a new system's architecture to solve it. Finally, performances of the proposed switching algorithm are evaluated in Sect. 4, considering the case of perfect channel knowledge via MATLAB simulations.

2   System Overview

In this work, we consider a simplified MIMO-OFDM (Orthogonal frequency division multiple access) system model with N_t transceiver and N_r receiver antennas as depicted in Fig. 1. Other than the basic components, a switching bloc is added to select between spatial multiplexing and diversity to enhance the BER performances.

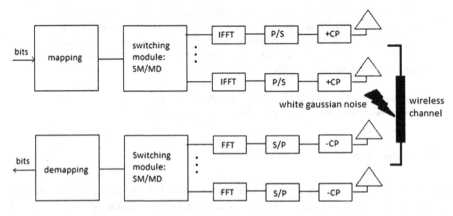

Fig. 1. System structure

After symbol's mapping, modulated symbols are encoded by the MIMO encoder (diversity or multiplexing) and OFDM samples are computed via IFFT (Inverse fast Fourier transform). Finally, these samples go through a parallel to serial converter and cyclic prefix is added.

After passing through a multipath channel with additional white Gaussian noise, the signal reaches the receiver to be decoded and demodulated.

2.1   Switching Module

Switching module is used to dynamically choose which MIMO technique offers better BER performances depending on the instantaneous channel state.

In this work, the considered MIMO techniques are:

- Diversity: It uses multiple antennas to send multiple copies of the required signal to ensure better wireless link quality [5, 6].
- Spatial multiplexing: It uses multiple antennas to send independent data streams each time to ensure greater throughput at a given signal to noise ratio (SNR) [7].

The used switching criterion is PPSNC (post-processing SNR Criterion) [12]. Several switching criterions are studied. The most known are the demmel condition number of the instantaneous channel matrix and the post-processing SNR. A comparison study given in [12] proved that post processing SNR based switching technique offers the best BER performances.

This technique consists on choosing the MIMO technique that offers the highest post-processing SNR weighted by the constellation's Minimum Euclidean distance. The spatial multiplexing is chosen if:

$$ppSNR_{MD}d_{MD}^2 < {}^{min}_{k}\left(ppSNR_{SM,k}\right)d_{SM}^2, \tag{1}$$

Where:

- $ppSNR_{MD}$: Post-processing SNR after MIMO diversity processing.
- $ppSNR_{SM,k}$: Post-processing SNR after Spatial multiplexing processing of the kth channel.
- d_{SM}^2: Minimum Euclidean distance of the constellation assigned to MIMO diversity.
- d_{MD}^2 Minimum Euclidean distance of the constellation assigned to spatial multiplexing.

Elsewhere, MIMO diversity must be chosen.

2.2 Mapping/Demapping

To maintain a fixed data rate for the mentioned MIMO techniques, we used two modulation's mapping sizes:

- 2^R- Constellation if diversity is selected.
- $2^{\frac{R}{T}}$ - Constellation for spatial multiplexing otherwise.

Where R is the number of bits per code and T is the number of symbol periods per space-time bloc code.

3 Proposed Embedded STBC Architecture

With the growth of antennas' number, conventional spatial architectures cannot be used for the switching techniques because at the same data rate, spatial multiplexing is much more efficient than diversity.

In fact, for the diversity, the bit error probability [12] is given by:

$$P_{MD} = N_{s_{MD}}N_{e_{MD}}Q\left(\sqrt{\frac{PPSNR_{MD}dmin_{MD}^2}{2}}\right) \tag{2}$$

Where:

- $N_{s_{MD}}$: Number of transmission chains

- $N_{e_{MD}}$: Constellation's nearest neighbors' number
- $PPSNR_{MD}$: SNR after signal decoding at the receiver
- $dmin^2_{MD} = \frac{12}{2^R-1}$: Constellation's minimum Euclidean distance with R is the number code word's bits in case of diversity technique.

With the increase of R, $dmin$ is decreased and so the bit error probability rises. Which means that to preserve the same data rate for diversity and spatial multiplexing, BER performances of the diversity technique is deteriorated.

Moreover, conventional Space-time bloc coding (STBC) is not defined for large-scale systems. Therefore, we propose a new MIMO encoder's architecture which is based on choosing a small conventional STBC for each bloc of two antennas depending on the instantaneous channel state then embedding them to obtain an adaptable and scalable STBC.

In this work, we consider two low complexity MIMO techniques which are Alamouti and spatial multiplexing with zero-forcing decoder.

Figure 2 represents the embedded STBC based on switching between Alamouti code and spatial multiplexing.

	Diversity			Spatial multiplexing	
first bloc :	x_1	$-x_2^*$	or	x_1	x_3
	x_2	x_1^*		x_2	x_4
	⋮	⋮		⋮	⋮
Nt/2 th bloc :	x_{N_t-1}	$-x_{N_t}^*$	or	x_{N_t-3}	x_{N_t-1}
	x_{N_t}	$x_{N_t-1}^*$		x_{N_t-2}	x_{N_t}

Fig. 2. Switching between Alamouti code and spatial multiplexing in an embedded spatial architecture

Let's pose the data stream $\{x_1, x_2, ..x_{N_t}\}$, the switching scenario will be as follow:
At the transmitter:

- For each group of two antennas, evaluate the switching criterion:

- If spatial multiplexing is the most appropriate x_1 is sent in the first antenna and x_2 in the second one for the first symbol's period. Then at the second period, x_3 is sent in the first antenna and x_4 in the second one.
- If diversity is the most appropriate, x_1 is sent in the first antenna. x_2 is sent in the second antenna at the first period. Then at the second period, $-x_2^*$ is sent in the first antenna and x_1^* in the second one.

- Repeat the first step for all the next groups of two antennas to get the STBC mentioned in Fig. 2.

At the receiver:

- Receive the signal during two symbol's periods

$$y_{T1} = HX_{T1} + N_{T1} \tag{3}$$

$$y_{T2} = HX_{T2} + N_{T2} \tag{4}$$

With $y_{Ti,i=1,2}$ is the received signal at the ith symbol's period T, $X_{Ti,i=1,2}$ is the transmitted signal at the ith symbol's period, N is a random white Gaussian noise vector and H is the channel state matrix. H is supposed to be constant for two symbol's periods.

Channel equalization

$$X_{T1} = H^{-1}y_{T1} \tag{5}$$

$$X_{T1} = H^{-1}y_{T2} \tag{6}$$

- For each group i of two antennas, decide the transmitted symbols s_i :
- In case of spatial multiplexing:

$$s_i = (X_{T1}(1), X_{T1}(2), X_{T2}(1), X_{T2}(2))$$

- In case of Alamouti:

$$s_i = \left[(X_{T1}(1) + X_{T2}^*(2))/2, (X_{T1}(2) - X_{T2}^*(1))/2 \right]$$

- The Final estimated symbols are given by embedding the estimated symbols of each group of two antennas:

$$s = \left(s_1 s_2 \ldots s_{N_t/2} \right)$$

4 Simulation Results

To analyze the proposed technique's performances, MATLAB simulations of the MIMO-OFDM system described in Sect. 2 is performed. Following IMT vision of 5G networks given in [1], we assume the smallest bandwidth possible which is 100 MHz at 30 GHz spectrum. Channel measurements are following the millimeter waves' specification given in [13]. BER is the mean of 100 realizations and we assume that perfect channel state information is available.

The first simulation is a comparison between conventional OSTBC (orthogonal space-time bloc coding) from [14] described in Fig. 3, the embedded STBC given in Fig. 4, the conventional spatial multiplexing and the proposed switching technique. We are limited to $N_t = 8$ and $N_r = 8$.

$$\begin{pmatrix} x_1 & x_2 & x_3 & x_4 & x_5 & x_6 & x_7 & x_8 \\ -x_2 & x_1 & x_4 & -x_3 & x_6 & -x_5 & -x_8 & x_7 \\ -x_3 & -x_4 & x_1 & x_2 & x_7 & x_8 & -x_5 & -x_6 \\ -x_4 & x_3 & -x_2 & x_1 & x_8 & -x_7 & x_6 & -x_5 \\ -x_5 & -x_6 & -x_7 & -x_8 & x_1 & x_2 & x_3 & x_4 \\ -x_6 & x_5 & -x_8 & x_7 & -x_2 & x_1 & -x_4 & x_3 \\ -x_7 & x_8 & x_5 & -x_6 & -x_3 & x_4 & x_1 & -x_2 \\ -x_8 & -x_7 & x_6 & x_5 & -x_4 & -x_3 & x_2 & x_1 \end{pmatrix}$$

Fig. 3. OSTBC scheme [14]

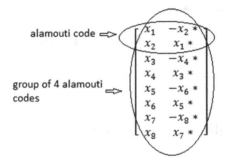

Fig. 4. Embedded STBC scheme

To ensure a fixed data rate, bpsk (Binary Phase Shift Keying) modulation is used for spatial multiplexing, qpsk for embedded STBC and 256-psk for conventional STBC.

Table 1 summarizes the simulation's configuration.

Table 1. Simulation 1 configuration

Spatial multiplexing modulation	Bpsk
Conventional STBC modulation	256-psk
Embedded STBC modulation	Qpsk
Number of transceiver antennas	8
Number of receiver antennas	8
Subcarrier bandwidth	0.87 MHz
Number of subcarriers	128
Mobile's speed	360 km/h

Simulation results are illustrated in Fig. 5.

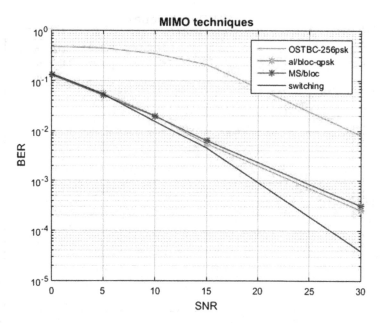

Fig. 5. BER performance of the switching algorithm in an embedded architecture 8×8

Figure 5 shows that the Alamouti embedded system presents better BER performance than MIMO OSTBC 8×8 at the same data rate in the order of 16 dB at BER $= 10^{-2}$. Besides, the switching technique offers a gain of 4 dB compared to spatial multiplexing and 3,5 dB compared to embedded STBC at BER $= 10^{-3}$.

A second simulation is performed in a larger architecture ($N_t = 32$ and $N_r = 32$). It aims to compare the BER of the described spatial multiplexing, embedded STBC and the switching between them. The new configuration is given by Table 2.

Table 2. Simulation 2 configuration

Spatial multiplexing modulation	Bpsk
Embedded STBC modulation	Qpsk
Number of transceiver antennas	32
Number of receiver antennas	32
Subcarrier bandwidth	0.87 MHz
Number of subcarriers	128
Mobile's speed	360 km/h

Simulation results are illustrated in Fig. 6.

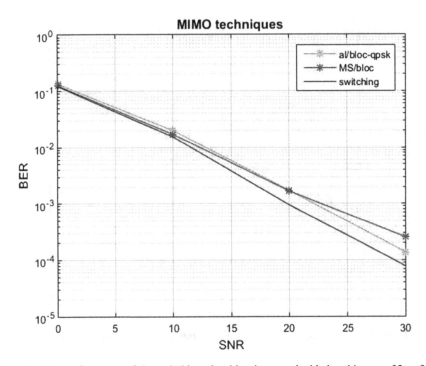

Fig. 6. BER performance of the switching algorithm in an embedded architecture 32×32

Simulation's result shows that the switching technique offers a gain of 2 dB compared to the spatial multiplexing and the embedded STBC at BER $= 10^{-3}$.

5 Conclusion

In this paper, we studied the effects of using MIMO techniques' adaptation in a large-scale MIMO system. First, we defined the system's architecture as well as the used technologies. Then, we explained the used adaptation technique, the simulation procedure and its results.

The major contribution of this work is proposing a new scalable and adaptable Diversity/multiplexing trade-off. It offers a better system's bit error rate performances and avoids the resources' waste in case of favorable channel state.

Further work will consider channel estimation problems in large scale MIMO and its effect on the adaptation techniques.

References

1. IMT Vision: Framework and overall objectives of the future development of IMT for 2020 and beyond, IMT 2020
2. FP7 Project MAMMOET, Massive (very large) MIMO systems (2017)
3. Larsson, E.G., Edfors, O., Tufvesson, F., Marzetta, T.L.: Massive MIMO for next generation wireless systems. IEEE Commun. Mag. **52**(2), 186–195 (2014)
4. Marzetta, T.L.: How much training is required for multiuser MIMO? In: Proceedings of IEEE Asilomar Conference on Signals, Systems, and Computers, October 2006
5. Gesbert, D., Shafi, M., Shiu, D., Smith, P.J., Naguib, A.: From theory to practice: an overview of MIMO space time coded wireless systems. IEEE J. Sel. Areas Commun. **21**(3), 281–302 (2003)
6. Alamouti, S.M.: A simple transmit diversity technique for wireless communications. IEEE J. Sel. Areas Commun. **16**(8), 1451–1458 (1998)
7. Adeane, J., Malik, W.Q., Wassell, I.J.: Error performance of ultrawideband spatial multiplexing systems. IET Microw. Antennas Propag. **3**(3), 363–371 (2009)
8. Heath Jr., R.W., Love, D.J.: Multimode antenna selection for spatial multiplexing systems with linear receivers. IEEE Trans. Signal Process. **53**(8), 3042–3056 (2005)
9. Han, C., Armour, S., Doufexi, A., Ng, K.H., McGeehan, J.: Link adaptation performance evaluation for a MIMO-OFDM physical layer in a realistic outdoor environment. In: Vehicular Technology Conference, vol. 74, pp. 1–5, September 2006
10. Muquet, B., Biglieri, E., Sari, H.: MIMO link adaptation in mobile WiMAX systems, Kowloon, pp. 1810–1813, Juin 2007
11. Forenza, A., McKay, M.R., Pandharipande, A., Heath Jr., R.W., Collings, I.B.: Adaptive MIMO transmission for exploiting the capacity of spatially correlated channels. IEEE Trans. Veh. Technol. **56**(2), 619–630 (2007)
12. Mlayah, Y.: Méthodes de commutation des techniques MIMO-OFDM robustes à la variation de l'état instantanée du canal de transmission sans fils dans les contextes mono et multi-utilisateurs. In: SUPCOM, p. 47 (2012)
13. Rappaport, T.S., MacCartney, G.R., Samimi, M.K., Sun, S.: Wideband millimeter-wave propagation measurements and channel models for future wireless communication system design. IEEE Trans. Commun. **63**(9), 3029–3056 (2015)
14. Tarokh, V., Jafarkhani, H., Calderbank, A.R.: Space–time block codes from orthogonal designs. IEEE Trans. Inf. Theory **45**(5), 1456–1467 (1999)

Cooperative Communication over a NS-3 PLC Module

Nouha Khyari[✉], Sofiane Khalfallah, Yosra Barouni,
and Jaleleddine Ben Hadj Slama

LATIS- Laboratory of Advanced Technology and Intelligent Systems,
ENISo University of Sousse, Sousse, Tunisia
nouha.khyari@gmail.com

Abstract. Taking advantage of the PLC module developed using NS-3 network simulator, we aim through this work to study a realistic model of a cooperative in-home network based on the MAC switching. To evaluate the QoS of the implemented system, we study the channel behaviour in terms of maximum capacity and bit error rate for the AF and DF relay protocols, in comparison with direct transmission. We also study the throughput obtained by our cooperative system. According to the simulations, and despite the short distances and the minimal variations, the cooperative transmission has proved its out-performance compared to the direct transmission protocol.

Keywords: Power line communication · In-home application
Cooperative communication · MAC layer · NS-3 simulator

1 Introduction

With the advent of renewable energy sources, the power grid is going through a major evolution. To take into consideration these new changes, old electrical equipments need innovative communications systems able to remotely control the intermittent production of renewable energies and optimize consumption. Technological intelligence was introduced in these networks, which led to the concept of Smart Grid (SG).

The Smart Grid is based on making data and power transmissions coexist within the same electrical support, mainly due to the power line communication technology (PLC). The modernization of the grid has used various information technologies in order to meet the communications requirements (reliability, data rates, throughput, security, etc.) in such environments, like the indoor and outdoor systems [1].

Cooperative transmission is one of the solutions to improve the efficiency and performance of the SG network with the presence of disturbing elements characterizing the electrical medium. This relaying technique consists in routing the information from the source to the destination via a relay node, through a

© Springer Nature Switzerland AG 2018
N. Boudriga et al. (Eds.): UNet 2018, LNCS 11277, pp. 58–68, 2018.
https://doi.org/10.1007/978-3-030-02849-7_6

different path, when the direct link connecting the source and the destination is affected by the fading effects. This cooperation offers flexibility, robustness and coverage to the whole network.

2   State of the Art

Several studies have investigated the application of cooperative communication in different environments. Most of them targeted the physical level, such as the energy consumption side [2], multiplexing/modulation techniques [3] and total capacity [4]. Different relay protocols have been used for this purpose, to which belong the Decode and Forward (DF) and Amplify and Forward (AF) [5]. In [6], a comparison of these two protocols was conducted in an in-home environment, based on a measuring campaign performed in an urban area in Juiz de Fora in Brazil. The results were used to compare the AF and DF protocols in terms of data rates.

Concerning the MAC layer, we found only few works working on it. In [7] the authors show the benefits of the cooperative transmission in terms of packet error ratio through a cooperative protocol for PLC link layer. Using this protocol, the relay sends a Want To Cooperate message to the source that has already received a negative acknowledgement (Nack) from the destination. We note that the simulations for this work were done with Matlab, which is the common evaluation environment used in the cited works. In our work we consider an in-home application based on cooperative communication. We chose to work with NS-3 simulator, which allows to simulate different topologies of the PLC network and offers more flexibility in the channel configuration than the other simulation tools [8]. Simulations in [9–11] were based on this module.

In [9], the authors have studied the characteristics of Linear-Periodic Time-Variant channel which they implement using PLC NS-3 module. Based on this characterization, they introduced an analytical model for MAC scheduler and evaluated its performance through simulations. In [10], a study of the channel transfer function for several PLC topologies was detailed and simulated using the NS-3 PLC module. Simulation results were compared with the output of the MATLAB simulator and the real measurements for broadband and narrowband PLC. Unlike the above-mentioned works which focused mainly on direct transmission schemes, we are treating in our work a cooperative PL communication.

An evaluation of an in-home PLC system was produced in [11] to measure some Quality of Service (QoS) metrics through this network. Based on this home model, we added to the direct communication system studied by the authors, a cooperative communication scheme using the NS-3 PLC module, where the data exchange is done in dual hop via a relay node.

3   Contribution

Our contribution consists on studying the contribution of the cooperative communication in an in-home environment, through the comparison of the AF and

DF protocols with the direct communication. Unlike the previous works, we are based on the PLC module developed using the NS-3 simulator, which is described in [8]. The QoS is evaluated in term of capacity, Bit Error Rate and network throughput. For the latter, we have implemented a new MAC Header facilitating cooperative communication between the different nodes. More details will be provided later.

Our paper will be organized as follows: In the first section we introduce the adopted topology and the NS-3 PLC elements used to build it, followed by a description for the cooperative system. In the second section we use different metrics to evaluate the QoS through the network. Finally, the simulation results are discussed in the third section.

4 Network Topology

The NS-3 simulator is a discrete-event network that includes several modules and features used to simulate network protocols with different topologies. Simulations can be visualized through a graphical interface. The PLC module, not being officially a part of the NS-3 standard distribution, is a module allowing various configuration of PLC networks and the simulation of realistic channels behaviour.

4.1 In-Home Topology

For our in-home application, we adopt the topology model used in [11] to take advantage of the cabling measurements and to compare the given simulations results with the cooperative transmission. More details on the design of this model can be found in the same reference. Figure 1 shows a layout of the network topology with stretching wires. It considers a $60\,m^2$ home composed of a bedroom, a living room, a kitchen and a bathroom.

The simulation of a communication between two nodes of this network goes through a defined channel configured using the PLC module.

4.2 NS-3 PLC Elements

This module is described in details in [8]. Establishing a communication between two nodes using the PLC module is done in several steps. **Nodes** are at first, created and connected through a **Cable**. The current PLC implementation includes three commonly used power cable types. We are using the NAYY150SE cable in this work.

The **Channel** is set up based on a **Spectral Model**. **Nodes** are connected to the channel using methods provided by a **Net Device** to enable communication between them.

To facilitate working with the **Net Device**, a **Device Helper** is defined and is usually responsible for creating **Transmitter** and **Receiver Interfaces**. **Outlets** are installed on the nodes, and a **PLC Physical** is installed on each **Outlet**.

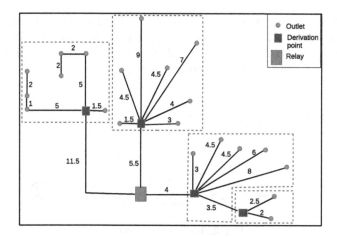

Fig. 1. In-home simulated topology

Once the topology is successfully created, the **Noise Floor** is set through **Interference** class at each **Physical Interface** installed on each **MAC**. To send a packet from one node to another, the **CSMA/CA** MAC protocol is enabled on nodes.

As mentioned in [8], the PLC module supports four **Impedance** types, which are fixed, frequency selective, time-selective, and frequency and time selective impedance. Fixed impedance is used in our simulation.

4.3   Cooperative Communication

As cited in [12], cooperative relaying is no longer limited in channel specification and physical layer but also investigated with MAC protocols. In our case, the relayed path is then decided at MAC layer as described in Fig. 2 (usually done based on routing tables).

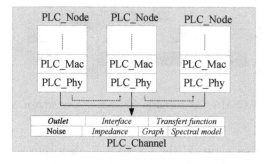

Fig. 2. Cooperative transmission through the MAC and physical layers

The PLC module provides two MAC protocols with different control mechanism which are the ARQ (Automatic Repeat Request) and the Hybrid ARQ. We are using in our network the ARQ MAC where a successful transmission is marked with a positive acknowledgement (Ack).

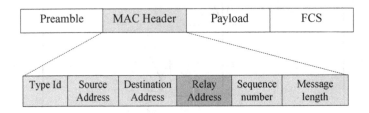

Fig. 3. PLC frame format

To do this, the decided relayed packet is retrieved by the intermediate node due to the new address field added to the MAC header indicating the relay's MAC address (see Fig. 3). The channel access in this module adopts the CSMA/CA mechanism. This mechanism is basically presented as follows: When the channel is free, the sending station executes its Backoff algorithm [14].

It is a counter started at the end of the DIFS (DCF interframe space) that decrements as long as the channel is free. When a collision is detected, this counter is suspended until the channel is released. Once the counter reaches 0, the station starts sending its packet and waits for the reception of an Ack from the destination station. The destination's response is sent after a short interframe space (SIFS). Once the Ack is received, the transmitting station will understand that the transmission was made without collisions. In the opposite case and at the expiration of the Backoff counter, the transmitter resends the same frame.

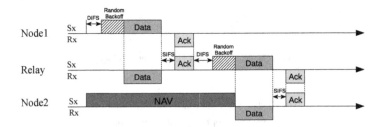

Fig. 4. CSMA/CA scenario for cooperative transmission

In our cooperative network, the CSMA/CA algorithm is performed twice: between the source and the relay, and then between the relay and destination. When the channel is sensed busy, an indicator called Network Allocation Vector (NAV) is maintained at each listening node to inform about the channel reservation status [14]. We have summarized the communication in Fig. 4. In the following sections, we will use this characterization of the network to evaluate its performance.

5   QoS Parameters

The purpose of our work is to evaluate the QoS on this cooperative network, through the quantification of some selected metrics, which are the capacity, the bit error rate and the transmission throughput.

Channel Capacity

Theoretically, the maximum achievable capacity C is given by the known Shannon formula:

$$C = B \log_2(1 + \gamma). \tag{1}$$

B refers to the bandwidth and γ to the received SNR. For a cooperative communication, capacity expression depends on the adopted relaying techniques. Extensive researches focused on the AF and DF protocols in dual or multi-hop communication and several maximization problems were posed. To defend the output of our system, we calculated the capacities of the AF and DF systems in order to compare their achievable rate with that of a direct communication. These capacities are defined by [13]

$$C_{AF} = B \log_2(1 + \gamma_{AF}) \quad with \quad \gamma_{AF} = \left(\sum_{i=1}^{N}(\gamma_i)^{-1}\right)^{-1} \tag{2}$$

$$C_{DF} = B \log_2(1 + \gamma_{DF}) = \min_{i=1..N}\{C_i\} \quad with \quad C_i = B \log_2(1 + \gamma_i)$$

where γ_i is the received SNR at the ith node.

Bit Error Rate

The Bit Error Rate (BER) is a value usually given in percentage and defines for every transmitted bit sequence the erroneous bit rate. Its expression depends on the adopted modulation scheme. Various forms of digital modulations can be applied in powerline communication. In Narrowband systems, Frequency Shift Keying (FSK), Phase Shift Keying (PSK) and Amplitude Shift Keying (ASK) are used. On the other side, for a transmission of high data rates (above 1 Mbps), M-ary PSK, M-ary QAM and OFDM are adopted for the spectral efficiency they offer [15]. For the BPSK modulation, the BER is given by:

$$BER = \frac{1}{2} erfc\left(\frac{E_b}{N_0}\right) \quad with \quad \frac{E_b}{N_0} = \frac{\gamma.B}{C} \tag{3}$$

We remind that $\frac{E_b}{N_0}$ is by definition the energy per bit to noise power spectral density ratio.

Network Throughput

By definition, the throughput is an average number of flow units per unit of time deducted after successive processing periods. Unlike the theoretical capacity, the throughput T is the output of packets transmission simulation through the network, which explains its lower values. It is calculated using the following formula:

$$T(bit/s) = \frac{8.TotalReceivedBytes}{RoundTripDelay} \tag{4}$$

The Round Trip Delay is defined by the total time spent by a signal to be transmitted from a node to another until the reception of the Ack.

The parametrization of these quantities according to the considered network is specified during the simulation.

6   Simulation Results

The NS-3 PLC module offers specific features to analyse the network and simulated channels behaviour. The installation of this module and basic steps to simulate a PLC system are described on the official website of the developers (see [8]). For the study of the communication channel, some estimations have been taken into account. Table 1 shows the values of the used variables.

Table 1. Numerical values used in simulation

Variable	Value
Nodes number	26
Frequency range	2–30 MHz
Noise Floor	15^{-9} W
Transmit PSD	10^{-6} W
Packet size	1024 Bytes

The channel transfer function is calculated using the method implemented in the PLC module. We first choose to study Shannon capacity C with and without a relay station. Figure 5 shows the variation of this capacity for an AF and DF relay systems versus direct transmission link.

Theoretically, the direct channel can reach a maximum capacity of 70 Mb/s, while DF reaches more than 100 Mb/s, thus exceeding the capacity given by the AF system. This is explained by the low value of the SNR of the direct transmission compared to the cooperative one.

Compared with Figs. 6, 7 and 8, we notice the decline in capacity values using M-QAM modulation with M = 2, 16, 64. It should be reminded that the constellation for M = 2 is the same for BPSK modulation. A higher QAM modulation allows carrying more bits through the channel, Fig. 6, 7 and 8 shows that

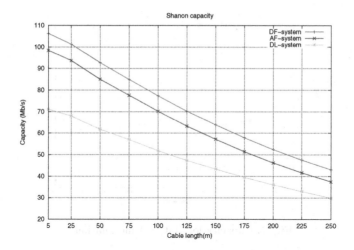

Fig. 5. Shannon capacity variation for cooperative and non cooperative communication

the capacity is proportionally increasing by moving to a higher-order constellation. Also, it is clear that the highest values of capacities are given in short distances. The cooperative communication proves its efficiency in terms of data rate compared to the direct link.

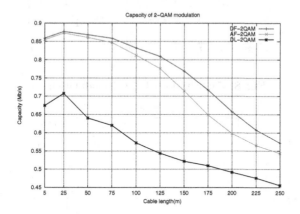

Fig. 6. Capacity for 2-QAM modulation

Concerning the error rate, Fig. 9 gives the BER function progression for the direct channel as well as those relayed. The percentage of error is certainly small in short distances, but the gap between the BER given with the relay compared to the direct transmission is important.

This is due to the better signal quality and the higher spectral efficiency provided by the cooperative transmission.

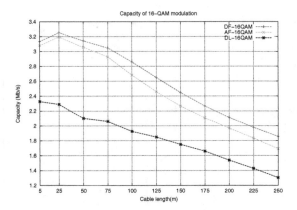

Fig. 7. Capacity for 16-QAM modulation

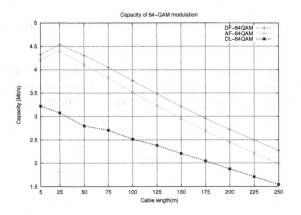

Fig. 8. Capacity for 64-QAM modulation

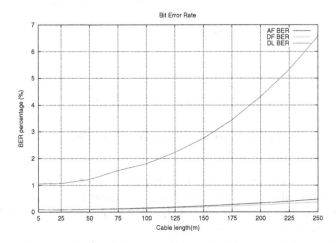

Fig. 9. BER percentage variation with cable length

The cooperative communication technique has been exploited at the MAC level by measuring the throughput value based on MAC forwarding without the use of an Internet stack.

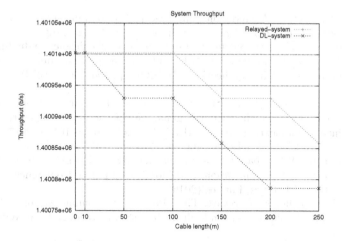

Fig. 10. Measured throughput for cooperative and direct link communications

Finally, Fig. 10 shows the comparison between the three simulated techniques. The improvement of the throughput is clear, although showing the difference between the values has required a precision to 6 digits after the decimal point because of the relatively short wiring adapted for our application. This throughput increasing should be better seen for long distances. Our application focuses on an in-home application where the cable length is limited.

This increase in throughput as well as in capacity has shown the advantage brought by the cooperative communication that we have introduced into this in-home system relative to the concurrent direct link.

7   Conclusion

In this paper, we chose to work on network simulators like the NS-3 simulator whose PLC module was recently developed and put in open source. Based on this module, and focusing on an in-home application, our work consisted in studying a cooperative system based on MAC forwarding by introducing a modification to the predefined MAC header. For the QoS evaluation across our network, we simulated the capacity of a direct channel connecting a source to a destination, as well as the capacities of two relayed channels using the AF and DF protocols while using different QAM modulations. The error percentage (BER) has also been simulated for these channels. The next quantity was the network throughput. The short distances did not prevent us from seeing a clear result on the out performance of cooperative communication compared to direct transmission. It will be interesting to collect these QoS measurements through the set up of a real PLC system and configuring a relay host. This will permit to compare the output of the real system to the results given by the NS-3 simulation.

References

1. Gungor, V.C., et al.: A survey on smart grid potential applications and communication requirements. IEEE Trans. Ind. Informat. **9**, 28–42 (2013)
2. Rabie, K.M., Adebisi, B., Salem, A.: Improving energy efficiency in dual-hop cooperative PLC relaying systems. In: IEEE International Symposium on Power Line Communications and its Applications (ISPLC), pp. 196–200. IEEE Press, Bottrop (2016)
3. Rabie, K.M., Adebisi, B., Yousif, E.H.G., Gacanin, H., Tonello, A.M.: A comparison between orthogonal and non-orthogonal multiple access in cooperative relaying power line communication systems. IEEE Access **5**, 10118–10129 (2017)
4. Ezzine, S., Abdelkefi, F., Bouallegue, A., Cances, J.P., Meghdadi, V.: Capacity analysis of an OFDM-based two-way relaying AF-PNC-PLC systems. In: International Wireless Communications and Mobile Computing Conference (IWCMC), pp. 205–210. IEEE Press, Paphos (2016)
5. Lampe, L., Tonello, A.M., Swart, T.G.: Power Line Communications: Principles, Standards and Applications from Multimedia to Smart Grid, 2nd edn. Wiley, Hoboken (2016)
6. Facina, M.S.P., Latchman, H.A., Poor, H.V., Ribeiro, M.V.: Cooperative in-home power line communication: analyses based on a measurement campaign. IEEE Trans. Commun. **11**, 1–12 (2014)
7. Oliveira, R.M., Facina, M.S.P., Ribeiro, M.V., Vieira, A.B.: Performance evaluation of in-home broadband PLC systems using a cooperative MAC protocol. Comput. Netw. **95**, 62–76 (2016)
8. Aalamifar, F., Schlogl, A., Harris, D., Lampe, L.: Modelling power line communication using network simulator-3. In: IEEE Global Communications Conference (GLOBECOM), pp. 2969–2974. IEEE Press, Atlanta (2013)
9. Tsokalo, I., Lehnert, R.: Modeling approach of broadband in-home PLC in network simulator 3. In: IEEE International Symposium on Power Line Communications and its Applications (ISPLC), pp. 113–118. IEEE Press, Austin (2015)
10. Mlynek, P., Hasirci, Z., Misurec, J., Fujdiak, R.: Analysis of channel transfer functions in power line communication system for smart metering and home area network. Adv. Electr. Comput. Eng **16**, 51–56 (2016)
11. Khach, R., Jacobsen, K.E., Skov, M.N., Hojholt, N.B., Sorensen, R.B.: Investigation of QoS in PLC and evaluation of a NS-3 PLC simulator. Technical report, Aalborg University, Danemark (2014)
12. Adam, H., Elmenreich, W., Bettstetter, C., Senouci, S.M.: CoRe-MAC: A MAC-protocol for cooperative relaying in wireless networks. In: IEEE Global Telecommunications Conference (GLOBECOM), pp. 1–6. IEEE Press, Honolulu (2009)
13. Levin, G., Loyka, S.: Amplify-and-forward versus decode-and-forward relaying: which is better? School of Electrical Engineering and Computer Science, Ottawa, Ontario, Canada (2012)
14. Yang, L.T., Waluyo, A.B., Ma, J., Tan, L., Srinivasan, B.: Mobile Intelligence. Wiley, Hoboken (2010)
15. Najarkolaei, A.H., Hosny, W., Lota, J.: Bit error rate performance in power line communication channels with impulsive noise. In: IUKSim-AMSS International Conference on Modelling and Simulation (UKSim), pp. 248–251. IEEE Press, UK (2015)

An Enhanced Evolutionary Approach for Solving the Nodes Migration Scheduling Problem

Fatma Moalla[1(✉)], Ali Balma[2], and Mehdi Mrad[3]

[1] ISG Tunis, University of Tunis, Tunis, Tunisia
fatma.moalla.fen@gmail.com
[2] National Higher Engineering School of Tunis, University of Tunis, Tunis, Tunisia
alibalma05@yahoo.fr
[3] Department of Industrial Engineering, College of Engineering,
King Saud University, Riyadh, Saudi Arabia
mmrad@ksu.edu.sa

Abstract. This paper deals with a scheduling problem in the telecommunication field, namely the node migration scheduling for an access network. The problem consists of migrating nodes from a former network to a new one affording the required services. The migration procedure needs the installation of a bridge between the two networks without disrupting current services. Nodes are moved sequentially one by one. Our objective is to minimize the cost of the required bridge. We describe an enhanced genetic algorithm based on a good initial population. Numerical experiments show that our method has good performance.

1 Introduction

In the telecommunications filed, operators are faced to new challenges such as emergence of new services and the traffic evolution. Indeed, the shift from a service to another obliges the operator to adjust the actual network configuration to support the new equipment installation. Technological capabilities are in perpetual evolution. Formerly, circuit switching was well repented before the emergence of internet and video technology. Nowadays, The mobile technology become the trend in the telecommunication sector. The operators interest is on deploying the 5G technology. Therefore, all these changes emphasizes the importance of the migration optimization strategies and the more specifically the migration scheduling problem. A migration decision can be taken at the strategic or the tactical level. In fact, For a medium term horizon links and nodes may be concerned. In a medium-term horizon, only nodes should migrate from a former network to a new one.

In this context, we consider the node migration process as a gradual stepwise move of the nodes which should be well planified in order to prevent the services interruption. For this aim, a temporary bridge should be installed between two networks linking the migrated nodes to those remaining in the ancient network

© Springer Nature Switzerland AG 2018
N. Boudriga et al. (Eds.): UNet 2018, LNCS 11277, pp. 69–81, 2018.
https://doi.org/10.1007/978-3-030-02849-7_7

(Fig. 1). Once all nodes are displaced to the new network, the bridge should be removed.

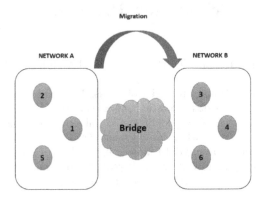

Fig. 1. A migration from ancient to new network

We extend the node migration scheduling problem addressed in [1] by proposing an enhanced genetic algorithm with a new strategy for generating the initial population. The paper is organized as follows. In Sect. 2, we present the migration process. Section 3 recall the problem formulation as presented in [1]. Section 4 presents some related works. Section 4 details the proposed method. In Sect. 5, we present computational results and finally we conclude.

2   Problem Description

Geographically spoken, three domains can be defined for the telecommunication networks which are the core, the metro and the access network. The access network which is connected to the end users consists of a set of transmission nodes connected to traffic processing nodes (Fig. 2). Two transmission nodes connect a processing nodes ensuring the continuity of services. In order to perform a migration, transmission nodes should be replaced by other nodes supporting the bandwidth growth.

As mentioned previously in the introduction, installing a bridge along the migration process present many advantages. First, it guarantees the interoperability between the networks. Second, it prevents also from the service rupture. From a technical perspective, it represents a gateway for the traffic between the nodes connected to the ancient and the new network. Our objective is to find minimal capacity cost connecting the two networks. Finding a good node ordering for a migration sequence is the success key for achieving our goal. More practical applications for the migration problem include the Virtual machine migration as well as evolving to a more capacitated network using IP routers. The following example highlights the influence of changing the nodes order in the migration sequence by considering two different orders. We note that the maximum value of the traffic on the bridge throughout the migration process is 15 for the first order. We now consider a second migration scenario. For this scenario, the value of the maximum traffic on the bridge is 12, entailing a capacity of the bridge less than the first scenario (Fig. 3).

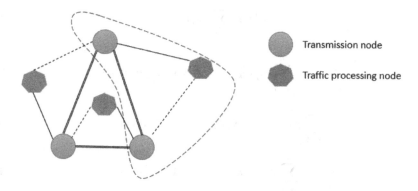

Fig. 2. Access network structure

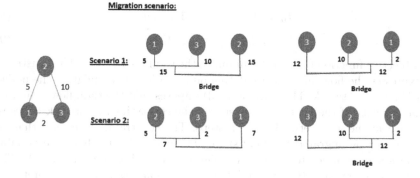

Fig. 3. Migration scenarios

3   Problem Formulation

Given an undirected graph $G = (V, E)$ with $|v| = n$ nodes and E the set of valuated edges. An edge corresponding to the traffic amount between two nodes i and j and is denoted d_{ij}. The capacity on the bridge is ensured via boards. A board w which belongs to the boards set W is defined by its modular capacity λ_w and its cost k_w. We denote by $O_i = \sum_{j=1}^{n} d_{ij}$ $\forall i$ the total flow issued from the node i. The decision variables are:

- x_{ik}: binary variables which take 1 if node i is migrated before or at the stage k and 0 otherwise.
- f_{ik}: the traffic amount on the bridge emanating from i at the stage k.
- c_w: the number of boards of type w.

We recall the problem formulation as presented in [1]:

$$Min \sum_{w \in W} k_w c_w \tag{1}$$

$$f_{ik} \geq O_i x_{ik} - \sum_{j=1}^{n} d_{ij} x_{jk} \qquad \forall k = 1, \ldots, n \forall i = 1, \ldots, n \tag{2}$$

$$\sum_{i=1}^{n} f_{ik} \leq \sum_{w \in W} \lambda_w c_w \qquad \forall k = 1, \ldots, n \tag{3}$$

$$\sum_{i=1}^{n} x_{ik} = k \qquad \forall k = 1, \ldots, n \tag{4}$$

$$x_{in} = 1 \qquad \forall i = 1, \ldots, n \tag{5}$$

$$x_{ik-1} \leq x_{ik} \qquad \forall i = 1, \ldots, n \forall k = 2, \ldots, n \tag{6}$$

$$x_{ik} \in \{0, 1\} \qquad \forall i, k = 1, \ldots, n \tag{7}$$

$$f_{ik} \geq 0 \qquad \forall i, k = 1, \ldots, n \tag{8}$$

$$c_w \in Z \qquad \forall w \in W \tag{9}$$

The objective function (1) aims to minimize the total boards cost. The constraint (2) expresses the flow amount circulating on the bridge if we migrate the node i at or before the stage k. The constraint (3) imposes that the total flow is limited by the capacity of the bridge at any stage. The constraint (4) forces k nodes to be moved in the new network after k steps. The constraint (5) ensure that all nodes should be migrated the final stage. The constraint (6) fixes the variable at 1 for stages superior to k, once we migrate a node i at a given stage k. The constraints (7), (8) and (9) are the integrity and non-negativity constraints.

4   Related Work

The network planning problem has attracted more attention in the telecommunications field. One of the most studied problems in the planning context is the migration problem. This problem encompasses a variety of network technologies such as traffic routing and transmission technology [3] and mobile access network technology [4]. The authors of [5] and [6] tackle the migration problem from an SDH to Ethernet network. The proposed migration consider both nodes and links. The Problem is solved using metaheuristics namely the ant colony [5] and a genetic algorithm in [6]. The authors of [7] suggests a mixed integer linear program to reduce the costs in a passive Optical Network. These costs are related to the capacity evolution. An empirical approach and mathematical model were proposed in [8] to address the migration in a mobile network with load balancing. The authors of [9] propose two algorithms for a virtual network in order to minimize the whole migration time. The authors of [10] take into account the virtual machines dependencies and the network structure to get a scheme. The objective of such migration is to decrease the traffic amount in the network. We study in this work the node migration scheduling problem for an access network in order to migrate from a 4G network to 5G network. In [1], a time-staged formulation and lower bound model were proposed to solve this problem. We should mention that exact method were not able to solve large sized instances. An approximate method was developed in [2] to solve this problem in virtual networks. Therefore, the objective of this work is to provide another approximate method combining the partition problem concepts and the standard elements of a genetic algorithm.

5 Proposed Method

Genetic algorithms are population based search techniques. They are among the most important class of evolutionary algorithms. The concept behind this technique introduced by Holland [11] is inspired by biological natural selection. This work is motivated by the fact that the use of the classical form of genetic algorithm (GA) may consume much time and could not converge to a global optimum. To remedy this weaknesses, many works focus on improvement on GA operators such as crossover and mutation. Other works consider that evolutionary algorithms with automatic parameter tuning is more performant than setting manually these parameters. Another important feature of the genetic algorithm is the population initialization since it accelerates the convergence of the algorithm. Population initialization has not received the attention it deserves despite its importance. In order to solve node migration scheduling problem, we propose a new genetic algorithm with an initial population based on problem knowledge.

Different approaches for generating initial population are suggested. An alternative random initialization in genetic algorithm was discussed by [12], authors of [13] proposed an opposition based learning initialization approach. Selective initialization is proposed in [14] to deliver better results. A state-of the-art population initialization techniques was proposed in [15]. The classification of these techniques is based on three categories which are randomness, compositionality and generality.

We propose a knowledge based procedure for our GA. The procedure starts by generating the first chromosome C1 in the initial population. This chromosome represents a bi-partition solution of the problem.

The pseudo-code of the overall proposed genetic algorithm is given in Algorithm 1.

We introduce quickly the bi-partitioning problem in Sect. 5.1 related to the graph theory and optimization problems.

Algorithm 1. Pseudo code of the genetic approach

1: **Input**: GA parameters:
2: **Output**: cost of the best migration order;
3: **Begin**
4: generate the initial population with knowledge based initialization procedure
5: While termination criterion is not met do
6:     select parents from the current population pop_k
7:     apply crossover
8:     apply mutation
9:     apply replacement
10: EndWhile
11:     compute the cost of the best migration order
12: **End**

5.1   The Graph-Partitioning Problem GPP

The graph-partitioning problem (GPP) is a combinatorial optimization problem, which belongs to the class of NP-hard. Cutting a graph into smaller parts is relevant since it presents many advantages for parallelization or complexity reduction. This problem concerns both the weighted and unweighted graph. Formally, Given an undirected graph $G = (V, E)$, where V represents the set of vertices and E refers the set of edges, a graph partitioning could be defined as division of V into k disjoint subsets $V_1, V_2, \ldots, V_k$ in order to minimize the cut value. Each disjoint subset is named a partition. The cut edges are those edges whose extremities belong to different partitions. For a weighted graph, the cut value C_i defines the cut edges weight sum. Considering k = 2 is a special case of partitioning problem where we divide the vertices set in only two subsets. This problem is called graph bi-partitioning or graph bisection. The GPP problem has proven its ability to solve real life such parallel processing, complex network, image processing, road network and VLSI design [16]. Much effort, as for [17], have been made to solve this problem exactly. When exact methods fail to deliver results, approximative methods are used such as lin Kernighan algorithm and more recently multilevel algorithms [16]. A fast running heuristic for the bi-partitionning problem from [18] is used to generate the chromosome C1.

5.2   Solution Representation

The sequence representation can be considered as permutation which refers to a sequence of integers where each number designates a migration order. Possible values are from 1 to n where n = $|N|$. The vector Perm(x) is the permutation order of a solution x as shown in Fig. 4.

5.3   Initial Population

A population is composed of a set of chromosomes as illustrated in Fig. 5. NP denotes the population size. As mentioned earlier, in order to generate the first

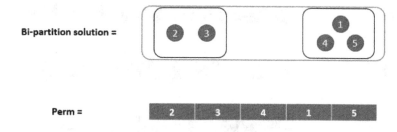

Fig. 4. A chromosome encoding

individual, we refer to the heuristic from [18]. The remaining population individuals ($|NP| - 1$) are generated following the Algorithm 2.

Algorithm 2. Knowledge-based algorithm for generating the initial population

---

1: **Input**: NP: population size, N: chromosome length
2: **Output**: initial population pop1;
3: **Begin**
4: solution ⟵ RunHeuristic (from [18])
5: generate the first chromosome C1 in the initial population
6: For all remaining individuals in this population
7:   swap two nodes position x and y to get the current individual Ck (with $x, y \in [1, \frac{N}{2}]$ or $x, y \in [\frac{N}{2} + 1, N]$)
8: EndFor
9: **End**

5.4 Selection

We use the classical roulette selection wheel. In this method, all the chromosomes in the population are placed on the roulette wheel according to their fitness values. Each individual is assigned a segment of roulette wheel. The size of each segment in the roulette wheel is proportional to the value of the fitness of the individual.

5.5 Crossover

One-point crossover works by selecting a common crossover point in the parent chromosome and then swapping the corresponding parts. We check the offspring chromosome feasibility in order to get a feasible potential solution.

5.6 Mutation

The purpose of mutation is to preserve and introduce diversity. It alters one or more gene values in a chromosome from its initial state.

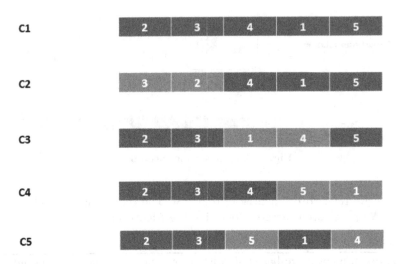

Fig. 5. Generating initial population

5.7   Replacement

The replacement operator consists of choosing the appropriate individual for removal. Replacement strategies have been studied in the literature. Several methods were discussed among them Steady State and elitism.

6   Experimental Tests

The proposed approach has been coded in C language and executed on a i7 processor machine with 1.8 GHz. Memory and 8 GB Ram. In this section, two benchmark sets are considered. The first set A refer to small size instances up to 40 nodes proposed firstly in [1]. The second set B deals with medium and large size instances from [2]. For all the instances a complete graph is considered. The overall Instances sets consist of a traffic matrix randomly generated between 100 Mb/s and 1 Gb/s which consider only the symmetric traffic.

Different versions of the genetic algorithm are considered:

1. SGA: simple genetic algorithm (random initial population).
2. ICPGA: genetic algorithm with combined initial population($\frac{1}{2}$ random, $\frac{1}{2}$ based bi-partitioning approach).
3. IPBBGA: genetic algorithm with initial population based bi-partitioning.

Defining the quality of this proposed evolutionary approach is crucial. In order to evaluate the results, we use the following performance measures which are the gap and ARPD metrics:

$$G = 100 * \frac{(GA_i - OPT)}{OPT}. \tag{10}$$

$$ARPD = \frac{1}{s} \sum_{i=1}^{s} \frac{A_i - bA_i}{bA_i} * 100 \qquad (11)$$

where GA_i denotes the solution value obtained by a version of genetic algorithm for its ith instance. bGA_i is the best solution value obtained for that instance among the three versions of GA (SGA, ICPGA and IPBBGA).A_i refer the solution value obtained by an approximative method (heuristic, genetic algorithm) for its ith instance. bA_i is the best solution value obtained for that instance among the fours methds of GA (SGA, ICPGA and IPBBGA and the heuristic). We denote by s the number of problem instances for a problem size. We should note that OPT is the solution of mathematical formulation f2 presented in [1].

Table 1. Average gap values for instances of set A

Size	G_{IPBBGA}	G_{SGA}
20	5.71	17.14
25	2.77	11.11
30	0	1.85
35	0	6.94
40	0	10.75

Table 2. Average ARPD values for instances of set B

Size	$ARPD_{IPBBGA}$	$ARPD_{ICPGA}$	$ARPD_{SGA}$	$ARPD_H$
50	0	0	7.73	2.77
60	0	0	2.62	0.76
70	0	0	5.99	0.28
80	0	0	4.78	0.21
90	0.16	0	5.89	2.2
100	0	0.15	5.5	2.03
200	0.04	0.06	4.34	1.17

The first column of Table 1 cites instances of type A. Column 2 and 3 report the average gap values between optimal solution and two versions of genetic algorithm namely the IPBBGA and the SGA. It is clear that the proposed approach outperforms the classical version of genetic algorithm. Indeed, the average gap value has decreased from 17.14 to 5.71 for $|v| = 20$ and from 11.11 to 2.77 for $|v| = 25$. The optimality is reached for all the instances of size 30, 35, 40. Mathematical formulation from [1] was not able to deliver results for instances

Table 3. Comparaison between initial population results

Size	IPBBGA		SGA	
	Min	Max	Min	Max
20	491.7	502.6	519.9	580.6
25	758.5	783.2	821.3	901.1
30	1098	1121.8	1187.3	1284
35	1515.4	1546.7	1636.5	1733
40	1992.5	2018.2	2153.7	2256
50	3191.1	3194.8	3414	3518.7
60	4577.9	4595.4	4868	5006.6
70	6229.1	6244.9	6660.7	6839.2
80	8176.5	8194.6	8730.2	8894.5
90	10404	10425.7	11059.8	11288.7
100	12849	12863.2	13642	13858.4
200	52312.8	52344.8	54698.4	54981.7

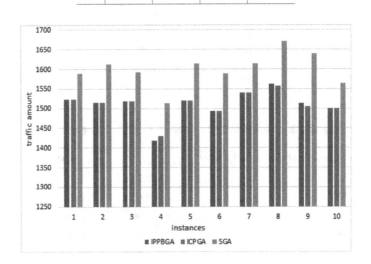

Fig. 6. Total traffic on the bridge for 10 instances ($|V| = 35$ nodes)

up to $|v| = 40$ nodes. Therefore, to assess the efficiency of the IPBBGA algorithm for medium and large size instances, we compare our results to Heuristic H from [2] which address the nodes migration problem for virtual machines. Table 2 presents the ARPD values for the instances set B. Results show that for the two versions using the initialization procedure (IPBBGA and ICPGA) perform better compared to basic version of genetic algorithm (SGA) and the heuristic H. Indeed, the proposed results in column 2 and 3 have small average

Table 4. Running time for IPBBGA

SEQ	t_{IPBBGA}
20	0.05
25	0.08
30	0.12
35	0.18
40	0.28
50	0.5
60	0.89
70	1.3
80	1.75
90	2.4
100	3.2
200	24.1

ARPD values near to zero for almost the cases. The SGA has the worst results among the considered methods i.e. an average ARPD from 2.62 to 7.73.

In order to confirm the robustness of the initialization procedure, average Best (Min) and worst (Max) chromosomes for the initial population are listed in Table 3 for both IPBBGA and SGA. The reported values disclose the competitivity of our initial population since for the overall considered sizes, the average worst chromosomes fitness for IPBBGA is always better to the average best chromosomes fitness for the SGA. The running time is reported in Table 4. For similar cost values, we should compare the total traffic values. Figure 6 reports the total traffic values for 10 instances of size $|V| = 35$ nodes. Based on these results, the initialization procedure proves its efficiency to deliver better results.

7 Conclusion

In this paper, the node migration scheduling problem for an access network is discussed. A genetic algorithm with initialization procedure is proposed. The originality of this proposed approach resides in using initial population based on a fast heuristic of the bi-partition problem. This problem was used in prior works to get effective bounding for our migration scheduling problem. The results show that our proposed approach is effective. It provides better results than other methods in a reasonable time. To extend this work, we will investigate more tight bounds for this problem as well as others application context.

References

1. Mrad, M., Balma, A., Moalla, F., Ladhari, T.: Nodes migration scheduling of access networks. IEEE Trans. Netw. Serv. Manag. **14**(1), 77–90 (2017)
2. Moalla, F., Balma, A., Mrad, M.: A rapid heuristic for the virtual machines migration scheduling problem. In: Proceeding of Engineering and Technology PET of The Fifth International Conference on Control and Signal Processing (CSP 2017), vol. 25, pp. 44–47 (2017)
3. Leiva, A., Machuca, C.M., Beghelli, A., Olivares, R.: Migration cost analysis for upgrading WDM networks. IEEE Commun. Mag. **51**(11), 87–93 (2013)
4. Haidine, A., Aqqal, A., Ouahmane, H.: Modeling the migration of mobile networks towards 4G and beyond. In: El Oualkadi, A., Choubani, F., El Moussati, A. (eds.) Proceedings of the Mediterranean Conference on Information Communication Technologies 2015, vol. 380, pp. 355–363. Springer, Cham (2016). https://doi.org/10.1007/978-3-319-30301-7_37
5. Türk, S., Radeke, R., Lehnert, R.: Network migration using ant colony optimization. In: 2010 9th Conference on Telecommunications Internet and Media Techno Economics (CTTE), pp. 1–6, June 2010
6. Türk, S., Radeke, R., Lehnert, R.: Improving network migration optimization utilizing memetic algorithms. In: 2013 Global Information Infrastructure Symposium, pp. 1–8, October 2013
7. Andrade, M.D., Tornatore, M., Sallent, S., Mukherjee, B.: Optimizing the migration to future-generation passive optical networks (PON). IEEE Syst. J. **4**(4), 413423 (2010)
8. Chardy, M., Yahia, M.B., Bao, Y.: 3G/4G load-balancing optimization for mobile network planning. In: 2016 17th International Conference on Telecommunications Network Strategy and Planning Symposium (Networks), September 2016
9. Ammar, M., Lo, S., Zegura, E.: Design and analysis of schedules for virtual network migration. In: 2013 IFIP Networking Conference, pp. 1–9 (2013)
10. Shrivastava, V., Zerfos, P., Lee, K.-W., Jamjoom, H., Liu, Y.-H., Banerjee, S.: Application aware virtual machine migration in data centers. In: 2011 Proceedings of INFOCOM, pp. 66–70 (2011)
11. Holland, J.H.: Adaptation in Natural and Artificial Systems: An Introductory Analysis with Applications to Biology, Control, and Artificial Intelligence. MIT Press, Cambridge (1992)
12. Kallel, L., Schoenauer, M.: Alternative random initialization in genetic algorithms, In Bäeck, Th. (ed.) Proceedings of the 7th International Conference on Genetic Algorithms, pp. 268–275. Morgan Kaufmann, Burlington (1997)
13. Rahnamayan, S., Tizhoosh, H.R., Salama, M.M.: A novel population initialization method for accelerating evolutionary algorithms. Comput. Math. Appl. **53**(10), 1605–1614 (2007)
14. Sivaraj, R., Ravichandran, T., Priya, R.D.: Boosting performance of genetic algorithm through selective intialization. Eur. J. Sci. Res. **68**(1), 93–100 (2012). ISSN 1450–216x
15. Kazimipour, B., Li, X., Qin, A.K.: A review of population initialization techniques for evolutionary algorithms. In: 2014 IEEE Congress on Evolutionary Computation (CEC), pp. 2585–2592. IEEE (2014)
16. Buluç, A., Meyerhenke, H., Safro, I., Sanders, P., Schulz, C.: Recent advances in graph partitioning. In: Kliemann, L., Sanders, P. (eds.) Algorithm Engineering. LNCS, vol. 9220, pp. 117–158. Springer, Cham (2016). https://doi.org/10.1007/978-3-319-49487-6_4

17. Liberti, L.: Compact linearization for binary quadratic problems. 4OR **5**(3), 231–245 (2007)
18. Wu, J., Jiang, G., Zheng, L., Zhou, S.: Algorithms for balanced graph bipartitioning. In: 2014 IEEE International Conference on High Performance Computing and Communications, 2014 IEEE 6th International Symposium on Cyberspace Safety and Security, 2014 IEEE 11th International Conference on Embedded Software and Systems (HPCC, CSS, ICESS), pp. 185–188. IEEE (2014)

Benchmarking Big Data OLAP NoSQL Databases

Mohammed El Malki[1]([⊠]), Arlind Kopliku[1], Essaid Sabir[2], and Olivier Teste[1]

[1] Institut de Recherche en Informatique de Toulouse, Toulouse, France
{elmalki,teste}@irit.fr, ArlindKopliku@yahoo.fr
[2] NEST Research Group, ENSEM, Hassan II University of Casablanca,
Casablanca, Morocco
e.sabir@ensem.ac.ma

Abstract. With the advent of Big Data, new challenges have emerged regarding the evaluation of decision support systems (DSS). Existing evaluation benchmarks are not configured to handle a massive data volume and wide data diversity. In this paper, we introduce a new DSS benchmark that supports multiple data storage systems, such as relational and Not Only SQL (NoSQL) systems. Our scheme recognizes numerous data models (snowflake, star and flat topologies) and several data formats (CSV, JSON, TBL, XML, etc.). It entails complex data generation characterized within "volume, variety, and velocity" framework (3 V). Next, our scheme enables distributed and parallel data generation. Furthermore, we exhibit some experimental results with KoalaBench.

1 Introduction

Several benchmarks have been proposed for information systems evaluation and specifically for decision support systems [1]. We particularly mention the well-known TPC-DS [18] and the TPC-H benchmarks [13, 24]. They provide data sets and usage scenarii allowing comparison of systems' behavior under equivalent conditions, thus permitting comparative evaluations. Recently, information systems have quickly evolved to support the growth of data Volume, Variety/diversity and Velocity (3 V) framework. However, the evaluation benchmarks have not evolved at the same rate. The existing solutions are still at the time where data warehouses were mainly stored in a single powerful machine and relational databases were mostly used. Besides, there are many other reasons to make us believe that a new DSS benchmark is required. For instance, we cite the following:

(i) *New Enabling Technologies:* Nowadays, there are different NoSQL ("Not only SQL") systems that ease Big Data management, which cannot be handled efficiently by existing relational systems [11, 20]. These systems enable the storage according to various data models (documents, columns, graphs, etc.), introducing a higher flexibility on the schema levels. We are facing a high diversity of solutions to jointly consider;

N. Boudriga et al. (Eds.): UNet 2018, LNCS 11277, pp. 82–94, 2018.
https://doi.org/10.1007/978-3-030-02849-7_8

(ii) **Multiple Data Models**: Every NoSQL solution supports different formats and data models [7]. On one hand, multidimensional data warehouses rooted with relational databases (ROLAP) favour data models like the snowflake schema (standardized schemas) or the star schema (non-standard schema). On the other hand, NoSQL systems are likely to use a flat model with a complete denormalization (can be related to the universal relationship) and could use imbrications. These approaches go against the principle introduced by the relational approach of strict separation between the data model and the data processing. The dependencies between data modelling and data processing make even more important to have a support for multiple data models adapted to multiple various treatments;

(iii) **Data Volume:** Before deciding which solution to adopt, it is important to check the system behaviour under a massive amount of data [11]. The larger the amount is, the more we are facing the memory limits on a single-computer configuration. Big Data's new solutions allow to scale up and balance the memory disorders. Data are settled on multiple computers forming a cluster. Then, when it reaches the storage limit, the system can be upgraded by simply adding new computers. This agile method costs less than increasing the storage capacity of a centralized computer. It is worth to mention that existing benchmarks generate the data only on one computer;

(iv) **Variety/Diversity:** NoSQL systems rely on new logical data models that promise higher flexibility. Some NoSQL systems are said "schemaless"; i.e. there is no fixed data schema. Data of the same class can have no schema or might have multiple schemas. Integration and analysis of those heterogeneous data sets is a complicated task that benchmarks dedicated to the existing decision-making systems are still struggling with;

(v) **Velocity:** As data is generated with an increasing rate, the architectures are compelled to adopt a system capable of processing such fast growing data.

Henceforth, related research community must consider new evaluation benchmarks supporting big data challenges. Data warehouses evaluation benchmarks (TPC-DS [18], TPC-H and SSB [19] are relatively out-of-date and do not consider the new challenges and technologies. These solutions are neither defined for a usage in a distributed environment, nor for NoSQL databases. Their data generating processes are quite sophisticated and interesting. However, they remain limited when it comes to data volume and data variety since they depend on the memory limit of the machine being used for data generation and they only generate one data model, one file format, and one schema. NoSQL systems work with different logical data models and different file formats and they can accommodate to diverse schemaless data. In other terms, a significant effort is needed to load data on NoSQL systems and to be able to assess some of their advantages such as support for data diversity.

In this paper, we propose a new benchmark for evaluating multidimensional data warehouses that take into consideration big data properties (i.e., 3 V paradigm). KoalaBench is an extension of TPC-H that tackles big data technologies and requirements. These new benchmark functionalities include:

– Support for relational databases system and NoSQL systems;
– Support for multiple logical models: snowflake, star schema, flat schema;

- Support parallel and distributed data generation natively in HDFS;
- Support for variety/diversity: multiple schemas at once;
- Support for velocity: able to process fast growing data.

The remaining is organized as follows. We provide in Sect. 2 a comprehensive overview on existing benchmark suites. Section 3 describes the proposed benchmark. We finally exhibit an extensive experimental work and results in Sect. 4. Concluding remarks and some future directions are drawn in Sect. 5.

2   Related Work

During the last few years, tremendous research efforts on information system benchmarks have been deployed. However, the technology evolution and the explosion of stored information are demanding novel and efficient benchmarks methods. We distinguish two benchmarking families with respect to distributed information systems and decision support systems. The first method details the TPC-D derived benchmarks, which focus on Decision Systems (DSS). Whereas, the second family tackles the benchmarks supporting NoSQL approaches.

2.1   Decision Benchmark Systems (DSS)

Benchmark approach edited by Transaction Processing Performance Council (TPC) is the most used to evaluate DSS systems. The well-known benchmark APB-1 was popular in the 90's. It quickly became obsolete because it was too simple and unsuitable for most experiences [4, 22].

The TPC-D benchmark was the first benchmark designed explicitly for DSS systems. Later, two sub-benchmarks were derived from it: TPC-H has been designed for ad-hoc queries and TPC-R has been designed for reporting. TPC-DS succeeds on TPC-H as the data model became richer, standardized and supports a total of 99 queries classified into 4 categories: interactive OLAP queries, ad-hoc decision support queries, extraction queries and reporting queries. The data model is a constellation schema composed of 7 fact tables and 17 shared dimensions tables. TPC-H is an alternative benchmark that simulates a decision support system database environment. It implements business-oriented queries and concurrent data access. These queries are performed on ultra large amounts of data and have a high degree of complexity.

In 2009, the Star Schema Benchmark (SSB) was proposed [19]. It is an extension of the TPC-H benchmark. Unlike TPC-DS, SSB introduces some denormalization on data for the sake of simplicity. It implements a pure star schema composed of a fact table and 4 dimension tables. In order to adapt a star-schema-oriented benchmark to NoSQL, two SSB-derived benchmarks were proposed. Namely, the CNSSB that supports column-oriented data models [6] and SSB that supports column-oriented as well as documents-oriented data models with different logical data modelling approaches [2]. TPC benchmarks remain the main reference for DSS evaluation. However, they are built for relational systems and cannot be easily implemented for NoSQL databases.

2.2 Big Data Benchmarks

Big Data benchmarks tend to compare the new systems that are storing massively distributed data and that support parallels computing. Yahoo Cloud service is one of the most popular tools. It is used to compare standard CRUD operations (Create, Read, Update and Delete) [3]. It already has been used by most of the NoSQL systems proving their capabilities for data loading, updates, etc. [3]. Similarly, Bigframe is a benchmark that primarily focuses on problems of volume, variety, and velocity in Big Data context [10]. With more functionalities than the first two, the authors of [8] propose BigBench which models command lines. It is composed of 3 types of data: structured (from TPC-DS), semi-structured (clicks streams on web sites), and unstructured (clients comments) and it is developed to measure and evaluate offline analytic using Hadoop. Hibench is a benchmark suite for measuring incomplete data using Hadoop and MapReduce. BigDataBench is a complete benchmark suite that evaluates the big data requirements centric on 4 V [14]. it supports the offline and online analysis using Hadoop and NoSQL.

As shown in Table 1 and unlike traditional benchmarks, big data benchmarks are oriented toward flexible information, massive data, and scalability. Even though these big data benchmarks have gained popularity in the last few years, they do not evaluate the same criteria as compared to DSS benchmarks (fact, dimensions, OLAP).

Table 1. Comparing Big Data benchmarking solutions.

Benchmark	Multidimensional scheme (fact – dimensions, OLAP)	Data scalability	Software
YCSB	No	Partial (volume, variety)	NoSQL
Bigbench	No	Partial (volume- variety)	Hadoop
BigDataBench	No	Total	NoSQL
HiBench	–	Partial (volume- variety)	Hadoop/hive
SSB+	Yes	Partial (volume)	NoSQL
TPCH	Yes	no	RDBMS
CN	Yes	Partial (volume)	NoSQL
Koalabench	Yes	Total	NoSQL

In this paper, we propose a new benchmark, an extension of TPC-H. This solution supports column-oriented models and document-oriented models. This effort is complementary to the Big Bench effort as it provides a simpler but fair framework to play with NoSQL and SQL-like technologies. Also this new benchmark is dedicated to multidimensional data warehouse.

3 KoalaBench Benchmark Tool

KoalaBench is a decision support benchmark for Big Data needs. It is derived from the TPC-H benchmark, the reference benchmark in research and industry for decision support systems. It has been adapted to support Big Data technologies such as NoSQL and Hadoop file systems. It generates data in different file formats following different data models. The data generator is developed using a Java development of TPC-H. It supports:

- different logical models (flat, star, snowflake and flexible models);
- different formats compatible with NoSQL and relational storage systems;
- parallel and distributed data generation through HDFS and MapReduce;
- diversity in data through flexible schemas;
- velocity of generated data.

3.1   Data Models

The KoalaBench benchmark can generate consistent data with 3 logical models [3, 4]. We detail them below:

Snowflake Data Model. This first data model is very close to the one used in the TPC-H benchmark with small modifications. In the snowflake model, data redundancy is minimized through data normalization; facts refer to dimensions which refer to other entities. For example, a customer can reference a country that references a region (Europe). The regions and the countries are generated in different files. The data schema is represented in. In this model, the data are generated in 9 files which will serve to supply the database.

Star Data Model. This data model corresponds to a star schema. It is a common data model for data warehouses [17, 21]. It is simpler than the snowflake schema. Here, we only consider one entity per fact and one entity per dimension. Dimensions themselves can have some redundancy (functional dependencies data). For instance, the customer is associated with a country that is associated with a region (e.g. EUROPE). In the star schema, we will not have a separate file for countries and regions. The customer file will include the country and the region even if the region is functionally dependent from the region. The data generation and data model are very similar to the Star Schema Benchmark (SSB) (Fig. 1).

We add a table entity. named *Date*. becomes an explicit dimension and it is described by multiple attributes such as "week number", "day of the week", "day in the year", ... The date table is common in traditional data warehouses. The *LineItem* fact is associated with 4 dimensions: Customer, Part, Date, and Supplier. This makes a simplification in the schema. The data schema is represented in Fig. 2.

Flat Data Model. This is the simplest data model we propose. It groups, in one entity, data about the fact and dimensions. This creates a considerable amount of redundancy in data, but it is known to be better for some NoSQL systems that do not support joins. We remove some attributes that are less important.

3.2   Complex Data

The new benchmark supports diversity of data, meant as variety of schema. It can generate data with diverse schemas i.e. data of the same class (table, collection) does not have to comply with one strict schema, different records of the same class can have

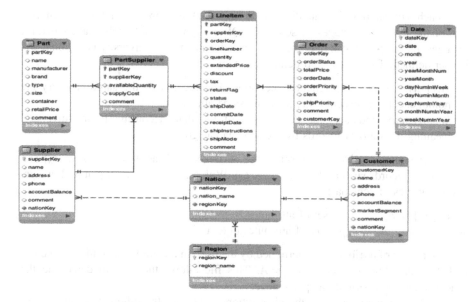

Fig. 1. Snowflake data model

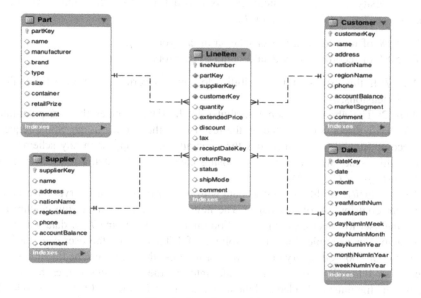

Fig. 2. Star data model.

different schemas. It is easy to think of instances of the class "products", where we can store *mobile phones* and *num supplier*. They can be described by common attributes such as *weight* and *brand* but they can have specific attributes such as *screen size*.

Benchmark support for data diversity is important as support of flexible schemas is one of the major advantages of some NoSQL systems. KoalaBench enables diverse data generation, which can help measure this advantage. Data diversity is optional and is user defined. The user has to define two parameters:

- *diversity*: the possible schema categories. The records of the same category are homogeneous in structure i.e. have the same attributes.
- *homogeneity*: indicates the distribution of the data according to the diversity, meaning the ratio of records by the schema category.

To illustrate, consider A the set of the attributes such as $A = [a_1, a_2 ..., a_n]$ and T the set of records such as $T = [t_1, t_2 ..., t_m]$. With a diversity level equal to 2, we get two categories of schemas:

- $C_{S1} = [b_1, b_2, ..., b_p]$ a set of attributes $b_j \in A$
- $C_{S2} = [c_1, c_2, ..., c_q]$ a set of attributes $c_j \in A$

The choice of attributes is determined by the user, in a configuration file of schemas and their distribution; $C_{S1} \cup C_{S2} = A$. This file allows the user to determine the schemas and the distributions percentage.

The homogeneity specifies the distribution of data for the different possible schemas; the level of homogeneity is proportional to the level of the diversity. For example, with a diversity level at 2, the homogeneity is equal to $1/2 + 1/2$, forming two sets of data such as $T_1 \cup T_2 = T$ et $T_1 \cap T_2 = \varnothing$:

- T_1: 50% of records with a data schema of category C_{S1}.
- T_2: 50% of records with a data schema of category C_{S2}.

Note 1: In this extension, the flexibility does not concern root attributes (identifiers) of the dimensions.

Note 2: The absence of some attributes in the data schemas that are potentially diverse, has a direct consequence on the results and the queries usage. Some requests can become invalid, if the attributes they contain do not appear in any schemas. To address this issue, we recommend choosing categories of schema that cover every attribute $(C_{S1} \cup C_{S2} = A)$.

Data Velocity. Ability to process data with regular or irregular interval refreshment is another contribution of this paper. The new benchmark considers this feature and allows the user to select the data generation interval and the time T for data loading in the system. For example, for a total volume of 1 TB of data, the user can specify a generation of 2000 GB every 60 s. Same for loading, the user can schedule a load at a regular time interval or not. For an irregular interval, the user only specifies the number of times the file must be loaded and the maximum time T_{max} to wait between two loads. The system implicitly generates a value $T \in [1, T_{max}]$.

3.3   File Formats and Supported Systems

Several file formats are possible: tbl, csv, json and xml. To optimize the data loading phase in the NoSQL systems, the generator gives the user the possibility to specify the appropriate format of the used NoSQL systems. For example, for the document-oriented model, MongoDB is a system storing data in bjson (binary json), it is optimized for a loading from json files. Loading a csv format file in MongoDB is possible but it will need a conversion in json that considerably increases the loading time. Koalabench has a special option for generating data compatible with ElasticSearch.

Regarding the formats and the data models generated, several data management systems are supported.

- Relational databases: *PostgreSQL, MySQL, Oracle* that takes files under *csv, tbl* or *xml* formats.
- XML databases or object-oriented supporting XML format files.
- Document-oriented databases: *MongoDB, CouchDB, ElasticSearch* that compliant with *json* format.
- Column-oriented databases: *HBase, Cassandra* that takes *csv* format files.
- Graph-oriented databases: *Neo4j* that takes files in csv format.

The supported systems are summarized in the following Table 2.

Table 2. Supported systems versus supported file formats.

Information system class	Supported databases (examples)	File formats
RDBMS	PostgreSQL, MySQL, SqlServer, Oracle, etc.	csv, tbl, xml
Document-oriented	MongoDB, CouchDB, ElasticSearch	json
Column-oriented	Hbase, Cassandra	csv, tbl
Graph-oriented	Neo4J	csv
XML, object-oriented	BaseX, ...	xml, json, csv

3.4   Distributed Data Generation

The data generator has been adapted to generate data on several computers in parallel. It is possible to generate data on the very popular distributed files system HDFS. The distributed generation is based on the two main components of the Hadoop distributed file systems:

- *MapReduce*: to ensure the parallel generation of data.
- *HDFS*: to ensure the distributed file storage.

3.5   Impact of Scale Factor

Here, we discuss the effect of the scale factor on data generation. We detail the data generation for scale factor *sf = 1*. For other scale factors, the proportions are linear

Snowflake Model: When we generate data with the snowflake data model, we generate 8 files for 8 entities. For each entity we have: 5247925 line items, 1500000 orders, 150000 customers, 800000 supplied parts, 200000 parts, 10000 suppliers, 25 nations, 5 regions. The total dataset size takes different amounts of memory depending on the data format. More precisely, it takes: 3.87 GB in .xml, 2.33 GB in .json, 1.16 GB in .tbl and 1.16 GBin .csv.

Star Model: When we generate data with the star data model, we generate 5 files for 5 entities. For each entity we have: 5247925 line items, 150000 customers, 200000 parts, 10000 suppliers and 255 dates. The total dataset size takes different amounts of memory depending on the data format. Yet: 2.52 GB in .xml, 1.47 GB in .json, 0.68 GB in .tbl and 0.68 GB in .csv.

Flat Model: When we generate data with the flat data model, we just generate 1 file. We have a total of 5247925 line items. The total dataset size takes different amounts of memory depending on the data format. More precisely, it takes: 8.21 GB in .xml, 4.67 GB in .json, 2.38 GB in .tbl and 2.38 GB in .csv.

Obtained results are summarized in Table 3.

Table 3. File size versus data model.

Model/format	.xml	.json	.tbl	.csv
Flocon	3.87 GB	2.33 GB	1.16 GB	1.16 GB
Star	2.52 GB	1.47 GB	0.68 GB	0.68 GB
Plat	8.21 GB	4.67 GB	2.38 GB	2.38 GB
Flat flexible	6.48 GB	4.12 GB	2.13 GB	2.13 GB

3.6 Queries Generator

Without loss of generality, we use the original *QGEN* query generator to generate queries written in SQL. Generating queries in other interrogation languages is tempting and certainly useful, but it would be challenging to cover all the NoSQL technologies out there. Moreover, this would likely be technology and version specific. The *QGEN* generator has a high number of queries; few of them could not be directly translated into NoSQL language specific queries. Some NoSQL systems are not suitable for non-standard data models (e.g. "joins" are not supported natively). Thus, it is up to the benchmark users to handle the adaptation work.

For our own experiments, we rewrote some queries to adapt them to the non-standard data models and we translated them into the targeted NoSQL database languages: *Hive* for *HBase usage*, *CQL* for *Cassandra usage,* in the *MongoDB* query language for a usage with *MongoDB* and in the *Cypher* language to be used with *Neo4j*. These queries can be classified according to two criteria:

- Dimensionality affects the dimensions number in the grouping clause (equivalent to the Group By clause in SQL): iD for i dimensions;
- Selectiveness affects the level of data filtering when some conditions are applied.

4   Experiments and Data Sets

In this section, we present the results of some experiments conducted using the proposed benchmark. More precisely:

- we analyze and compare data generation with respect to the memory usage;
- we analyze and compare data generation with respect to the execution time;
- we analyze and compare loading times in *Cassandra* and *MongoDB* NoSQL.

For the different configurations, we change the scale factor to enable comparison at different scale levels.

Hardware. The used cluster includes three nodes (machines). Each node has 4-core CPU, 3.4 Ghz (i5-4670), 8 GB RAM, 2 TB SATA disk (7200RPM), 1 Gb/s network. Each node acts as a worker. One node acts also as dispatcher.

Software: Every machine runs on a CentOS operating system. We test data loading on two NoSQL data stores: Cassandra (v.3) and MongoDB (v.3.2) [5]. The latter represents respectively column-oriented storage and document-oriented storage.

Experiment 1: Memory Usage on Different Configurations. In Table 4, we report the time needed to generate data under different scale factors (*sf* = *1, 10, 100, 1000*) for the different data models. The file format impacts drastically the memory usage, as we can see in Table 3. For instance, at *sf* = *1000* and under the flat model, we have got 2380 GB for CSV file format and 4670 GB (almost double) for the JSON format. This difference impacts significantly the generating time, as files with a more expressive format (JSON or XML) may need 3 to 4 longer time. This way, using flat model at *sf* = *1000*, we need around 17883 s to generate a CSV file versus 69872 s for a JSON file. Another observation can be noted about the fixed or flexible generation on the flat model. Indeed, we notice that the flexible generation is faster, which is explained by the minor volume generated Table 6.

Table 4. Memory usage (in GB) by factor and by scale model

		sf1	*sf10*	*sf100*	*sf1000*
Snowflake	*xml*	3.87 GB	38.7 GB	387 GB	3870 GB
	json	2.33 GB	23.3 GB	233 GB	2330 GB
	csv	1.16 GB	11.6 GB	116 GB	1160 GB
	tbl	1.16 GB	11.6 GB	116 GB	1160 GB
Star	*xml*	2.52 GB	25.2 GB	252 GB	2520 GB
	json	1.47 GB	14.7 GB	147 GB	1470 GB
	csv	0.68 GB	6.8 GB	68 GB	680 GB
	tbl	0.68 GB	6.8 GB	68 GB	680 GB
Flat flexible	*xml*	6.48 GB	64.8 GB	64.8 GB	6480 GB
	json	4.12 GB	41.2 GB	412 GB	4120 GB
	csv	2.13 GB	21.3 GB	213 GB	2130 GB
	tbl	2.13 GB	21.3 GB	213 GB	2130 GB
Flat	*xml*	8.21 GB	82.1 GB	821 GB	8210 GB
	json	4.67 GB	46.7 GB	467 GB	4670 GB
	csv	2.38 GB	23.8 GB	238 GB	2380 GB
	tbl	2.38 GB	23.8 GB	238 GB	2380 GB

Table 5. Time of generation (in seconds) by scale factor and by model.

		sf1	*sf10*	*sf100*	*sf1000*
Snowflake	*xml*	50.2 s	386 s	3634 s	35902 s
	json	39.2 s	298 s	2873 s	27453 s
	csv	23.7 s	173 s	1877 s	17832 s
	tbl	23.7 s	173 s	1877 s	17832 s
Star	*xml*	30.5 s	192 s	2028 s	18973 s
	json	40.5 s	244 s	2351 s	21839 s
	csv	20.8 s	123 s	1312 s	12893 s
	tbl	20.8 s	123 s	1312 s	12893 s
Flat flexible	*xml*	122 s	1143 s	11165 s	104321 s
	json	71 s	561 s	5835 s	56348 s
	csv	21 s	136 s	1560 s	14902 s
	tbl	21 s	136 s	1560 s	14902 s
Flat	*xml*	154 s	1372 s	13767 s	132756 s
	json	87 s	691 s	7003 s	69872 s
	csv	31 s	164 s	1873 s	17883 s
	tbl	31 s	164 s	1873 s	17883 s

Table 6. Loading time per model and per scale factor with Cassandra and MongoDB.

	sf = 1	*sf* = 10	*sf* = 100
Cassandra (star)	672 s	6643 s	69025 s
MongoDB (flat)	3967 s	38632 s	381142 s

Experiment 2: In Table 5, we report the loading time under different scale factors (*sf* = *1, 10, 100*) for different data models. We only have proceeded to the necessary loading for each tool, JSON for MongoDB and CSV for Cassandra. We notice that the required loading time in Cassandra is lower than in MongoDB. For example, at *sf* = *1*, we need 672 s for Cassandra versus 3976 s for MongoDB, which means 4 times longer. This can be explained by the file's format used. In MongoDB, the JSON format used is 4 times more voluminous than a CSV file. In addition, it led to more transfers between the master node and the slave node. The communication in Cassandra via its master-master architecture seems much less expensive. MongoDB creates an important number of indexes to optimize the querying phase.

5   Concluding Remarks

This paper presents the KoalaBench benchmark built to address the issues of decisions support systems based on big multidimensional data warehouses (Big Data). It is based on an extension of the reference benchmark TPC-H. The data can be generated in different formats (TBL, CSV, XML, JSON) and in different data models. It is worth to mention that KoalaBench is not restricted to relational models; it can also generate data in several NoSQL systems. This novel benchmark solution is suitable for columns-oriented, graph-oriented and documents-oriented NoSQL systems. Moreover, data can be generated under a fixed or a flexible schema, in a distributed architecture using the Hadoop platform. KoalaBench proposes a specific loading script for every evaluated system. Conducted experiments show that the KoalaBench brings numerous advantages compared to the original version TPC-H. It simplifies the loading phase and allows data loading in a Hadoop distributed environment. It also permits evaluating the schemas' diversity, which is specific to NoSQL approaches. This functionality enables dynamic data generation.

References

1. Chaudhuri, S., Dayal, U.: An overview of data warehousing and OLAP technology. SIGMOD Rec. **26**(1), 65–74 (1997)
2. Chevalier, M., El Malki, M., Kopliku, A., Teste, O., Tournier, R.: Document-oriented data warehouses: models and extended cuboids, extended cuboids in oriented document. In: 10th International Conference on Research Challenges in Information Science (RCIS 2016), Grenoble, France, pp. 1–11. IEEE (2016)
3. Chevalier, M., El Malki, M., Kopliku, A., Teste, O., Tournier, R.: Implementation of multidimensional databases in column-oriented NoSQL systems. In: Morzy, T., Valduriez, P., Bellatreche, L. (eds.) ADBIS 2015. LNCS, vol. 9282, pp. 79–91. Springer, Cham (2015). https://doi.org/10.1007/978-3-319-23135-8_6
4. Chevalier, M., El Malki, M., Kopliku, A., Teste, O., Tournier, R.: Implementation of multidimensional databases with document-oriented NoSQL. In: Madria, S., Hara, T. (eds.) DaWaK 2015. LNCS, vol. 9263, pp. 379–390. Springer, Cham (2015). https://doi.org/10.1007/978-3-319-22729-0_29
5. Cooper, B.F., Silberstein, A., Tam, E., Ramakrishnan, R., Sears, R.: Benchmarking cloud serving systems with YCSB. In: Proceedings of the 1st ACM Symposium on Cloud Computing, Series. SOCC 2010. ACM, pp. 143–154 (2010)
6. Darmont, J.: Data warehouse benchmarking with DWEB. In: Taniar, D. (ed.) Progressive Methods in Data Warehousing and Business Intelligence: Concepts and Competitive Analytics. Advances in Data Warehousing and Mining (2008)
7. Dede, E., Govindaraju, M., Gunter, D., Canon, R.S., Ramakrishnan, L.: Performance evaluation of a MongoDB and hadoop platform for scientific data analysis. In: Proceedings of the 4th ACM Workshop on Scientific Cloud Computing, Series, pp. 13–20 (2013)
8. Dehdouh, K., Boussaid, O., Bentayeb, F.: Columnar NoSQL star schema benchmark. In: Ait Ameur, Y., Bellatreche, L., Papadopoulos, George A. (eds.) MEDI 2014. LNCS, vol. 8748, pp. 281–288. Springer, Cham (2014). https://doi.org/10.1007/978-3-319-11587-0_26
9. Dehdouh, K., Bentayeb, F., Boussaid, O., et al.: Using the column oriented NoSQL model for implementing big data warehouses. In: PDPTA. The Steering Committee of The World Congress in Computer Science, Computer Engineering and Applied Computing (World-Comp), p. 469 (2015)
10. Ghazal, A., et al.: BigBench: towards an industry standard benchmark for big data analytics (2013)
11. Iu, M.-Y., Zwaenepoel, W.: HadoopToSQL: a mapReduce query optimizer. In: Proceedings of the 5th European Conference on Computer Systems. ACM, pp. 251–264 (2010)

12. Ivanov, T., Rabl, T., Poess, M., Queralt, A., Poelman, J., Poggi, N., Buell, J.: Big Data Benchmark Compendium. In: Nambiar, R., Poess, M. (eds.) TPCTC 2015. LNCS, vol. 9508, pp. 135–155. Springer, Cham (2016). https://doi.org/10.1007/978-3-319-31409-9_9
13. Jacobs, A.: The pathologies of big data. Commun. ACM **52**(8), 36–44 (2009)
14. Kim, K., et al.: MRBench: a benchmark for mapReduce framework. In: 2008 14th IEEE International Conference on Parallel and Distributed Systems. ICPADS 2008, pp. 11–18, December 2008
15. Hacigumus, H., Iyer, B., Mehrotra, S.: Providing database as a service. In: 2002 Proceedings of 18th International Conference on Data Engineering. IEEE, pp. 29–38 (2002)
16. Lee, K.-H., Lee, Y.-J., Choi, H., Chung, Y.D., Moon, B.: Parallel data processing with mapReduce: a survey. SIGMOD Rec. **40**(4), 11–20 (2012)
17. Lee, R., Luo, T., Huai, Y., Wang, F., He, Y., Zhang, X.: YSmart: yet another SQL-to-mapReduce translator. In: 2011 31st International Conference on Distributed Computing Systems (ICDCS), pp. 25–36, June 2011
18. Moniruzzaman, A.B.M., Hossain, S.A.: NoSQL database: new era of databases for big data analytics - classification, characteristics and comparison. CORR abs/1307.0191 (2013)
19. Morfonios, K., Konakas, S., Ioannidis, Y.: ROLAP implementations of the data cube. ACM Comput. Surv. (CSUR) **39**(4), 12 (2007)
20. Poess, M., Nambiar, R.O., Walrath, D.: Why you should run TPC-DS: a workload analysis. In: Proceedings of the 33rd International Conference on Very Large Data Bases. VLDB 2007 (2007)
21. O'Neil, P.E., O'Neil, E.J., Chen, X.: The star schema benchmark (SSB). In: PAT, vol. 200, p. 50 (2007)
22. Stonebraker, M.: New opportunities for new SQL. Commun. ACM **55**(11), 10–11 (2012)
23. Ravat, F., Teste, O., Tournier, R., Zurfluh, G.: Algebraic and graphic languages for OLAP manipulations. In: Strategic Advancements in Utilizing Data Mining and Warehousing Technologies: New Concepts and Developments, p. 60 (2009)
24. Vassiliadis, P., Sellis, T.: A survey of logical models for OLAP databases. ACM SIGMOD Rec. **28**(4), 64–69 (1999)
25. Wang, J., et al.: BigDataBench: a big data benchmark from internet services. In: 2014 IEEE 20th International Symposium on High Performance Computer Architecture (HPCA), pp. 488–499, February 2014
26. Zhang, J., Sivasubramaniam, A., Franke, H., Gautam, N., Zhang, Y., Nagar, S.: Synthesizing representative I/O workloads for TPC-H. In: Software, IEEE Proceedings, pp. 142–142, February 2004
27. Zhao, H., Ye, X.: A practice of TPC-DS multidimensional implementation on NoSQL database systems. In: Nambiar, R., Poess, M. (eds.) TPCTC 2013. LNCS, vol. 8391, pp. 93–108. Springer, Cham (2014). https://doi.org/10.1007/978-3-319-04936-6_7

IoT Network Management and Applications

Multihop Transmission Strategy Using Dijkstra Algorithm to Improve Energy Efficiency in WSNs

Maha Abderrahim[1(✉)], Hela Hakim[1,2(✉)], Hatem Boujemaa[1(✉)], and Farid Touati[3(✉)]

[1] COSIM LAB, SUPCOM, Carthage University, Tunis, Tunisia
[2] Digital Research Center, University of Sfax, Sfax, Tunisia
{maha.abderrahim,hela.hakim,hatem.boujemaa}@supcom.tn
[3] Department of Electrical Engineering, Qatar University, Doha, Qatar
touatif@qu.edu.qa

Abstract. Thanks to the development in the wireless communication technologies and the microelectronics domain, Wireless Sensor Networks (WSNs) are more and more omnipresent. The most important challenge of WSN is how to extend its lifetime. For long distance communication, using one hop transmission causes the dissipation of a lot of energy. To avoid this dissipation, an energy-efficient multihop transmission strategy based on Dijkstra algorithm is proposed in this paper. We consider a WSN organized into clusters, each cluster is composed of N sensor nodes classified as follows: source node, cluster head (CH) node as the destination, group of active nodes and group of sleeping nodes. The selection of CH node is based on the position of nodes within the cluster and their residual energy. Then, the CH groups the remaining nodes into active or sleeping nodes according to a reference distance. We suppose that the transmitting symbol is correctly received only if the Signal-to-Noise Ratio (SNR) at the receiver is above a threshold γ_{th}. Our main objective is to define a new transmission technique minimizing the power consumption using multihop communication. The selected relays which cooperate to aid the source-destination communication are those offering the least transmit power while maintaining SNR equal to the threshold γ_{th}. We use Dijkstra algorithm to select the reliable relays. Simulations results demonstrate that the proposed transmission technique can reduce enormously the power consumption.

Keywords: Wireless Sensor Network · Multihop transmission
Dijkstra algorithm · Energy saving

© Springer Nature Switzerland AG 2018
N. Boudriga et al. (Eds.): UNet 2018, LNCS 11277, pp. 97–107, 2018.
https://doi.org/10.1007/978-3-030-02849-7_9

1   Introduction

With the development of internet of things technology, Wireless Sensor Networks are in use everywhere today.[1] In fact, a WSN is described as a network of nodes connected via wireless links, often powered by batteries of limited energy. Each sensor accomplishes three main functions: collecting, processing and transmitting collected data to one collection point called the Cluster-Head. To ensure conviviality, this network can be divided into groups called clusters. The application of the WSN involves several fields to facilitate the human life and preserve the nature. A wide examples of WSN applications cited in [1–3], the traffic monitoring, environmental surveillance, infrastructure control, healthcare, etc. According to the application, wireless sensors can be deployed in difficult to reach locations, (ex: submarine, underground, sahara, forest...). So, it is troublesome to replace their batteries. Generally, inaccessible sensors are left away once their batteries have been exhausted. They are called dead nodes. The number of dead nodes greatly influences the network performance and sometimes, if this number is important, the network will be totally disabled. Thus, one of the most important challenges of WSN is how we can extend the WSNs lifetime as long as possible. Several techniques and approaches are adopted in WSN to reduce the energy consumption. Among these techniques, those who use clustering. Authors in [4] and [5] present a state of the art survey on clustering algorithms and classify them based on various metrics such as convergence rate, cluster stability, cluster over-lapping, location awareness and support for node mobility. In [6], authors proposed a clustering algorithm based on cell combination for the networks. This clustering algorithm consists of dividing the monitoring area into hexagonal cells based on the geographic location information of nodes. In [7], authors proposed a clustering algorithm which uses an associated weight function and tries to regroup the sensor nodes so that a minimum number of clusters with maximum number of sensor nodes in each cluster could be obtained. Authors in [5] and [8], present a survey about LEACH protocol and its descendant as F-LEACH, SLEACH, Sec-LEACH, SS-LEACH, RLEACH, A-LEACH, and V-LEACH in [9]. Routing techniques are also considered as a good approach to minimize the energy consumption in WSNs. In fact, the aim of routing in WSNs is to find out and maintain routes in WSNs to transmit data between nodes. There are many routing protocols have been proposed in the literature to make the availability of WSNs for a long period with a low power. Among these protocols, we can cite, P-SEP presented in [10], this algorithm is a modified Stable Election Protocol (SEP), allows to prolong the stable period of Fog-supported sensor networks by maintaining balanced energy consumption. In [11], authors proposed an energy aware routing algorithm for cluster based WSNs. This algorithm is based on a cluster head (CH) selection strategy according to residual energy of the CHs and the intra-cluster distance for cluster formation. In [14], a new multihop

---

[1] This publication was made possible by NPRP grant #8-1781-2-735 from the Qatar National Research Fund (a member of Qatar Foundation). The statements made herein are solely the responsibility of the authors.

transmission strategy is proposed. This strategy allows to select a set of reliable nodes collaborate to transmits data to the destination node with the minimum possible power. Authors in [15], propose an energy-efficient transmission strategy with cluster organization phase to improve energy saving in WSNs. This technique allows firstly classifying the nodes within the cluster, then applies a relay selection algorithm to choose the relays that offers the minimum transmit power.

In this paper, we propose a new multihop transmission strategy based on SNR threshold. This transmission strategy is done in two steps. During the first step we try to elect the appropriate node as cluster head based on the distance to the cluster center and the residual energy of nodes. Then, we classify the remaining nodes within the cluster into sleeping nodes and active nodes. The second step is dedicated to select the set of reliable relays which offering the least transmit power while maintaining the SNR at the receiver equal to the threshold γ_{th}. The relays selection algorithm is based on Dijkstra algorithm. This set of nodes participates in the transmission to aid the source-destination communication.

We present this paper as follows: In Sect. 2, we present our system model. In Sect. 3, we present the CH election procedure. Section 4 is devoted to clarify the relay selection strategy based on Dijkstra algorithm and Sect. 5 to define the transmission strategy. Numerical results are shown and discussed in Sect. 6, followed by our conclusions in Sect. 7.

2   System Model

This section is devoted to present the system model of our network. We consider a clustered WSN which is established for both cooperative and non-cooperative transmission schemes. As shown in Fig. 1, all nodes within the cluster are placed randomly. They have the coordinates x and y between [−a, a] and [−b, b] respectively. Each cluster is composed of one source node noted S, one destination node (in our work we will consider that the elected CH is the destination node) and the remaining nodes within the cluster are grouped into active nodes and sleeping nodes according to the decision of CH. Based on this model, we propose a multi-hop transmission technique based on Dijkstra algorithm to minimize the energy consumption in WSNs. In fact, we suppose that when a sensor node detects relevant information, it tries to transmit it to the destination node via multi hop transmission scheme. The selected relays which participate in this transmission are those offering the least transmit power while maintaining SNR equal to the threshold γ_{th}. This set of nodes is obtained by applying Dijkstra algorithm. The elected CH has to transfer the received data to a center of supervision and maintenance in order to take the necessary intervention. The matrix distance between nodes is calculated using this formula:

$$d(i,j) = \sqrt{[x(i) - x(j)]^2 + [y(i) - y(j)]^2} \qquad (1)$$

We suppose that each node is equipped with a single antenna and limited battery source. The communication between nodes is in half-duplex mode. So, the sensor cannot transmit and receive data simultaneously. The transmitting signal is noted X_S. The set of active relays within the cluster can participate in the transmission by forwarding the received signal X_R to the elected CH using Decode-and-Forward relaying strategy. To combine the signals from selected relays and source node, the elected CH uses the Maximum Ratio Combiner (MRC). The received signal from a node i to a node j can be as:

$$Y_{i,j} = \sqrt{P_i} h_{i,j} X_i + n_{i,j} \tag{2}$$

Where P_i is the transmitting signal, $h_{i,j}$ is the channel coefficient modeled as a Rayleigh fading channel, ($h_{i,j} = \nu_{i,j} d_{i,j}^{-\alpha/2}$, where $d_{i,j}$ is the distance between i and j, α is the path loss exponent and $\nu_{i,j}$ is the fading coefficient modeled as a circular symmetric complex Gaussian random variable with variance 1). X_i is the transmitted signal and $n_{i,j}$ is a White and Additive Gaussian Noise with variance N_0. We suppose that the transmitting symbol is correctly received by the destination only if the SNR at CH equal to γ_{th}. Therefore, to have the SNR at CH equal to γ_{th}, the transmitter must use a power equal to:

$$P_i = \frac{N_0 \gamma_{th}}{|h_{i,j}|^2} \tag{3}$$

We suppose that the maximum power available for a transmission is P_{max}, so if the power in Eq. (3), exceeds P_{max}, the transmission will not take place and the system is considered in outage state.

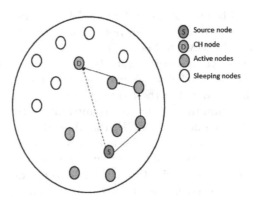

Fig. 1. An example of a cluster

3   The CH Election Procedure

In this section, we explain firstly the procedure of CH election and then the principle of classification of nodes within the cluster.

The elected CH is responsible for forwarding the receiving data from the source node to a center of maintenance and supervision. The process of election CH consists of selecting the appropriate node as cluster head based on two criteria: the distance to the cluster center and the residual energy of nodes. In fact, the ignorance of residual energy in this process causes the rapid death of certain nodes. Because, if the elected CH has low energy, this accelerates its death and shortens the WSN lifetime. To elect the CH, we firstly sort the nodes in descending order according to its residual energy. Then we choose from the two nodes that have the most energy which is closest to the cluster center. After, the election of CH, this last classifies the remaining nodes within the cluster into active nodes and sleeping nodes according to a reference distance d_{ref}. The nodes that have a distance from S less than d_{ref} will be notified to be active nodes and will be used in the application of Dijkstra algorithm to select the set of reliable nodes which will participate in the multi hop transmission to minimize the transmit power. The nodes which don't receive a notification message from the elected CH stay in sleeping mode and conserve its residual energy. The election of the better CH node and the classification of remaining nodes within the cluster alleviate the processing and avoid the unnecessary transfer of messages between the nodes.

4   Relay Selection Algorithm

In this section, we present our proposed relay selection strategy based on Dijkstra algorithm. So, firstly we define the Dijkstra algorithm and its steps.

4.1   Dijkstra Algorithm

Dijkstras algorithm is an algorithm for finding the shortest paths between nodes in a graph. There are different variants of this algorithm. The original variant consists of finding the shortest path between one source node and one destination node. An alternative variant fixes a single node as the "source" and finds shortest paths from the source to all other nodes in the graph [12].

We consider that the source, the CH and the active nodes form a completely connected graph G(X, A, C), where X is the set of vertices, A is the set of arcs and C is the cost of arcs. X will be divided into two groups, a group of visited nodes which have found the shortest path to the source node and a group of unvisited nodes, called the unvisited set, contains the node set that has not determined the vertices of the shortest path. Dijkstras algorithm calculates the shortest paths between two nodes in a graph as follows: [13].

Step 1: set the cost to zero for the source node and infinity for all other nodes.
Step 2: for the node in question, consider all of its neighbors and calculate their costs. Compare the newly cost to the assigned value and attribute the smallest one. For example, if a node N1 is marked with a cost of 5, and the edge connecting it with a neighbor N2 has length 3, then the cost to N2 (through N1) will be 5 + 3 = 8. If N2 was previously marked with a cost greater than 8 then change it to 8. Otherwise, keep the current value.

Step 3: remove this node from the unvisited set and add it to the visited set.

Step 4: repeat step 2 and step 3 until the destination will be marked as visited node.

4.2 Relay Selection Algorithm

Our objective is to define a transmission technique aiming to maintain a minimum SNR equal to γ_{th} at the elected CH node while minimizing the overall consumed power. For that we define a new transmission strategy to aide source node to transmit the detected data to the elected CH with the minimum possible power. The set of selected relays is found by applying Dijkstra algorithm. So, in our work, the source node and the elected CH node and the set of active nodes constitute a completely connected graph G(X, A, C), where X is the set of vertices, A is the set of arcs and C is the cost of arcs. We define the cost as the transmit power that keeps SNR equals to γ_{th}. Figure 2 shows an example of a cluster composed of 7 nodes. Node 1 is the source node and node 5 is the elected CH. Algorithm 1 details the process of selecting the adequate relays that offer us the minimum power consumption.

Algorithm 1

Initialization: C(S) =0

                 C(i)=∞; where belongs to active nodes set

                 Previous (S)=S

                 Visited_nodes=[S]

While (CH doesnt belong to Visited_nodes)

     For each i belongs to active nodes set

         If C(S)+P(S,i)< C(i)

            C(i)= P(S,i)+ C(S)

            Previous(i)=S

            Visited_nodes=[Visited_nodes, i]

         End if

            Update S=i

     End for

End while

After running Dijkstra algorithm, we calculate the transmit power through the scheme composed of the set of visited nodes using this formula:

$$P_c = P_{S,R_1} + \sum_{i=2}^{L-1} P_{R_i,R_{i+1}} + P_{R_L,CH} \tag{4}$$

Where R = $\{R_1, R_2, \ldots, R_L\}$ is the set of relays selected as result of applying Dijkstra algorithm.

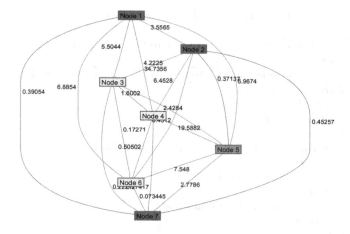

Fig. 2. Dijkstra algorithm

5   Transmission Strategy

In this section, we explain the proposed transmission technique. In fact, our transmission strategy combines the cooperative and the non-cooperative schemes to reduce the transmit power. The transmitted symbols are assumed to be correctly detected by the CH node only if the SNR at the CH is above a threshold γ_{th}, otherwise, the transmission is interrupted. After the election of CH node, we calculate the transmit power P_d considering that S will transmit using direct link. If P_d exceeds the maximum power authorized to use P_{max}, the source information could not been transmitted and the system suffers from an outage state. Then, we carry out the relay selection strategy based on Dijkstra algorithm to select the set of suitable relays R = $\{R_1, R_2, \ldots, R_L\}$. This set will participate in the transmission in order to aid the source-destination communication. We calculate afterward the transmit power using the cooperative scheme P_c.

$$P_c = P_{S,R_1} + \sum_{i=2}^{L-1} P_{R_i,R_{i+1}} + P_{R_L,CH} \tag{5}$$

As we mentioned previously, our transmission strategy uses cooperative and non-cooperative schemes. So, we will compare between P_d and P_c and choose the one that gives us the smallest value. Table 1 is given to facilitate the comprehension of the proposed strategy.

Table 1. Proposed transmission strategy

1- Election of CH node based on the distance to the cluster center and the residual energy of nodes.
2- Classification of remaining nodes into active nodes and sleeping nodes.

3- Choose of transmission scheme
    If ($P_d > P_{max}$)
       ⇒ Outage state
    Else
       Calculate the transmit power: $P_T = \min(P_d, P_c)$
       If ($P_T = P_d$)
          ⇒ Direct transmission
       Else
          ⇒ Cooperative transmission
       End if
    End if

6   Numerical and Simulations Results

In this section, we display the simulation results of our proposed transmission strategy to demonstrate how far it can save energy in the network. So, to evaluate its performance, we use Monte-Carlo simulations. We suppose that the channel corresponds to the Rayleigh channel. We set the path loss exponent α to 3 and the variance of the AWGN N_0 to 0.01. We use 10^3 samples for each simulation. We fix the coordinates a and b to 4, so all relays are randomly distributed within the cluster, whose the coordinate are between $[-4, 4]$. The reference distance d_{ref} which will be used to classify the nodes equal to $3/2 * d_{S,CH}$.

The energy saving percentage is calculated as follows:

$$ES(\%) = \frac{(P_c - P_d)}{P_d} * 100 \tag{6}$$

Where P_c is the transmit power via cooperative scheme and P_d is the transmit power using direct link. We carry out our simulations for many random topologies and we present the average result.

In Fig. 3, we have shown the comparison of energy consumption between direct transmission and our multi hop transmission strategy for N = 10 (N represents the number of sensors within the cluster). The results illustrate that the total energy consumption is reduced significantly using multi hop transmission. This reduction in power consumption thanks to the election of the appropriate node as CH and the classification of nodes into active nodes and sleeping nodes is translated into energy saving. In Fig. 4, we present the percent of the energy saved thanks to our proposed strategy compared to the transmission where the CH is randomly chosen within the cluster for N = 10. Thus the energy saving attains more than 75% in high SNR values. As shown, the saved energy increases proportionally with the SNR. Because, when the SNR increases, the amount of

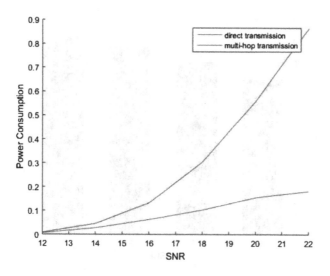

Fig. 3. Power consumption comparison for N = 10

the authorized power P_{max} also increases. This increases the probability to find a set of relays which cooperate to transmit data with transmit power less than P_d. Moreover, the number of nodes within the cluster influences the total energy consumption and consequently the percent of energy savings. In fact, by increasing the number of nodes per cluster, more energy savings can be found. Because when N increases, we will be more likely to select the best set of relays which provides the minimum transmit power. We see clearly in Fig. 5 this increase when we change N from 10 to 25 for SNR = 20 dB.

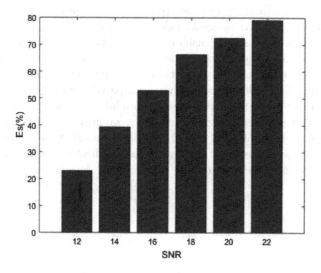

Fig. 4. Energy saving

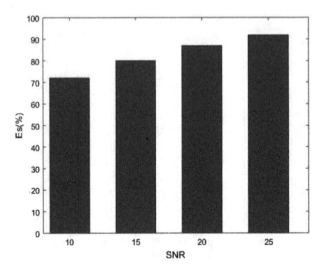

Fig. 5. Energy saving for N = [10:25]

7 Conclusion

In this paper, a new multi hop transmission strategy which is based on Dijkstra algorithm is applied to a clustered WSN. This approach considered that the transmission achieves the destination without interruption only if the SNR at the CH is above an SNR threshold. Otherwise, the system is considered in an outage state. The main purpose of our proposed strategy is to improve the energy saving in order to extend the network lifetime. So, we define a new transmission technique consisting of electing the appropriate node as CH according to its residual energy and its distance to the cluster center. Then, classify the remaining nodes into active nodes and sleeping nodes to alleviate the processing and minimize the unnecessary transfer of messages between the nodes within the cluster and to reduce the duration of data transmission to the maintenance center. After that, we apply the relay selection strategy based on Dijkstra algorithm to select the set of reliable relays. We have compared the results between direct transmission and cooperative transmission, simulations prove that our proposed transmission strategy offers a significant energy savings (can reach up to 80% in high SNR). The percent of energy savings varies proportionally with the number of nodes within the cluster. As future work we will investigate the multi-source case where more than one source node can transmit data simultaneously.

References

1. Ojha, T., Misra, S., Raghuwanshi, N.S.: Wireless sensor networks for agriculture: the state-of-the-art in practice and future challenges. Comput. Electron. Agric. **118**, 66–84 (2015)
2. Al-Fuqaha, A., Guizani, M., Mohammadi, M., et al.: Internet of Things: a survey on enabling technologies, protocols, and applications. IEEE Commun. Surv. Tutor. **17**(4), 2347–2376 (2015)
3. Rashid, B., Rehmani, M.H.: Applications of wireless sensor networks for urban areas: a survey. J. Netw. Comput. Appl. **60**, 192–219 (2016)
4. Kumar, V., Jain, S., Tiwari, S., et al.: Energy efficient clustering algorithms in wireless sensor networks: a survey. IJCSI Int. J. Comput. Sci. Issues **8**(5), 259 (2011)
5. Mamalis, B., Gavalas, D., Konstantopoulos, C., Pantziou, G.: Clustering in wireless sensor networks. In: RFID and Sensor Networks, pp. 323–354 (2009)
6. Chang-ri, L., Yun, Z., Xin-Hua, Z., Zi-bo, Z.: A clustering algorithm based on cell combination for wireless sensor networks. In: 2010 Second International Workshop on Education Technology and Computer Science, ETCS, vol. 2, pp. 74–77, March 2010
7. Zainalie, S., Yaghmaee, M.H.: CFL: a clustering algorithm for localization in wireless sensor networks. In: International Symposium on Telecommunications, IST 2008, pp. 435–439. IEEE (2008)
8. Tandel, R.I.: Leach protocol in wireless sensor network: a survey. Int. J. Comput. Sci. Inf. Technol. **7**(4), 1894–1896 (2016)
9. Manjusha, M.S., Kannammal, K.E.: Efficient cluster head selection method for wireless sensor network. Int. J. Comput. Eng. Res. **04**, 43–49
10. Naranjo, P.G.V., Shojafar, M., Mostafaei, H., et al.: P-SEP: a prolong stable election routing algorithm for energy-limited heterogeneous fog-supported wireless sensor networks. J. Supercomput. **73**(2), 733–755 (2017)
11. Amgoth, T., Jana, P.K.: Energy-aware routing algorithm for wireless sensor networks. Comput. Electr. Eng. **41**, 357–367 (2015)
12. Dahiya, A., Kumar, V.: Performance measurement of Dijkstra using WSN: a review. Int. J. Eng. Appl. Manag. Sci. Paradig. **26**, 29–34 (2015)
13. Ya-Qiong, Z., Yun-Rui, L.: A routing protocol for wireless sensor networks using K-means and Dijkstra algorithm. Int. J. Adv. Med. Commun. **6**(2–4), 109–121 (2016)
14. Abderrahim, M., Hakim, H., Boujemaa, H., Al Hamad, R.: Multihop transmission strategy to improve energy efficiency in WSNs. In: IEEE International Conference on Advanced Information Networking and Applications Proceeding (2018, Accepted)
15. Abderrahim, M., Hakim, H., Boujemaa, H.: Energy-efficient transmission strategy with cluster organization phase to improve energy saving in WSNs. In: IEEE International Conference on Advanced Information Networking and Applications Proceeding (2018, Accepted)

Two Vice-Cluster Selection Approach to Improve Leach Protocol in WSN

Kamel Tebessi[1(✉)] and Fouzi Semchedine[2(✉)]

[1] Department of Mathematics and Computer Science, Research Unit
(RTESMPEFVS), University of Oum El Bouaghi, Oum El Bouaghi, Algeria
kameltebessi@yahoo.fr
[2] Institute of Optics and Precision Mechanics (IOMP), University of Setif,
Sétif, Algeria
fouzi.jams@gmail.com

Abstract. A Wireless Sensor Network (WSN) consists of a set of sensor nodes which have a limited energy, processing and memory capabilities. The applications of WSN in some hostile environment make the sensor nodes difficult to replace once their battery resources exhaust. The wireless transmission is the most energy consuming operation and designing an energy efficient routing protocol becomes the main goal for the wireless sensor network. LEACH is considered as the most popular routing protocol which has better performance in saving the energy. However, it has some limits. This paper presents a new variant of LEACH protocol called TV-LEACH that aims extending the lifetime of the network. The simulation results show that the network lifetime in the improved protocol is better than that of the LEACH Protocol.

1 Introduction

Wireless sensor network consists of hundreds and even thousands of small tiny devices called sensor nodes distributed autonomously to observe physical or environmental conditions like temperature, pressure, vibration and motion at different locations such as landslides [3]. Every node in a sensor network usually is equipped with one sensor, a wireless communication device like radio transceiver, a small micro-controller, and an energy supply or a battery. Since the nodes are based on battery, the energy plays a vital role.

The application of the WSN involves several fields, like military battleground, fire detection, and other hostile environments. In these situations, it is difficult to replace the dead nodes caused by energy's depletion with new ones to operate the network. Therefore, making the sensor nodes operational as long as possible is the main challenge to maximize the network lifetime. The energy consumption of sensor nodes primarily is due to the long distance of data transmission. So, an efficient routing protocol could preserve such energy. Hence, how to design an energy efficient routing protocol becomes the main objective for the wireless sensor networks [5].

© Springer Nature Switzerland AG 2018
N. Boudriga et al. (Eds.): UNet 2018, LNCS 11277, pp. 108–115, 2018.
https://doi.org/10.1007/978-3-030-02849-7_10

The basic objective of any routing protocol is to make the network operational as longer as possible. A cluster-based routing protocol is one of the existing schemes. It groups the sensor nodes where each group of nodes has a Cluster Head (CH). The sensed data are sent to the CH rather than the sink. The CH performs some aggregation functions on the received data and sends them to the sink. LEACH [6] is considered as the most popular routing protocol that uses cluster-based routing mechanism in order to minimize the energy consumption.

The main contribution of this paper is a modified protocol design called TVLEACH that uses two Vice-Cluster Head (V-CH). The first V-CH will take the role of the CH even if the CH is still alive, which will decrease the energy spent on the re-clustering process by delaying the coming of the new round. The second V-CH will be the alternate CH only when the new CH is died.

The remainder of the paper is organized as follows: Sect. 2 presents the LEACH variant protocols. Section 3 presents the proposed protocol. Section 4 shows the simulation results and we conclude the work in Sect. 5.

2 LEACH Variants

LEACH, is a low-energy adaptive clustering hierarchy for WSN. The operation of LEACH can be divided into rounds (Fig. 1).

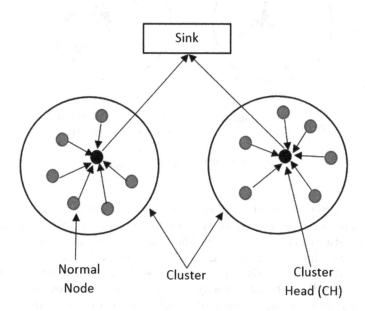

Fig. 1. LEACH network model

Each round begins with a set-up phase in which the clusters are organized and followed by a steady-state phase where several frames of data are transferred from the nodes to the cluster head and thus, to the sink [1]. Its main objectives are prolonging the network lifetime, reducing the consumed energy, and using the data aggregation to reduce the number of exchanged massages.

In the standard LEACH, the CH always receives the data from the cluster members, aggregates them and then, sends them to the sink that might be located far away from it. Thus, the CH will die earlier than the other nodes in the cluster. When the CH die, the cluster will become useless because the data gathered by the cluster nodes will never reach the sink. In order to overcome this problem, a modified version of LEACH was proposed in the literature and called V-LEACH. In V-LEACH protocol [1], there is a vice-CH that takes the role of the CH (Fig. 2) when the CH dies. By considering these vices-CH, the cluster nodes' data will always reach the sink and there is no need to elect a new CH each time the CH dies. Consequently, this will extend the network lifetime.

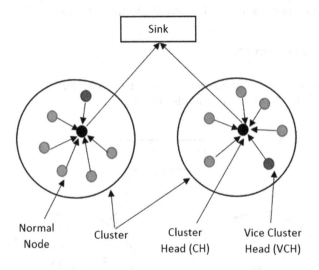

Fig. 2. VLEACH network model

In [2], an extended vice-CH selection is proposed to improve the V-LEACH protocol. The selection process of the vice-CH is based on three factors: the minimum distance, the maximum residual energy, and the minimum energy. In [3], another improvement of V-LEACH was proposed. The vice-CH will be the node that has the maximum energy in the cluster. The vice-CH will take the role of the CH in the later steady-state phase of the current round. Then, the CH itself will become a standard member node because of the too much energy consumption. This will decrease the frequency of the re-clustering process and extend the time of being in the steady-state phase, which could prolong the network lifetime. Although the V-LEACH protocol acts in a very sensible manner, it also suffers from several limits, such as: In the first rounds of the network lifetime (before that the first CH dies), the calculation of the VCH in

[1,2] (which consumes energy) is useless, because the VCH will be operational only when the CH dies. When the CH dies, the VCH will take its place. So, the common nodes will consume much more energy to send their data to the new CH than to the previous CH, if the new CH is situated at the border of the cluster.

3   The Proposed Protocol TV-LEACH

In our improved TV-LEACH protocol, besides having a CH in the cluster, there are two VCH (Vice-Cluster Head), as it is shown in Fig. 3.

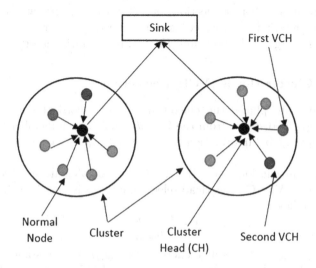

Fig. 3. Proposed TV-LEACH

In fact, the Vice CH selection criteria are: the maximum residual energy and the minimum distance from the CH. Thus, the protocols proposed in [2,3] combine this two criteria. We have found that the protocol in [2] was better than the protocol in [3] in the first rounds of the network lifetime. However, the protocol in [3] was better than that of [2] in the last rounds of the network lifetime. From this, it come the idea of using 2 vice-CH since we have only two criteria.

3.1   Cluster Heads (CHs) Selection (Set-Up Phase)

LEACH ignores the residual energy of each node during the CH selection process. The better results were obtained by just taking the ratio of the current energy and the initial energy instead of taking the square root in the formula for the threshold calculation T(n) [8]:

$$T(n) = \begin{cases} \frac{P}{(1-P*(r\ mod(1/P)))}) * \frac{E_{residual}}{E_{initial}}, n \in G \\ 0\ otherwise \end{cases} \tag{1}$$

Based on such threshold, we propose a new formula, which will increase the probability of nodes having the higher residual energy to become the cluster head. The threshold is set as follows:

$$T(n) = \begin{cases} ((\frac{P}{(1-P*(r\ mod((1/P)))}) * ((1 + \frac{E_{residual}}{E_{initial}}) * ((1 - P) \\ + (1 + \frac{E_{residual}}{2*E_{initial}})))), n \in G \\ 0\ otherwise \end{cases} \tag{2}$$

Where: p is the percentage of cluster heads over all the nodes within the network, r: is the number of selection rounds in the current time, G: is the set of nodes that haven't been selected as cluster heads in the round $\frac{1}{P}$, $E_{residual}$: is the residual energy of the node and $E_{initial}$: is the initial energy of each node.

3.2 Vices Cluster Heads (VCHs) Selection

In the steady-state phase, the cluster head will record the residual energy ($E_{residual}$) and the distance from the CH (d_{toCH}) to each member node. Thus, the CH can have global information (id_{node}, $E_{residual}$, d_{toCH}) about its member nodes.

Using this information, the CH will be able to calculate its vices-CH. The process of the 1st Vice-Cluster Head selection criteria is based on the value of λ considered as follows:

$$\lambda = \frac{E_{residual}}{d_{toCH}} \tag{3}$$

Where $E_{residual}$ is the residual energy and d_{toCH} is the distance of the node from the CH. λ is only calculated among cluster heads. The node that has the highest value of λ will become the 1st Vice-Cluster Head. The 2nd Vice-Cluster Head will be the node with the highest residual energy in the cluster. The CH broadcasts a message containing the VCHs id to all the member nodes. The heavy tasks on CH will cause an excessive amount of consumed energy. So, to delay the arriving of a new round which will increase the energy spent on the re-clustering process, the first vice-CH will take the role of the CH and the CH itself will become a standard member node. The new CH also consumes too much energy as the previous CH. A new round begins and new clusters are going to be rebuilt in the set-up phase. The second V-CH will act as a CH only if the new CH dies in order to guaranty the deliverance of the data gathered by the cluster nodes.

4   Simulation

In order to show the effectiveness of the proposed variant, we simulate LEACH variant protocols that use a vice-CH scheme and the improved protocol (Two

V-LEACH). The test network parameters are shown in Table 1. The simulation parameters is inspired from previous works [2,3] to give a fair comparison. Since the network density causes messages' overhead, we choose a dense network (1000 nodes) to show the effectiveness of the new variant.

Table 1. Simulation parameters

Parameter	Variables
Node number	1000 nodes
Initial energy	1 Joule
Network size	$100 \times 100\,\text{m2}$
Sink location	200×50
CH probability	0.01
Nodes distribution	Randomly distributed
Number of rounds	800
ETX	50 * 0.000000001
ERX	50 * 0.000000001
Efs	10 * 0.000000000001
Emp	0.0013 * 0.000000000001
EDA	5 * 0.000000001

Figure 4 shows the result for the energy consumption between VLEACH1 [2], VLEACH2 [3] and TVLEACH. The results show that our proposed TVLEACH protocol is better than the two variants VLEACH1 and VLEACH2 since it consumes less energy.

Figure 5 illustrates the performance of our protocol comparing to VLEACH1 and VLEACH2 in terms of network lifetime. As shown in Fig. 5, the sensor network performs longer with TVLEACH in comparison to VLEACH1 and VLEACH2.

In fact, the TV-LEACH protocol is better because in the first rounds when the CH dies, the first Vice-CH (selected on the basis of the distance to the CH and the remaining energy) will be the new CH. So, the common nodes of the cluster will consume less energy when sending their data to the new CH (since it is close to the old CH) than the VLEACH2 protocol where the Vice-CH (selected only on the basis of the remaining energy) could be at the border of the cluster. In the last rounds, TV-LEACH will deliver more data to the sink than VLEACH1 where the nodes at this phase exhaust their energy. On the other hand, the Vice-CH selected only by using the remaining energy has a better chance to send its data to the sink (as is the case of the second Vice-CH of our TV-LEACH protocol) than the Vice-CH selected by using the distance to the CH and the remaining energy.

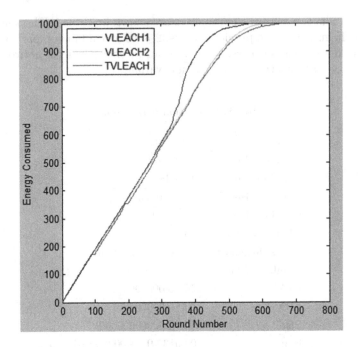

Fig. 4. Consumed energy

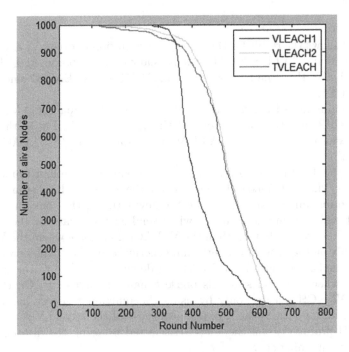

Fig. 5. The network lifetime

5 Conclusion

Wireless Sensor Networks consists of a huge number of small self-contained devices with limited computational, sensing and wireless communication capabilities. LEACH is the earliest cluster-based routing protocol. Compared to the flat network where multi-hop algorithm is adopted, it gains features of low energy consuming, self-adaptive and cluster-organized. However, when the CH die, the cluster will become useless since the data gathered by the cluster nodes will never reach the sink. Many improvements were proposed to overcome this problem. This paper proposed a new improved protocol which uses two Vice-Cluster Head to extend the lifetime of the entire network. The new improved protocol is simulated. The simulation results shown that the energy efficiency of the proposal is better than that of the LEACH variants.

References

1. Yassein, M.B., Khamayseh, Y., Mardini, W.: Improvement on LEACH protocol of wireless sensor network (VLEACH). Int. J. Digit. Content Technol. Appl. (2009)
2. Ahlawat, A., Malik, V.: An extended vice-cluster selection approach to improve VLEACH protocol in WSN. In: 2013 Third International Conference on Advanced Computing and Communication Technologies, ACCT, pp. 236–240. IEEE (2013)
3. Manjusha, M.S., Kannammal, K.E.: Efficient cluster head selection method for wireless sensor network. Int. J. Comput. Eng. Res. 4(2), 43–49 (2014)
4. Parmar, B., Munjani, J., Meisuria, J., et al.: A survey of routing protocol LEACH for WSN. Int. J. Sci. Res. Publ. 4(1) (2014)
5. Li, J.-Z., Gao, H.: Research advances in wireless sensor networks. J. Comput. Res. Adv. 45(1), 1–15 (2008)
6. Khamforoosh, K., Khamforoush, H.: A new routing algorithm for energy reduction in wireless sensor networks. In: 2nd IEEE International Conference on Computer Science and Information Technology, ICCSIT 2009, pp. 505–509. IEEE (2009)
7. Kansal, S., Bhatia, T., Goel, S.: Performance analysis of LEACH and its variants. In: 2015 2nd International Conference on Electronics and Communication Systems, ICECS, pp. 630–634. IEEE (2015)
8. Naregal, K., Gudnavar, A.: Improved cluster routing protocol for wireless sensor network through simplification. In: 2012 18th Annual International Conference on Advanced Computing and Communications, ADCOM, pp. 1–3. IEEE (2012)

Developing IoT Spark-Streaming Applications by Means of StreamLoader

Luca Ferrari, Stefano Valtolina(✉), and Marco Mesiti

Department of Computer Science, University of Milano, Milan, Italy
{ferrari1,valtolina,mesiti}@di.unimi.it

Abstract. Nowadays there is a great interest in the development of cross-domain IoT applications that are able to gather an high number of observations taken from sensors belong to heterogeneous IoT platforms and efficiently combine them in flows that can be exploited for conducting analysis. However, their realization poses several concerns. From one side, graphical interfaces are needed for facilitating the specification and composition of the data acquisition operations. From the other side, facilities are required to manage big data streams, to check the application correctness, and to set up and configure clusters of machines. Starting from the graphical facilities of the StreamLoader system for the development of Data Acquisition Plans (*DAPs*) from sensors belonging to heterogeneous IoT platforms, in this paper we show the approach developed for translating DAPs in a Spark-Streaming application. Experiments are shown for assessing the scalability of the developed applications.

Keywords: Spark-streaming · Cross-domain IoT applications

1 Introduction

According to a recent survey [7], more than 600 Internet of Things (IoT) platforms have been recently developed for the management of streams of sensor data produced in different domains (e.g. environment monitoring, healthcare service, Smart Cities and Homes). However, these solutions are characterized by the use of hardware and software of a specific industry and the interoperability with other applications is rarely supported. Even if many standards are currently proposed (e.g. oneM2M, OMA NGSI 9/10, ETSI M2M), none of them is currently well accepted and is predominantly adopted by the entire community. Many efforts are nowadays devoted to the creation of virtual bridges among these platforms in order to guarantee the development of cross-platforms (also named *horizontal*) applications, that is applications able to connect sensors belonging to different platforms. European projects (like OpenIoT, BIG-IoT, Biotope, INTER-IoT, SymbIoTe) are moving in this direction and their idea is to offer facilities across all layers of the network stack in order to improve the interoperability among the different components involved in the management of sensors, actuators and network infrastructures. These projects share the need to

© Springer Nature Switzerland AG 2018
N. Boudriga et al. (Eds.): UNet 2018, LNCS 11277, pp. 116–127, 2018.
https://doi.org/10.1007/978-3-030-02849-7_11

easily handle the millions of events that the monitored sensors can produce in an effective, efficient and scalable manner.

Starting from the possibility that many IoT platforms offer to expose the datastreams produced by their sensors by means of publish-subscribe context brokers (like Mosquitto, RabbitMQ, Apache Kafka), in the context of a phD thesis [2] we have developed the *StreamLoader* system that supports domain experts in the graphical development of *Data Acquisition Plans (DAPs)* for the integration of sensor data that are exposed by IoT platforms by means of publish-subscribe interaction models. By means of the DAPs, the domain experts can define the operations needed for filtering, integrating and enhancing (by means of external knowledge) the sensor observations and make them in a suitable format for conducting different kinds of analysis. Once a DAP is considered soundly specified and coherently adhering to the concepts expressed in a Domain Ontology, it can be easily translated in a scalable Apache Spark Streaming script for its distributed execution in a cluster of machines.

The development of graphical facilities for working on data streams is an active research field. Commercial systems such as Talend Studio (www.talend. com), StreamBase Studio (www.streambase.com), Waylay.io (www.waylay.io), and Node.Red (nodered.org) offer graphical interfaces for designing dataflows as graphs of connected nodes representing tasks and data-sources. While Talend works on static data coming from fixed data-sources, StreamBase, WayLay and Node.Red can receive and analyze continuous data streams and are specifically designed for IoT. These systems offer a composition paradigm based on the use of graphs for representing the flow of data that are generated by sensors and services. This notation fits very well the mental model of IoT experts who are used to adopt a visual representation where nodes representing data inputs, outputs, and functions are connected with edges that define the data flow between components [1,3]. However, some specific features (like the management of STT dimensions, the multi-granularities, the verification of sound specification of a DAP) are not provided and need to be manually implemented along with the configuration of the underlying network. Moreover, these systems are not able to support multidisciplinary requirements of the stakeholders at all different levels of the IoT design chain. What is missing in these solutions is an integration between tasks related to the configuration of a network of data sources, with tasks for supporting domain experts in expressing policies for managing dataflows and for detecting relevant events. Finally, these systems do not provide a translation of the services in advanced stream processing systems able to scale when the size of events to handle increases. For these reasons, in our solution we propose to integrate graphical data-flow design and execution strategies with network configurations in a simple and effective way.

In the paper we present the overall organization of the StreamLoader system (Sect. 2) and then focus on how the DAPs are automatically translated in an Apache Spark Streaming application (Sect. 3). Specifically, we focus the presentation in the configuration of the environment and the communication with Apache Kafka, the translation of the single services contained in a DAP, and the strategy for the translation of the overall DAP. Finally, Sect. 4 discusses the experiments for assessing the scalability of the proposed system.

2   StreamLoader Overview

StreamLoader offers a GUI by means of which domain experts can register new sensors and graphically design data acquisition plans (*DAPs*) for accessing in real time to the sensors events and combine them by means of a set of services. In the StreamLoader system we assume the presence of monitors for checking the presence of new sensors in the considered IoT context brokers. When new sensors are detected, it is possible to specify (when available) the Spatial-Temporal granularities and Thematics according to which the sensors produce the events. Moreover, since these values can be organized in a record, the record structure and its fields can be better specified by means of our interface (details in [2]). This process, named *Semantic virtualization* of sensors, requires the interaction with the domain expert and aims at discovering the presence of new sensors, extracting the sensor schema (i.e. the attributes that are generated by the sensor according to a given format), semantically annotating and characterizing the sensor schema and attributes by means of concepts of a Domain Ontology. This process results in a semantic description, also partial, of each sensor schema according to the spatial, temporal and thematic dimensions. Once the sensors are semantically virtualized, the GUI depicted in Fig. 1 is dedicated to the graphical specification of the DAP. The Domain expert can select the sensors from which he/she wishes to collect data and then specify the data acquisition services for generating a final single data stream that is stored in a database for analysis.

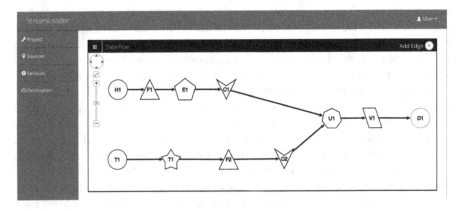

Fig. 1. StreamLoader main GUI with the DAP for computing the Humidex factor

Example 1. Suppose that we wish to compute the Humidex factor [4] per hour in different zones of the city of Hammamet according to the following formula

$$HD = [T + (0.555 \cdot (H - 10))]$$

where, T is the temperature (expressed in $°C$ and relevant for the computation only when the values are in the range $20°C$ to $55°C$) and H is the humidity degree (expressed in hPa). Suppose that in the area of Hammamet there are many temperature and humidity sensors, but the sensors belong to two different IoT platforms and return the events using different spatio-temporal granularities and unit of measure. A first platform contains sensors of type H_1 that allow to gather the humidity expressed in hPa every 10 min. The sensor observations are associated with the sensor identifier but no geo-spatial locations of the sensors are provided (but we have a database that associates each sensor with its longitude and latitude). A second platform contains sensors of type T_1 for gathering the temperature every 15 min in Fahrenheit degree for each zone of the city. These sensors provide the needed information for computing the Humidex, but the sensor data need to be transformed, converted in coarser spatio-temporal granularities, integrated and enhanced in order to correctly compute the formula. Figure 1 shows the DAP designed for collecting the data from the two types of sensors and for computing the average temperature per hour and per zone of Hammamet and for storing the result in MondoDB.   □

StreamLoader adopts a flexible spatio-temporal multigranular data model in which the events generated by the sensors are represented according to the spatio-temporal-thematic (STT) dimensions. The events can be represented as JSON values in which both values of simple types and list of values can be specified. We adopt this rich data model to represent both simple values generated by physical sensors (like a simple temperature) and complex values generated by social sensors or obtained by the aggregation of simple values (like the list of tweets of a given topic and its cardinality, or the temperatures recorded in the last hour). The model points out the thematic and spatio-temporal granularities of the values in order to make them comparable and decide whether their composition is legal (e.g. union, join, etc.). The model is also flexible in the sense that none of the STT dimensions is mandatory. This feature is useful to handle partial information that can be enriched later.

Example 2. Consider sensors of type T_1 and H_1 of previous example. The following is their representation in our internal model (pointing out the temporal, spatial, and thematic granularity, the interval of time in which events are collected, the legal values for the spatial dimension and the type of collected events):

- $\langle$ 10 min, $\bot$, humidity, ["1/1/2018-00:00", "1/1/2019-00:00"],
  $\bot$, $Event_{\langle 10\ min, \bot \rangle}^{\{humidity\}}$(humVal:real)$\rangle$
- $\langle$ 15 min, zone, temperature, ["1/1/2018-00:00", "1/1/2019-00:00"], HamZone,
  $Event_{\langle 15\ min, zone \rangle}^{\{temperature\}}$(tempVal:real)$\rangle$

where HamZone represents the zones in which sensors of type T_1 are located among the five zones (named z1, .., z5) in which the city can be divided. Each zone is delimited by boundary lines.   □

Several services have been developed for the manipulation of the events produced by the sensors and are classified in non-blocking (i.e. they can be applied

Table 1. Graphical representation and description of StreamLoader services

Service	Symbol	Description	Service	Symbol	Description
transform		transformation functions are applied to the value of some attributes	filter		events that do not adhere to specific conditions are removed
enrich		events are enriched with information taken from external databases	union		events produced by different sensors are merged together
aggregate		an aggregation function is applied to selected attributes of the events collected in a specific time interval	join		An SQL join is applied between the events collected in a specific time interval from two incoming streams
virtual property		a new property is created relying on an arithmetic expression	convert		Spatial-temporal aggregations are applied relying on the granularities of the incoming stream

event by event) and blocking services. The main services are reported in Table 1. Blocking services are window-based, that is they require to maintain a cache of events for a temporal interval. At the end of the interval, the events in the cache are processed by the operator and the obtained result produced to the upcoming operators. Transform, filter, virtual property and convert are non-blocking services while the others are blocking services.

Example 3. In our running example, humidity values produced by sensors of type $H1$ lack the geo-references in the city. This information can be included by means of a relational table that contains the latitude and longitude of each sensor (through the enrich service). Moreover, the database contains the zones of the city along with their boundaries. Therefore, by means of the convert service it is possible to change the spatio-temporal granularity of each event from ⟨10 min, point⟩ to ⟨1 h, zone⟩. Only the temperatures in the range $20\,°C$ to $55\,°C$ and humidity greater than 20 hPa should be considered (filter service) for the computation. Then, they need to be converted in the granularity ⟨1 h, zone⟩, make the union with the humidities and aggregate them per hour/zone. The virtual property with the expected result is thus generated.   □

3   Automatic Translation in Spark Streaming

Once the DAP has been graphically drawn, several conditions (related to the used services and the entire topology) can be evaluated for considering it *sound*.

When they are met, the plan can be translated in a script in Apache Spark Streaming. We have chosen this framework because it allows to handle both stored and stream data. However, also other frameworks can be adopted (with a slightly modification of the supported services). Among the possible languages that support Apache Spark Streaming we decided to translate the DAP in Scala code because of its functional programming support.

Figure 2 explains the execution model of the generated script. The script is configured for consuming the events that are exposed in the channels of the Kafka server. The server to use, the channels and the formats of the events are known since the semantic virtualization of the sensors. The events are processed according to the services reported in the DAP in a Spark engine. The engine is formed by a cluster of machines (of different size) in order to properly scale depending on the amount of events that need to be processed. The result of the computation is a stream that can be stored for further processing.

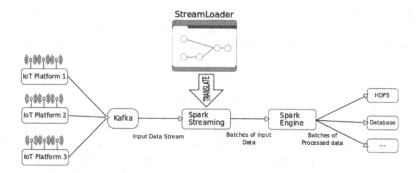

Fig. 2. StreamLoader execution model

3.1 Configuration

In order to efficiently manipulate the information coming from the sensors, each sensor is treated as a scala `case class` with attributes that represent the STT dimensions. Specifically, the `Location case class` models the `latitude`, `longitude` and zone, province or region `name` where an event has been generated. The STT dimensions are defined by the `case class Stt` that contains the `spatial`, `temporal` and `thematic` properties that are instances of the `case class Spatio`, `Time` and `Thematic`.

For what concern the Spark and Kafka communication, it is necessary to configure the Spark cluster and the Kafka server correctly. The `sparkConf` property provides the Spark Context, the host of the Master node in the Spark cluster, while the `ssc` property sets the size of the streaming batch. The size of the batch is defined manually by the domain expert and it is a multiple of the temporal granularity of the last service Applied in the DAP. Code 1.1 presents the case classes and the configuration of the Spark/Kafka environment.

```
case class Thematic(name: String, metadata: JObject)
case class Time(unit: String,count: Double,metadata: JObject)
case class Spatio(unit: String,metadata: JObject)
case class Stt(spatial: Spatio,temporal: Time,thematic: Thematic)
case class Location(latitude: Double,longitude: Double,name: String)

val sparkConf = new SparkConf().setAppName("myApp").setMaster("spark://0.0.0.0:7077")
val ssc = new StreamingContext(sparkConf, Hours(1))

val kafkaParams = Map[String, Object](
  "bootstrap.servers" -> "http://0.0.0.0:9092",
  "key.deserializer" -> classOf[StringDeserializer].getCanonicalName,
  "value.deserializer" -> classOf[StringDeserializer].getCanonicalName,
  "group.id" -> "test", "auto.offset.reset" -> "latest")
```

Code 1.1. The case classes are used to represent the information provided by the sensors. In order to consume data from Kafka and to be executed in an environment, the script needs some configuration settings.

Internally, the Apache Spark script works as follows. Spark Streaming receives live input data streams and divides the data into batches of a fixed dimension specified in the **StreamingContext**. Spark Streaming provides a high-level abstraction called *discretized stream* or *DStream*, which represents a continuous stream of data. DStreams, in our case, are input streams generated by Kafka.

3.2 Translation of Sources and Destination

Since each sensor presents a specific schema of data and topic, two case classes are created for each sensor included in the DAP. The first one, named **Data** concatenated to the **Id** of the sensor, contains the properties (name and type) of the sensor. The second one, named **Sensor** concatenated to the **Id** of the sensor, contains the sensor name, the interval of time in which the sensor produces data, the schema, spatio-temporal granularity and the thematic of the sensor. Moreover, a specific topic is created in Kafka for gathering the data produced by the sensor and made available through Kafka. An example of a sensor in our running example is provided by the code below.

```
case class Data_s1(location:Location, timestamp:String, humVal:Double)
case class Sensor_s1(sensor_name:String, start_date:String, end_date:String,
                     data:Data_s1, stt: Stt)
val topics_s1 = Array("topics1") //Topic s1
val stream_s1 = KafkaUtils.createDirectStream[String, String](ssc, PreferConsistent,
    Subscribe[String, String](topics_s1, kafkaParams))
val s1 = stream_s1.map(record => {implicit val formats = DefaultFormats
    parse(record.value).extract[Sensor_s1]})
```

Code 1.2. The code shows how a sensor is initialized and parsed. Spark provides the createDirectStream class for consuming data from Kakfa.

Kafka acts as the central hub for real-time data streams. Each sensor needs to "consume" data of a specific topic and for this reason sensors need to be initialized as Kafka Consumers. The **KafkaUtils.createDirectStream** takes as parameters the Spark Context, a **LocationStrategies.PreferConsistent**, in order to distribute partitions evenly across available executors and a **Subscribe** method, where information about the topic and the Kafka environment must be provided and a new Kafka stream is instantiated.

For what concern the `destination`, besides providing configuration information, it contains also information about the storage of the processed data into a database. `MongodbConfig.Host`, `mongoDbDatabase` and `mongoDbCollection` contain the configuration of the DB while in the `foreachRDD` every processed tuple is converted into a specific schema and then saved on MongoDB.

```
val mongoFormat = "com.stratio.datasource.mongodb"
val mongoDB = "StreamLoader"
val mongoCollection = "Results"
val MongoOptions = Map(MongoConfig.Host −> "http://0.0.0.0:27017",
    MongoConfig.Database −> mongoDB,
    MongoConfig.Collection −> mongoCollection)
val dest = j1.foreachRDD { rdd =>
    val dest=spark.read.schema(Sensorj1).json(rdd)
    dest.write.format(mongoFormat).mode(SaveMode.Append).options(MongoOptions).save()}
```

Code 1.3. The settings for the database name and location are provided in this code. The foreachRDD method iterates on every RDDs and store them on the MongoDB.

3.3   Translation of Services

Each DAP service is translated in Spark Streaming instructions that read values from the output variable of the incoming service and generates a stream for the subsequent service. In the remainder we describe the translation of some services that we use in our scenario. Other services are discussed in [2]. The variables PN, PN1 or PN2 are used to define the `id` of the incoming node (or nodes) associated with the service. The operations are executed on each *DStream* that is a sequence of Spark RDD collected in a batch.

Transform. This operator applies transformation functions taken from a list stored on MongoDB. It takes in input an array composed of: (*i*) the attribute on which the function must be applied; (*ii*) the name of the function; (*iii*) for the *replace* function, the value to replace and the replaced value (optional, used on the *replace* function); and (*iv*) the Spark code of the function. The code is omitted for specific transformations (like Celsius to Fahrenheit and vice-versa). By means of this approach, it is easy to include new transformation functions.

In our example, the sensors that produce temperatures in Fahrenheit need to be transformed in the corresponding temperatures in Celsius. Code 1.4 presents this transformation applied to the `tempVal` attribute.

```
val t1 = PN.map { r => new Sensor_PN(r.sensor_name, r.start_date, r.end_date,
        new Data_PN(
            new Location(r.data.location.latitude, r.data.location.longitude,
                r.data.location.name), r.data.timestamp,
                r.data.tempVal.*(1.8).+(32)),
        new Stt(new Spatio(r.stt.spatial.unit, r.stt.spatial.metadata),
            new Time(r.stt.temporal.unit, r.stt.temporal.count,
                r.stt.temporal.metadata),
            new Thematic(r.stt.thematic.name, r.stt.thematic.metadata)))}
```

Code 1.4. The transformation uses the map method and the operation is done only on the specific attribute.

Union. This service takes in input two incoming streams. If their schema is exactly the same, it does not introduce a new **sensor case class** otherwise it has to be defined. The new class contains all the common attributes between the two sensors, taken only one time, and the specific attributes.

Consider our running example. Sensors H_1 and T_1 need to be included in a single stream to subsequently compute the Humidex factor. The STT dimensions of the two sources are the same but **tempVal** is missing in H1 and **humVal** is missing in T_1. Then, when an observation is read, the value of the corresponding attribute is modified and the other is set to 0.0. Code 1.5 shows the creation of the new class and how the two sources are mapped to it. After that the Spark union primitive is applied every hour on the two *DStreams*.

```
case class Data_u1(location : Location, timestamp : String, tempVal : Double, humVal :
       Double)
case class Sensor_u1(sensor_name: String, start_date: String, end_date: String, data:
       Data_u1, stt: Stt)
val u1PN1 = PN1.map { r => new Sensor_u1(r.sensor_name, r.start_date, r.end_date,
                       new Data_u1(
                         new Location(r.data.location. latitude ,
                             r.data.location .longitude,
                             r.data.location .name), r.data.timestamp, 0.0,
                             r.data.humVal),
                         new Stt(new Spatio(r.stt. spatial .unit,
                             r.stt . spatial .metadata),
                         new Time(r.stt.temporal.unit, r.stt .temporal.count,
                             r.stt .temporal.metadata),
                         new Thematic(r.stt.thematic.name,
                             r.stt.thematic.metadata)))}
val u1PN2 = PN2.map { r => new Sensor_u1(r.sensor_name, r.start_date, r.end_date,
                       new Data_u1(
                         new Location(r.data.location. latitude ,
                             r.data.location .longitude,
                             r.data.location .name), r.data.timestamp,
                             r.data.tempVal, 0.0),
                         new Stt(new Spatio(r.stt. spatial .unit,
                             r.stt . spatial .metadata),
                         new Time(r.stt.temporal.unit, r.stt .temporal.count,
                             r.stt .temporal.metadata),
                         new Thematic(r.stt.thematic.name,
                             r.stt.thematic.metadata)))}
val u1 = u1PN1.union(u1PN2).window(Hours(1), Hours(1))
```

Code 1.5. A new case class is created and the information from each sensor are mapped to the new class. This is required because the union method does not allow to merge DStream of different types.

Enrich. This service is a special case of a **join** between stream and static data. It is done by defining a join attribute between the stream and the static information. The first thing that we have to do is load a table and cache it so that it can be joined with streams. Then we need to identify the "join" attributes for the stream and for the static data. In the JSON representation of this service, the enrich predicate is specified along with the kind of enrich to be applied and the dimension of the enrich window.

In our running example we wish to associate the information of latitude and longitude of sensor H1 through the sensor identifier, with data stored in the Identifier table in a MongoDB. Code 1.6 is generated.

```
val idInfo = sqlContext.table("Identifier").rdd.map(row => (row(0).toDouble(),
    row(1).toDouble())).partitionBy(partitioner).cache()
val e1PN1 = PN1.map(x => (x.data.location.name, (x)))
val e1PN2 = idInfo.map(x => ((x.(0), x.(1)), (x)))
val e1PN1win = e1PN1.window(Minutes(10), Minutes(10))
val e1pre = e1PN1win.join(e1PN2)
case class Data_el(location : Location, timestamp : String, humVal : String)
case class Sensor_el(sensor_name: String, start_date: String, end_date: String, data:
    Data_el, stt: Stt)
val e1 = e1pre.map { r => new Sensor_el(r._2._1.sensor_name, r._2._1.start_date,
    r._2._1.end_date,
                        new Data_el(new Location(r._2._2._1, r._2._2._2,
                            r._2._1.data.location.name), r._2._1.data.timestamp,
                            r._2._1.data.humVal),
                        new Stt(new Spatio(r._2._1.stt.spatial.unit,
                            r._2._1.stt.spatial.metadata),
                        new Time(r._2._1.stt.temporal.unit, r._2._1.stt.temporal.count,
                            r._2._1.stt.temporal.metadata),
                        new Thematic(r._2._1.stt.thematic.name,
                            r._2._1.stt.thematic.metadata)))}
```

Code 1.6. The code shows how static data is mapped and how is joined with the streaming information. After the join operation, it is required to map the result to a new case class that contains the new attribute.

3.4 The Overall Translation Algorithm

The most important issue in the translation of a DAP is to maintain the order of the operators as defined in the DAP. Each service provides information about the id of the incoming node (or nodes). Therefore it is easy to establish the incoming and outgoing variables. Then, the right "ordering" of the DAP is demanded to the internal way of handling RDDs by Apache Spark. Indeed, Spark adopts a *stage-oriented scheduling* for transforming a Logical Execution Plan (i.e. RDD lineage of dependencies) to a Physical Execution Plan through a *DAG scheduler* [5] that is able to reorder the dependencies automatically. In this way the execution order is maintained also if the operations are written in the Spark script without following the right order as they appear in the DAP.

With the aim of creating a clearer an more maintainable script, in the translation phase we report the imports of packages and libraries that are required for the right execution of the code, the configuration of the Spark and Kafka environment, and all the classes associated with sensors accessed in the script. The nodes that represent the operations are then translated and included in the code while in the last part we provide the translation of the storage information defined by the destination node.

4 Experimental Validation

We conducted a set of experiments for evaluating the performances of the Spark Streaming scripts generated by means of StreamLoader when it is executed locally and on clusters of different dimension (5 and 10 nodes). These experiments are focused on the evaluation of the performances of the generated scripts and to determine the number of events that can be handled per second. We use virtual machines that reside on an **Ovirt** Datacenter (https://www.ovirt.org/) that are equipped with Ubuntu 16.04 LTS (GNU/Linux 4.4.0-96-generic x86_64), 8 GB RAM, 2 core processor, 250 GB HDD and 2799.202 MHz CPU clock speed. In each cluster, a node acts as master and the others as slaves.

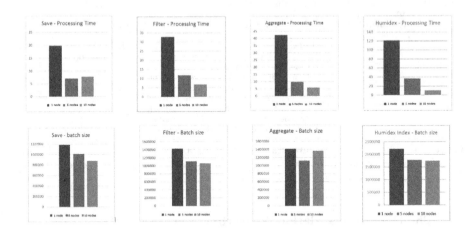

Fig. 3. Processing time and batch size of different DAPs

Figure 3 reports for each row the processing time and the size of the batch for different DAPs executed on a single node, a cluster of 5 nodes, and a cluster of 10 nodes. The DAPs contain both non-blocking and blocking services at increasing complexity. The first is a simple DAP that reads data from a sensor and store the obtained value in a file. The second one applies a filter condition and only the events that meet the condition are stored in the file. The third one applies an aggregation on the considered events and the aggregated events are stored in the file. The last one compute the humidex factor described in this paper. For the first four DAPs we have considered a single flow of 10 million events, whereas for the last one we have considered two flows of 10 millions events each.

As we can note from all the considered DAPs the processing time is deeply affected by the number of machines in which the DAP is executed. In the passage from one node to 5 nodes, the average processing times is reduced of at least one third. The reduction is less in the passage from the cluster of 5 to the one of 10 nodes, but we believe that this is due to the reduced number of processed events. Moreover, by increasing the complexity of the DAP (from the one in the first row to the last raw) the processing time increases but not linearly with respect to the number of services that are included in the DAP. This is an important factor for dealing with DAPs of different complexity.

For what concern the computation of the Humidex factor, we can note that Spark is able to process 222.000 tuple per second. Moreover, the processing time improves deeply by considering clusters with 5 and 10 nodes. The local execution of a 10 s batch (with a range of events between 1.8 millions and 2.2 millions) requires an average time of 121 s, whereas in a cluster of 5 nodes requires 37 s, and 10 s in the cluster of 10 machines (thus an improvement of 12 times w.r.t. the local execution). Note that the scheduling delay is null for the cluster of 10 nodes (the average processing time – 3 ms – is equal to the batch size), wheres this time is around 13 s. for the cluster of 5 nodes and 114 s. for the single node.

5   Conclusions and Future Works

In this paper we have presented the main characteristics of the StreamLoader Web application for graphically composing different services that work on streams of data produced by sensors. Then, we have shown how the DAP generated by an user can be automatically translated in an Apache Spark Streaming script that can be easily made in execution in a cluster of machines with limited user interventions. At the current stage, depending on the parameter specified by the user, the script is automatically loaded in one of our clusters and executed. Finally, we have reported some experimental analysis of the automatically generated scripts that point out their efficiency and scalability. We are currently carrying out further experiments, looking on how automatically tuning parameters depending on the characteristics of the DAP to be processed, and improving the graphical interface for monitoring the execution of the DAP.

References

1. Blackstock, M., Lea, R.: Toward a distributed data flow platform for the web of things (distributed node-red). In: Proceedings of 5th International Workshop on Web of Things, WoT 2014, pp. 3439, ACM, New York (2014)
2. Ferrari, L.: Ontology-based consistent specification and scalable execution of sensor data acquisition plans in cross-domain IoT platforms. Ph.D. Dissertation on Computer Science, Department of Computer Science, University of Milano (2018)
3. Guinard, D., Trifa, V., Mattern, F., Wilde, E.: From the internet of things to the web of things: resource-oriented architecture and best practices. In: Uckelmann, D., Harrison, M., Michahelles, F. (eds.) Architecting the Internet of Things, pp. 97–129. Springer, Heidelberg (2011). https://doi.org/10.1007/978-3-642-19157-2_5
4. Masterton, J., Richardson, F.: Humidex: a method of quantifying human discomfort due to excessive heat and humidity, CLI,1–79, Environment Canada, Atmospheric Environment Service, Downsview, Ontario, 45 p.(1979)
5. Laskowski, J.: DAGScheduler - Stage-Oriented Scheduler. http://jaceklaskowski.gitbooks.io/mastering-apache-spark/spark-dagscheduler.html
6. Laskowski, J.: RDD Lineage - Logical Execution Plan. http://jaceklaskowski.gitbooks.io/mastering-apache-spark/spark-rdd-lineage.html
7. IoT Analytics. List of 640+ Enterprise IoT Projects. http://iot-analytics.com/product/list-of-640-iot-projects/

Mobile Edge Networking and Fog-Cloud Computing

Road Congestion Analysis
in the Agglomeration of Sfax Using a Bayesian
Model

Ahmed Derbel[(✉)] and Younes Boujelbene

Sfax University, (FSEG) of Sfax, 3018 Sfax, Tunisia
derbelamd@gmail.com

Abstract. This study provides a road traffic portrait in urban areas to compare the congestion level of certain sections. In view of a better exploitation, we proposed a Bayesian network (BN) analysis approach to modeling the probabilistic dependency structure of congestion causes on a particular road segment and analyzing the probability of traffic congestion. In this case, two steps are also necessary, the macroscopic traffic flow modeling and the traffic simulation for which empirical measurements can be developed and tested. The BN method is used to analyze the uncertainty and probability of traffic congestion, and is proved to be fully capable of representing the stochastic nature of road network situation. This approach is used to represent road traffic knowledge in order to build scenarios based on a practical case adapted in the city of Sfax.

Keywords: Macroscopic traffic flow model · Bayesian network
Measuring road congestion

1 Introduction

With a population of about 955,500 inhabitants in 2012, Sfax is the second largest Tunisian agglomeration in terms of population. It is the second populated region in Tunisia. In terms of transport, the city of Sfax is today confronted with a growing urban sprawl. The problem of transport has always been a handicap for the displacement of inhabitants in regional centre or urban area. At peak times, the difficulty of transport has become more and more difficult. The congestion of traffic is due to the increased use of private vehicles and the existing road infrastructure is also poorly organized. The public transport share is decreased from 30% in the early 1990s to around 21% in 2016. The traffic in central areas is generated by the spatial concentration of economic activities and administrative services. The situation is aggravated by the flagrant lack of parking spaces in these areas as well as the non-realization of scheduled interchanges. This situation can be explained by several factors, including the level of public transport service that is inefficient: low frequencies and the gradual deterioration of commercial bus speeds. In addition, the port of Sfax is located near the city center, the traffic is therefore booming and the containers are brought by all types of vehicles: automobile, truck, recreational vehicles, etc. The access to this port is directly through the city center and the different types of vehicles have increased the flow of goods and

© Springer Nature Switzerland AG 2018
N. Boudriga et al. (Eds.): UNet 2018, LNCS 11277, pp. 131–142, 2018.
https://doi.org/10.1007/978-3-030-02849-7_12

services, which generates significant noise and visual disturbances caused by the congestion on our city streets and on our highway. In summary, despite the socioeconomic role of the city of Sfax, the transport system in this city remains insufficient, congestion increases the problem of air pollution in the city. Faced with the increase the problems of road traffic mobility, the management of vehicle flows has become an important issue that gives rise to many practical studies. Our research is based on the traffic congestion analysis in the agglomeration of Sfax. The available data in our application is based from general circulation census in 2017 with a very large spatial and temporal dimension. The available data come essentially from general traffic census in 2017 presented in the form of a macroscopic traffic situation. Based upon the available data, the variables has been concluded for measuring the road traffic on a very wide scale and enables the evolution of certain road axis in Sfax city. The temporal dimension is based from the annual average time such as the flow and the density are calculated in annual average during all the year of 2017 and the taking accounts of the spatial dimension are based on the kilometers flown. By defining the spatial and temporal boundaries, the macroscopic level seems more appropriate, instead to evaluate the traffic flow. In the rest of the procedure, we presented the framework and the methodology used to collect and analyze data from two steps such as modeling and simulation. The both stages are used to identify the road traffic variables by a macroscopic presentation. The macroscopic model is mainly done on the basis of three variables: speed (km/hours), density (vehicles/km) and flow (vehicles/hours). We used these three variables to know the traffic state in the Sfax city, as a fundamental tool to prevent, control and diagnose the congestion situation. We used also a Bayesian network (BN) approach which aims to propose a conceptual and methodological framework for this purpose and to analyze the probabilities of urban congestion.

2 Defining Variables in a Modeling Study

Traffic congestion is a critical problem which happens on roads which make traffic busy because roads full of cars and buses. Traffic congestion challenges traffic flow in urban area and is prevented smooth traffic. The literature of traffic phenomena is already extensive and is characterized by contributions covering different aspects of modeling. Theorists of the road traffic are interested in developing simple and efficient models to represent the traffic flows modeling [1]. The data collected and presented in our application are related to macroscopic modeling for this reason that we started to define the context and understand the macroscopic situation.

2.1 The Macroscopic Model of Road Traffic

However, in order to control a road traffic sector the macroscopic point of view seems the most adequate choice. It doesn't require a large set of variables compared to other type of models, and thus it leads to a shorter decision time. Furthermore, it permits a general representation of a traffic network, offering access to a global view of the entire system [2]. The model is typically used for planning and control operations involving large networks with a long periods. Road traffic is represented in a compact manner using a series of interrelated variables such as flow $Q(x, t)$, density $K(x, t)$ and average speed of the flow $V(x, t)$. In the case of a macroscopic model, the temporal evolution of macroscopic quantities circulations are represented by nonlinear editing systems called conservation laws presented by the following equation:

$$\begin{cases} Q(x,t) = K(x,t) \times V(x,t) \\ \frac{\partial Q(x,t)}{\partial x} + \frac{\partial K(x,t)}{\partial t} = 0 \\ V(x,t) = V_e(K(x,t)) \end{cases} \tag{1}$$

The three basic variables of road traffic examine the relationships between many possible indicators of congestion and estimated congestion level in an attempt to identify and validate indicators for area wide congestion measurement purposes. From three basic variables of road traffic we can identify other indices that are directly related to macroscopic modeling. In order to achieve this, we determined the standard time delay (STD) and the rate of travel speed (RTS). The two main components are used to measure traffic congestion comparing reference or actual velocities with free flow velocity (FFV) on the same section. The road users tend to compare their actual speed with free-flowing speed. Another relevant variable that can be defined in the analysis of urban congestion is the share of private cars (SPC). This index made some progress in the structure of road traffic, so that a steady increase in motorized traffic can lead to traffic congestion, a shortage of parking spaces and consequently causing a progressive increase in atmospheric and noise pollution. A congestion measure should also be simple, well explained, and easily understood and interpreted among two variables. For example, the congestion can be expressed by the ratio between supply and demand or by the relative quality of traffic flow between ideal conditions and the prevailing traffic situations. The scale of measure may be a set of discrete classes [level of service (state) = class A, B, C] or with a continuous value explained by the (RTS) variable (e.g., a number between 0 and 1). The (RTS) is near to 0, the rate of travel speed is low indicated the fluid circulation. On the contrary, if the (RTS) becomes higher and close to 1 then the traffic is probably saturated, the road is blocked and the traffic volume (TV) is increasing rapidly. Subsequently, we were able to identify the variables that made it possible to measure the traffic situation in the agglomeration of Sfax. For these analyzes, we indicated a brief description of the 9 components that are present by their definition (Table 1 below).

3 Simulation of Road Traffic via a BN

Bayesian networks (BN) are usable in fields where the proceeding raises a state of uncertainty and the outcome is difficult to predict. Instead of just 'guessing', Bayesian networks help its users make intelligent, quantifiable and justifiable decisions. It is now the method of choice for reasoning under uncertainty. The BN provides a comprehensive set of commonly used tools for artificial intelligence, applied mathematics or engineering. Bayesian modeling techniques offer several advantages in the field of analysis and dynamic data management. BN has been applied successfully in several applications, textual classification [3], medical diagnosis [4], environmental

Table 1. Variables and state definitions for the proposed BN model.

Variable: symbol	Description	Definition of states
Share of private cars (SPC)	The proportion of motorized traffic (light + heavy) in percentage	Low: <=80% High: >81%
Traffic flow Q(x, t)	The traffic flow represents the number of vehicles having crossed a point between two given times. It is measured by the number of vehicles per hour (v/h)	Low: <=1315 v/h High: >1315 v/h
Density K (x, t)	This variable expresses the distribution of vehicles in space. It is measured by the number of vehicles per kilometer (v/km)	Low: <=59 v/km High: >59 v/km
Average speed of the flow (ASF)	It is the speed at which most vehicles move in a traffic lane. The speed is defined as the distance it travels during a unit of time interval. ASF variable is measured per kilometer per hour (km/h)	Low: <=15 km/h High: > 15 km/h
Free flow velocity (FFV)	(FFV) variable represents the optimal speed for a given section, a counterfactual speed based on ideal traffic conditions	Low: <=30 km/h High: >30 km/h
Rate of travel speed (RTS)	(RTS) variable is used to measure the valuation of the speed at the risk of arriving late due to congestion. This indicator expresses the level of congestion of a road section with respect to free flow conditions. It is a non-negative value and it is between 0 and 1: $RTS = \frac{V_{freeflowvelocity} - V_{theaveragespeedoftheflow}}{V_{freeflowvelocity}}$ (2)	Free: <=0.5 Congestion: >0.5
Standard time delay (STD)	It is the ratio of the travel time at a defined time to the free flow time. It is usually expressed in km per vehicle $STD = Q(x,t) \times \left(\frac{1}{ASF} - \frac{1}{FFV}\right)$ (3)	Low: <=60 km/v High: >60 km/v
Traffic volume (TV)	(TV) variable provides an estimate of the traffic volume in the road. This is the distance traveled by all the vehicles circulating on the network taken into account during a given period	Low: 0% High: 1%
Road traffic situation (TS)	The (TS) variable provides an estimate of traffic conditions and quality of service. It is the ability to convey in good conditions a given type of traffic, in terms of speed on the network	Class A: fluid Class B: dense Class C: congestion

management [5] and the traffic modeling [6]. Generally the searches of traffic management are oriented towards two aspects:

Prediction of Congestion: The management of vehicle flows is an important issue, which gives rise to numerous studies. The system for traffic congestion forecasting is set up to know the network status in real time, reduce the risk of failure and it should be possible to deal with congestion problems in various ways. The research of [7] proposes a traffic prediction model called "Jam Bayes". This model exploits the past states of congestion and to estimate the likely evolution in the future. This predictive analysis system allows to act upstream of the problems, in order to prevent traffic jams and accidents related to a traffic density. Recently, Kim and Wang [8] presented an analytical framework that uses a BN to diagnose and predict traffic congestion to measure the congestion causes on the road segment and to analyze the probabilities of road congestion based on different scenarios and assumptions.

Incident Prediction: Due to the pressure on the road network, any incident can quickly lead with huge delays and the incoming traffic might grow considerably. Traffic incident management exists to control incidents and minimize their impact on traffic safety. Incident management involves detecting, verifying and eliminating traffic incidents, as well as minimizing this impact on communities and traffic. The research of [8] is established to accurately predict the incident duration for preventing future conflicts in the road. Yang's research [9] focused on highway accident detection equipment to propose the latest generation equipment based on video images systems, to its customers.

3.1 Basic Concept

The BNs are models that can be used to represent probabilistic reasoning situations based on the Bayes theorem. Given data x and parameter θ, a simple Bayesian analysis starts with a prior probability $P(\theta)$ and likelihood $P(x/\theta)$ to compute a posterior probability expressed by the formula (4):

$$P(\theta/x) \propto P(x/\theta)P(\theta) \tag{4}$$

Often the prior on θ depends in turn on other parameters φ that are not mentioned in the likelihood. So, the prior $P(\theta)$ must be replaced by likelihood $P(\theta/\varphi)$, and a prior $P(\varphi)$ on the newly introduced parameters φ is required, resulting in a posterior probability is as follows:

$$P(\theta, \varphi) \propto P(x/\theta)P(\theta/\varphi)P(\varphi) \tag{5}$$

BNs are directed acyclic graphs that specify dependencies between random variables. For the BN to be easily used, its graphic part provides a visual means of knowledge representation that shows the dependencies and independence between the variables. For example, if an arc connects two nodes, then these variables are dependent on one another. The topology of the graph exploits any conditional independence between the variables, and this induces a factorization of the overall joint probability distribution (Eq. 5). This factorization, combined with Bays' Rule, allows for computationally efficient belief propagation algorithms. When we receive a new piece of evidence regarding one of the random variables in the network, these belief propagation algorithms allow us to update the probabilities in all of the variables through causal reasoning. Thus, the BN associates a qualitative part that is the graphs and a quantitative part representing the conditional probabilities associated with each node of the graph relative to the parent. The qualitative part expresses conditional independence between variables and causal links thanks to an acyclic oriented graph whose nodes correspond to random variables. The motivation to use the BN is numerous, the graphical part of BN gives a visual tool which indicates not only the potential regulations between the road traffic variables, but also the orientation of these regulations (directed arcs). In addition, we need to calculate the probability of an uncertain cause given some observed evidence. For example, we would like to know the probability of a congested road when we observed a remarkable increase in the share of private cars. A Bayesian approach is appropriate in these cases, while Bayesian networks, or alternatively graphical models, are very useful tools for dealing not only with uncertainty, but also with the complexity and the importance of establishing causality.

3.2 Defining Dependency and Relationships

The BN is a probabilistic graphical model that represents the probabilistic relationships between a set of variables via a directed acyclic graph (DAG). Our BN has composed a set of 9 variables, whose nodes are random variables and the arcs represent the dependencies of causalities. After setting the variables, the second step is to determine a qualitative property of the BN and to find the links of causalities. To measure the dependencies between the variables, basic concepts of a macroscopic model must be taken into account. The proportion of motorized traffic is an essential element in the modeling of road traffic. We can see that the variable (SPC) is a cause variable, the flow and the density are two evidence variables since an increase in (SPC) makes it possible to influence on the flow and density indices. From these two variables $Q(x, t)$ and $K(x, t)$ can be directly determine the average flow velocity (ASF) according the rules in (Eq. 1). There is a fundamental law that links the mean flow rate with density. The two variables $Q(x, t)$ and $K(x, t)$ have a direct impact on the variable (ASF). Moreover, the variable (RTS) is used to measure the difference between the flow velocity and the free flow velocity. It also expresses the level of a road congestion section with respect to free flow conditions using the (Eq. 2) in Table 1. Furthermore, (STD) is the ratio of the travel time at a defined time to the free flow time. This standard time delay is used to assess the extent to which the length of time a motorist traveled there. In order to arrive at an estimate of cumulative delays for a given road section, we needed to know the speed profile of the vehicles traveling and the number of vehicles likely to be delayed, which is expressed by the average hourly flow index. The formula that links the three variables can indicate the periods when there is a slowdown in traffic speed (Eq. 3). Finally, the variable (TS), designates the traffic service levels, it is determined from the operating thresholds of the curves (speed-velocity) which defines 3 service levels (fluid, dense and congestion) based on the diagram fundamental connecting the flow rates to the corresponding speeds.

3.3 Machine Learning to Determine CPT

A rigorous likelihood based statistical method is proposed for estimating the model parameters from a general road traffic census in 2017 (see Fig. 1). From this data, we can automatically estimate the probability of using a multi-hypothesis algorithm. The first assumption is linked by the share of private car, if $(SPC >= 80)$ then we have proposed that the mobility demand is high. The variables $Q(x, t)$ and $K(x, t)$ follows a normal distribution with mean θ_i and σ is a standard deviation presented with $x_i \sim N(\theta_i, \sigma^2)$. In this case, $Q(x, t) - N(1224, 417)$ and $K(x, t) - N(153, 59)$.

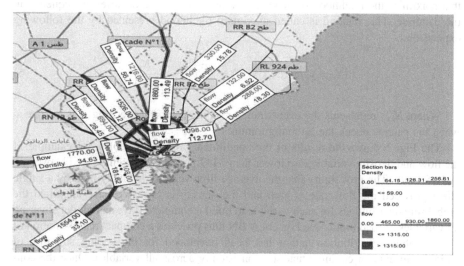

Fig. 1. According to data taken from the general circulation census of 2017, the variables presented in these figure correspond to the density and flow rate.

On the other hand, in the case where the demand is weak, the flow follows a normal distribution with $Q(x, t) - N(947, 589)$ and $K(x, t) - N(31, 19)$. The average speed of flow is determined directly by the ratio between the flow and the density and it must necessarily be maintained between [0 km/h, 50 km/h] because the general speed limit of the circulation in the urban areas is limited between these two values. In addition, the free flow velocity is followed by the normal distribution $(FFV) - N(50, 7)$ and the (RTS) is calculated directly from (FFV) and (ASF). The volume of traffic (TV) is determined from the moment the following three conditions are met, if the density is high, the delay is high and the rate of displacement is high then the traffic volume is increasing rapidly. From the assumptions, it is possible to deduce from the observation of the traffic conditions on a road infrastructure, the class A is consonant with a high speed which corresponds to a fluid situation, the class B indicates that the (ASF) is between [15, 30] km/h which corresponds to a dense situation and finally the class C is characterized by a high density and it corresponds to a congestion situation. Subsequently, we collected the information on the different possible traffic situations below and we wanted to transform them into an algorithm. The algorithm aims to determine the probabilities of the hypotheses generated over a set of 10,000 possible values and it generates all conditional probability tables (CPT) in an automatic way.

Using a multi-hypothesis algorithm, we can quantify conditional and marginal probabilities for all variables. This is done by calculating a conditional probability distribution for each node of all possible combinations in relation to parent nodes. For example, the CPT of node (*ASF*) represents the probability values for all possible configurations $P(ASF$ = low or high | Flow = low or high, Density = low or high). The statistical estimation is a method of estimating the parameters given the observations that maximize the likelihood of making parameters given the occurrence frequency in the database. This method is called maximum likelihood presented by the following expression:

$$\widehat{P}(X_i = x_k/Pa(X_i) = x_j) = \widehat{\theta_{i,j,k}}^{MV} = \frac{N_{i,j,k}}{\sum_k N_{i,j,k}} \qquad (6)$$

Where $N_{i,j,k}$ represents the events number in the database checking x_i is in state x_j when his parents check the x_k configuration.

The Fig. 2 shows the results of the conditional probability tables, for example, if the flow and density variables are lower than 3447 points have been located between 0 and 15 km/h. The probability that the average flow velocity is totally high by a single effect provided the flow rate is high and the density is low. We have identified the probability distributions for each variable to build a complete Bayesian model covering all variables of road traffic (see Fig. 3). A BN thus provides a compact representation of the probability distribution and it has been developed for the coding structure of variables to explain certain situations consistently across all variables. Once the conditional probability tables are processed, then we can finally specify the structure and parameters of our application.

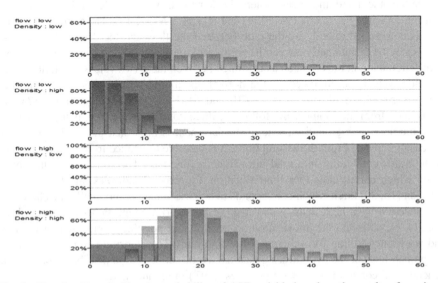

Fig. 2. The algorithm decides the probability of *ASF* variable based on the results of previous condition

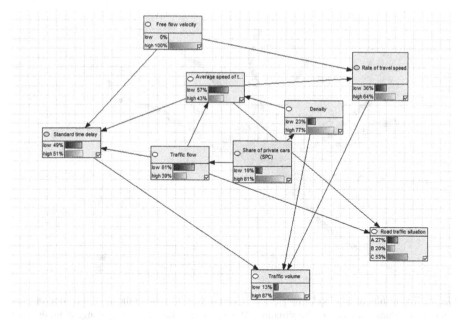

Fig. 3. Modeling traffic information using BN to analysis the probabilistic dependency structure of congestion road

3.4   Presentation Analysis and Interpretation of Results

Figure 3 illustrates the results of the probability distributions. The *SPC* and *FFV* are important marginal variables in our application. The modification of these two variables makes it possible to change all the probabilities in the system. The share of private cars in the agglomeration of Sfax is quite high (81%), the flow is low, 61% below 1315 v/h and the density is practically acute, 77% of a value higher than 59 v/km. These two observations have a considerable influence on the flow speed. The average flow of speed is 57% low to moderate. Finally, we found not only a higher value of traffic volume, but also more than 53% of the trips are classified in the category of congestion (class C) (see Fig. 4). In this case, we can see that the volume of traffic in the agglomeration exceeds the road capacity and the vehicles cannot circulate and the displacement becomes in this case slower and suffer a delay to finish eventually a complete block in the road. The traffic situation in the agglomeration of Sfax has deteriorated is characterized by a non-efficient transport system with an intense and congested traffic. Mobility is also assessing in the agglomeration that it generates today significant negative effects among which were some recommendations will be made in the consideration to further improve the reliability of the displacement. The transport system in the city can be risky, if it's not properly managed these missions. However, the public authority should take into account road transportation alternatives, including other non-road modes in their search for possible solutions.

A BN therefore makes it possible to represent a set of random variables for which we can model a certain number of dependency relationships. The BN allows the

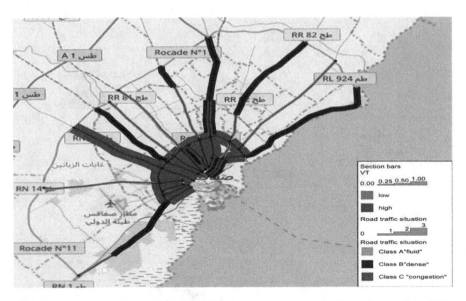

Fig. 4. The results of BN model for detection the congestion zone in the agglomeration of Sfax in terms of volume and road traffic situation. The red zone indicates a strong congestion, the blue zone indicates a dense circulation and the green section indicates a fluid situation (Color figure online)

calculation of the posterior probability distribution for a set of variables, given an observed event. X calls the set of variables and $P(X)$ the probability distribution on this set of rules. If we have new information ε on one or more observation variables (E), then we want to update the knowledge $P(X)$ in the light of this new information. This update, which will of course be done using the Bayes rule, is called probabilistic inference. Mathematically speaking, the inference in a BN is the computation of $P(X|E)$, that is to say the calculation of the posterior probability of the network knowing ε. We used the exact method for performing probabilistic reasoning in a BN illustrated in the Eq. 7:

$$P = (X/E) = \frac{P(X, E)}{P(E)} = \frac{\sum_{\varepsilon} P(E = \varepsilon, X)}{\sum_{\varepsilon} P(E = \varepsilon)} \tag{7}$$

The reasoning can be carried out in two different approaches, is known or observed causes and the effects are unknown (predictive reasoning) and known effects and the causes are unobserved (diagnostic reasoning). The characteristics of BN are powerful tools to diagnose and predict traffic congestion under uncertainty. From that perspective, to quantify congestion in the agglomeration of Sfax examples of issues that can be challenged. What is the probability of having congestion when the share of private cars is high (prediction of congestion) and to calculate the probability of (SPC) when we observed the congestion (diagnosis of congestion). The objective is to understand the relationships between the target variables and the scenario variables by performing various diagnostic and predictive reasoning tasks. The diagnostic reasoning was made from the posterior probability distribution of each scenario variable $S = \{SPC, Flow, Density, FFV, ASF, STD$ and $RTS\}$ knowing that the congestion was observed P(S | TS = class C, TV = high). In this case, the probability of (TS) and (TV) are 100%, which means that we have updated our belief about the congestion state and therefore there is no uncertainty. We compared the distributions of the earlier probabilities P (S) and presented the modifications that were made to the probability distributions. In the case of congestion, the probability P(SPC = high) was increased by 91%, the probability P($density$ = high) was increased by 13% and the probability P(ASF = low) was increased by 43%. On the contrary, in the case of road traffic fluidity the probability P(SPC = high) was decreased by 60%, the probability P($density$ = high) decreased by 77% and the probability P(ASF = high) was increased by 57%.

4   Summary and Conclusion

The mobility of people in the Grand Sfax has been estimated at 1.2 million trips per day, 79% of travel in intra-city, 30% of movements are registered between the city center and the other 6 commons, while travel between commons and out-of-town only correspond to 14%. This growth in mobility, especially in urban areas, has resulted in the saturation of the road network during peak hours. The city suffers from congestion, and traffic jams in the morning and evening are particularly important. Congestion is generated by the spatial concentration of economic activities and administrative services and it is aggravated by the flagrant lack of parking spaces in these areas. The failure of intra-urban public transport services in terms of comfort, frequency and punctuality has led to an imbalance in the transport system. Therefore, our study on the problem of urban congestion in the Greater Sfax agglomeration has shown that: the average speed of traffic in urban areas is 57% below than 15 km/h, the share of private cars is greater than 80%, the traffic volume is more than 87%, 53% of urban roads are in the state of congestion. The problems of road transport are therefore numerous and have been the subject of much analysis. Precisely because of the current congestion situation, we should focus on other recommendations. First too completely decongestion roads, it is necessary to reduce the share of private cars by 56%. To ensure this regression and to curb car use, the public authorities have made it necessary to change the current traffic policy and to introduce an adequate traffic system favoring sustainability of transport, notably in communities where it is possible to encourage people to use the bike share system, or to develop automobile demand constraint strategies, such as taxes, congestion charging and parking policies. The analysis approach using a static BN offers the possibility to integrate these variables on a particular road segment and to analyze the probability of traffic congestion. The implementation of a Bayesian model is very easy to program and its practical implementation is easy matter for which the data urban are collected and processed in the database. The analysis approach using a static BN offers the possibility to integrate these variables on a particular road segment and to analyze the probability of traffic congestion. The implementation of a Bayesian model is very easy to program and its practical implementation is easy task to determine the relative contribution of the urban activity being considered in our analysis.

The next step is to develop a dynamic model that aims to relate variables each other over adjacent time steps in order to predict the congestion situation in the coming years. The limits of our research are the unavailability of instantaneous data for covering all types of current problems in real time.

References

1. Ni, D.: Traffic Flow Theory, 1st edn. Butterworth-Heinemann, Oxford (2015)
2. Martins, C., da Conceição Fonseca, M., Pato, M.V.: Modeling the steering of international roaming traffic. Eur. J. Oper. Res. **261**(2), 735–754 (2017)
3. Altheneyan, A.S., Menai, M.E.B.: Naïve Bayes classifiers for authorship attribution of Arabic texts. Comput. Inf. Sci. **26**(4), 473–484 (2014)
4. Yang, M.C., Huang, C.S., Chen, J.H., Chang, R.F.: Whole breast lesion detection using Naive Bayes classifier for portable ultrasound. Ultrasound Med. Biol. **38**(11), 1870–1880 (2012)
5. Fusco, G., Colombaroni, C., Isaenko, N.: Short-term speed predictions exploiting big data on large urban road networks. Transp. Res. Part C: Emerg. Technol. **73**, 183–201 (2016)
6. Horvitz, E.J., Sarin, R., Liao, L.: Prediction, expectation, and surprise: methods, designs, and study of a deployed traffic forecasting service. Microsoft, Indrix, University of Washington (2006)
7. Kim, J., Wang, G.: Diagnosis and prediction of traffic congestion on urban road networks using Bayesian networks. Transp. Res. Rec. J. Transp. Res. Board 108–118 (2016)
8. Chen, C., Zhang, G., Wang, H., Yang, J., Jin, P., Walton, C.M.: Bayesian network-based formulation and analysis for toll road utilization supported by traffic information provision. Transp. Res. Part C: Emerg. Technol. **60**, 339–359 (2015)
9. Yang, H., Shen, L., Xiang, Y., Yao, Z., Liu, X.: Freeway incident duration prediction using Bayesian network. In: 4th International Conference on Transportation Information and Safety (ICTIS), Canada, pp. 974 – 980 (2017)

A Survey on Data Center Network Topologies

Zina Chkirbene[1(✉)], Ridha Hamila[1], and Sebti Foufou[2,3]

[1] College of Engineering, Qatar University, Doha, Qatar
`zina.chk@qu.edu.qa`
[2] LE2i Lab, University of Burgundy, Dijon, France
[3] Computer Science, New York University Abu Dhabi,
Abu Dhabi, United Arab Emirates

Abstract. Data centers are the infrastructures that support the cloud computing services. So, their topologies have an important role on controlling the performance of these services. Designing an efficient topology with a high scalability and a good network performance is one of the most important challenges in data centers. This paper surveys recent research advances linked to data center network topologies. We review some representative topologies and discuss their proprieties in details. We compare them in terms of average path length, network fault tolerance, scalability and connection pattern techniques.

Keywords: Cloud computing services · Survey
Data center topology · Network performance

1 Introduction

Massive data centers are being built around the world to provide various cloud computing services such as Web search, online social networking, online office and IT infrastructure out-sourcing for both individual users and organizations [1,2]. Microsoft, IBM, Google, Amazon, Yahoo and eBay are running data centers with at least 60,000 nodes for each one of them [3]. Data center infrastructure must be well designed to maintain the consumed energy and the cost of both deployment and maintenance at an acceptable level [4]. In addition, data availability and scalability are considered as critical criteria in the design of a data center topology because of their big impact on the infrastructure cost. In fact, massive data centers with millions of nodes (servers)[1] has a high cost including the cost of network switches, number of server, cables and power consumption [5]. For instance, according to industry estimates, the cost of United States data center market has been increased by 23 billion USD in four years between 2005 and 2009. It reached almost 39 billion USD in 2009. Hence, the data center topology is considered as an important factor that controls the network performance in terms of

---

[1] In this document we will use the words "node" and "server" interchangeably.

© Springer Nature Switzerland AG 2018
N. Boudriga et al. (Eds.): UNet 2018, LNCS 11277, pp. 143–154, 2018.
https://doi.org/10.1007/978-3-030-02849-7_13

average path length, latency, fault tolerance and cost [4]. According to the configurability of the topology, there are two types of data center interconnections: flat and recursive topologies. Flat topologies have a maximum network degree of two (degree ≤ 2). These include FatTree [6], FlatNet [7] HyperFltaNet [8], ScalNet [9], VacoNet [10]. Recursive topologies, in the other hand, are characterized with a high network degree and require more layers to scale up to big number of nodes. DCell [11], BCube [12] and LaCoDa [13] are representative examples of recursive topologies.

There are several surveys about data center configurations and data center topologies. [14] focus on wireless data center networks, [15] focuses on data center energy consumption. This survey considers wired data center topologies. We give an overview of flat and recursive data center topologies and compare them in terms of designs, average path length (APL), scalability as well as bandwidth. This paper is organized as follows: In Sect. 2, we present representative example of data center topologies, then compare them in Sect. 3 from different perspectives. Section 4 concludes the survey.

2   Topologies of DC Networks

The topologies presented in this section are classified into two categories: flat and recursive. If the servers in the topology have a maximum of 2 ports, we classify the topology as a flat topology; otherwise it is a recursive topology. We denote by n the number of ports per switch and k the number of ports per server in a topology.

2.1   Flat Topologies

Flat Topologies use intelligent switches for a smart routing of packets in a DC and some servers act as routers. Examples of data center topologies in this category are FatTree [6], FlatNet [7], HyperFltaNet [8], ScalNet [9], VacoNet [10].

FatTree

FatTree is an extension of tree topology. FatTree contains three switch levels which are the core, edge and aggregation levels and it has $\frac{n}{2}^2$ n-port switches. FatTree uses the same kind of switches in the thee levels with a maximum connected nodes equals to $\frac{n^3}{4}$ for n port per switch. Each switch in the edge level has n ports: $\frac{n}{2}$ are connected to the servers and the rest ($\frac{n}{2}$) are linked to the switches in the aggregate level. *pod* is the basic element in FatTree. One *pod* can be considered as the some of servers that are linked to $\frac{n}{2}$ edge switches which are linked to $\frac{n}{2}$ aggregation-level switches.

FlatNet

FlatNet was proposed to increase the network scalability compared to FatTree. The total number of connected nodes in the network is equal to n^3 nodes. FlatNet contains two network layers where the first layer is composed of one n-port switch that connects n nodes. The second layer can be regarded as n^2 1-layer FlatNet. Every n servers are directly connected to an "external" switch (denoted by cluster). The connection pattern of theses clusters are proposed in [7]. One major problem is FlatNet is the connection pattern which was qualified as inefficient in terms of APL and latency.

HyperFlatNet

HyperFlatNet was proposed to improve the connection pattern in FlatNet. It connects n^3 nodes using LCM algorithm [8] which improves the network performance in terms of latency and APL. LCM algorithm increases the number of directly connected cluster compared to FlatNet so it reduces the APL [8]. For instance, if 2 clusters are not directly connected (.i.e. indirectly connected) meaning that they do not have an intermediate switch between them, the path between any servers from these clusters is equal to 8 hops. HyperFlatNet reduces the number of indirectly connected clusters which reduces the APL. Figure 1 shows an example of HyperFlatNet network for n = 4.

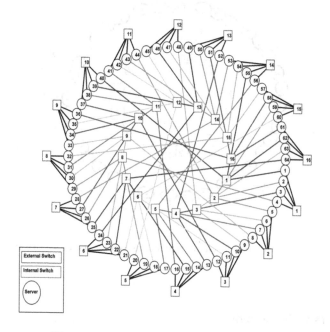

Fig. 1. A HyperFlatNet network for $n = 4$.

ScalNet

ScalNet is proposed to improve network scalability compared to HyperFlatNet. The connection pattern in ScalNet is inspired from LCM algorithm proposed in [8]. This topology is able to connect $\frac{n^4}{2}$ servers. For example for (n = 16),

ScalNet connects 32768 servers which means that ScalNet increases the number of servers by 700% compared to FlatNet while using the same number of links by server.

VacoNet

VacoNet reduces the number of unused node in the network. It scales up to $\frac{n^4}{2}$ according to the needed number of servers. VacoNet presents a solution for the server consolidation problem while reducing the infrastructure cost and the energy consumption. VacoNet increases the number of directly connected clusters and avoids the redundant cluster connections repetitions. Figure 2 shows a 36-server 2-layer VacoNet constructed by using 3-port switches.

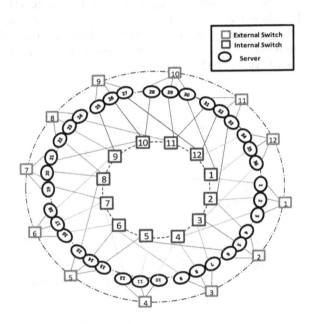

Fig. 2. A 36-server 2-layer VacoNet constructed by using 3-port switches.

2.2   Recursive Topologies

Several recursive topologies are proposed to interconnect nodes in date center including DCell [11], BCube [12], HyperBcube [16] and LaCoDa [13].

DCell

DCell is a recursive structure where the first layer is called DCell$_0$. Each server in a DCell$_k$ has $k+1$ links where the first one (called also level$_0$ link) is linked to a switch in DCell$_0$, the level$_i$ link is used to connect servers located in the same DCell$_i$. DCell has computational servers with several interface cards (NICs) that act as routers. One major drawback of DCell is the wiring complexity and the double exponentially scalability.

BCube

BCube is a server-centric topology. $BCube_1$ is composed by n-port switches and n $BCube_0$. n switches are used in $BCube_1$ and they connect one server in each $BCube_0$. $BCube_1$ can be built by connecting n $BCube_0$ with n extra switches. A $BCube_k$ is built from n $BCube_{k-1}$ with n^k extra n-port switches (Fig. 3). The extra switches are used to connect servers in $BCube_{k-1}$. Both DCell and BCube require servers with $(k+1)$ NICs.

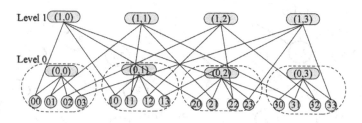

Fig. 3. A BCube structure [17].

HyperBcube

HyperBcube is a recursive topology [16]. The first layer of the HyperBcube is composed by one n-port switch connecting n servers. Starting from the second layer ($k \geq 2$), HyperBcube can be considered as an $n^2 * n^{(2 \times k - 3)}$ matrix having $n^{(2 \times k - 3)}$ columns, where each column contains exactly n^2 servers which belong to a n^2 (k-1)-layer HyperBcube. n-port switches are used to connect the n^2 servers located at the same column.

LaCoDA

Similarly to DCell, the first layer of LaCoDA contains n servers and one n-port switch. For ($k \geq 2$), LaCoDA links $n^2 * n^{(2 \times k - 3)}$ nodes. LaCoDA was been proposed to increase the number of directly connected clusters in HyperBCube so to reduce the APL while connecting the same number of nodes. LaCoDA strikes also a compromise between the high cost of BCube and high scalability of DCell. Figure 4 presents LaCoDA with $n = 2, k = 3$.

3   Comparisons of Topologies

3.1   Comparison Criteria

- **Degree of the servers:** It is the number of ports per server in the DC. For flat topologies, the degree is less or equal to 2. However, the number of ports in recursive topologies varies according to the required levels.

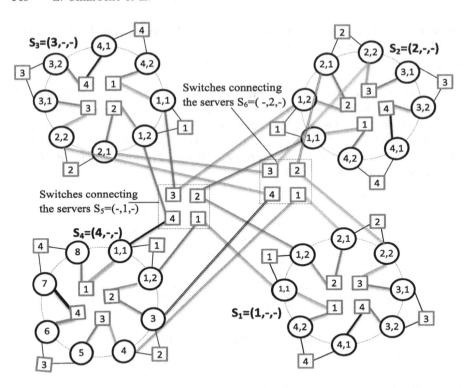

Fig. 4. A LaCoDA structure for $n = 2, k = 3$.

- **Scalability:** It presents the number of servers in the topology. In general, a topology must have a good scalability that supports the incremental expansion of nodes without affecting the existing ones.
- **Diameter:** The diameter is defined as the maximum of the shortest distances between all pairs of notes. A smaller diameter proves that the topology has an effective routing algorithm, and low transmission latency.
- **Fault tolerance:** A fault-tolerant topology is able to continue working even in the presence of failures. Fault-tolerant routing algorithms are needed to improve the topologies against the network failure.
- **Average Path length:** In a network, the APL shows the efficiency of the routing algorithms in terms of packet transmission.
- **Bandwidth:** It is used to characterize data transfer rate, i.e. the amount of data that can be carried from one point to another. There are four types of data bandwidths that can occur under different traffic patterns: One-to-One, One-to-All, One-to-Several and All-to-All bandwidth.

3.2   Performance Comparison

Some quantitative structural properties of existing topologies are presented in Tables 1 and 2. BCube and DCell have good scalability. However, DCell has a high wiring complexity and BCube requires more than three layers to connect big number of nodes. For instance, using a 5-port switch and 4 layers we can connect $5^4 = 625$ nodes. A 4-layer BCube network requires 4 NICs per node, which is costly and hard to control in practice. Consequently, BCube has scalability problems for cost-effective small degree node and small-port-count switches. Table 3 shows also that both DCell and HyperBcube/LaCoDa provide bigger number of nodes than BCube and flat topologies.

Table 1. Comparison between flat topologies.

	FatTree	HyperFlatNet/FlatNet	ScalNet	VacoNet
Nodes number	$\frac{n^3}{4}$	n^3	$\frac{n^4}{2}$	N
Link number	$3 \times \frac{n^3}{4}$	$2 \times n^3$	n^4	$2 \times N$
Link number per node	3	2	2	2
Switches number	$5\frac{n^2}{4}$	$2 \times n^2$	$2 \times \frac{n^3}{2}$	$2 \times \frac{N}{n}$
Switches number per node	$\frac{5}{n}$	$\frac{2}{n}$	$\frac{2}{n}$	$\frac{2}{n}$
Network diameter	6	4	5	4

Table 2. Comparison between layered topologies.

	HyperBcube/LaCoDA	DCell	BCube
Nodes number	n^{2k-1}	$a_1 = n(k = 1)$ $a_k = a_{k-1}(a_{k-1}+1)(k \geq 2)$	n^k
Node degree	k	k	k
Link number	kn^{2k-1}	$(k+1)\frac{a_k}{2}$	kn^k
Switches number	kn^{2k-2}	$\frac{a_k}{n}$	kn^{k-1}

Moreover, a data center network consists of switches, nodes and links [18] and there are three types of links in a data center topology (See Fig. 5): α link which connects two nodes, β link connecting a node and a switch and γ linking two switches. DCell topology uses both α and β links. BCube uses only β links. However, BCube has a low scalability for small network layers and DCell has a high wiring complexity [16]. FatTree uses γ links which connects only switches and decreases the network scalability [6]. An α link can be considered as the most simple connection between a pair of nodes. A major advantage of β link is the multiple non-blocking paths which increases the network diversity. However, β link needs an additional switch for inter node communication. So, a good tradeoff between cost and performance would be to use β links and small-port-count switches.

For the bandwidth, the one-to-one, one-to-several and one-to-all bandwidths are limited by the number of ports on each node (k). So, for a flat topology, the bandwidth does not exceed 2, while for a recursive topology the bandwidth equals k. Consequently, the flat topology has the smallest all-to-all bandwidth

Table 3. Scalability comparison between different topologies under different configurations.

n	Flat topology			k	Recursive topology		
	FlatNet/HyperFlatNet	FatTree	ScalNet		DCell	BCube	HyperBcube/LaCoDa
4	64	3	128	2	20	16	64
				3	420	64	1024
				4	176820	252	16384
6	216	16	684	2	42	36	216
				3	1806	216	7776
				4	3×10^6	1269	823543
8	512	54	2048	2	72	64	512
				3	5252	512	32768
				4	27×10^6	4096	2×10^6
16	4096	128	32768	2	272	256	4096
				3	74256	4096	1×10^6
				4	5514×10^6	65536	268×10^6

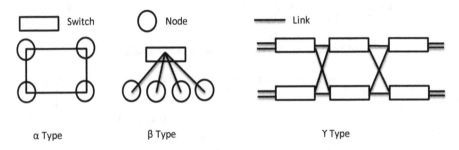

Fig. 5. Link types in a data center network.

because of the limited number of ports. In addition, this indicates that recursive topologies offers a great bandwidth performance under any traffic configuration ($k \geq 2$).

Figure 6 shows an APL comparison between flat topologies. The number of servers varied between 1 to 1000. We can remark that the APL of HyperFlatNet, FlatNet FatTree and VaCoNet does not exceed 3.5 even for 1000 severs. In the other hand, ScalNet has a high APL. For example, for 1000 nodes, ScalaNet increases the APl by 30% compared to all the other topologies. ScalNet connects bigger number of nodes than HyperFlatNet, FlatNet, FatTree and VaCoNet which has a big impact on its APL.

Figure 7 shows an APL comparison between recursive topologies. The number of servers varied between 100 to 1000. We can note that the LaCoDa, which has the same number of connected nodes as HyperBcube, has the smallest APL compared to DCell, BCube and HyperBcube. DCell has a higher APL compared to the other topologies because of its high wiring complexity.

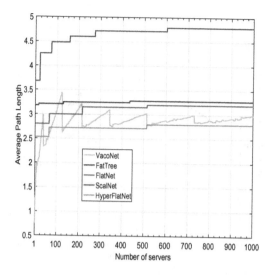

Fig. 6. APL comparison between flat topologies.

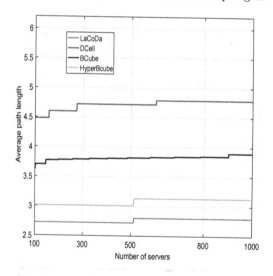

Fig. 7. APL comparison between recursive topologies.

Figure 8 shows the connection failure rate in function of the link failure rate of some flat topologies. The link failure rate is varied from 10% to 20%, while the number of nodes is fixed at 1000. For each failure rate value, we measure the connection failure rate as the proportion of failure to finding routes. If the connection failure rate increases slowly compared to the link failure rate, then this is a good indication that the network can maintain acceptable performances under faulty conditions. We can note that the HyperFlatNet is the most resistant

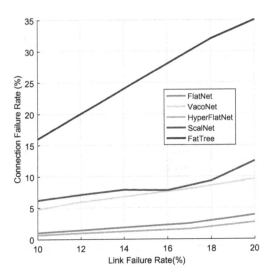

Fig. 8. The connection failure rate in function of the link failure rate of some flat topologies

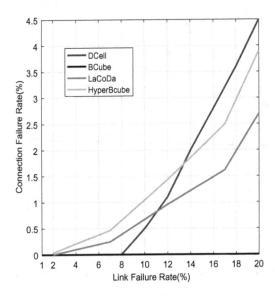

Fig. 9. The connection failure rate in function of the link failure rate of some recursive topologies.

topology against the link failure. However FatTree is more sensitive to link failure compared to ScalNet, FlatNet and VaCoNet.

Figure 9 shows the connection failure rate in function of the link failure rate of some recursive topologies. The link failure rate is varied from 1% to 20%, while the number of nodes is fixed at 1000. We can note that the BCube is the most unaffected topology against the link failure compared to the other topologies.

4 Conclusion

In this survey, we discussed representative examples of data center network topologies. We discussed the properties of these topologies, their connection patterns and fault tolerant performances. Comparisons between the properties of some representative topologies have been presented. We showed that any topology has to strike a compromise between performance and scalability due to the impact of the scalability on the network performances.

Acknowledgment. This publication was made possible by NPRP grant 6-718-2-298 from the Qatar National Research Fund (a member of Qatar Foundation). The statements made herein are solely the responsibility of the authors.

References

1. Carter, A.: Do it green: media interview with Michael Manos. http://edge.technet. com/Media/Doing-IT-Greel
2. Rabbe, L.: Powering the Yahoo! network. http://yodel.yahoo.com/2006/11/27/ powering-the-yahoo-networl
3. Ruiu, P., Bianco, A., Fiandrino, C., Giaccone, P., Kliazovich, D.: Power comparison of cloud data center architectures. In: 2016 IEEE International Conference on Communications (ICC), May 2016, pp. 1–6 (2016)
4. Stroh, S., Schröder, G., Gröne, F.: Keeping the data center competitive six levers for boosting performance, reducing costs, and preparing for an on-demand world, November 2012
5. Popa, L., Ratnasamy, S., Iannaccone, G., Krishnamurthy, A., Stoica, I.: A cost comparison of datacenter network architectures. ACM, New York (2010)
6. Al-Fares, M., Loukissas, A., Vahdat, A.: A scalable, commodity data center network architecture. In: SIGCOMM 2008 Conference on Data Communication, pp. 63–74, August 2009
7. Lin, D., Liu, Y., Hamdi, M., Muppala, J.: FlatNet: towards a flatter data center network. In: 2012 IEEE Global Communications Conference (GLOBECOM), December 2012, pp. 2499–2504 (2012)
8. Chkirbene, Z., Foufou, S., Hamdi, M., Hamila, R.: Hyper-FlatNet: a novel network architecture for data centers. In: 2015 IEEE International Conference on Communication Workshop (ICCW), June 2015, pp. 1877–1882 (2015)
9. Chkirbene, Z., Foufou, S., Hamdi, M., Hamila, R.: ScalNet: a novel network architecture for data centers. In: 2015 IEEE Globecom Workshops (GC Wkshps), December 2015, pp. 1–6 (2015)
10. Chkirbene, Z., Foufou, S., Hamila, R.: VacoNet: variable and connected architecture for data center networks. In: 2016 IEEE Wireless Communications and Networking Conference, April 2016, pp. 1–6 (2016)
11. Guo, C., Wu, H., Tan, K., Shi, L., Zhang, Y., Lu, S.: DCell: a scalable and fault-tolerant network structure for data centers. In: SIGCOMM 2008 on Data Communication, pp. 75–86, August 2008

12. Guo, C., Wu, H., Tan, K., Shi, K., Zhang, Y., Lu, S.: BCube: a high performance, server-centric network architecture for modular data centers. In: SIGCOMM 2009 on Data Communication, pp. 63–74, August 2009

13. Chkirbene, Z., Foufou, S., Hamila, R., Zahir, T., Zomaya, A.Y.: LaCoDa: layered connected topology for massive data centers. J. Netw. Comput. Appl. **83**, 169–180 (2017)

14. Baccour, E., Foufou, S., Hamila, R., Hamdi, M.: A survey of wireless data center networks. In: 2015 49th Annual Conference on Information Sciences and Systems (CISS), March 2015, pp. 1–6 (2015)

15. Baccour, E., Gouissem, A., Foufou, S., Hamila, R., Tari, Z., Zomaya, A.Y.: An energy saving mechanism based on vacation queuing theory in data center networks. In: Hu, J., Khalil, I., Tari, Z., Wen, S. (eds.) MONAMI 2017. LNICST, vol. 235, pp. 188–202. Springer, Cham (2018). https://doi.org/10.1007/978-3-319-90775-8_16

16. Lin, D., Liu, Y., Hamdi, M., Muppala, J.: Hyper-BCube: a scalable data center network. In: 2012 IEEE International Conference on Communications (ICC), June 2012, pp. 2918–2923 (2012)

17. Chen, T., Gao, X., Chen, G.: The features, hardware, and architectures of data center networks: a survey. J. Parallel Distrib. Comput. **96**(Suppl. C), 45–74 (2016)

18. Liu, Y., Muppla, J., Veeraghavan, M., Lin, D., Hamdi, M.: Data center network (2013). http://www.amazon.ca/Data-center-Network

Optimization on Ports Activation Towards Energy Efficient Data Center Networks

Zina Chkirbene[1]([⊠]), Ridha Hamila[1], Sebti Foufou[2,3], Serkan Kiranyaz[1],
and Moncef Gabbouj[4]

[1] College of Engineering, Qatar University, Doha, Qatar
zina.chk@qu.edu.qa
[2] LE2i Lab, University of Burgundy, Dijon, France
[3] Computer Science, New York University Abu Dhabi,
Abu Dhabi, United Arab Emirates
[4] Tampere University of Technology, Tampere, Finland

Abstract. Nowadays, Internet of thing including network support (i.e. checking social media, sending emails, video conferencing) requires smart and efficient data centers to support these services. Hence, data centers become more important and must be able to respond to ever changing service requirements and application demands. However, data centers are classified as one of the largest consumers of energy in the world. Existing topologies such as ScalNet improves the data center scalability while leading to enormous amounts of energy consumption. In this paper, we present a new energy efficient algorithm for ScalNet called Green Scal-Net. The proposed topology strikes a compromise between maximizing the energy saving and minimizing the average path length. By taking into consideration the importance of the transmitted data and the critical parameters for the receiver (e.g. time, energy), the proposed topology dynamically controls the number of active communication links by turning off and on ports in the network (switches ports and nodes ports). Both theoretical analysis and simulation experiments are conducted to evaluate its overall performance in terms of average path length and energy consumption.

Keywords: Internet of thing · Data center network
Network architecture · Average path length · Energy consumption

1 Introduction

The increasing growth of the Internet of Things (IoT) presents challenges in different areas such as capacity, security as well as analytic. Consequently, the design of data-center networks became an interesting topic for IoT management [1]. In fact, date center must restructure how it holds and processes data to effectively handle all that the IoT has in store. In addition, a recent report by

© Springer Nature Switzerland AG 2018
N. Boudriga et al. (Eds.): UNet 2018, LNCS 11277, pp. 155–166, 2018.
https://doi.org/10.1007/978-3-030-02849-7_14

the Gartner Inc. research firm [2] shows that the IoT with its massive network connections and data requires an optimally-sized data centers to effectively manage capacity and forwards data in low latency. Moreover, the IoT will include 26 billion units installed by 2020, which has a big impact on the size, cost and the energy consumption in data centers. In fact, the studies prove that with the experiential growth of IoT, the installed base of servers on data centers has been growing by 12% year, from 14 million in 2000 to 35 million in 2008 [3]. Consequently, IoT data centers are becoming one of the biggest energy consumers in the word. Several architectures such as DCell [4], BCube [5], AdyNet [6] and FlatNet [7] have been proposed to interconnect nodes in IoT data centers. However, these data centers topologies are usually constructed with large numbers of links and network devices where the average link utilization is only between 5% and 25% and varies largely between daytime and night [8]. In addition, the traditional routing algorithms forward packets to the destinations without caring about the amount of consumed energy. In fact, generally only a subset of network devices and links can suffice to forward data packets to their destinations, and hence significant energy saving can be obtained by reducing the number of network hop.

ScalNet has been proposed in [9] to interconnect a massive number of servers in a way that makes the network scale faster than FlatNet, BCube and DCell which has a big impact on the energy consumption. For instance, ScalNet consumes around 12 million watts for a network with 525×10^3 nodes. Such observations inspired us to design a new energy efficient algorithm for ScalNet called Green ScalNet. The proposed algorithm uses only some subset of network links to forward packets to their destinations, and the remaining ones will be powered off for more energy saving. The amount of energy consumed by Green ScalNet is proportional to the importance of the transmitted data and the critical parameters for the receiver (time, energy) presented by the parameter α ($\alpha \in [0,1]$). The algorithm computes the number of ports per cluster to be powered off, for n-port switch, the number of powered off port per cluster is equal to $n \times \alpha$ and the Powered Off Port rate per Cluster (denoted by $POPC$) is $100 \times \alpha$. Moreover, a new dynamic routing algorithm is proposed to forward data to their destinations using only a set of the available links.

The main contributions of this paper can be summarized as follows:

1. Proposing a new IoT data center energy saving algorithm for ScalNet called Green ScalNet, capable of reducing the energy consumption compared to the original ScalNet.
2. Minimizing the port energy consumption by considering switch and server ports activation while taking into consideration the receiver transmission conditions.
3. Guaranteeing the data center traffic demand satisfaction by proposing a new cluster routing algorithm for packet transmission using available servers.
4. Various simulations to evaluate the proposed solution and strengthen the theoretical analysis.

The rest of the paper is organized as follows. A brief literature review on related work in this field is presented in Sect. 2. The proposed Green ScalNet is described in Sect. 3. In Sect. 4, the system evaluation is presented to evaluate the performance of the proposed algorithm. Finally, conclusions are drawn in Sect. 5.

2   Related Work

Numerous architectures based on parallel computing have been recently proposed to interconnect massive data centers such as DCell [4], BCube [5] and FlatNet [7].

DCell is a recursive structure whom the most basic element is called $DCell_0$. Each server in a $DCell_0$ is connected to the switch in the same $DCell_0$. In a $DCell_k$, each server will eventually have $k + 1$ links: the first link or the $level_0$ link connected to a switch when forming a $DCell_0$, and $level_i$ link connected to a server in the same $DCell_i$. Servers in DCell are acting as routers: they are equipped with multiple interface cards (NICs). In fact, just computational servers are also considered as the routers in the system. As a result, the DCell architecture scales double exponentially, and an additional cost will be introduced because of additional and lengthy wiring communication links between switches and servers.

BCube is a server-centric network structure, where a $BCube_1$ is constructed from n $BCube_0$s. It makes use of more switches when constructing higher level architecture. It requires n switches to construct a $BCube_1$. In fact, it connects one server in each $BCube_0$. Hence, a $BCube_1$ contains n $BCube_0$s and n extra switches. More generally, a $BCube_k$ is constructed from n $BCube_{k-1}$ and n^k extra n-port switches. These extra switches are connected to exactly one server in each $BCube_{k-1}$. BCube requires more switches when constructing higher level structures, and DCell uses only $level_0$ n-port switches. However, both require servers to have $k + 1$ NICs. The implication is that servers will be involved in switching more packets in DCell than in BCube.

FlatNet is a recursive architecture. The first layer of the FlatNet contains n servers and one n-port switch and the second layer consists of n^2 1-layer FlatNet. A two layers FlatNet can be considered as an $n^2 * n$ matrix and every n servers (denoted by cluster) are directly connected to an "external" switch and these clusters are connected using the connection pattern proposed in [7].

3   Green ScalNet

3.1   Motivation

ScalNet has been proposed to scale the network faster than FlatNet, BCube and DCell with only two layers of network. It reduces the number of non-connected clusters compared to FlatNet. However, it suffers from high port energy consumption. Table 1 presents the consumed energy for 25000-nodes with different topologies. We use the values of 12 (Watts) per port server and switch [10].

Table 1. Cost comparison between different architectures.

	DCell	BCube	FlatNet	ScalNet
n-port switch	158	159	29	15
Servers number	25122	25281	24389	25313
Ports energy consumption	75366	101124	97556	101250

With small n-port switch, ScalNet increases the number of servers compared to other topologies in cost of energy consumption as all the network ports are activated ($2n^4$ ports including servers and switches). Moreover, only a subset of network is used in the routing process and the rest can be considered as an underutilized resources.

Such observations motivate us to design a new energy saving algorithm for ScalNet called Green ScalNet, which power-off the idle links and ports. The links will be divided on two types:

Critical links: links between the servers and the external switch which aims to avoid the problem of disconnected nodes/clusters.
Uncritical links: links between the servers and the internal switches that connects ScalNet clusters. These links are divided on *Used links* employing during the packets transmission and *Unused links* which can be deactivated without lost in network performance in terms of routing.

Green ScalNet minimizes the energy consumption by deactivating a set of the uncritical links by deactivating the end ports of each one of them to save energy, while avoiding the problem of having disconnected nodes and activating the critical links.

3.2 Problem Formulation

In order to minimize the network energy consumption, Green ScalNet reduces the number of active ports by closing a subset of the uncritical links. We denote by p_i the energy consumed by the active port i, n the number of ports per switch and k the number of ports per server. The energy consumption Eg of a topology can be computed as:

$$Eg = N_{sw} \sum_{i=1}^{n} p_i + N_{sv} \sum_{j=1}^{k} p_j \tag{1}$$

where N_{sw} denotes the total number of switches and N_{sv} denotes the total number of servers in the network. For ScalNet, N_{sw} and N_{sv} can be expressed as:

$$N_{sw} = n^3 \tag{2}$$

$$N_{sv} = \frac{n^4}{2}$$

By considering that the critical links will remain active (*critical links* $= \frac{N_{sw}}{2}$) and that only a subset from the uncritical links will be deactivated, Eg becomes:

$$Eg = \frac{N_{sw}}{2} \sum_{i=1}^{n} p_i + N_{sv} \sum_{j=1}^{k} p_j \tag{3}$$

$$= \frac{n^3}{2} \sum_{i=1}^{n} p_i + \frac{n^4}{2} \sum_{j=1}^{k} p_j$$

$$= \frac{n^4}{2} \left(\frac{1}{n} \sum_{i=1}^{n} p_i + \sum_{j=1}^{k} p_j \right)$$

So, minimizes the total consumed energy is equivalent to minimize the active ports in the network denoted by P_a:

$$P_a = \sum_{i=1}^{n} p_i + \sum_{j=1}^{k} p_j \tag{4}$$

$$= \sum_{i=1}^{n} \left(2 - floor \left(\frac{min(i-1,k)}{k} \right) \right) p_i$$

The objective is to find a set of optimal routing paths that minimizes P_a:

Minimize: $\sum_{i=1}^{n} \left(2 - floor \left(\frac{min(i-1,k)}{k} \right) \right) p_i$

3.3   Overview

ScalNet generates a $(\frac{n^3}{2} \times n)$ matrix denoted by R such that:

$$\forall i \in \{1..\frac{n^3}{2}\}, \forall j \in \{1..n\},$$

The server (i,j) is connected to the switch number $R(i,j)$.

In the first layer, the ScalNet network contains n nodes and one n-port switch. The second layer contains $\frac{n^3}{2}$ first layers. Thus, the $\frac{n^4}{2}$ connected servers can be considered as $\frac{n^3}{2}$ groups of n servers (clusters). In particular, the different servers network can be regarded as $\frac{n^3}{2} \times n$ matrix. The row and column indexes in the matrix correspond to the cluster number (denoted by Coordinate 2) and the index in the cluster (denoted by Coordinate 1), respectively. Every n servers are directly connected to an "external" switch (cluster) and referred by $(C2, C1)$ where *C1* and *C2* correspond to its coordinate 1 and 2, respectively.

3.4 Ports deactivation

Although powering off idle ports for more energy saving and increasing the average link utilization is an attractive technique, there is a conflict between powering off links and maintaining the network connected. Consequently, there must be a tradeoff between power conservation and the network connectivity. ScalNet uses a special physical connection algorithm that interconnect each cluster to its next neighbor by using the first and the second ports from each switch cluster. So, the minimum number of port per switch that should be active to guarantee the connectedness of the network called network connectedness links, is equal to 2. We propose a new algorithm Algorithm 1 that selects L_d from $(n-2)$ links in each cluster (based on the network requirements) to be deactivated by deactivating the end ports of each one of them denoted by P_d^c. The performance of Green ScalNet can be improved by selecting which link from the uncritical links will be deactivated based on the analysis of the nodes transmission load. However, this analysis will require centralized decision i.e. all nodes need to send their transmission load information to the decision center to be able to decide which links to be deactivated. This becomes impracticable for big number of nodes. So, by tacking advantages from the ScalNet network symmetry and the high bisection bandwidth, we prove by simulation (Sect. 5) that green ScalNet increases the energy saving while keeping high network performance and avoiding the problem of transmission load information synchronization.

The algorithm Algorithm 1 manages the network performance according to the importance of the transmitted data and the critical parameters for the receiver (time, energy). Basically, the bigger α results in a bigger $POPC$ and consequently more energy saving. However, for low α the number of active ports increases and the APL and latency decrease. L_d is computed such that:

$$L_d = floor(\alpha \times n) \tag{5}$$
$$L_d \leq (n-2) \tag{6}$$

$GetConnetRoutes(R)$ is the function that identify the set of the network connectedness links. $GetCriticalLinks(R)$ is the function that identify the set of critical links.

3.5 Routing Algorithm

The proposed algorithm divides the total nodes in two categories:

Master server (denoted by S^M): It provides services to the network and it is involved in the routing from source to destination.
Idle server: It is an inoperative server that uses Master server to transmit its data to the destination. The idle server is an energy saving node.

Figure 1 presents an example of two Master and two idle servers per cluster. n-port switch is 4, α is 0.5.

Algorithm 1. Ports deactivation algorithm

function $PowerOffPorts((R,n,\alpha))$

    Input:

    R is the matrix connection.

    n is the number of ports per switch.

    α presents the network requirements in terms of the number of active ports.

    Output:

    R_{up} is the new connection matrix with the deactivated links.

    $N_c \leftarrow$ GetCriticalLinks(R)

    $L_c \leftarrow$ GetCriticalLink(R)

    $R_{up} \leftarrow poweron(N_c, L_c)$

    $L_d[\ ] \leftarrow \emptyset$

    while $L_d \leq$ (n-2) **do**

        $L_d \leftarrow floor(\alpha \times n)$

        Select randomly L_d links to be powered off

        for each cluster c_j=1 to $\frac{n^3}{2}$ **do**

            $R(c_j) \leftarrow poweroff(L_d)$

            $P_d^c \leftarrow poweroff(L_d)$

        end for

    end while

    $R_{up} \leftarrow R(c_j)$

    return (R_{up})

end function

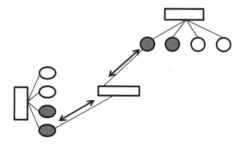

Fig. 1. ScalNet cluster with n-port switch = 4: 2 idle servers and 2 master server (alpha = 0.5).

3.6 Cluster Adaptive Routing Algorithm

Cluster routing algorithm Algorithm 2 is proposed for packets transmission in Green ScalNet. In case of deactivated link, the algorithm Algorithm 2 proposes the function $FindMasterservers$ to find the nearest master server S^M which becomes a new source to forward the packet $S2_{new}$. Then, it uses function $Routing$ to complete the routing packets to destinations.

Algorithm 2. Cluster routing algorithm

1: **procedure** CLUSTER ROUTING$((S_2, S_1),(D_2, D_1),\Omega)$
2:     Input:
3:     Ω is the vector of directly connected clusters
4:     (S_2, S_1) is the source coordinates
5:     (D_2, D_1) is the destination coordinates
6:     Output:
7:     $\overline{Path}$ is the path from the source to the destination

8:     **if** (link(S2,S1),(D2,D1) = active link) **then**
9:         $Path \leftarrow Routing((S_2, S_1),(D_2, D_1),\Omega)$
10:     **end if**
11:     **if** (link(S2,S1),(D2,D1) = closed link) **then**
12:         Find the nearest Master server C_s of $S2$
13:         $S2_{new} \leftarrow FindMasterservers(\text{R},C_s)$
14:         $Path \leftarrow Routing((S2_{new}, S_1),(D_2, D_1),\Omega)$
15:     **end if**
16: **end procedure**

17: **function** $FindMasterservers(\text{R},C_s)$
18:     V is the source row
19:     Input:
20:     $\overline{R}$ is the matrix connection
21:     C_s is the source cluster
22:     Output:
23:     $\overline{S_s^M}$ is the set of master servers
24:     Extract the source row
25:     $V = R(C_s,:)$
26:     **for** $i = 1$ to length V **do**
27:         Find the set of master severs in V
28:         $V(i)! = 0$
29:         $S_s^M i = S^M$
30:     **end for**
31:     **return** (S_s^M)
32: **end function**

33: **function** $Routing((S_2, S_1),(D_2, D_1),\Omega)$
34:     **if** $S_2 = D_2$ **then**
35:         The source and the destination are directly connected via an external switch
36:         $Path \leftarrow (S_2, S_1) \rightarrow (D_2, D_1)$
37:     **else**
38:         **if** $mod(S_2 - D_2, \frac{n^3}{2}) \in \Omega$ **then**
39:             The source and the destination are connected via one internal switch
40:             Find T_2^1 and T_1^1 such that $P \leftarrow (S_2, S_1) \rightarrow (S_2, T_1^1) \rightarrow (D_2, T_2^1) \rightarrow (D_2, D_1)$.
41:         **else if** $mod(S_2 - D_2, \frac{n^3}{2}) \notin \Omega$ **then**
42:             The source and the destination are not directly connected and are linked only by the intermediate of 2 switches
43:             Find T_1^1, T_2^1, T_1^2 and T_2^2 such that $P \leftarrow (S_2, S_1) \rightarrow (T_2^i, T_1^i) \rightarrow (T_2^j, T_1^j) \rightarrow (D_2, D_1)$ where (i, j) is an arrangement of $\{1,2\}$

44:        **else**
45:              The source and the destination are not directly connected and are linked only by the intermediate of 3 switches
46:              Find T_1^1, T_2^1, T_1^2, T_2^2, T_1^3 and T_2^3 such that $P \leftarrow (S_2, S_1) \rightarrow (T_2^i, T_1^i) \rightarrow (T_2^j, T_1^j) \rightarrow (T_2^k, T_1^k) \rightarrow (D_2, D_1)$ where (i, j, k) is an arrangement of $\{1,2,3\}$.
47:        **end if**
48:    **end if**
49:    $Path \leftarrow P$
        return Path
50: **end function**

4   System Evaluation

4.1   Average Path Length

The average path length measures the efficiency of a packet transmission on a network. Table 2 compares Green ScalNet with other topologies. Note that when $\alpha = 0$, Green ScalNet has the same number of active ports as ScalNet. With only $n = 6$, Green ScalNet connects bigger number of nodes compared with the other topologies. For $\alpha = 0.18$, it reduces the energy consumption by 8620 (watts) compared with BCube while increasing the APL by only 0.6 which still smaller than the APL of DCell (4.7).

Table 2. A comparison between different topologies

	Number of servers	n	APL	Total active ports	Energy Consumption
BCube	625	25	3.75	2304	27648
DCell	600	24	4.7	1950	23400
FlatNet	512	8	3.1	2048	24576
Green ScalNet	648	$n = 6$ & $\alpha = 0$	4.11	2592	31104
	648	$n = 6$ & $\alpha = 0.18$	4.35	1586	19020
	648	$n = 6$ & $\alpha = 0.6$	5.7	770	9234

4.2   Energy Consumption

Figure 2 shows the energy saving rate under different POPC. The switches port-count is varied between 8, 10, 32 and 64. Note, that the bigger is the n-port switch the bigger is the energy saving rate. In addition, we remark that when $n = 64$, the energy saving rate starts to increase from 2.02×10^8 (Watts) to reach 2.15×10^9 (Watts) so more than 1930×10^6 (Watts) energy has been saved. Thus,

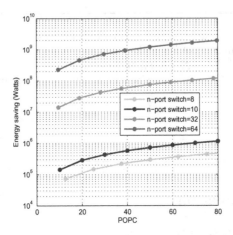

Fig. 2. Energy saving rate under different configurations of port count switches.

Green ScalNet increases largely the energy saving compared to ScalNet without any additional cost.

Figure 3 shows the energy consumption of Green ScalNet compared with ScalNet under different port count switches configuration. We remark that the energy consumption of ScalNet is constant for a fixed n-port switch and by increasing the POPC, the energy consumption of Green ScalNet starts decreasing from 1.67×10^7 when $n = 64$ to attain 1.83×10^6 when the rate of POPC = 80% and the energy consumption of ScalNet is fixed to 1.67×10^7 for the same number of switches $n = 64$. Hence, the POPC has a great impact on the energy saving. In fact, the bigger is the POPC, the bigger is the energy saving.

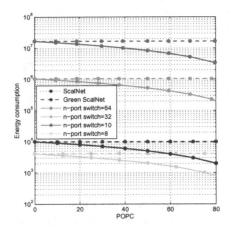

Fig. 3. Energy consumption of Green ScalNet compared with ScalNet under different configurations of port count switches.

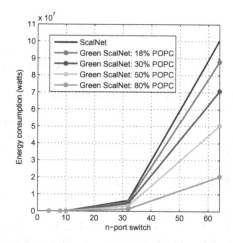

Fig. 4. Energy consumption of Green ScalNet under different n-port switch.

Figure 4 shows the energy consumption of Green ScalNet under different n-port switch (varies between 4, to 64). We remark that the energy consumption is an increasing function of POPC. It reaches 8.8×10^7 when $n = 64$ and POPC $= 18\%$ and 2.04×10^7 when $n = 64$ and POPC $= 80\%$. This means that the new algorithm can reduce more than 5 times the energy in ScalNet without increasing the cost and while reducing the APL.

5   Conclusions

In this paper, we propose Green ScalNet that minimizes the energy consumption of the ports involved in ScalNet packet transmission. The number of ports per cluster to be power off has been computed as a function of α and the energy saving problem has been formulated in terms of the number of ports. Moreover, a new design for routing algorithm has been proposed to find a set of optimal routing paths through the master servers. Simulation results proved the efficiency of the proposed algorithm. As our future work, we intend to investigate the impact of the randomness of the port deactivation and the priority of specific ports activation.

Acknowledgment. This publication was made possible by NPRP grant 6-718-2-298 from the Qatar National Research Fund (a member of Qatar Foundation). The statements made herein are solely the responsibility of the authors.

References

1. Voices of the Industry: Gartner-internet-of-things-will-disrupt-the-data-center (2016). http://datacenterfrontier.com/data-centers-support-the-iternet-of-things/. Accessed 8 Feb 2016
2. Sverdlik, Y.: Gartner-internet-of-things-will-disrupt-the-data-center (2014). http://www.datacenterdynamics.com/servers-storage/gartner-internet-of-things-will-disrupt-the-data-center/85635.article. Accessed 19 March 2014
3. Donston-Miller, D.: Internet of Things will require data centers of all sizes (2014). https://powermore.dell.com/technology/internet-of-things-will-require-data-centers-of-all-sizes/. Accessed 8 Feb 2014
4. Guo, C., Wu, H., Tan, K., Shi, L., Zhang, Y., Lu, S.: DCell: a scalable and fault-tolerant network structure for data centers. In: SIGCOMM 2008 on Data communication, pp. 75–86, August 2008
5. Guo, C., Wu, H., Tan, K., Shi, K., Zhang, Y., Lu, S.: BCube: a high performance, server-centric network architecture for modular data centers. In: SIGCOMM 2009 on Data communication, pp. 63–74, August 2009
6. Chkirbene, Z., Foufou, S., Hamila, R.: Integrating variability management in data center networks. In: 2017 IEEE Wireless Communications and Networking Conference (WCNC), pp. 1–6, March 2017
7. Lin, D., Liu, Y., Hamdi, M., Muppala, J.: FlatNet: towards a flatter data center network. In: 2012 IEEE Global Communications Conference (GLOBECOM), pp. 2499–2504, December 2012
8. Heller, B., et al.: Elastictree: saving energy in data center networks. In: Proceedings of the 7th USENIX Conference on Networked Systems Design and Implementation, Berkeley, CA, USA, NSDI 2010, p. 17. USENIX Association (2010)
9. Chkirbene, Z., Foufou, S., Hamdi, M., Hamila, R.: ScalNet: a novel network architecture for data centers. In: 2015 IEEE Globecom Workshops (GC Wkshps), pp. 1–6, December 2015
10. Popa, L., Ratnasamy, S., Iannaccone, G., Krishnamurthy, A., Stoica, I.: A cost comparison of datacenter network architectures. In: ACM, New York 2010

A Two Objective Linear Programming Model for VM Placement in Heterogenous Data Centers

Rym Regaieg[(✉)], Mohamed Koubàa, Evans Osei-Opoku, and Taoufik Aguili

Laboratoire des Systèmes de Communications,
Département des Technologies de l'Information et de la Communication,
École Nationale d'Ingénieurs de Tunis, Université de Tunis El Manar,
BP 37, Le Belvédère, 1002 Tunis, Tunisia
{rym.regaieg,mohamed.koubaa,evans.oseiopoku,taoufik.aguili}@enit.utm.tn

Abstract. Virtual Machine Placement (VMP) is one of the challenging problem arising in cloud computing data centers. VMP is the process of selecting the most suitable Physical Machine (PM) to host the Virtual Machines (VMs). The placement goal can be either maximizing the usage of existing available resources or it can be saving power by being able to shut down some servers (PMs). In this paper, we propose a new Two-Objective Integer Linear Programming (TOILP) model to solve the VMP problem aiming, for the first time as far as we know, at maximizing simultaneously the usage of PM resources while ensuring power efficiency. We also assume heterogeneous configuration for the data center which has been proven, through recent research work and industrial experience, to be more cost-effective for some applications especially those with intensive I/O operations. Two heterogeneous data center configurations are studied in order to ascertain the impact of each configuration on the performance of the proposed model. Simulation results point out the benefits brought by the TOILP model with an average number of used PMs gain of 32.45% and an average total potential cost of resource wastage gain of 60.62%. It was also reported that the cloud provider should not choose the PMs' configuration independently of the offered virtual machines.

Keywords: Cloud computing · Heterogeneous data centers
Virtual Machine Placement · Integer Linear Programming
Power consumption · Resource wastage

1 Introduction

Cloud Computing is defined as a model for enabling ubiquitous, convenient, on-demand network access to a shared pool of configurable computing resources (e.g., networks, servers, storage, applications, and services) that can be rapidly provisioned and released with minimal management effort or service provider interaction [1]. Infrastructure as a Service (IaaS), Platform as a Service (PaaS)

© Springer Nature Switzerland AG 2018
N. Boudriga et al. (Eds.): UNet 2018, LNCS 11277, pp. 167–178, 2018.
https://doi.org/10.1007/978-3-030-02849-7_15

and Software as a Service (SaaS) are the common categories of cloud computing service models. For IaaS model, cloud provider offers different kinds and amounts of virtualized computing resources (e.g., storage, processing, networks, etc.) gathered into a virtual machine (VM) over the Internet [1]. This provisioned VM allows customers to deploy and run the appropriate application in a personalized and isolated runtime environment.

The decision to place a VM into a particular host is known as the VM placement (VMP) problem [2]. The key challenge here is to maximize the number of cohosted VMs while optimizing a given placement goal. The VMP algorithms can be broadly classified into two categories with respect to their placement goal which fall under one of the following assumptions: maximizing the usage of existing resources or minimizing the power consumption in the data center by shutting down some of the physical machines (servers).

This paper proposes a Two-Objective Integer Linear Programming (TOILP) model that simultaneously optimizes the usage of PMs and power consumption. The TOILP model attempts, given a set of VMs to be set up, to place the VMs in the more suitable server without any VM migration. As the VMP problem has become a particularly challenging task in non homogeneous hardware infrastructures due to the resource variability of PMs, the performances of the proposed TOILP model are evaluated in two different heterogeneous data centers configurations. Two data center configurations are considered in order to study the impact of each PM combination over the different performance metrics (potential cost of resource wastage, number of used PMs, VM rejection ratio). The former configuration has an almost even distribution number of the PMs' configuration whereas the latter is characterised by a different distribution number.

The rest of the paper is organized as follows. Section 2 describes the problem tackled in this paper, Related works is given in Sect. 3. In Sect. 4, we define the notations used to present the proposed model described in Sect. 5. Section 6 shows the experiments evaluating our proposed model and their results. Section 7 concludes the paper.

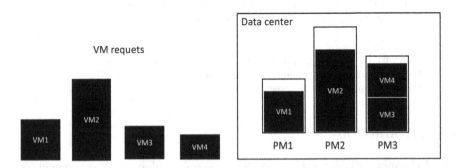

Fig. 1. The VM placement problem in a heterogeneous data center

2   Description of the Problem

The VMP problem can be stated as follows: for a set of PMs and the resource requirements of VMs, the VMs should be hosted on the PMs with respect to a given placement goal. Figure 1 shows an example of VMP with 4 VMs and 3 PMs in a heterogeneous data center with an end-goal of maximizing the PM usage. As it can be seen, after deploying the VMP process, VM_1 is hosted in $PM1$, VM_2 is hosted in PM_2 due to the insufficient resource capacity in PM_1 and VM_3 and VM_4 are hosted in PM_3 as a result of limited resources in both $PM1$ and $PM2$.

Actually, the VMP process usually produces a large amount of wasted resources due to the underutilization of the PMs. As a consequence, an increase in the number of active PMs is noticed leading to a high power consumption in the data center. In this paper, we look for the optimal VM-PM mapping so that the PMs can be used to their maximum efficiency while the energy consumption is minimized by hibernating or shutting down some of the PMs depending on the load conditions.

3   Related Work

The VM placement (VMP) problem has been well explored in cloud computing literature and mostly has been considered similar to the vector bin packing problem which is NP-hard [3,4]. The individual PMs can be considered as bins having different dimensions, corresponding to the resource capacities of the PMs. Similarly, the VMs can be considered as objects to be packed into these bins. For each VM, the amount of required resources (dimensional requirements of objects) is specified. The vector bin packing problem aims at allocating a given set of objects of known sizes into a minimum number of needed bins in order not to exceed each bin's capacity. Therefore, the VMP problem is strongly NP-hard.

Many existing algorithms have been proposed to solve the VMP problem. These algorithms include deterministic (eg. integer programming, constrained programming) [5–7], meta-heuristics (eg. randomized greedy, simulated annealing, genetics and evolution) [8–10] and heuristics.

In this paper, we review works which have focused only on the objectives of this paper (maximization of both PM usage and power consumption efficiency) and which have used deterministic algorithms to solve the offline VMP problem. In [11,12], Shi et al., have considered maximizing the cloud provider revenues, under the placement constraints such as full deployment, anti-colocation and security and also resource capacities constraints such as VM requirements and PM capacities. An Integer Linear Programming formulation is proposed to compute the exact solution. The authors have demonstrated that the proposed VMP approach was practical for the offline VM placement in both small and/or medium data centers. Both works [11,12], have evaluated the proposed VMP approach with the VMs of commercial pattern (i.e, predefined VMs resource capacities) in a homogeneous data center. In [4], Ribas et al., have considered minimizing the active physical machines number, under the PMs resource capacity constraints. A Pseudo-Boolean Constraint is proposed to obtain the exact solution. In [13], Sun et al., have considered minimizing power consumption, under the PM resource reservation constraints. A matrix transformation algorithm is proposed to obtain the exact solution. The proposed solution is evaluated with VMs of customized pattern, i.e., the Cloud user defines the VM resource requirements and in a heterogeneous data center. Most of the above-mentioned works use a VM placement approach with a single-objective to achieve resource utilization maximization or power consumption minimization. This paper addresses two challenges. Firstly, it proposes a new two-objective ILP model to address the offline VMP problem that simultaneously maximizes the usage of PM resources and power consumption efficiency. Finally, the solution is performed in two heterogeneous data centers with different configurations to ascertain the impact of each configuration.

4   Notations

We use the following notations and typographical conventions:

Index conventions

– i and j as subscript denote a virtual machine request and a physical machine index respectively.

The parameters

– N corresponds to the number of virtual machines arriving at the Data Center to be hosted. The VM request numbered i, denoted v_i, $\forall\ 1 \leq i \leq N$, is defined by the tri-tuple $(c_i,\ r_i,\ s_i)$ where c_i, r_i and s_i are the CPU, memory and storage requirements of VM v_i.
– M corresponds to the number of physical machines in the Data Center. The PM numbered j, denoted P_j, $\forall\ 1 \leq j \leq M$ is characterized by the tri-tuple $(C_j,\ R_j,\ S_j)$ where C_j, R_j and S_j are the CPU, memory and storage capacities of PM P_j.

The variables

– The binary variable λ_{ij}. $\lambda_{ij} = 1$ if the VM v_i is hosted by the physical machine P_j. $\lambda_{ij} = 0$, otherwise.
– The binary variable ϕ_j. $\phi_j = 1$, if there is at least one virtual machine hosted by physical machine P_j. $\phi_j = 0$, otherwise.

5   The Model

The Two-Objective ILP model relies on two separate steps to compute the optimal VM-PM mapping, as shown in Fig. 2. Using the previous notations, Step 1 and Step 2 are given in Table 1.

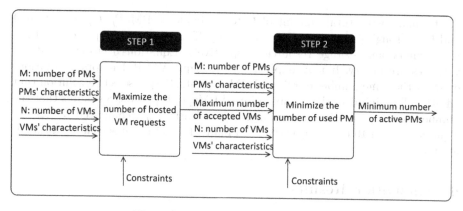

Fig. 2. The two-objective ILP model

Table 1. The two-objective ILP model

Step 1	Step 2
Given N, M, C_j, R_j, S_j, c_i, r_i and s_i	**Given** N, M, C_j, R_j, S_j, c_i, r_i, s_i and ψ_{max}
Maximize	**Minimize**

$$\psi_{max} = \sum_{i=1}^{N}\sum_{j=1}^{M} \lambda_{ij} \qquad (1)$$

$$\theta = \sum_{j=1}^{M} \phi_j \qquad (7)$$

$$\sum_{j=1}^{M} \lambda_{ij} \leq 1, \quad \forall 1 \leq i \leq N \qquad (2)$$

$$\psi_{max} \leq \sum_{i=1}^{N}\sum_{j=1}^{M} \lambda_{ij} \qquad (8)$$

$$\sum_{i=1}^{N} c_i \lambda_{ij} \leq C_j, \quad \forall 1 \leq j \leq M \qquad (3)$$

$$\lambda_{ij} \leq \phi_j, \quad \forall 1 \leq i \leq N, \forall 1 \leq j \leq M \qquad (9)$$

$$\sum_{i=1}^{N} r_i \lambda_{ij} \leq R_j, \quad \forall 1 \leq j \leq M \qquad (4)$$

$$\phi_j \leq \sum_{i=1}^{N} \lambda_{ij}, \quad \forall 1 \leq j \leq M \qquad (10)$$

$$\sum_{i=1}^{N} s_i \lambda_{ij} \leq S_j, \quad \forall 1 \leq j \leq M \qquad (5)$$

2, 3, 4, 5 and 6

$$\lambda_{ij} \in \{0,1\}, \quad \forall 1 \leq i \leq N, \forall 1 \leq j \leq M \qquad (6)$$

$$\phi_j \in \{0,1\}, \quad \forall 1 \leq j \leq M \qquad (11)$$

Step 1 computes the VM-PM mapping with the objective of maximizing ψ_{max}, the number of hosted VM requests. Equations 2 ensures that each VM request v_i is hosted by at most one physical machine P_j. Equations 3 ensures that the total amount of CPU consumed by the VMs hosted at a PM P_j is at most equal to the total amount of CPU available at PM P_j, C_j. Equations 4 and 5 are roughly similar to 3 in that, the CPU resource is replaced by both the memory and storage resources respectively. Equations 6 ensures that λ_{ij} variables are binary. It may happen that multiple VM-PM mapping solutions exist for the same number of rejected VM requests. Step 2 selects a solution that additionally minimizes the number of used PMs, θ. Equations 8 ensures that the number of accepted VM requests must be at least ψ_{max}, computed by Step 1. Equations 9 and 10 define ϕ_j variables. Finally, Eqs. 11 ensures that ϕ_j variables are binary.

6 Simulation Results

In this section, we experimentally evaluate and compare the performance of the TOILP model in two heterogeneous data center configurations with 20 PMs each. The PMs' characteristics for both configurations, called C1 and C2, are given in Table 2(a) and (b) respectively. One may notice that both configurations have almost the same total amount over the CPU, RAM and disk resources. C2 exceeds C1 with 2.5% and 2% over the total usages of CPU and disk respectively.

Table 2. Hetrogeneous data center configurations

(a) First DC Configuration

		C1		
PM	CPU	RAM	DISK	COUNT
PM$_1$	32	64	500	7
PM$_2$	64	128	1500	7
PM$_3$	96	256	3000	6

(b) Second DC Configuration

		C2		
PM	CPU	RAM	DISK	COUNT
PM$_1$	32	64	500	5
PM$_2$	64	128	1500	10
PM$_3$	96	256	3000	5

We generated 50 test-scenarios, that is, 50 different VM requests instances each of which consists of N VM requests generated randomly from a predefined set of VM types (Small (S), Medium (M), Large (L) and XLarge (XL) according to the details given in Table 3. Figure 3 gives a detailed information on the average number of generated VMs of type S, M, L and XL for each value of N. The reason why the TOILP model cannot solve the VMP problem with over 290 VM requests is due to the NP-hardness of the problem. We used Optimization Programming language (OPL) [14] with CPLEX 12.6.3 [15], to solve both steps. The CPLEX solver is run on a windows 10 machine with an Intel Core i7, 2.6 GHz processor and 16 GB RAM. In the following, each couple of figure shows the same simulation results obtained by the TOILP model, considering both data center configurations respectively.

Figure 4 plots the average number of hosted VMs on each PM for both DC configurations for N = 130. Each bar in the plot shows the total number of VMs of type S, M, L, and XL hosted by each of the PMs. Subfigures (a) and (b) show the VM placement computed by Step 1 whereas subfigures (c) and (d) show the

Table 3. The VM configuration.

VM	Vcore	Memory (GB)	Disk (GB)
S	3	4	50
M	4	8	100
L	5	12	150
XL	6	24	250

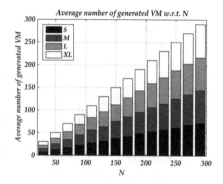

Fig. 3. The average number of generated S, M, L and XL w.r.t. N

VM placement computed by Step 2. One may notice that the number of used PMs computed by Step 2 is lower than the one computed by Step 1.

Figure 5 shows the CPU, RAM and disk usages on each PM for both DC configurations. Subfigures (a) and (d) show the CPU usage. Subfigures (b) and (e) plot the RAM usage. Subfigures (c) and (f) show the disk usage. The top-subfigures from (a) to (f) plot the resource usage computed by Step 1. The subfigures below plot the resource usage computed by Step 2. The height of the white bar shows the amount of available resource at the PM when no VM are hosted. The height of the black bar shows the amount of the consumed resource after hosting some VMs. One may observe that the PM resources are efficiently used in C1 compared to C2. The resource usage is almost equal in each of the PM's dimension. We also notice that the number of used PMs computed by C1 is lower than the one computed by C2. This last result will be investigated in the following.

Figure 6 plots the average number of used PMs w.r.t. N, the total number of VMs to be hosted. We report that Step 2 performs efficiently in both DC configurations with average gains (Step 2 achievement against Step 1 achievement) of 32.45% and 27.53% in C1 and C2 respectively. We notice that the average number of used PMs in C1 is lower than the number of used PMs considering configuration C2. Consequently, configuration C1 should hopefully lead to a better power consumption efficiency compared to C2.

Figure 7 shows the average VM rejection ratio w.r.t. N. The average VM rejection ratio is computed as the ratio of the total number of rejected VMs to the total number of VMs arriving at the DC. We used errorbar plots to show the main VM rejection ratio information for each N. In this plot, the top and bottom bars are the highest and the lowest VM rejection ratio among the fifty generated test-scenarios, while the mid-points denote the average. We notice that in both DC configurations, the number of rejected VMs increases with N as the capacity of available resources per PM is decreasing. We also notice that the average VM rejection ratio computed for configuration C1 is lower than C2, as shown

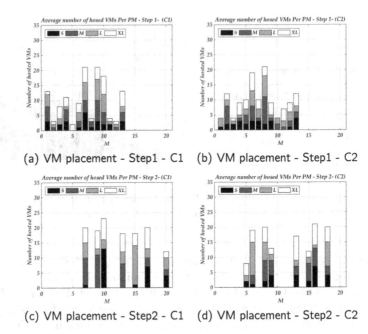

(a) VM placement - Step1 - C1   (b) VM placement - Step1 - C2

(c) VM placement - Step2 - C1   (d) VM placement - Step2 - C2

Fig. 4. The average number of hosted VMs per PM, N = 130

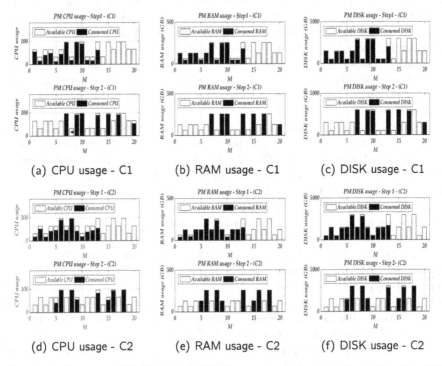

(a) CPU usage - C1   (b) RAM usage - C1   (c) DISK usage - C1

(d) CPU usage - C2   (e) RAM usage - C2   (f) DISK usage - C2

Fig. 5. The averages CPU, RAM and DISK usage on each physical machine, N = 130

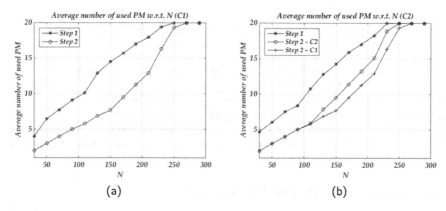

Fig. 6. The average number of used PMs w.r.t. N

in Fig. 7(b). The above results will be explained in details in the subsequent section. Table 4 shows the average rejection ratios for VMs of type S, L, M and XL w.r.t. N. The average rejection rate for each VM type $(T, T = S/M/L/XL)$ is computed as the number of VM rejected of type (T) to the total number of VM requests of type (T). We notice that in both configurations, the VM requests of type L and XL are the most rejected ones. This is mainly related to one of the TOILP's objectives which aims at maximizing the number of hosted VMs. Since, VM of type L and XL are more resource consuming.

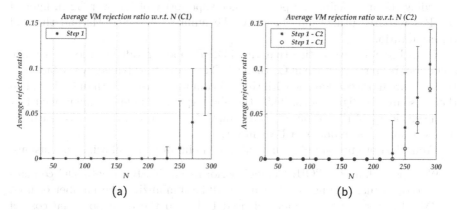

Fig. 7. The average VM rejection ratio w.r.t. N

Figure 8 plots the average total potential cost of resource wastage w.r.t. N. The total potential cost of resource wastage is computed as the sum of all the resource wastage amounts of PMs in the data center. The potential cost of

Table 4. The average rejection rates of S, M, L and XL VM requests

N	C1								C2							
	Step 1				Step 2				Step 1				Step 2			
	S	M	L	XL	S	M	L	XL	S	M	L	XL	S	M	L	XL
230	0	0	0.00008	0.00042	0	0	0	0.00052	0	0	0.00008	0.00668	0	0	0	0.00678
250	0	0.00008	0.00008	0.0116	0	0	0	0.01176	0	0.00008	0.00008	0.03528	0	0	0	0.03544
270	0	0	0	0.04036	0	0	0	0.04036	0	0.00006	0.00014	0.06844	0	0	0.00006	0.06858
290	0	0	0.00006	0.07792	0	0	0	0.078	0	0.00006	0.00012	0.10516	0	0	0	0.10536

resource wastage of the jth PM, RW_j is given by [16]:

$$RW_j = \sum_{l!=k}(R^l - R^k), \qquad \forall 1 \leq j \leq M, \forall 1 \leq l, k \leq 3$$

where, R^l denotes the normalized residual capacity of the lth resource dimension (CPU, RAM, disk), i.e., the ratio of residual resource to total resource. R^k denotes the smallest residual resource rate of all dimensions. We notice that the average total potential cost of resource wastage gain in C1 (60.62%) is higher than in C2 (50.21%) (Step 2 achievement against Step 1 achievement). We also observe that in both DC configurations, the benefit gain of the total potential cost of resource wastage decreases sharply when a set of VMs starts to be rejected ($N \geq 230$). This is due to Step 2's difficulty of balancing the resource usage of each PM as one or more may be exhausted, and others remain unused. This preceding result explains the performance superiority of C1 over C2 in light of the PM resource utilization efficiency, the number of used PMs and the VM rejection ratio.

From Fig. 8(b), we notice that the TOILP model produces a lower average amount of resource wastage in C1 than C2. This can be explained by the fact that the VMs are more compatible with the PM combinations of C1 than C2 based on their resource configurations. This, thereby, explains the above-mentioned fact of the efficiency of PM resource utilization in C1. As a result, more VMs can be hosted using a less number of PMs in C1.

From the obtained simulation results, we point out the following conclusions:

- We report that the TOILP model performs efficiently in both DC configurations, in maximizing the PM usage while minimizing the number of used PMs. In average, the number of used PMs and the total potential cost of resource wastage are reduced by 32.35% and 60.62% respectively.
- The cloud provider should not choose the PM configurations independently of the offered virtual machines. This is due to the degree of compatibility between the VM-PM resource configurations as it has an impact on the amount of resource wastage in the DC.
- We realized that as the amount of the resource wastage is reduced in the DC, the VM rejection is lowered and the number of used PMs is also minimized. This should hopefully lead to lower power consumption in the DC.

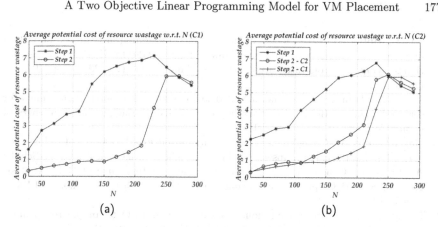

Fig. 8. The average potential cost of resource wastage w.r.t. N

7 Conclusion and Future Work

In this paper, we proposed a new two objective ILP model to address the VM placement problem in cloud service provider (CSP) data centers with heterogeneous PM configurations. The objectives are to improve the resources usage of physical machines while reducing energy consumption in a data center. We evaluated and compared the performances of the proposed solution in two heterogeneous data centers configurations to ascertain the impact of each configuration. Through extensive simulation scenarios, we reported the benefits brought by the TOILP model in both average gains of total potential cost of resource wastage and number of used PMs. We also reported that the cloud provider should not choose the PM configurations independently of the offered Virtual machines. In the future work, we will compare the performances of the TOILP model in both data center architectures (homogeneous and heterogeneous) in order to assess which of the architectures produces a better trade-off between the resource utilization and power consumption efficiency.

References

1. The NIST Definition of Cloud Computing, pp. 2–3 (2018). http://nvlpubs.nist.gov/nistpubs/Legacy/SP/nistspecialpublication800-145.pdf
2. Lopez-Pires, F., Baran, B.: Virtual machine placement literature (2018). https://arxiv.org/pdf/1506.01509.pdf
3. Li, Y., Tang, X., Cai, W.: Dynamic bin packing for on-demand cloud resource allocation. IEEE Trans. Parallel Distrib. Syst. **27**(1), 157–170 (2016)
4. Ribas, B.C., Suguimoto, R.M., Montano, R.A.N.R., Silva, F., Castilho, M.: PBFVMC: a new pseudo-Boolean formulation to virtual-machine consolidation. In: Brazilian Conference on Intelligent Systems (BRACIS), pp. 201–206 (2013)
5. Chaisiri, S., Lee, B.S., Niyato, D.: Optimal virtual machine placement across multiple cloud providers. In: IEEE Asia-Pacific Services Computing Conference (APSCC), pp. 103–110 (2009)

6. Shi, L., Butler, B., Botvich, D., Jennings, B.: Provisioning of requests for virtual machine sets with placement constraints in IaaS clouds. In: IFIP/IEEE International Symposium on Integrated Network Management (IM 2013), pp 499–505 (2013)

7. Van, H.N., Tran, F.D., Menaud, J.M.: Autonomic virtual resource management for service hosting platforms. In: Workshop on in Software Engineering Challenges of Cloud Computing, pp. 1–8 (2009)

8. Geyer-Schulz, A., Ovelgönne, M.: The randomized greedy modularity clustering algorithm and the core groups graph clustering scheme. In: Gaul, W., Geyer-Schulz, A., Baba, Y., Okada, A. (eds.) German-Japanese Interchange of Data Analysis Results. SCDAKO, pp. 17–36. Springer, Cham (2014). https://doi.org/10.1007/978-3-319-01264-3_2

9. Dhingra, A., Paul, S.: Green cloud: heuristic based BFO technique to optimize resource allocation. Indian J. Sci. Technol. **7**(5), 685–691 (2014)

10. Tang, M., Pan, S.: A hybrid genetic algorithm for the energy-efficient virtual machine placement problem in data center. Neural Process. Lett. **41**(2), 611–621 (2015)

11. Shi, L., Butler, B., Wang, R., Botvich, D., Jennings, B.: Optimal placement of virtual machines with different placement constraints in IAAS clouds. In: Symposium on ICT and Energy Efficiency and Workshop on Information Theory and Security (CIICT), pp. 202–206 (2012)

12. Shi, L., Butler, B., Botvich, D., Jennings, B.: Provisioning of requests for virtual machine sets with placement constraints in IaaS clouds. In: IFIP/IEEE International Symposium on Integrated Network Management (IM), pp. 499–501 (2013)

13. Sun, M., Gu, W., Zhang, X., Shi, H., Zhang, W.: A matrix transformation algorithm for virtual machine placement in cloud. In: IEEE International Conference on Trust, Security and Privacy in Computing and Communications (TrustCom), pp. 1778–1783 (2013)

14. Modeling with OPL (2018). http://www-01.ibm.com/software/commerce/optimization/modeling/

15. IBM Cplex Optimizer, January 2018. http://www-01.ibm.com/software/commerce/optimization/cplex-optimizer/

16. Xu, J., Fortes, J.A.B.: Multi-objective virtual machine placement in virtualized data center environments. In: IEEE/ACM Conference on Cyber, Physical and Social Computing (CPSCom) Green Computing and Communications (Green-Com), pp. 179–188 (2010)

Towards an Optimized Energy Consumption of Resources in Cloud Data Centers

Sara Diouani[(⊠)] and Hicham Medromi

Engineering Research Laboratory (LRI), System Architecture Team,
ENSEM, Hassan II University, Casablanca, Morocco
diouanisara19@gmail.com, hmedromi@yahoo.fr

Abstract. Over the last few years, cloud computing has become a prominent paradigm. It promises to offer to users cost-effective and on-demand decentralized services, in terms of computing, memory, storage, etc., without the need for large infrastructure investments. Moreover, with the growing number of data centers resources, much higher levels of energy are being consumed. Also, the increasing level of associated carbon dioxide is emitted in the air, which consequently, raises the costs. Considering that there is an extreme growth in demand for Data Centers cloud computing requiring high computational complexity, there is an utmost need to take sufficient measures to lower the risk of energy demand. Hence, efficient energy-aware techniques are required to assure proper performance with regards to Service Level Agreements (SLA). In this work, we highlighted the issue of Virtual Machines (VMs) allocation in cloud computing data centers, and how to better manage the placement of VMs in order to optimize performance and reduce energy consumption. In our proposed solution, we will focus on minimizing the number of Physical Machines (PMs) hosting the VMs and utilize them as sufficient as possible.

Keywords: Cloud computing · Data center · Energy consumption
Virtual machine · Physical machine · OpenStack · VM placement
SLA · Virtualization · Optimization · Resource allocation · Migration
Consolidation

1 Introduction

Cloud computing is spreading more and more into different fields of our everyday life. It is a sophisticated technology that is used everywhere without being totally conscious of it. IT Companies, developers, or even simple individuals could employ cloud computing services by the use of infrastructure as a service (IaaS) and platform as a service (PaaS) [1]. This technology permits the small and big companies such as Amazon and Microsoft to obtain good infrastructure for data storing with a high computing performance through Internet network. Moreover, even the traditional Web services including Web search, Webmail, e-learning, millions of Internet of Things (IoT) devices and tools also transfer their billions of generated data to the cloud computing.

© Springer Nature Switzerland AG 2018
N. Boudriga et al. (Eds.): UNet 2018, LNCS 11277, pp. 179–185, 2018.
https://doi.org/10.1007/978-3-030-02849-7_16

Technically speaking, one or multiple data centers are necessary to offer to the end users the cloud computing needed services, since the data volume is under an extreme and speedy growth and evolution. In fact, every data center is composed of servers with multiple of PMs that can host hundreds or even thousands of VMs. For example, to preserve its cloud services, Google, which is one of the huge public cloud computing providers, uses more than 15 data centers all over the world [2].

The cloud computing is based on the Virtualization technology. This concept allows the cloud provider to run multiple operating system instances at the same time by the use of a single PM. We can have many advantages on the VMs side including an easier maintenance, better portability, etc. Also, the isolation of operating systems is offered by the Virtualization technology and which enhance the security system. Since essential hardware components are shared between VMs, they are optimized; they are and should always be used at their maximum range and capability. Without forgetting that the computing resources in data center affect the VM performance during the VM creation, migration, and maintenance.

2 Problem Statement and Formulation

Running multiple large and big data center in cloud computing consumes a high margin of energy and electrical power for processing data, storage, and network communication [3, 4]. In fact, different previous studies have proven that data centers consume more power than they really require [5].

This issue harmfully influences the energy crisis and brings tremendous economic problems. Also, any data center generates a considerable amount of heat which must be dispersed by adoption of high power cooling systems. The negative environmental impact of these systems is the resulting carbon dioxide emission in the air.

As a result, the reduction of energy consumption in cloud data center is a very important goal to achieve. Actually, most of the proposed solutions and techniques targeting energy efficiency improvement in Infrastructure as a Service (IaaS) cloud data centers primarily focalize on managing computing elements, particularly on server consolidation techniques [6, 7] and by changing the mode of idle resources to a power saving or to operating mode. Considering CPU and RAM as energy parameters, in [8], the researchers select VMs to consolidate from the overloaded or underloaded host for migrating them to another appropriate host. Also, the idle hosts are turned into energy saving-mode [9]. Also, in [10], VMs are selected to be migrated from overloaded hosts by taking into account CPU, RAM, and Bandwidth. After, the empty hosts are switched to the sleep mode.

By adopting this approach, the number of turned on physical servers and machines hosting the active virtual ones is clearly minimized. Also, the resources dynamic regulation of performance level may efficaciously decrease their energy consumption.

Moreover, according to the most notable researchers in the last years, and which are related to the minimization of energy consumption in datacenter cloud computing, all of the major energy parameters (e.g. CPU, memory and so forth) necessary to ensure an ideal energy efficiency are not taken into consideration.

3 Proposed Solution

In this work, we propose our architecture for optimized resource management, considering all major energy parameters that influence the efficiency of the cloud data center energy.

In fact, the main energy parameters include the CPUs, the memory amount, the disk storage space, the quantity of transmitted message in the network (bandwidth) and the available amount of input/output operations per second (IOPS) on the physical machine.

Moreover, the VM placement relies on some distinct Service Level Agreement constraints including:

- The affinity constraint: between couples of VMs refer to the aim to get an optimal placement which considers the fact that two VMs for instance, must be allocated on the same physical machine. This constraint is related to interdependent VMs that use jointly data with each other in short predefined deadlines.
- The security constraint: could be, for instance, separating two VMs on different servers (or even two data centers), so as to ensure their isolation.
- The migration constraint: could be related to executing the VM placement only on a set of accurately stated machines, or even to keep a VM on the same server (or even same data center).

We also, defined other energy parameters including the total number of VMs allocated on a PM, the total number of PMs used, the number of reallocations or displacements of a VM, the period of time of VM interruption in the migration phase, the percentage of maximum and minimum use of VMs/PMs and the response time of a task at the level of a VM (SLA).

The aspect of the sustainability of data is also interesting; assuring in real time the replication of each data to multiple hosts/data centers (such as a primary and backup host).

Our solution uses a system model that knows the state of the system at any moment. It is based on dynamically managing VM distribution in the data center, in terms of performance, cost, availability system and energy instantly consumed. This is done by adopting optimized resource allocation and live migration through a decision mechanism. Also, the approach must effectively manage the strict SLA requirements.

As the Fig. 1 shows, the proposed Cloud model platform follows various management stages including collecting monitoring data, exploiting these data to calculate a better VMs placement, draw a plan to reallocate and manage virtual machines in the physical machines, and at the end applying the proposed actions.

The data resources consumption collection module is responsible for periodic monitoring, and collection of consumption data and load resources usage from the cluster's physical machines. These data could be CPU, disk, and memory usage, etc. Also, the electricity collection is achieved by the use of power consumption measurement tools, such as Power Meter or Wattmeter.

The analysis component uses a built-in scheduler algorithm to make decisions. This model determines whether to trigger the implementation of the algorithm by evaluating

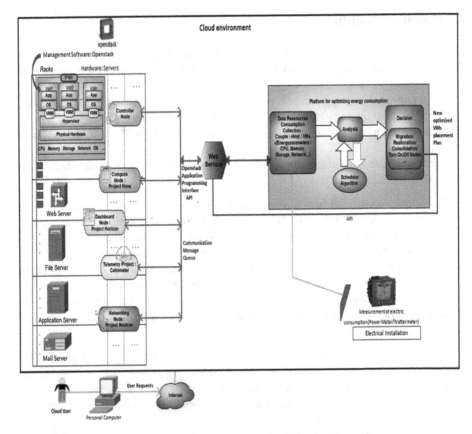

Fig. 1. Overview of the proposed solution architecture

the results of resource data use. We designed this algorithm in a way that it does not depend on a particular type of workload and does not require any knowledge of the applications running on the VMs. And its execution requires accurate power usage parameters and high-resolution measurements.

The input of the algorithm is the set of each host with its VMs allocated, the collected results of the different resource information and the specified energy consumption parameters in order to decide which VM to migrate and where to migrate it. The execution of this algorithm provides us, as output, a new optimized VMs placement plan with a set of nodes under loaded to be exploited further (which one we can deactivate, and turn on later ...).

The decision component is responsible (based on the results obtained from the scheduler algorithm) for migrating the VMs to the specified hosts according to the instructions of the analysis model.

Technically speaking, the architecture applies the modules of OpenStack which provides a large range of metrics and power consumption information on the use of resources for energy consumption estimation. Also, it is an open source platform for cloud computing that offers Infrastructure as a Service (IaaS) which may be used as a private, public or hybrid cloud [11], where we integrate our algorithm and benefit from the Application Programming Interface (APIs) to communicate with the outside and to control the allocation using Kernel-based Virtual Machine (KVM).

In fact, in this work, we integrated our proposed monitoring solution with a cloud platform OpenStack, which is very rewarding to the computing community research and cloud practitioners that wish to work in this field.

OpenStack is a collection of components that cooperate to provide IaaS functionality. Each component manages a different aspect of the cloud and uses a message bus to communicate with other components. All components generate notification messages when events occur (such as instances created or destroyed). Capturing these messages was the first data source for the component named Ceilometer.

The Ceilometer provides a collection of metering data on managed virtual resources based on the use of the controlling monitor [12]. The exploitation of these collected data takes place during the analysis phase by the use of the Nova_scheduler which is an OpenStack component to determine on which host a VM instance is going to be executed.

Also, our platform uses the Dashboard component named Horizon, which is a web application that allows us to interact with the services OpenStack and monitor them (launch VMs, configure IP addresses and manage access ...).

In the analysis phase and for the management of the computes on OpenStack, the exploitation of the collected data takes place by the use of the Nova component. It is also used for the communication with different hypervisors, and the execution of the instances requested by the user. This stage also involves the execution of the programmed scheduling algorithm.

The algorithm consists essentially of two major phases: first, we begin by calculating the use of resources on the input physical machines to ignore the filled one with all VMs that turn above, and then we select the list of those that need to reallocate their VMs. Each time, we check if there are any empty physical machines (if there is an empty PM, we turn it off by IPMI call).

It is necessary to begin by calculating the use of resources on a physical machine, not to start the computation by the VMs, because, as long as the physical machine is filled, it can be ignored and ignore all the VMs that turn above.

The use of retrieved resources (CPU, memory, network, disk, IOPS usage) and the number of all VMs on the PM are used as a reference to be compared with minimum and maximum limits of the parameters already defined.

Also, we calculate the VMs IOPS sum of the host and store it (this information is used as reference to compare with a limit of IOPS sum). If the use of resources retrieved is lower than the limits defined, we select this host for migration and add it to a list of hosts. And if not, we go to the next host on the host's list. Ultimately, we will have the list of hosts with limited use of defined resources.

Second, we take the first host from the returned list and we search in the list of VMs which one to migrate to this host. And we check if the host is empty (if it is empty, we turn it off by IPMI call). And each time we test if this host can receive another VM of this list or not (in case of host saturation, we pass to another one in the host's list to be reallocated).

Also, we check on the VMs list if the first VM cannot be migrated (according to SLA constraints). In that case, we remove it from the VMs list as long as the list is not empty. We check whether the use of the resources of the host's VMs with those of the selected VM exceeds or is below the minimum defined limit. If the use of resources retrieved is lower than the limits defined, we select this VM for migration. And if not, we go to the next VM on the VMs list.

The proposed algorithm is threshold-based; we opt for migrating virtual machines on hosts that have low use of defined energy parameters such as CPU. If we migrate VMs to a host that has a high CPU usage, we can overload the host and block it. In a concrete manner, the PM resource parameters must reach 70 to 85% (ideally). It is useful to mark each host as saturated one (a host with resource use of 90% approximately: no possibility to add another VM on this host). That is why we define the minimum and maximum limits used during the execution of the algorithm. Also, it should be checked each time if there are empty hosts to turn them off by IPMI calls, or even turn them whenever needed.

4 Conclusion and Future Works

In cloud computing, the data center performs the storage, retrieval, recovery and the processing of the cloud user data. And since the cloud demand is increased, and its data centers infrastructure is growing too overtime, an enormous amount of electrical energy is consumed with the emission of a large amount of carbon dioxide in the air.

Therefore, it is necessary to optimize the physical data centers for energy efficiency and thus contributes to the environmental protection. Multiple energetic efficiency techniques based essentially on virtualization, migration, and consolidation have been implemented.

In fact, in this paper, we have proposed an optimized resources management solution which considers major energy parameters and major possible constraints of VMs allocation in physical machines so as to ensure energy efficiency by keeping energy-performance trade-off in concern.

To continue our work, we will detail and implement the scheduler algorithm while respecting the defined Service Level Agreements.

References

1. Armbrust, M., et al.: Above the Clouds: A Berkeley View of Cloud Computing. University of California, Berkeley UCBEECS-2009-28 February, vol. 28, January 2009
2. Gordin, I., Graur, A., Balan, D.: Development of eco-friendly cloud computing environments. In: 2017 14th International Conference on Engineering of Modern Electric Systems (EMES), pp. 140–144 (2017)
3. Baliga, J., Ayre, R.W.A., Hinton, K., Tucker, R.S.: Green cloud computing: balancing energy in processing, storage, and transport. Proc. IEEE **99**(1), 149–167 (2011)
4. Greenberg, A., Hamilton, J., Maltz, D.A., Patel, P.: The cost of a cloud: research problems in data center networks. SIGCOMM Comput. Commun. Rev. **39**(1), 68–73 (2008)

5. Delforge, P.: America's data centers are wasting huge amounts of energy. National Resources Defense Council, Issue Paper, 06 February 2015
6. Beloglazov, A., Buyya, R.: Optimal online deterministic algorithms and adaptive heuristics for energy and performance efficient dynamic consolidation of virtual machines in cloud data centers. Concurr. Comput. Pract. Exp. **24**, 1397–1420 (2012)
7. Mastroianni, C., Meo, M., Papuzzo, G.: Probabilistic consolidation of virtual machines in self-organizing cloud data centers. IEEE Trans. Cloud Comput. **1**(2), 215–228 (2013)
8. Yadav, R., Zhang, W., Chen, H., Guo, T.: MuMs: Energy-aware VM selection scheme for cloud data center. In: Proceedings of the 28th International Workshop on Database and Expert Systems Applications (DEXA), Lyon, France, pp. 132–136, August 2017
9. Rossigneux, F., Lefevre, L., Gelas, J.P., de Assuncao, M.D.: A generic and extensible framework for monitoring energy consumption of OpenStack clouds. In: 2014 IEEE Fourth International Conference on Big Data and Cloud Computing, pp. 696–702 (2014)
10. Khoshkholghi, M.A., Derahman, M.N., Abdullah, A., Subramaniam, S., Othman, M.: Energy-efficient algorithms for dynamic virtual machine consolidation in cloud data centers. IEEE Access **5**, 10709–10722 (2017)
11. Rani, A., Peddoju, S.K.: A workload-aware VM placement algorithm for performance improvement and energy efficiency in OpenStack cloud. In: 2017 International Conference on Computing, Communication and Automation (ICCCA), pp. 841–846 (2017)
12. Cima, V., Grazioli, B., Murphy, S., Bohnert, T.M.: Adding energy efficiency to Openstack. In: Sustainable Internet and ICT for Sustainability (SustainIT), pp. 1–8 (2015)

Ubiquitous Internet of Things: Emerging Technologies and Breakthroughs

Temperature Monitoring and Forecast System in Remote Areas with 4.0G LTE Mobile Technologies

Kevin Alexandre Riaño Vargas[1], Octavio José Salcedo Parra[1,2(✉)], and Lewys Correa Sánchez[1]

[1] Faculty of Engineering, Universidad Distrital "Francisco José de Caldas", Bogotá, D.C., Colombia
{karianov, lcorreas}@correo.udistrital.edu.co,
osalcedo@udistrital.edu.co

[2] Department of Systems and Industrial Engineering, Faculty of Engineering, Universidad Nacional de Colombia, Bogotá, D.C., Colombia
ojsalcedop@unal.edu.co

Abstract. The need to monitor areas of high risk in terms of temperature indexes has included two important elements for its compliance: monitoring and forecast of records in an environment. Performing this procedure manually is inefficient as it provides a flat perspective and can't predict the state of the environment rigorously. Software systems are contemporary elements in constant refinement which satisfy the emerging needs within a certain context. The monitoring and forecasting processes can be hence automated and that tends to lead to a better supervision of the risks present in the environment. This article presents a proposal for the supervision of high-risk areas, through temperature records that can be managed through the design of a software system with the implementation of mobile 4.0G LTE technologies, aimed at efficiency and effectiveness in the notification of the environmental status. Finally, the development of a remote temperature monitoring and forecast system using mobile technologies leads to conclude that the fuzzy logic prediction system's quadratic error is lower than 2.6%. Additionally, future work is presented from the research standpoint according to the emergence of new perspectives related to this developing software system.

Keywords: Mobile technologies · Predictive system · Software engineering
Telematics · Temperature monitoring

1 Introduction

Colombia's interest in forestry has been booming lately, as the media are becoming more and more aware of environmental catastrophes, but it is clear that the response times for these calamities are still inefficient.

A rapid assessment of the situation in the department of Arauca shows that the number of forest fires is small, yet there was great damage over a large area. Meanwhile, in Cundinamarca, the number of fires is high but the number of damaged

© Springer Nature Switzerland AG 2018
N. Boudriga et al. (Eds.): UNet 2018, LNCS 11277, pp. 189–201, 2018.
https://doi.org/10.1007/978-3-030-02849-7_17

hectares is lower, making it possible to emphasize on the urban characteristic as an advantage to act immediately once the fire is detected. Of course, such characteristic is specifically treated from a technological point of view. A more detailed assessment shows that the relationship between the number of fires and the number of affected hectares per department is closely related. Each fire is causing direct damage to the hectares within risk-prone areas specially when fires are not prevented but dealt with once they have been detected in the surrounding area.

In addition to the environmental damage caused by fires within the country, each case shares a preventive detection factor which can potentially lead to the efficient control of fires in order to regulate stability in risk-prone environments. The key to analyze the causality of these events consists on reading the temperature in the environment before, during and after the fire, because it shows intrinsic contrast with the environment's stability. Gathering these data essentially allows generating statistical reports in order to provide information and analysis. Bringing together this research with environmental processes as an alternative forest fire detection and prediction strategy would mean a significant advance in the social and ecological development of the country.

The present research is carried out with the motivation to contribute on a social scale so that the technological resources truly constitute a tool of progress for the community. The duty of every Computer Engineer consists on bringing effective software-based solutions for a specific population. It is important to mention that the project is born from the evidence of an increasing contemporary problem which is expanding on a nation-wide (and possibly international) scale such as forest fires. It requires a strategic approach that goes beyond research and analysis, managing to implement a system with the necessary components to transcend in the world of software technologies and bring with it an effective solution to a problematic of great importance.

Furthermore, the project is also developed so that the proposed methodology can have multiple effects on society in terms of knowledge, leading to new proposals for the surveillance of areas risking fires or any scenario that requires development-oriented software for structuring and documentation. Initially, it is important to establish the two fundamental axes of research rationale: methodological justification and practical justification, since the characteristics used in each section are essential to demonstrate the motivation and need to adopt this project.

Arguing in terms of methodological justification, the present research project is essentially a software engineering project, based on the development with nuances of quality and documentation directed towards a field of action, and it is precisely this feature that makes it somewhat formal within the scientific institution. It is unconceivable to speak of a development process that is built on the pillars of software engineering, without being strict with this branch of human knowledge as a globally accepted science.

However, it is not enough to mention software engineering explicitly as a form of motivation; all the techniques required for research must be outlined, understanding that it is an institution that is constantly evolving within short periods of time. Yet, it is possible to establish that the main instruments are quality and software documentation, in the sense that they are the two most outstanding properties that currently identify software engineering projects. From such instruments, *methodologies* are derived by the knowledge community. Finally, the reasoning for *practical justification* becomes more understandable once the pragmatic objective of software design is agreed upon as well as its functionality.

2 Background

The surface area of forest forests has been changing during the last 25 years, fires, pests, indiscriminate felling or winter seasons are the main causes of their decline. According to figures from the Food and Agriculture Organization of the United Nations (FAO) in 2015, a total of 3999 million hectares of forest area were registered, a figure that in years much later was significantly higher, annually by percentage The rate of change can be represented as 0.13 decremental, which generates an alarming situation and a broad field of research to present solutions and manage to slow or at least gradually reduce that damage.

Many research and developments in different parts of the world are aimed at providing and giving significant contributions to the problem of forest fires understood as one of the worst consequences of the prevention, control and timely reaction of these natural or intentional disasters. Independent models of the technologies aim to analyze different fire elements, current environmental elements or generate knowledge bases for the creation of systems for increasingly accurate predictions and with the minimum error rate.

The use of Sensor Networks and Wireless Actors (WSANs) (Fig. 1) as a strategy for detecting and extinguishing fire represent a great contribution, due to its form of implementation seeking the minimum of energy consumption and obtaining Expected results [2].

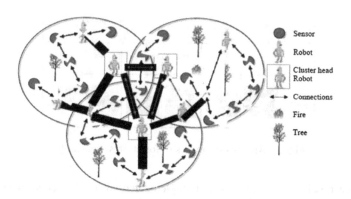

Fig. 1. WSAN implementation. Source: [2]

On the other hand, the direct analysis of the smoke resulting from the first fires generates a starting point to be able to predict new possible scenarios or fire activity, to identify key factors in the smoke and to carry out a corresponding morphological processing. Then, analyzing the rate of false 2 positives and the rate of recognition of the results of these experiments, it selects the combination of direction of motion, high frequency energy based on the wavelet transformation and compactness to constitute the final recognition vectors [3, 4].

On the other hand, the construction of Unmanned Aerial Vehicles (UAVs), solves the problem of the surveillance and detection of forest fires, even when a failure occurs in one or more UAV within the perimeter of surveillance and control. Having a scenario similar to the Fig. 2 with a fault included and presenting the reaction of the UAVs involved in the attention of the natural disaster [5].

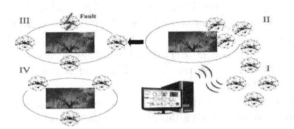

Fig. 2. Forest fire monitoring. Source: [5]

The design of an intelligent platform developed for the recognition and response to disasters using a deep forest-based forest fire monitoring technique using images acquired from an unmanned aerial vehicle with an optical sensor. Through training for the set of images (see Fig. 3) of past forest fires, the proposed deep learning based forest fire monitoring technique is designed to make human judgment for a new image of Entry is automatically whether the forest fire exists or not [6].

Label-2	Fire			Non-fire		
Label-6	Fire-nighttime	Fire-daytime	Smoke	Spring-fall	Summer	Winter
Training images						

Fig. 3. Analysis of images of forest fires. Source: [6]

Another possibility developed and implemented, using the concept of thermal infrared channel (TIR), which contains wavelengths sensitive to the emission of heat. And taking advantage of the fact that forest fires can be characterized by peaks of intensity in TIR images. A fully automatic method of detecting forest fires from TIR satellite images based on the theory of the random field [7] is proposed (Fig. 4).

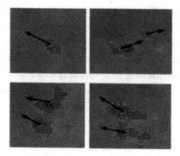

Fig. 4. Detection of forest fire and possible propagation. Source: [7]

The work developed in 'ESS-IM applied to forest fire prediction: Parameters tuning for a heterogeneous configuration' represents a study of calibration of the evolutionary-statistical system with the evolutionary parameters of the island model (Evolutionary-Statistical System with Island Model ESS-IM) (Fig. 5).

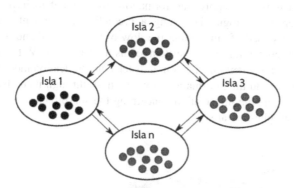

Fig. 5. Island-based parallelization scheme. Source: [8]

ESS-IM is a general-parallel uncertainty reduction method applied to the prediction of forest fire propagation [8].

The prevention work not only remains to be able to predict a possible fire, but on the contrary goes beyond, to the point of analyzing the possible propagations or factors that can greatly increase the current emergency, therefore, the implementation and construction of A system based on and expressed in cellular automata capable of simulating and effectively predicting the propagation tendency of the forest fire in various conditions represents a vital support for the treatment of fires already generated and at risk of propagation in the affected area [9].

Within the proposal of design and appropriation of the different existing techniques that contribute to the construction of a much more robust device, it has the work of fuzzy logic, where the possibility to predict and anticipate scenarios of forest disasters, includes the current proposal as an important and key component for greater support and better intervention in the different frameworks in which they can be presented. This is how the work developed in [10] is a great investigative and supportive contribution Where an "approach on board fuzzy logic" is presented to identify and detect active fire spots in the Brazilian Amazon forest considering the separability of the spectral characteristics of the fire considering it a valuable contribution to the current research and development of a device that includes knowledge And accurate predictions of possible forest risks.

3   Methodology

Figure 6 is the representation of the methodology that will allow the development of research, in terms of its most representative components during the management phases, and the relationships of the main components associated to the proposed system. It has an objective context, which can be understood as the plant where there will be installation of a physical assembly, which will allow to manage sensorial data flows, through a temperature sensor, to bring the notion of the state in which the environment is That you want to monitor and follow up. The system will be able to capture this data flow, and apply transformations to its input to have the prediction module based on fuzzy logic, i.e. using a predictive component, can extend the monitoring properly made from reading the flow of information, and to follow up the possible states of temperature as the system learns its data entry. With this, the system will reproduce the competent information to its telecommunication module with mobile devices, in order to send the information flow to a user, through its mobile technology, so that it can consume the information concerning the surveillance and supervision of A potential catastrophe risk area.

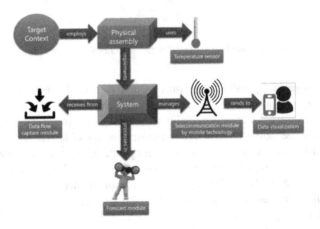

Fig. 6. Illustration on research methodology. Source: Authors

In this sense, it is also proposed to make a process specification, which is contained within the framework in Scrum, and is the life cycle in Cascade, for the moment of implementation, since it is expected that by that time A complete specification of requirements, and have an advantage over the progress in software development in terms of quality and documentation.

In the Table 1 it is possible to appreciate the structure of 4 the data to be handled during the experimental development of the system. This table contains specific aspects about the details that will be taken into account for the presentation of the implementation and results obtained for the eventual analysis. This information establishes how each of the methods and techniques that will allow the monitoring and monitoring of temperature through the system will be performed in the sense presented by the experimentation documented here and the process to be followed to consume the product information. It is necessary to clarify that in the data of capture pulsations, it is a configuration available for the sending of data obtained sensorially, by reason of each interval of time, so that the amount of registers exposed for the experiment covers a period of time in the That the correct analysis can be provided and thus offer the services developed in the system.

Table 1. I data structure

Description of the data		
Concept	Datatype	Units
Temperature	Numerical	Celsius Degrees [°C]
Description of the experiment		
Capture	Sensor LM35	
Technology	4.0G LTE	
Visualization	Mobile device (Android)	
Capture pulses	Ten (10) seconds (sec.)	
Number of records	One hundred (100)	
Description of the experimental plant		
Dimension	13.4 m^3	
Window	On a wall with 1.5 m^2	
Door	On a wall with 1.5 m^2	
City	Bogotá D.C.	
Season	May 2017	

4 Implementation

4.1 Deployment of the Project

The deployment of the project is possible to understand it through the diagrams of nodes and artifacts, being a software system according to the standardization of documentation and the quality of development.

(1) Node Diagram: It should be mentioned that the communication flow between the nodes follows a sequential pattern, as the information is traveling from a server to a client, however, it is understood that there is a constant data capture from the microcontroller device, which causes The flow of communication is continuous and provides a more appropriate and sustainable use of software.

(2) Artifact Diagram: In Fig. 7 it is possible to observe a more concrete representation of the final devices that are part of the software deployment. These devices are the ones that make possible the transformation of the information through the flow of processes, to arrive from a capture in a zone of study, towards a visualization of the information.

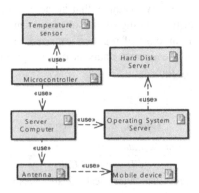

Fig. 7. Deploy through the artifact diagram. Source: Authors

4.2   Application on Android

In the same order of implementation, I conceived the construction of a mechanism to achieve the emission by the software system and the reception by the Android customers, through the notifications that this operating system provides. Thus, the operation established for the creation, sending and reading of notifications is displayed, as the software system is in its monitoring and control work. Within this operation it is highlighted the assignment of a single token or identifier to each client, which is registered by the server provided on the server side of the software, which then uses the messaging service provided by Google called Firebase Cloud Messaging Who is responsible for sending the notification created from the control and monitoring proposed by the application built.

Therefore, each user interested in receiving such notifications complies with this procedure and is subscribed to receive notifications of the process of recording and controlling temperatures in the area that is of interest to them.

4.3 Calculations for the Transmit Antenna

Due to the need to transmit the information to a mobile device, it is necessary to implement an antenna with 4G technology, and for this, it is necessary to calculate some parameters in order to obtain the desired assembly.

(1) Initial Parameters: In the Eqs. 1a and 1b the initial parameters are presented, so that it is possible to begin by indicating the desired transmission frequency and the function associated with the transmission of the signal.

$$f = 3Ghz \tag{1a}$$

$$U = \cos^5 \theta \tag{1b}$$

(2) Main Values: In the set of Eqs. 2 the calculation for the APBW and FNPW standards is made, first with the declaration of assignments to the functions of the proposed signal in the part 2a; And then finding the values for 2θ in each standard in the part 2b.

$$\cos^5 \theta = 0 \quad \cos^5 \theta = \frac{1}{\sqrt{2}} \tag{2a}$$

$$2\theta = \pi \quad 2\theta = 0,736098 \tag{2b}$$

(3) Radiation power: In the set of Eqs. 3 the procedure is performed to calculate the expected radiation power for the antenna, according to the initial parameters, so that in the part 3a the associated declaration is made with the equation of the radiating power [17] in the part 3b the substitution is made by the initial function of the signal; And in the part 3c the result associated with the radiative power is displayed, after operating on the proposed calculation.

$$P_{rad} = \int_0^{2\pi} \int_0^{\frac{\pi}{2}} U \sin(\theta) \, . \, d\theta \, . \, d\Phi \tag{3a}$$

$$P_{rad} = \int_0^{2\pi} \int_0^{\frac{\pi}{2}} \cos^5(\theta) \sin(\theta) \, . \, d\theta \, . \, d\Phi \tag{3b}$$

$$P_{rad} = \frac{\pi}{3} \tag{3c}$$

4.4 Experimental Test with Field Data

In the Fig. 8 the result of the implementation on the developed system, in terms of the temperature captures in an experimental field room, located in the city of Bogota D.C., in Colombia during the present year, is exposed. In this figure the temperature values in degrees celsius [oC] can be seen at different times, captured at ten [10] min pulsations between registers. It is important to note that the times were taken in negative due to the use of this information as an empirical element to demonstrate the operation of the fuzzy system later. The Fig. 8 places the time variable in the iterations of the hundred records established during the data structure, to transform this region to the dimension of the temperature variable recorded during the experiment. The understanding of the values of these variables is equated between 14 °C minimum and 20 °C maximum during the collection of information within the system, and the statistical mean of these numerical values is concentrated at 17 °C. This graph interprets the scenario of the experimentation without allusion to the totality of the records and supports the comparison with the result of the fuzzy system of prediction implemented.

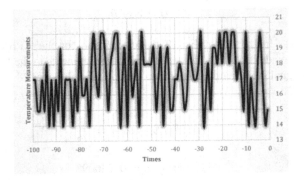

Fig. 8. Experimental temperature records. Source: Authors

5   Analysis of Results

Table 2 sets forth the result of the calculation related to the sum of the quadratic error obtained from the field test with the fuzzy logic based prediction system, rather than for service automation systems for the monitoring and supervision of Remote areas is an emerging research challenge, whether they are dealt with computational elements for the analysis of forest environments [3, 5, 9], or through the learning of machines using cybernetic automata [6, 10, 11].

Table 2. Sum of the quadratic error during the experiment

E	220, 85

From the analysis related to the analysis of forest environments [3, 5, 9] it was able to interpret environmental variables, such as temperature, atmospheric pressure, carbon dioxide level in air; And environmental contexts of the plants on the physical assemblages, which were not parameterized for the experimentation of this research project, at the same time that this research concentrated its interest in the independence by the scenario of implementation and in the domain of the system of Software itself.

While machine-directed analysis using cybernetic automata [6, 10, 11] interpreted the problem from a more control approach, and certainly with a more dense mathematical rationale, In spite of the fact that in this research the value of being implemented under the ideology of software development in the provision of computer services was added on the environmental states that represent a study area that can potentially be forest or high risk relative to temperature, With the systemic implications that include more scenarios than those proposed when establishing a data plan.

In fact, in each work that is directed to the resolution of a problem with some criterion of uncertainty, it must contemplate the scenario of the tolerable error of the designed system, so that the future work is the optimization of this factor to increase the credibility of the product.

6 Conclusions

The presentation of the temperature monitoring and forecast system has defined the software development process, insofar as it has met the project's goal with the implementation of mobile 4.0G LTE technologies to offer a remote computer service. This provided a predictive analysis for system feedback with the intention of providing decision-making support for high-risk areas, measurable through their temperature records.

The development of the research software included in the nuances of analysis with previous research works has contributed to a refined system to provide computer services without surpassing a 2.6% quadratic error under experimental conditions. The information management procedure has been overseen leading to the reduction of the quadratic error from 2.2085% to 0.0013%. The control of the variables in the software model supports any practical scenario where it is installed.

These figures related to the total quadratic error are intended to justify the importance of the integrity of the information provided by the fuzzy-based predictive system stating that it does not exceed a high error rate and also allows tuning parameters under multiple implementation conditions, with the idea of reducing the impact of the error under the desired prediction, as evidenced by the changes from 7, 10, 14 and 16, to 0.024, 0.004, 18.131, and 25.076 in the constants B1, B2, B3 and B4, respectively, within the logic-based compressor.

However, the system for temperature monitoring and surveillance in remote areas with mobile 4.0G LTE technologies challenges research fields with interest on improving the conditions for decision making in environments that represent a problem for a specific population. The methodology described above refers to the continuous improvement of the system which defines a candidate variable as it requires the on-demand installation in different plants. It can handle aspects such as atmospheric pressure, carbon levels in the air and circulation patterns of wave motion which can lead to a more sophisticated surveillance; Introducing new variables into the fuzzy system based on logical rules could avoid the constant shift of parameters necessary for error reduction so the model would be oriented towards $X(t-1)$, $X(T)$ and $X(t+1)$.

References

1. IDEAM, Estad'ısticas de Incendios en el 2010. Ministerio de Ambiente y Desarrollo Sostenible de Colombia (2012)
2. Afzaal, H., Zafar, N.A.: Robot-based forest fire detection and extinguishing model. In: 2016 2nd International Conference on Robotics and Artificial Intelligence (ICRAI), pp. 112–117, November 2016
3. Cai, M., Lu, X., Wu, X., Feng, Y.: Intelligent video analysis-based forest fires smoke detection algorithms. In: 2016 12th International Conference on Natural Computation, Fuzzy Systems and Knowledge Discovery (ICNC-FSKD), pp. 1504–1508, August 2016
4. Ganesan, P., Sathish, B.S., Sajiv, G.: A comparative approach of identification and segmentation of forest fire region in high resolution satellite images. In: 2016 World Conference on Futuristic Trends in Research and Innovation for Social Welfare (Startup Conclave), pp. 1–6, February 2016
5. Ghamry, K.A., Zhang, Y.: Fault-tolerant cooperative control of multiple UAVs for forest fire detection and tracking mission. In: 2016 3rd Conference on Control and Fault-Tolerant Systems (SysTol), pp. 133–138, September 2016
6. Kim, S., Lee, W., Park, Y.S., Lee, H.W., Lee, Y.T.: Forest fire monitoring system based on aerial image. In: 2016 3rd International Conference on Information and Communication Technologies for Disaster Management (ICT-DM), pp. 1–6, December 2016
7. Lafarge, F., Descombes, X., Zerubia, J.: Forest fire detection based on gaussian field analysis, In: 2007 15th European Signal Processing Conference, Sept 2007, pp. 1447–1451
8. Mendez-Garabetti, M., Bianchini, G., Caymes-Scutari, P., Tardivo, M.L.: ESS-IM applied to forest fire spread prediction: parameters tuning for a heterogeneous configuration. In: 2016 35th International Conference of the Chilean Computer Science Society (SCCC), pp. 1–12, October 2016
9. Xuehua, W., Chang, L., Jiaqi, L., Xuezhi, Q., Ning, W., Wenjun, Z.: A cellular automata model for forest fire spreading simulation. In: 2016 IEEE Symposium Series on Computational Intelligence (SSCI), pp. 1–6, December 2016
10. Leal, B.E.Z., Hirakawa, A.R., Pereira, T.D.: Onboard fuzzy logic approach to active fire detection in Brazilian amazon forest. IEEE Trans. Aerosp. Electron. Syst. 52(2), 883–890 (2016)
11. Bolourchi, P., Uysal, S.: Forest fire detection in wireless sensor network using fuzzy logic. In: 2013 Fifth International Conference on Computational Intelligence, Communication Systems and Networks, pp. 83–87, June 2013
12. Renubala, S., Dhanalakshmi, K.S.: Trust based secure routing protocol using fuzzy logic in wireless sensor networks. In: 2014 IEEE International Conference on Computational Intelligence and Computing Research, pp. 1–5, Dec 2014
13. Mohapatra, S., Khilar, P.M.: Forest fire monitoring and detection of faulty nodes using wireless sensor network. In: 2016 IEEE Region 10 Conference (TENCON), pp. 3232–3236, November 2016
14. Fred, "¿que es la metodología scrum?", Febrero 26 de 2017. http://cryptodevelopments.com/2017/02/26/que-es-la-metodologia-scrum/
15. Muthu, B.: What is client-server architecture?: Client-server architecture (2014). http://hitechtube.blogspot.com.co/2014/12/what-is-client-server-architecture.html
16. Sparx Systems Pty Ltd, "Enterprise architect," 2015, version 12.0.1215(Compilacion: 1215). Usado en Abril de 2017. http://www.sparxsystems.com/products/ea/12/

17. Balanis, C.A.: Antenna Theory, 3rd edn. John Wiley & Sons Inc, Hoboken (2005)
18. Mendel, J.: Fuzzy logic systems for engineering. IEEE, **83**(3), 4–32 (1995). https://ewh.ieee.org/cmte/cis/mtsc/ieeecis/FLSEngrTutorialErratacopy.pdf
19. Barati, R.: Application of excel solver for parameter estimation of the nonlinear Muskingum models. KSCE J. Civil Eng. **17**(5), 1139–1148 (2013). https://doi.org/10.1007/s12205-013-0037-2

Development of Prototype for IoT and IoE Scalable Infrastructures, Architectures and Platforms

Farid Touati[1(✉)], Hasan Tariq[1(✉)], Damiano Crescini[2], and Adel Ben Mnaouer[3]

[1] Qatar University, Doha, Qatar
{touatif,hasan.tariq}@qu.edu.qa
[2] University of Brescia, Brescia, Italy
damiano.crescini@unibs.it
[3] Canadian University of Dubai, Dubai, UAE
adel@cud.ac.ae

Abstract. IoT is the third wave of economy after the first and second being agriculture and industry, respectively, paving the way for the fourth industrial revolution (4IR). IoT is a combination of all the revolutionary technologies in the last two decades. More than a billion of smart devices have been developed across the world by more than 10 vendors to satisfy billions of needs that are trusted by 98% of economic actors. This study describes design and implementation of IoT architectures stressing on scalability, integration, and interoperability of heterogeneous IoT systems. It gives answers to (i) how systems can be designed to become easily configurable and customizable for a specific IoT infrastructure? And (ii) how Investors, producers and consumers can be integrated on the same page of an IoT platform?

We have developed a master database and directories from top chart IoT nomenclature, frameworks, vendors, devices, platforms and architectures and integrated data from 27 big online resources commonly used by Forbes, Businessweek and CNBC. Also, datasheets of IoT equipment by vendors (e.g. Intel, IBM, ARM, Microchip, Schneider, and CISCO), used tools (e.g. Labcenter Proteus, AutoCAD and Excel), and platforms (e.g. Visual Studio, Eclipse) are combined to build directories of plethora of data. The main outcome of this work culminates in providing a seamless solution and recommendations for various infrastructures (hardware and software) for effective and integrated resource utilization and management in a new IoT paradigm.

Keywords: IoE · WoT · SoT · IoT · Infrastructure · Architectures

1 Introduction

By 2020, the number of connected machines is estimated to reach more than 34 billion-more than four folds the globe population. A smart IoT solution potentially delivers significant benefits such as reduced device support and maintenance costs, customer engagement and satisfaction, and new business models.

© Springer Nature Switzerland AG 2018
N. Boudriga et al. (Eds.): UNet 2018, LNCS 11277, pp. 202–216, 2018.
https://doi.org/10.1007/978-3-030-02849-7_18

In a green and blue ecological metropolitan analysis by [2, 3], infrastructure refers to the entire set of systems and subsystems including transportation, energy, education, health and food etc., buildings and industries that define eco-system of a region and country. Recent IoT work by [4] based on UrbanSense (DCU), BusNet and its effective integration using REST API, ESTI and FIWARE is very impressive. Geo-mapping used by [4] is an excellent infrastructural tool, although lacking addressing cost benchmark. On the other hand, Government, public and private sector are three Internet of Everything (IoEs) that govern all the lower corporate and enterprise IoEs with trees of IoTs such as army, police, law, oil and gas, pharmaceutical, chemical and industries [6, 10, 11]. An excellent analysis from Figs. 1, 2, 3, 4, 5, 6, 7, 8 and 9 and Table 1 comparison [6] among openMTC, FIWARE, SiteWhere and Webinos, the proprietary AWS IoT, IBM's Watson IoT, Microsoft's Azure IoT Hub and Samsung's Smart-Things platforms. However, [6] lacked discrete recommendations and solution of their Integration of Middleware (IoM) analysis. Huge gaps in terms of authentication and identifications addressed by [7] based on XingQR need more elaboration with respect to multiple signatures. Also, compression and smart character generation for scalability can handle billions of users. Interoperability and integration proposed in [8, 9] should be improved in terms of real-world devices information. Excellent contribution in terms for Identity and Access Management (IAM) by [14] in terms of comparison of SAML, OAuth, OpenID Connect & SSO for mobile devices has been used by us in a different ubiquitous sense at D2D level lacked addressing hardware implementation and specifications of systems. HTTP 1.1, HTTP2 and SPDY comparison as new alternatives by [15] were interesting. This has fostered better understating prospect in [16]; Tables 1, 2 and 3 in terms of transmission and energy constraints of MQTT, CoAP, AMQP, TCP and Websockets on Intel and ARM ISAs. However, the work in [16] needs to be improved in terms of verification on some ready-to-go IoT topology in GNS3, Wireshark and VMware based platforms. Hand-Off time calculations by [17] proved that AMQP is better than MQTT for 0.5 KB to 1.2 KB. Nonetheless, the work in [17] needs to be matured for HTTP, CoAP, and Websockets. A very noticeable and referable effort by [18] for TinyOS, RIOT and ContikiOS control engine; however, this needs to address the effect of database used. Green aspect, energy harvesting and nano-power implementations by [19, 20] and the SERENO module for air quality monitoring [21, 22] needs to be assessed for mass production from scalable aspects and digital infrastructure definitions, being an excellent novel contribution. Finally, the glue. Things mash-up platform [24] developed WoTKit, Paraimpu and servIoTicy. Cloud virtualization design proposed by [27] for education and for community used by [25] using thin clients had limited applications as compared to capability of hardware. Web of things (WoT) has got a plenty of attention in market as per its flexibility and diversity. Private information sources of layman are now only three [26]. This challenge increases in terms of involving SMS and email.

In our work, we have tried to fill few of the potential gaps discussed above and proposed two scalable IoT models, namely Infrastructure-Centered Model and Agent Centered Model. Key advantages of our designs and implemented systems are:

- Infrastructure Definitions and Parametric Model
- Device and Implementation Cost Scaling

- IoT Integration of Middleware Scalability
- Multiple Digital Signatures, Identification & Authentication
- Runtime Data Compression and Reduced Network Traffic
- Systems & Network Simulation and Design onboard
- SQL and non-SQL (SQlite, MySQL, PostgreSQL, noSQL, JSON, XML)
- Utility Billing and Service Integrity
- Multiple IoT Platforms, Architectures and Hardware/Software Options
- Multiple Open Source IoT Brokers
- Multiple Enabling Technologies (Wired, Wireless, Fiber and SAT)
- Infrastructure Driven User Interface (UI) and User Experience (UX)
- Multiple Analytics, AI and ML Algorithms Integration Options
- Commercial grade hardware safety and operations
- Financial Flexibility as per Infrastructures and Consumer Category
- Hardware Architecture Characterization and Classification
- Time stamped SMS, Email and Social Media Posting.

Our IoT system design and implementation offers financial scalability in three levels of parameters called parameters sets (PS) where (PB: population basic, PV: population value and PP: population premium) based on sensor cards (SC-SXT-CATX) where (S: size of enclosure, X: number of parameters and T: PCB topology and CAT: category). Revision has two parts (X: set of alphabets and 0: sub revision, set of natural numbers). Table 1 describes the classification in details.

Table 1. IoT/IoE packages classification

Parameters	Basic packages	Value package	Premium package	Revision
PS-PB	SC-37F-PDAB	SC-37F-PDAB	SC-37F-PDAB	X - 0
PS-PV	X	SC-35F-PDAB	SC-35F-PDAB	X - 0
PS-PP	X	X	SC-68F-PDAB	X - 0

2 Scalable and Interoperable Models

2.1 Infrastructure-Centered Model (ICM)

Integrated design for implementation of MQTT, CoAP, AMQP and XMPP multiple brokers for IoE and IoT, OPC UA for IIoT and one block using DDS and Websockets is our contribution to ensure QoS and interoperability at the same time. MQTT (Message Queuing Text Transfer) and CoAP (Constrained Application Protocol) due to size smallest of packet and processing requirements have been implemented for M2M and D2D communication. XMPP (Extensible Messaging and Presence Protocol) strength in data representation and format communication i.e. XML (Extended Markup Language) qualified it for H2H, D2H, H2D, M2H and H2M communication i.e. M: Machine and H: Human. The potential of several bytes with reliability and security advantages AMQP (Advanced Message Queuing Protocol) has enabled us to implement it as our S2S, IoTM2IoTM and IoTM2S and S2IoTM bottlenecked communication, i.e. S: Server, IoTM: IoT Middleware. Finally CoAP over TCP/TLS provides a practicable solution until IPv6 becomes ubiquitous, making CoAP the preferable protocol for C2C, S2C and C2S. Information model for hard coded primitive infrastructures is the first step of infrastructure centered model (ICM). Brokers for these four protocols are given in Fig. 1 with the naming convention we used in our code.

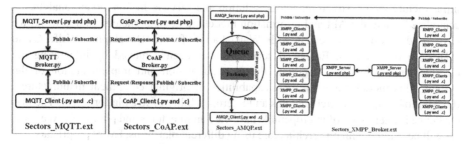

Fig. 1. Multiple brokers for sectors infrastructure

Many IoT infrastructures are available in the market by top vendors ARM, Intel (IntelIoT), CISCO (Cisco-IoE), Telit (Telit-IoT), Jasper (Jasper-IoT), Cumulocity (IoT), Davra Networks, Samsung, Qualocomm and HP with various features. The proposed model is shown in Fig. 2. In order to utilize any infrastructure, first the information model of real infrastructures (e.g. Smart Energy, Smart Industry, Smart Government, Smart Academia, Smart Health) has to be designed using database engines.

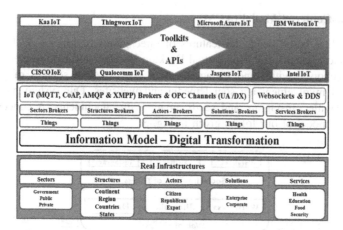

Fig. 2. Infrastructure-centered model (ICM)

Secondly, a generic application-programming interface (API) for a given IoT architecture is available by top IoT vendors to communicate with a particular database management system. The API customizes the entire IoT infrastructure with respect to real infrastructures. A novel datasheets approach to populate our database using the datasets of a given infrastructure as been used by us. The hardware architecture is static as per things in a particular infrastructure. The sensor cards are mentioned in Table 1 and parameters will remain static or fixed as defined in the datasheet of a particular object of class in the infrastructure, e.g., an object truck's datasheet will define which variables have to be measured by which sensors.

The datasheets can only be provided by the regulatory authority for a given infrastructure sector, structure, actors, solution and service. In this model, analytics is centralized where the API and information model are key parameters. In this work, we have used a top-down design with Water-Fall Software Development Life Cycle (SDLC) approach [16]. Enhanced scalability has been achieved by integrating the documentation support to facilitate the easy adaptation and implementation of the system. This model scales the best capabilities of original equipment manufacturers (OEMs) IoTs [6], OEM architectures and interoperability of IoT platforms [7]. The first challenge is integration of interoperable hardware architectures and platforms. At a time, we will be dealing with one architecture using different platforms. Every proprietary IoT framework has its own definitions to classify sensor-cards nodes, cables, drivers, network switches, IoT gateways, computers, servers and all the architecture specific software and hardware of a single vendor [8]. Specifically PLC, PAC and DCS based nodes OPC (OLE for Process Control) is used for scalability and flexibility of merging IIoT and IoT as we have an infrastructure of Industry 4.0 (Smart Industry) also. At gateway or in parallel to broker layer we have used OPC DX (Data Exchange) and as whole middleware we have used OPC UA (Unified Architecture) giving added feature to use i.e. (FactoryTalk, WinCC, Citect and third parties Indusoft WEBSCADA, WinTr and Tracemode SCADA systems is available in our work.

2.2   Agent-Centered Model (ACM)

The approach is based using the features of three giants of IoE i.e. Web of Things (WoT), Cloud Virtualization (for Virtual Desktop Interface (VDI)) and Social Web of Things (Facebook, twitter and Instagram etc.). An excellent sources of population attention and involvement are social media and websites. Our system publishes on Facebook, Twitter, Instagram and sends emails with attachments. A conceptual and implemented model of our IoE is given in Fig. 3.

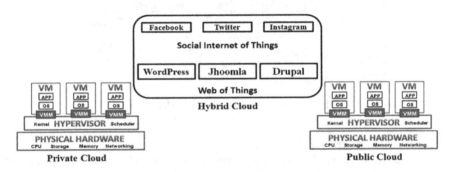

Fig. 3. Hybrid cloud and web of things

Cloud is used as infrastructure as a service (IaaS) to achieve scalability of workflow and management. Thick, thin and zero clients are the most powerful tools for utilizing scalability of hardware at lowest costs. A brief understating of thick, thin and zero clients is given in Fig. 4.

	Thick Clients	Thin Clients	Zero Clients
Definition	PCs with Operating System and Clients Software	Stations for Virtual Desktops hosted in Data Center / Server.	Stations for Virtual Desktops hosted in Data Center / Server.
Life Span	4 years	7 years	10 years
Hardware	A Complete PC	Atom PCs (at max)	(No Processor, No Hard disk, No RAM)
Set Up Time	2 hours (Average)	5 minutes (Average)	5 minutes (Average)
Operating Systems	Web Browser or Windows OS	Windows or Linux OS	No OS or Application
Security Level	10%	40%	100%
Ease of Management	10%	50%	100%
Power Consumption	300W+	80W+	30W+
Level of Maintenance Required	40%	5%	0%
Bandwidth Requirement	<100Mpbs	<50Mpbs	<50Mpbs
Latency	150ms+	300ms+	125ms+
Application	Multiple Displays, OS and level of user needs		

Fig. 4. Scalability (thick, thin and zero clients)

First of all the sensors or data acquisition points or variables will have impact factors or roles for a particular applied agent or object (e.g. SmartGrid and Smart Academia). Then, every infrastructure set or class of agents [8] will have its specific protocols depending on the data nature and bandwidth requirement (e.g. MODBUS, CANBUS, SNMP, PROFINET, and BACnet). In this context, every network address will be enough to identify the infrastructure being addressed. This serves two-fold purpose: (i) independence of design and implementation of the architecture and (ii) increase flexibility of platform. Every agent will have its marshalling (I/O Standardized Clusters) for remote I/Os.

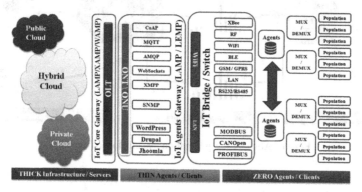

Fig. 5. Agent-centered model

In the proposed design, we used IP68 junction boxes and UL508 certified panels with IPC610A approved PCBs or embedded systems for commercial grade. This model is more ubiquitous and device-safety centric. Here, the agents will be distributed as per population of citizens and concerned subjects all over the globe. A pooling mechanism will be used on the basis of fittest-to-include and then keep continuously updating data to the cloud using relevant authentications and protocols. Then all the agents connected to the ADA (Agent Data Acquisition) bridge will keep processing the data. This concept is more suitable for highly populated countries where requirement is resource constrained.

3   Information Model and Physical System

3.1   Information Model and Datasheet Design and Development

Let us start with the infrastructure-centered model. The diversification of things is used as "Datasheet". The central command will have one datasheet to address; all infrastructures create the path of accessibility of resources this way. It ensures the swift transaction or movement of things moving upstream the infrastructure. It is an evolved infrastructure concept for entities like GCC, US, and EU. Let us apply this model for GCC; everybody will first become member of GCC, then he/she can physically be in GCC anywhere as per requirement, instead of directly coming to Doha and start working. This suggests then that first assign a GCC tag and proceed to any organ like Qatar, Oman, Kuwait, Saudi Arabia UAE, or Bahrain. The central portal will take the datasheet of an actor as a specified format and the actor will be placed in the system in the relevant structure, solution, or services.

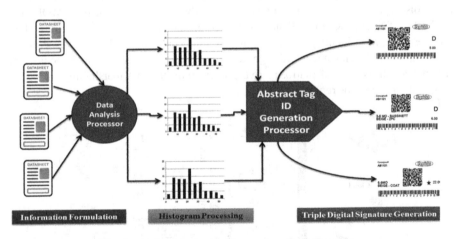

Fig. 6. Abstract tag generation system for IoT actors

Actors have to update their datasheet instead of manual appealing. Every attribute of an actor is the arrangement or placement parameter in the infrastructure as per points. The success of this model is speed, accuracy, automation and uniformity of framework. This model will crash wherever the individual state tried to over-rule its priorities of evaluation criteria.

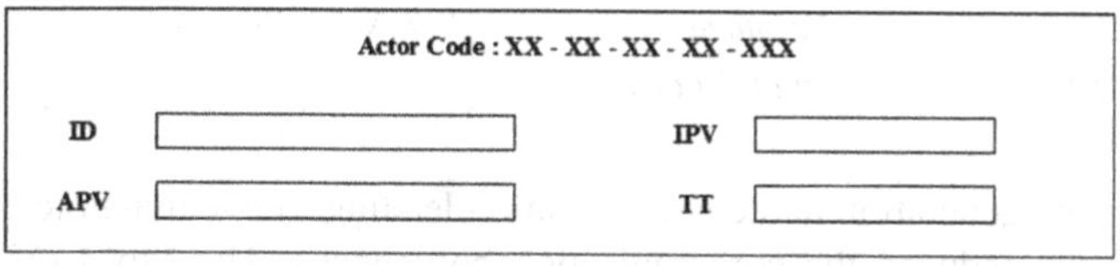

Actor Code : XX - XX - XX - XX - XXX

ID   [   ]   IPV   [   ]

APV   [   ]   TT   [   ]

Fig. 7. IoT actor: thread and session structure

In Fig. 6, the actor code gives the lifetime exact information about its position in the entire IoT no matter what is the size of IoT; the actor is traceable. The ID is 28 characters, is a dynamic value, is the current state as per location, structure, solution and all the attributes are defined as per the model in Fig. 2. The IPV stands for IoT Priority Value, as per services or sensors used by the actor. The IPV is a dynamic value and system-generated and routed. The APV is 28 characters and stands for Appealed Priority Value, which means that the sensors or system values need to be varied as per client request. It only addresses specific cases associated with health or safety of actors and state normally stays NULL. The TT is 20 digits and stands for Transition Time, in other words it determines the duration of APV and IPV in its 10:10 digit fields. This defines how long this actor stays in this state, after which the value of IPV or APV is truncated or assigned to a new actor. The entire IoT attributes revolve around this scheme as any actor can only be at one place and in one system and structure at a particular time second. The geo-plot clearly updates based on GIS of actors. It handles all the events and infrastructure situations. Every actor has NIC sized 4 mm thickness color screen pager or symbian device instead of a national id card. This symbian device will have 5/8 portion size as battery, 2/8 portion size solar panel and piezoelectric trigger circuits rest all the integrated device electronics (IDE). We implemented and tested this approach for 99,999,999 actors. Results showed that this approach is very effective in terms of efficient resource utilization, time, and cost saving per individual and aggregation. The concept used 'datasheet' is unique and has no resemblance with bio-data, CV, resume or company profile and portfolio. It strictly deals with alphanumeric using histogram based character allocation of last 8 characters. The highest amplitude will refer to the mass population involvement and thus using the smallest ASCII value for that leading to best real-time compression. This reduces the cost of infrastructure as well as increases the density of persons per area. Example parameters are shown in packages table is shown in Table 2.

Table 2. DAB tagging schema

Enclosures size (inches) (Length × Width × Depth)	Parameters (B, V and P)	PCB topology (No. of I/O Headers)		
Revision (X - 0)				
3: 3 × 3 × 2	*Current^B*	*4 = F for Basic*	*A*	*0*
6: 6 × 3 × 2	*Voltage^B*	*7 = S for Value*	*B*	*1*
10: 10 × 6 × 2	*Frequency^B*	*9 = N for Premium*	*C*	*2*
14: 14 × 10 × 6	*Digital Lock^B*		*D*	*3*

Dynamic data generation and characterization leading to live dynamic compression has automatically reduced the communication bottlenecks. The MoM (Message Oriented Middleware) technique has been enhanced in our work using compression and reducing the alphanumeric character set by reducing the load on brokers and middleware at the same time. The Master Database at the IoE/IoT side has its primary keys integrated in things databases as foreign keys in D2D communication. It facilitates both scalable IoE/IoT design and implementation.

3.2 Physical System Architecture and Marshalling Design and Development

This technique focuses on the physical presence of IoT agents in form of equidistant meshes of BLE and WiFi fogs. Assume that our cities are planned or planned in terms of homes and colonies, factories and chambers, that is, heterogeneous infrastructures where handling a population is dynamic as well as non-uniforms densities are possible due to multi-cultural environment even at un-accountable level. One DAB (Data Acquisition Box) in every home/communal unit consists of 6+ people acquiring all the utilities and needs data. 6+ people are the most basic social unit (2x grandparents/guardians, 2x parents/guardians, 2x children). This DAB is stackable and incase of additional services, one needs to buy an extra stacking board. Adding services is accomplished through bank payments and agents center. Water, gas, electricity, education, security, health all cards are printed upon request and penalty payment. Agent center is a small 8 ft × 6 ft × 4ft (L × W × H) cabin with automatic card printers and voucher-sticker teller machines. Just get the education card, get the sticker for new process keep on the name plate that school teacher will see, containing all the info like the subjects you paid for and hours. Put solar panels at your top of your home generate the electricity and get the payment voucher as a documentation proof and deliver it to the bank and get the cash. Card printers can print vouchers also, so only one mentioned in drawing. Agent center with zero client is only to guide and assist in system clarification or process to be initiated or terminated. Zero client-based agents cannot correct or amend anything of population element being DA (Data Acquisition) node only. Marshalling reduces load on service centers. Service centers provide monthly and annual detailed reports plus activation of promotion services like complete user/operator manual, saving plans and rights transformation. Service centers cannot even add/remove data. Size of services center is 30 ft × 20 ft × 15ft (LWH). 6 components, shown in the Fig. 8, are fixed for all 3 packages and remaining are added as per member and utility cards purchasing.

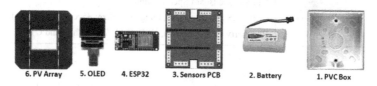

Fig. 8. PDAB components and assembly order (used)

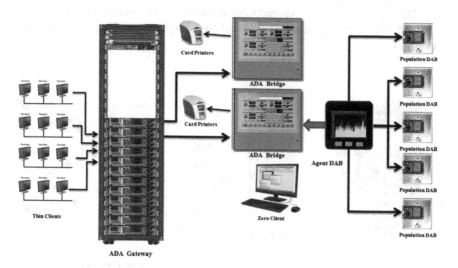

Fig. 9. Ubiquitous layers and integrity

4   Results and Discussion: Case Study-Qatar University

Structural health monitoring (SHM) has been used as a case study for testing the developed ICM and ACM. The safest infrastructure parameter is its protection and awareness towards big patches damage that has 10 km+ area of effect and 3000+ human lives loss threat. A ± 0.000X accuracy early warning system that can alarm the population and authorities quite before the disaster happens is the solution. The system designed and tested has the following components as shown in Table 3.

Table 3. SHM IoE specifications

DUAL AXIS	Early Warning Node Specification (Protocol, Transceiver, Sensor, Size: 43.8 x 65.4 x 14.35 (mm)) (CAN-Open, STM32F10RBT6, MMA8451Q)
	Out Surface Board Specification (SBC, OS and Interfaces, Language, Size: 85 x 56 x 18 (mm)) Raspberry Pi 3, Raspbian, USB and LAN, Python and C++

The distance constraint that the infrastructure has is handled using long distance physical layer protocols. We have chosen CAN-Open being as it can support cable length of 5000 m at 10 kb/s. Five CANOpen nodes were used in each cluster and connected through a CANOpen-to-USB converter to connect to Raspberry Pi 3 processor. The topology of the developed system hardware and software is summarized in Fig. 10, left with raspberry pi is hardware and on the right with IoT client, gateway and server is software.

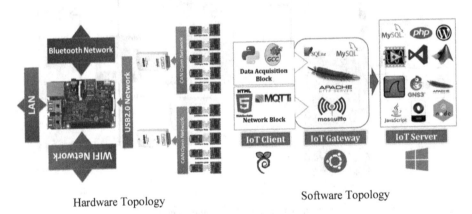

Hardware Topology   Software Topology

Fig. 10. SHM core topology

Tests results are shown in Fig. 11 for ThingSpeak IoT platform. The displayed sensors values from inclinometers using CAN-Open nodes demonstrate a typical operating example of ICM that is a proprietary platform on public cloud.

The physical site chosen for this system was Qatar University bridge as shown in Fig. 12. Line plots are time-stamped in sub-windows 'Field 3', 'Field 4', 'Field 5' and 'Field 6' which show a reading accuracy of 0.005 of sensors values which supports accurate decision making and warnings.

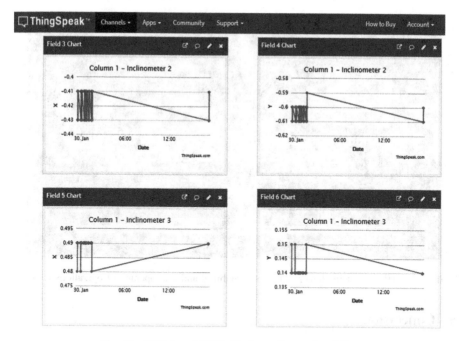

Fig. 11. ICM based SHM (Package 3) tested and live

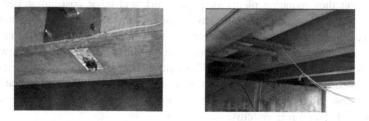

Fig. 12. SHM installed as scalable package 3 (ACM)

The system was at a remote location in form of CAN-Open based tiltmeter nodes connected to Raspberry Pi 3 and accessed through Wifi. The Wifi was linked to optical network terminal (ONT) and all the nodes through ONTs form an optical network. This Optical network was sending data to optical line terminals (OLTs). The WoT implementation can be seen in private cloud zero client screen in Fig. 13.

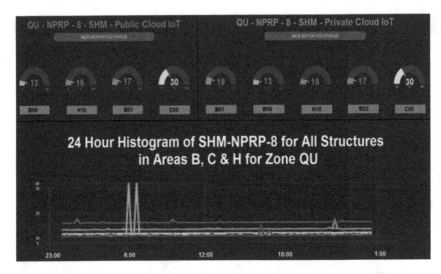

Fig. 13. SHM based Implementation for scalability and interoperability operations testing

5   Conclusion

In the present paper, we have presented two novel scalable infrastructure models based on IoT and IoE. Both cover the gap of digital transformation and convergence using information model by datasheet based input dataset and actor id generation with triple authentication thus reducing plenty of paper work and labor cost along with information security. A commercializable IoE solution can be built by combination of proprietary and open source IoT hardware and software architecture. Structural health monitoring system has been used as a case study with real-time results shown with continuous operation of the system for 2 months. The data from inclinometers with ±0.000X accuracy can be also seen in real-time plots of public and private cloud implementation. Nevertheless, the rest of the infrastructures would be implementable on our novel IoT and IoE systems.

Acknowledgments. This publication was made possible by NPRP grant # 8-1781-2-735 from the Qatar National Research Fund (a member of Qatar Foundation). The statements made herein are solely the responsibility of the authors.

References

1. da Silva, J.M.C., Wheeler, E.: Ecosystems as infrastructure. Perspect. Ecol. Conserv. **15**, 32–35 (2017)
2. Jin, J., Palaniswami, M., Gubbi, J., Marusic, S.: An information framework for creating a smart city through internet of things. IEEE Internet Things J. **1**, 112–121 (2014). https://doi.org/10.1109/jiot.2013.2296516

3. Santos, P.M., Rodrigues, P., Guilherme, J., Cruz, S.B.: PortoLivingLab: an IoT-based sensing platform for smart cities (2018). https://doi.org/10.1109/jiot.2018.2791522
4. Tamburini, L., Rossi, M., Brunelli, D., Barros, T.J.: Electronic and ICT solutions for smart buildings and urban areas. In: Renewable and Alternative Energy: Concepts, Methodologies, Tools, and Applications, January 2017. https://doi.org/10.4018/978-1-5225-1671-2.ch064
5. Guth, J., et al.: A detailed analysis of IoT platform architectures: concepts, similarities, and differences. In: Di Martino, B., Li, K.-C., Yang, Laurence T., Esposito, A. (eds.) Internet of Everything. IT, pp. 81–101. Springer, Singapore (2018). https://doi.org/10.1007/978-981-10-5861-5_4
6. Hertlein, M., Manaras, P., Pohlmann, N.: Smart authentication, identification and digital signatures as foundation for the next generation of eco systems. In: Linnhoff-Popien, C., Schneider, R., Zaddach, M. (eds.) Digital Marketplaces Unleashed, pp. 905–919. Springer, Heidelberg (2018). https://doi.org/10.1007/978-3-662-49275-8_80
7. Gravina, R., Palau, C.E., Manso, M., Liotta, A., Fortino, G.: Erratum to: integration, interconnection, and interoperability of iot systems. In: Gravina, R., Palau, C.E., Manso, M., Liotta, A., Fortino, G. (eds.) Integration, Interconnection, and Interoperability of IoT Systems. IT, p. E1. Springer, Cham (2018). https://doi.org/10.1007/978-3-319-61300-0_11
8. Afzal, B., Umair, M., Shah, G.A., Ahmed, E.: Enabling IoT platforms for social IoT applications: vision, feature mapping, and challenges. Future Gener. Comput. Syst. (2017)
9. Fafoutis, X., Elsts, A., Piechocki, R., Craddock, I.: Experiences and lessons learned from making IoT sensing platforms for large-scale deployments. IEEE Access **PP**(99), 1 (2017). https://doi.org/10.1109/access.2017.2787418
10. Klein, S.: IoT Solutions in Microsoft's Azure IoT Suite. Apress, Berkeley, CA (2017). https://doi.org/10.1007/978-1-4842-2143-3
11. Banafa, A.: The Internet of Everything (2014). https://doi.org/10.13140/2.1.3805.2487
12. Abeyratne, R.: The Internet of Everything, August 2017. https://doi.org/10.1007/978-3-319-61124-2_7
13. Naik, N., Jenkins, P., Newell, D.: Choice of suitable identity and access management standards for mobile computing and communication. In: 24th International Conference on Telecommunications (ICT), May 2017. https://doi.org/10.1109/ict.2017.7998280
14. Naik, N., Jenkins, P., Davies, P., Newell, D.: Native web communication protocols and their effects on the performance of web services and systems. In: 2016 IEEE International Conference on Computer and Information Technology (CIT), December 2016. https://doi.org/10.1109/cit.2016.100
15. Mun, D.-H., Le Dinh, M., Kwon, Y.W.: An assessment of internet of things protocols for resource-constrained applications. In: 2016 IEEE 40th Annual Computer Software and Applications Conference (COMPSAC), June 2016. https://doi.org/10.1109/compsac.2016.51
16. Luzuriaga, J.E., Boronat, P., Perez, M., Manzoni, P.: A comparative evaluation of AMQP and MQTT protocols over unstable and mobile networks. In: 2015 Annual IEEE Consumer Communications and Networking Conference (CCNC), Las Vegas, NV, vol. 12, January 2015. https://doi.org/10.1109/ccnc.2015.7158101
17. Ruckebusch, P., Van Damme, J., De Poorter, E., Moerman, I.: Dynamic reconfiguration of network protocols for constrained internet-of-things devices. In: Mandler, B., et al. (eds.) IoT360 2015. LNICST, vol. 170, pp. 269–281. Springer, Cham (2016). https://doi.org/10.1007/978-3-319-47075-7_31
18. Alghisi, D., Touati, F., Crescini, D., Ferraricmar, M.: Single and multi-source battery-less power management circuits for piezoelectric energy harvesting systems. In: Sensors and Actuators, July 2017. https://doi.org/10.1016/j.sna.2017.07.027

19. Alghisi, D., Touati, F., Crescini, D., Mnaouer, A.B.: A new nano-power trigger circuit for battery-less power management electronics in energy harvesting systems. In: Sensors and Actuators, June 2017. https://doi.org/10.1016/j.sna.2017.06.025

20. Touati, F., Galli, A., Crescini, D., Mnaouer, A.B.: Feasibility of air quality monitoring systems based on environmental energy harvesting. In: IEEE Instrumentation and Measurement Technology Conference 2015, pp. 266–271, July 2015. https://doi.org/10.1109/i2mtc.2015.7151277

21. Touati, F., Legena, C., Galli, A., Mnaouer, A.B.: Environmentally powered multiparametric wireless sensor node for air quality diagnostic. Sens. Mater. **27**(2), 177–189 (2015)

22. Touati, F., Legena, C., Galli, A., Mnaouer, A.B.: Renewable energy-harvested sensor systems for air quality monitoring, March 2015. https://doi.org/10.1109/icm.2014.7071831

23. Kleinfeld, R., Steglich, S., Radziwonowicz, L., Doukas, C.: glue.things – a mashup platform for wiring the internet of things with the internet of services. In: 5th International Workshop on the Web of Things, Cambridge, MA, USA, vol. 5, October 2014. https://doi.org/10.13140/2.1.3039.9049

24. Xu, W., Yuan, D., Xue, L.: Design and implementation of intelligent community system based on thin client and cloud computing. Int. J. Ad Hoc Ubiquitous Comput. (IJASUC) **5**(4), (2014)

25. Farseev, A., Chua, T.-S.: TweetFit: fusing multiple social media and sensor data for wellness profile learning

26. Mbuki, K.J., Osero, B.O.: Cost efficient education delivery by using zero clients, a case study of useful multi-seat platform

The Content Placement Problem in D2D Networks Under Coupling Distributed Caching and Distributed Storage

Basma Nissar[✉], Ahmed El Ouadrhiri, and Mohamed El Kamili

LIMS, Faculty of Sciences Dhar Mahraz, Sidi Mohammed Ben Abdellah University, Fez, Morocco
basma.nissar@usmba.ac.ma

Abstract. In this paper, we address the distributed caching device-to-device (D2D) network in which the popular contents are cached proactively as chunks in the storage of users' devices (referred to as "helpers") in order to offload the content delivery traffic and reduce the transmission delay. If a content is cached as a chunk-based content, the requester has to download all the chunks of this content, thus, he may encounter a case wherein the consumed energy for obtaining this chunk-based content exceed the one for obtaining the same content as single-based content, if any. As the dissemination of a content as a single-based content can considerably impact the helper energy expenditure, the chunk-based caching may incurs additional energy burden owing to the limited battery capacity. So, in order to optimally trade-off between energy consumption and transmission delay, we propose a hybrid strategy wherein each content is cached simultaneously as single-based strategy and chunk-based strategy. We show through simulations that the proposed strategy outperforms these two strategies and achieves the trade-off.

Keywords: D2D · Caching · Chunk-based · Energy

1 Introduction

It is widely acknowledged that the large amount of connected devices coupled with the rapid proliferation of social networking dominate the exponential growth of data traffic in wireless networks which is expected to exceed 30 exabytes per month by 2020 [1].

Such a dramatic increase of traffic demands has led to a significant congestion in the backhaul connection, and as a result many research communities are motivated to propose caching the most popular data in the small base stations, which later was no longer sufficient to offload network traffic and alleviate the burden on the network. One of the ideas, to deal with that, was caching proactively the contents directly in the users' devices, during the off-peak time based on the contents popularity and correlations among users and contents patterns

© Springer Nature Switzerland AG 2018
N. Boudriga et al. (Eds.): UNet 2018, LNCS 11277, pp. 217–228, 2018.
https://doi.org/10.1007/978-3-030-02849-7_19

[2]. Besides the presence of D2D links which opens up a possibility to exchange the locally cached contents between a user and his nearby devices who have the desired content via device-to-device (D2D) communications, the distributed caching at users' devices became a crucial issue [3].

Meanwhile, the capacity of storage appeared, concurrently with the increasing popularity of ultra-HD contents, as a significant issue owing to the limited storage capacities of the devices. Hence, it will become progressively difficult to cache the content of interest as single-based content in a single device and this motivated the researchers to the consideration of distributed storage regime [4]. A single-based content cannot be cached on one device, which means that it is stored as several chunks among different devices, and that a typical device may have to download content, as several portions, from multiple nearby devices in a network (named helpers). And such an idea, of chunk-based caching/distributed storage, is not only offloads the traffic but it enhances the transmission delay, this is due to the fact that the several chunks are downloaded in parallel, on the other hand it increases the energy consumption compared to the single-based caching.

The natural question in such a network is what makes the user helper wastes its energy to enhance the quality of experience of the other users' devices?, with take into consideration the limited battery capacity of mobile devices [5], which make the energy consumption at a helper user a big concern in D2D communications with caching in general and caching coupled with distributed storage in particular. Thus, it is a significant issue to evaluate the energy consumption besides delay of transmission at a transmitter device (helper) to transmit the content, at both single-based strategy and chunk-based strategy, in trying to achieve the trade-off.

1.1   Related Works

Generally, there is a substantial amount of studies on distributed caching in users' devices as a promising function of D2D system in order to improve quality of experience of users [6–10,16] and improve network performance [11,12]. The concept of helper is introduced in [10] for the first time to denote the femto-base stations which support the distributed caching, but because of the miss of scalability and flexibility the authors were motivated to consider the devices as caching helpers in [13]. For the concept of influential user, it is introduced in [2], in which the authors consider a proactive caching paradigm and propose a procedure to determine the influential users, based on the social networks, to cache the content and deliver it through D2D communications. In [4] the authors study two different distributed storage strategies in the users' devices in order to compare their expected costs of obtaining the complete content. The first one is the uncoded strategy in which the parts/chunks of the content are stored in different devices and the second is the coded strategy, which is based on using coded data, in which the chunks of the content are stored as random linear combination in each device. The results show that the coded strategy perform better than the uncoded one. There is Prior works focusing on caching on devices coupled with distributed storage such as [14] which considers a distributed caching device-to-device (D2D) network in which the storage of the content is distributed in the devices. The authors show, using a simple stochastic geometry model, that the performance bottleneck, caused by the dominant interferers, can be loosened and this is a result of the user mobility as a crucial factor of lower likelihood of having dominant interferer. In [9] the authors consider a randomly storage of the portions of the contents and discuss the coverage probability and average delay from two equivalent viewpoints, this work shows the importance of caching contents closer to the requesters in order to achieve better networks performance.

1.2 Our Contribution

In this work, we consider two strategies of caching a content in helpers that are supposed to be identified as influential users [2], the first strategy is that the contents are cached as a single-based content which means that each content is cached completely in one helper, the second one assume that the same contents are cached as chunk-based content, in other words we suppose that each content is split into chunks, hence, each chunk is cached in a different helper and each helper caches chunk of each content. We compare the two strategies with regard to the energy consumption and the transmission delay. The second strategy outperforms the first one in terms of transmission delay but still not efficient in all the cases of obtaining the content chunks compared to obtaining the single-based content, in terms of energy consumption in the helpers. Our main contribution, in order to achieve a trade-off between the energy and the transmission delay, is a new strategy of caching which combines the other strategies. The proposed strategy consists of caching each content as single-based content (with probability x) and as chunk-based content (with probability $1 - x$) simultaneously, and limit the choices of the requester to download a content between the single-based content and the good cases of chunk-based content. In other words, if downloading a chunk-based content consume a higher energy than downloading a single based content, then the requester should download the single-based content. As expected the third strategy is efficient and able to achieve the desired trade-off.

2 System Model

Using this model, we aim to study the impact of the three strategies mentioned above concerning the energy consumption and the transmission delay of caching a content on devices. Supposing a content is split into chunks and cached in the helpers, the transmission delay for obtaining this content will decrease compared to obtaining its as a single-based content because all the chunks are downloaded simultaneously, wherein the proportion of decreasing the transmission delay depends on the number of the chunks and the distance between the transmitters and the receiver. However, caching a chunk-based content influence the energy consumption as well, wherein the requester may encounter different situations in order to download a content, taking into consideration the different distances away from each chunk and since the energy depends on the distance, the question that arises is how the energy is influenced in chunk-based strategy regarding each situation compared to a single-based strategy. In the following, we introduce some notations and assumptions which will be used throughout the paper.

Consider that each small base station SBS can track and learn the set of influential users from the underlying social graph, and store the contents in the cache of those influential users during off-peak times [2], so that the peak traffic demands can be substantially reduced by proactively serving predictable user demands via caching at users' devices. Consider one SBS, with range L, coordinates the D2D communications between users where user location follows a Poisson Point Process (PPP) with density λ. Each influential user has local cache to store contents and acts as helper. We consider a catalog C with a set of N contents $C = c_1, \cdots, c_N$ where c_i is the i-th most popular content, and H helpers, each helper has cache memory size of M_s number of contents. The contents are assumed to have equal unit size F Bits. The popularity distribution of contents is modeled using Zipf's law:

$$q(i) = \frac{1}{i^\beta \sum_{i=1}^{N} (\frac{1}{i^\beta})} \tag{1}$$

where β is the skewness of the popularity distribution. We consider that the probability of devices who act as helpers (D2D transmitters) is $\rho \in [0, 1]$ which makes the probability of requesters as follows $1 - \rho$, the distributions of requesters and helpers follow homogeneous PPPs with intensity $(1 - \rho)\lambda$ and $\rho\lambda$, respectively. Each helper device independently caches content c_i with a certain probability $p_c(i)$, we assume that all the contents have the same probability of caching given by:

$$p_c(i)) = \begin{cases} M_s/N, & \text{if } N \geq M_s \\ 1, & \text{otherwise.} \end{cases}$$

Owing to the storage limit, we have $\sum_{i=1}^{N} p_c(i) \leq M_s$. Therefore, the distribution of helpers devices who has the content c_i follows a homogeneous PPP with intensity $p_c(i)(\rho)\lambda$. If a user can find its requested content in its own cache, which is the case of helpers, then the consumed energy will be zero, else if the user requests a content from its nearby helpers within a certain distance d, then the probability to find the desired content c_i is [8]:

$$p_f(i) = 1 - e^{-p_c(i)\rho\lambda\pi d^2} \tag{2}$$

Thus, the offloading ratio with a distance d is given by:

$$p_{off}(d) = \sum_{i=1}^{N} q(i)p_f(i) \tag{3}$$

If there are more than one helper which have the requested content, this content is transmitted from the nearest one. Otherwise, the user needs to fetch the content from the SBS. In order to investigate the efficiency of both caching strategies, we need to compare their transmission delay and their energy consumption. This comparison is the subject of the next section.

3   Transmission Delay and Energy Consumption

3.1   Single-Based Caching Strategy

Once a D2D link is established between the transmitter and the receiver, they will be able to transfer the content. We assume power-law path loss with exponent $\alpha > 2$ and Rayleigh fading. The transmit power P_t of a user and its average data rate R are coupled by Shannon's capacity theorem [15]:

$$R = w \log_2(1 + SINR)$$

We consider that the interference among the D2D links as noise, owing to the fact that the users who follow random locations request randomly the contents which are cached randomly. Hence, we can express the signal to interference plus noise ratio (SINR) as following:

$$\gamma(d) = \frac{P_t \mid h \mid^2 d^{-\alpha}}{\sigma_0^2},$$

where P_t is the transmit power, h is the channel coefficient of the D2D link, w is the spectral bandwidth. Thus, the average data rate will be expressed as [16]:

$$R(d) = w \log_2(1 + \frac{P_t \mid h \mid^2 d^{-\alpha}}{\sigma_0^2}), \tag{4}$$

and as mentioned above, we consider that all the contents have the same size F bits, so we can express the transmission delay of a content as following:

$$T_s(d) = F/R(d) = \frac{F}{w \log_2(1 + \frac{P_t \mid h \mid^2 d^{-\alpha}}{\sigma_0^2})} \tag{5}$$

Then, the energy consumed to transmit content via a D2D link with the distance d is formulated as in [16]:

$$E_s(d) = T_s(d)(\frac{P_t}{\eta} + P_c), \tag{6}$$

where P_c is the circuit power consumed at the receiver, and η is the power amplifier efficiency. Thus, the total consumed energy for the offloading is given by:

$$E_{ts}(d) = E_s(d)p_{off}(d) \tag{7}$$

3.2   Chunk-Based Caching Strategy

In this case, we consider that each content will be cached as a chunk-based content with k chunks, we assume that each chunk size is equal to: $F_c = F/k$. We compare the consumed energy to transmit a content cached as single-based content with a predefined distance d and the average of the consumed energy by all the possible cases in chunk-based caching. To clarify what we means by a "case" let's take an example:

Example. we assume that a content is split into 3 chunks and those chunks are situated at 10, 20 and 30 meters away from the receiver. we denote $(10, 20, 30)$ as a case, we assume that all the possible cases are determined using a predefined function.

For simplicity, we assume that the chunk-based content has the same offloading ratio as a single-based content. We consider a case $m = (r_1, ..., r_j, ..., r_k)$ where $m \in [1, M]$, the transmission delay of each chunk is $T_j(r_j) = F_c/R(rj)$, $j \in [1, k]$, where r_j is the distance between the requester and the $j - th$ chunk. Then, the average consumed energy for a chunk j is given by:

$$E_j(r_j) = T_j(r_j)(\frac{P_t}{\eta} + P_c)$$

and the consumed energy by the content in the case m is:

$$E_m = \sum_{j=1}^{k} E_j(r_j)$$

In order to evaluate the average consumed energy for the offloading by all the cases we have:

$$E_{tc} = p_{off}(d)/M \sum_{m=1}^{M} E_m \tag{8}$$

and

$$T_{tc} = \max_{1 \leq m \leq M} T_m, \tag{9}$$

where

$$T_m = \max_{1 \leq j \leq k} T_j(d_j)$$

3.3   Hybrid Strategy of Caching

In this work, we try to show the effectiveness of caching the same content in the two strategies: single-based content and cached-based content in order to avoid wasting energy consumption. To this end the requester should choose a strategy, in terms of energy, to download the content, given that the content is available as single-based content and chunk-based content.

For example, a small cell is shown in Fig. 1, we consider a content c with a size of F bits is cached simultaneously at both single-based caching and chunk-based caching using 3 chunks which have the same size $F_c = F/3$. In the Fig. 1(a) we show that it is efficient, in terms of energy consumption of transmission, that the content is downloaded as a chunk-based content, which marked using a green color, compared to single-based content, which marked using a red color, while, in Fig. 1(b), it is efficient that the content is downloaded as a single-based content. The distributed storage in Fig. 1(a) and (b) denote the good case and the bad case, respectively.

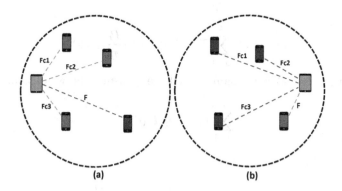

Fig. 1. (a) good case of chunks, (b) bad case of chunks (Color figure online)

In the following, we will explain how to identify the efficient strategy for downloading the desired content. Now let's assume that we have a cached single-based content c_i a distance d away from the requester and the same content is cached as chunk-based content and each chunk j is a distance d_j away from the requester, which means, in terms of energy consumption, that there are bad cases and good cases of obtaining the chunk-based content compared to the single-based content. We consider that the probability that the requester encounters good cases is p_{gc} and the probability that he encounters bad cases is $(1 - p_{gc})$. As mentioned above, each content can be cached with a probability $p_c(i)$, given that a content is cached at both strategies. We consider that p_s is the probability that the desired content can be found as single-based content and $(1 - p_s)$ is the probability that the desired content can be found as chunk-based content. Therefore, the probability that the desired content can be found in good cases will be $p_{gc}(1 - p_s)$ which make the probability that the desired content can be found in bad cases will be $(1 - p_{gc})(1 - p_s)$. We assume that if the requester doesn't find the content in the good cases he will download it as a single-based content, thus, the probability that the desired content can be obtained as single-based content will be $p_s + (1 - p_{gc})(1 - p_s)$. As a result, the offloading with a distance d in single-based content and chunk-based content will be, respectively, as follows:

$$p_{offs}(d) = (p_s + (1 - p_{gc})(1 - p_s))p_{off}(d), \qquad (10)$$

$$p_{offC}(d) = (1 - p_{gc})(1 - p_s)p_{off}(d) \qquad (11)$$

First we need to differentiate the good cases from the bad ones. The good cases are when the consumed energy by one of those cases is less or equal to the consumed energy by the single-based content, therefore, we have:

$$E_m \leq E_s(d)$$

which implies that:

$$\sum_{j=1}^{k} E_j(r_j) \leq E_s(d)$$

$$(\frac{P_t}{\eta} + P_c) \sum_{j=1}^{k} T_j(r_j) \leq T_s(d)(\frac{P_t}{\eta} + P_c)$$

By considering that P_t is the same for all the transmitters, we obtain,

$$\sum_{j=1}^{k} T_j(r_j) \leq T_s(d),$$

and since $F = F_c k$ so,

$$\sum_{j=1}^{k} \frac{F_c}{w \log_2(1 + \frac{P_t|h|^2 r_j^{-\alpha}}{\sigma_0^2})} \leq \frac{F_c k}{w \log_2(1 + \frac{P_t|h|^2 d^{-\alpha}}{\sigma_0^2})},$$

by denoting $\frac{P_t|h|^2}{\sigma_0^2} = b$ we obtain

$$\sum_{j=1}^{k} \frac{1}{\log_2(1 + br_j^{-\alpha})} \leq \frac{k}{\log_2(1 + bd^{-\alpha})}, \qquad (12)$$

where r_j is the distance between the requester and the j-th chunk-based content and d the distance between the requester and the single-based content.

Thus, the scenario of requesting a content is given by Algorithm 1.

Let's consider a set of G different good cases $g = 1, \ldots, G$, the average consumed energy by all the good cases in chunk-based caching and the transmission delay are considered, respectively, as following:

$$E_{tc} = p_{offC}(d)/G \sum_{g=1}^{G} Eg, \qquad (13)$$

$$T_{tc} = \max_{1 \leq g \leq G} T_g \qquad (14)$$

and the average consumed energy by the single-based content and the transmission delay are expressed, respectively, as following:

$$E_{ts}(d) = E(d)p_{offS}(d), \qquad (15)$$

Algorithm 1

---

if the content C is in the nearby devices **then**
    if C exist only as a chunk-based content **then**
        if there is a good case g **then**
            C is downloaded according to g
        else
            C is downloaded from the other cases
        end if
    else if C exist only as single-based content **then**
        C is downloaded as single-based content
    else if C is single-based content / chunk-based content **then**
        if condition (12) is True **then**
            C is downloaded as chunk-based content
        else
            C is downloaded as single-based content
        end if
    end if
else
    the user needs to download the content from the SBS
end if

$$T_{ts}(d) = F/R_d \tag{16}$$

Hence, the average consumed energy is given by:

$$\bar{E} = E_{tc} + E_{ts}(d) \tag{17}$$

4   Simulation

To evaluate the performance of our proposed strategy, we use Matlab simulator. Considering the users' location follows PPP distribution with $\lambda = 0.03$, we consider a social community of 100 users, in which $\rho = 10\%$ of the users act as helpers. The remaining 90% of users will request for a random content c_i in the catalog C according to the request probabilities $q(i)$, which follows the Zipf distribution with parameter $\beta = 1$. We consider the path loss exponent $\alpha = 4$. The device cache size capacity is $M_s = 2$ contents. The content library has a size of $N = 10$ contents, where each content is with a size of 30 Mbytes. The D2D searching distance is ≤ 100 m. The device transmission power and the background noise power are $P_t = 199.5$ mW and $\sigma_0^2 = -95$ dBm, respectively. The channel coefficient h=1, W $= 20$ MHz, the amplifier efficiency $\eta = 0.2$, and the circuit power is $P_c = 115.9$ mW. We consider a number of chunks k $= 3$ and each one has a size $F_c = 10$ Mbytes.

In Fig. 2(a), we represent the consumed energy while varying the distance d in a single-based content and the **average** energy consumed by all the possible cases in chunk-based content. When the distance d is less than 50 m, we can see that the transmission of a single-based content consumes less energy than chunk-based content, and this is because the possibilities of bad cases are more than those of the good cases. Contrariwise, when the distance d is higher than 50 m, the consumed energy by a single-based content becomes bigger than the consumed energy by a chunk-based content. Whatever, the transmission delay of chunk-based content stills more efficient than single-based content. The Fig. 2(b) shows that the maximum transmission delay in chunk-based caching doesn't exceed 0.32 s. However, it reaches about 0.95 s at 100 m. In Fig. 3, we show that when a requester downloads a chunk-based content, encountering a bad case, the consumed energy for transmission will be higher than when the requester downloads a single-based content, which is the opposite if the transmission encounters a good case. We notice that there is no bad cases at d=100 m, this is because the average energy consumed by all the cases is less than the energy consumed by a single-based content.

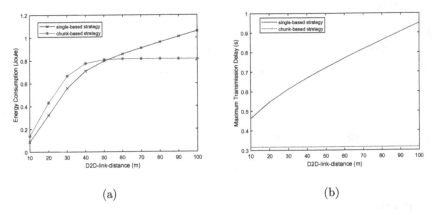

(a)   (b)

Fig. 2. The consumed energy and maximum transmission delay for the two strategies

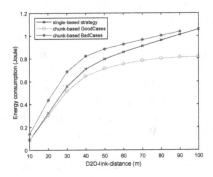

Fig. 3. The energy consumption of a chunk-based content (good cases and bad cases)

Figure 4 shows the energy consumption wherein we limited the choices of the requester, who looks for the content of interest, between the single-based content and the good cases of chunk-based content with different percentages. As expected we can maintain the consumed energy wherein it doesn't exceed the energy consumed by a single-based content and at the same time benefit from the distributed storage in terms of both energy consumption and transmission delay. Therefore, the trade-off is achieved.

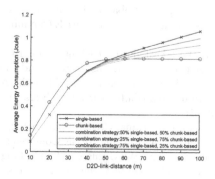

Fig. 4. The average energy consumption in the hybrid strategy

5 Conclusion

In this paper, we focused on the content placement problem in a D2D network formed by users' devices who act as helpers and requesters and where distributed caching coupled with distributed storage are employed. We proposed a new caching strategy which takes the advantages of the two already existing strategies: the single-based caching and the chunk-based caching. We have developed the necessary equations that characterize our proposed strategy *the Hybrid strategy of caching*, then we have proposed an algorithm illustrating the scenario of requesting a content. We showed, through simulations, that the new strategy is more efficient and can achieve a trade-off between the energy consumption and the transmission delay.

References

1. Cisco: Visual networking index forecast. 2015–2020 (2015)
2. Bastug, E., Bennis, M., Debbah, M.: Living on the edge: on the role of proactive caching in 5G wireless networks. IEEE Comm. Mag. SI Context Awareness **52**(8), 82–89 (2014)
3. Jin, H., et al.: Information-centric mobile caching network frameworks and caching optimization: a survey. EURASIP J. Wirel. Commun. Netw. **2017**, 33 (2017)

4. Altman, E., Avrachenkov, K., Goseling, J.: Distributed storage in the plane. In: Proceedings of the IFIP Networking Conference (2014)
5. Golrezaei, N., Molisch, A.F., Dimakis, A.G., Caire, G.: Femtocaching and device-to-device collaboration: a new architecture for wireless video distribution. IEEE Commun. **51**, 142–149 (2013)
6. Wang, W., Wu, X., Xie, L., Lu, S.: Joint storage assignment for D2D offloading systems. Comput. Commun. **83**, 45–55 (2016)
7. Chen, B., Shen, H., Cao, X.: Cooperative caching placement in cognitive device-to-device networks. J. Commun. **11** (2016)
8. Pappas, Z.C.N., Kountouris, M.: Probabilistic caching in wireless D2D networks: cache hit optimal versus throughput optimal. IEEE Commun. Lett. **21**(3), 584–587 (2017)
9. Krishnan, S., Dhillon, H.S.: Distributed caching in device-to-device networks: a stochastic geometry perspective. In: Signals Systems and Computer (2015)
10. Shanmugam, K., Golrezaei, N., Dimakis, A.G., Molisch, A.F., Caire, G.: wireless content delivery through distributed caching helpers. IEEE Trans. Inf. Theor. **59**(12), 8402–8413 (2013)
11. Kang, H.J., Park, K.Y., Cho, K., Kang, C.G.: Mobile caching policies for device-to-device (D2D) content delivery networking. IEEE Conference on Computer (2014)
12. Bai, B., Wang, L., Han, Z., Chen, W., Svensson, T.: Caching based socially-aware D2D communications in wireless content delivery networks: a hypergraph framework. IEEE Wirel. Commun. **23**, 74–81 (2016)
13. Golrezaei, N., Molisch, A.F., Dimakis, A.G., Caire, G.: Femtocaching and device-to-device collaboration: a new architecture for wireless video distribution. IEEE Commun. Mag. **51**(4), 142–149 (2013)
14. Krishnan, S., Dhillon, H.S.: Effect of user mobility on the performance of device-to-device networks with distributed caching (2017)
15. Mumtaz, S., Rodriguez, J. (eds.): Smart Device to Smart Device Communication. Springer, Cham (2014). https://doi.org/10.1007/978-3-319-04963-2
16. Chen, B., Yang, C.: Energy costs for traffic offloading by cache-enabled D2D communications. In: IEEE Wireless Conference and Networking Conference (2016)

An Interactive Business Model for Green Energy Production in Smart Grid

Youssef Moubarak[(✉)] and Mohamed Sadik

NEST Research Group, LRI Lab., ENSEM, Hassan II University of Casablanca,
Casablanca, Morocco
{youssef.moubarak, m.sadik}@ensem.ac.ma

Abstract. The prosumers represent a new profile of consumer/producer of energy that deploy the renewable technology to produce a pure quantity of energy oriented for internal Household demand, or for grid injection (Grid Connected PV). Based on decentralized structure, several studies discuss the requirement efficiency to enhance yield results and reduce energy loss in the grid while the moment of injection and distribution. On this paper, we use a game theory approach to incentivize prosumers to participate in a market game-based quantity of PV energy injected to maximize incomes profit and reduce the energy consumed from the grid by implementing Cournot-Nash equilibrium approach.

Keywords: Self-consumers · Prosumers · PV system · PV rooftop
Grid connected PV · Demand responses · Smart grid · Game theory
Nash equilibrium · Cournot oligopoly · Non-cooperative game
Pure game

1 Introduction

The use of renewable energies by replacing conventional energy, whose production is based on fossil fuels, brings several advantages in developing countries in this trend of energy saving and CO2 culture. From an economic point of view renewable energy generation does not require fossil fuels for their operation, so fuel price variations affect neither the quantity of electricity produced nor the performance of the energy system. Their diffusion improves the local employment situation during the installation, operation and maintenance phases. From an environmental point of view, renewables technologies do not emit greenhouse gases (GHG) during the electricity production phase and their uses allow the reduction of health impacts on the population.

According to the present plan, total PV power installations will reach 1.8 GW by 2020 and 600 GW by 2050. According to forecasts made by the Chinese Electric Power Research Institute, renewable energy installations will account for 30% of the total electric power installations in China by 2050, of which PV installations will account for 5%. In Morocco, the authorities launched a National Renewable Energy and Efficiency Strategy in 2008 which may improve a good promotion of energy efficiency and meet a 42% (14% solar, 14% wind, 14% hydraulic) target of green energy production by 2020 [1].

© Springer Nature Switzerland AG 2018
N. Boudriga et al. (Eds.): UNet 2018, LNCS 11277, pp. 229–240, 2018.
https://doi.org/10.1007/978-3-030-02849-7_20

Distributed photovoltaic systems connected to the grid can be installed to provide energy to a specific consumer or directly into the grid, increasing reliability of the systems. According to [2], the benefits of solar energy production include increased production capacity, avoided transmission and distribution costs, reduction of transformer losses and transmission lines, possibility to control reactive power and the fact that they are environmentally friendly. Environmental benefits can be measured in terms of greenhouse gas emissions. A 5 MW PV power plant operating in Saudi Arabia eliminated the emission of roughly 914 t of greenhouse gases, considering its substitution of a coal fired power plant of the same size [3]. Carbon emissions from photovoltaic cells are the result of electricity use during manufacturing [4]. [5] documented that, with the conservative European average electricity mix, energy payback time (EPBT) is 2–6 years and CO_2 payback time is 4–6 years for the photovoltaic system. The decreasing prices of photovoltaic systems have been driven by solar cell efficiency improvements; manufacturing-technology improvements; and economies of scale.

Decentralized renewable energy technologies have several advantages over grid extension, such as their proximity to the consumer, which considerably reduces operating costs in terms of energy transmission, which includes the costs of energy loss, expansion of transmission capacity, etc.

A grid-connected PV system can result in a considerable reduction in capital cost and maintenance cost by eliminating the need for battery bank storage. The grid can act as a storage bank for solar PV systems, where the excess electricity can be deposited to and, when necessary, also with drawn from. When a PV system is employed for domestic use, the PV modules are commonly mounted on the rooftop, which can reduce the size of the mounting structure and land requirements.

Self-consumers side is being the core of energy systems transition and development, in order to increase energy efficiency and security of supply, with the use of endogenous resources by decentralizing production into consumers and make them a Self-consumers or Prosumers and give them the choice to develop the energy market. With that in mind, using renewable resources for self-consumption is spreading all over Europe, supported by different national policies, either on small or large-scale generation. In this way the consumer is no longer a passive agent, he become a prosumer: an active consumer and producer [2, 6].

In this paper, we promote a new economic model of decentralizing PV energy production into Low Voltage (LV) consumer. In this case, the quantity produced is going to be use of internal demand, or in other way, be injected into the grid. So, the prosumer can consume or inject his energy produced with taking into account the total energy injected by all other prosumer into the market, the infrastructure costs, the balance between his own production price and that of the provider, etc.

This production is organized as follow: Model formulation of self-consumer steady behavior in Sect. 2; Utility model based on a fixed price quantity game in Sect. 3; Sect. 4 for developing PV energy market game injected at fixed price approach with computation of Cournot-Nash equilibrium and Sect. 5 to conclude this work.

2 Model Formulation: Self-consumer Steady Behavior

Grid connected photovoltaic (PV) systems, in particular low power on this case, mostly single-phase PV "rooftop" systems are generally privately owned in a power range of up to 10 KW. The main aim to maximize its energy yield, issues such as low cost, reliability, long life time (20 years and longer), high (part-load-) efficiency and good environmental conditions (availability of solar radiation) are hence of importance to the private operator.

In this system we consider a decentralized structure in Low Voltage regime (LV) for renewable energy production based Photovoltaic technology. For a number of Prosumers (self-consumers) (Players) N, the Fig. 1 shows the architecture proposed for this model. Each self-consumer A_i^c, as $i = \{1; 2; \dots; n\} \in N$ has a production unit Ph_i characterized by installed capacity X_i.

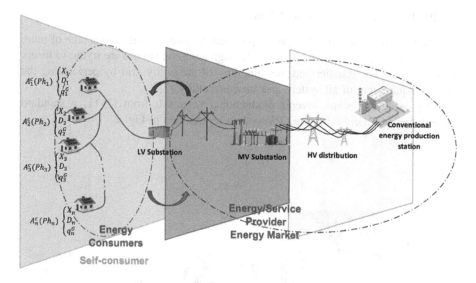

Fig. 1. Proposed architecture of PV energy market between self-consumer and energy provider.

The self-consumer profile, represents a LV customer profile connected to the network of a conventional energy supplier that authorize and regulate the integration of a direct-to-consumer photovoltaic production unit (no storage), and/or an injection of a quantity of energy into the Grid. In this case an Internal Demand Management is an encouraged approach by the distribution network manager, where the customer incentivized by a Dynamic Pricing [4]. In this case, the consumer is invited to schedule his daily consumption by referring to the current situation of the network, for example period of the peak of load [6], the choice of periods when the cost of a conventional unit of energy is the lowest (in the case of a liberalization of the energy market) compared to the cost of self-generated photovoltaic energy...

In a Prosumers energy market, [4] discuss the impact of Energy Consumption Scheduling (ECS) between consumers in order to avoid the excessive charging of load and which thus influences the pricing of the energy unit.

So that, it is up to us to summarize that a good approach of internal demand management in our case [5], contributes to the reduction of consumption costs, and to the reduction of energy costs and thus the creation of profit. In this case the consumer will combine two different energy sources: conventional energy $E_{\bar{G}}$ and photovoltaic E_{pv}; whose choice depends on the internal consumption profile in relation with the price of each energy source during the energy consumption cycle (24 h).

In fact, the consumer could be incentivized to invest on this model of Photovoltaic self-consuming connected to the grid and participate in the generation of profit on the report of the energy management and thereafter be part of the game that this paper will address and will propose the strategic elements to success this finality.

2.1   PV Production and Demand Model

Grid structure interconnecting PV power production system has the advantage of more effective utilization of generated power. Although a several studies are trying to insure the safety of the PV installer and the reliability of the utility grid by performing the technical requirement of all system and structure utility [7].

While consulting some several productions, we result from [8–11] a standard representation of a Grid connected PV system represented in Fig. 2.

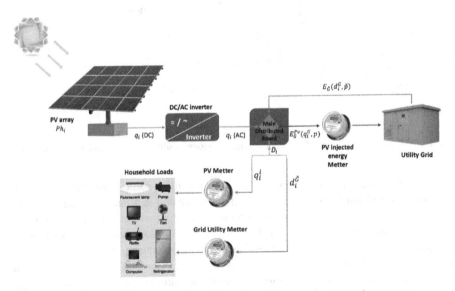

Fig. 2. Photovoltaic system connected to the grid source in prosuming process

In our case study, we are deploying photovoltaic energy production technology for direct consumption and injection (the absence of batteries). This condition comes to imply the self-consumer to depend directly, at first, on the energy provider. This implies that the coverage rate of the system must ensure maximum performance and efficiency during self-consumption.

The production of a photovoltaic unit depends on several dimensions: PV field surface (PV plate area), the minimum power of the module and the annual Radiation rate [6, 12].

The estimate of the quantity of energy q_i produced is expressed as follows:

$$E_{pv} = q_i = X_i * e_{pv} * \frac{br}{br_0} * 365 \tag{1}$$

X_i *represent the Maximum capacity installed of PV unit*
e_{pv} *represent the Efficiency of the PV*
br *represent the annual average rate of solar radiation*
br_0 *represent the rate of radiation standard for each region measured in* $(kWh/m^2/day)$.

In our case, we consider that the yield is maximum on all PV modules per customer, so $X_i = q_i$.

Given the production of the photovoltaic unit, the quantity produced is composed as follows:

$$q_i = q_i^i + q_i^G, i = \{1; 2; \ldots; n\} \in N \tag{2}$$

q_i^i *represent The quantity of internal PV energy consumption.*
q_i^G *represent The quantity of aditionnal quantity injected into the Grid.*

In terms of demand side, each consumer is characterized by their own demand for internal consumption:

$$D_i : D_1 \neq D_2 \neq \cdots \neq D_n, i = \{1; 2; \ldots; n\} \in N \tag{3}$$

The demand response (DR) is managed by the deployment of the two available resources: the internal production in original Photovoltaic E_{pv} quantity q_i, and a quantity of energy of the network (grid) $E_{\bar{G}}$ demand $d_i^{\bar{G}}$ for $i = \{1; 2; \ldots; n\}$.

The combination of energy demand is represented as follows:

$$D_i = d_i^{\bar{G}} + q_i^i, i = \{1; 2; \ldots; n\} \in N \tag{4}$$

The quantity value of the total demand side is subject to the conditions that are chosen by the prosumer for each consumption situation:

$$\textbf{Condition N}°\textbf{1}: D_i \geq q_i \Rightarrow \begin{cases} q_i = q_i^i \text{ and } D_i = d_i^G + q_i \text{ with } \left(q_i^G = 0\right) \\ q_i = q_i^i \text{ and } d_i = q_i \text{ with } \left(q_i^G = 0\right) \\ q_i = q_i^i + q_i^G \text{ and } D_i = d_i^G + q_i^i \text{ with } \left(q_i^G > 0\right) \\ q_i = q_i^G \text{ and } D_i = d_i^G\left(q_i^i = 0\right) \end{cases} \quad (5)$$

$$\textbf{Condition N}°\textbf{2}: D_i < q_i \Rightarrow \begin{cases} q_i = q_i^i + q_i^G \text{ and } D_i = q_i^i \\ q_i = q_i^G \text{ and } D_i = d_i^G \\ q_i = q_i^i + q_i^G \text{ and } D_i = d_i^G + q_i^i \end{cases} \quad (6)$$

The conditions (1) and (2) represent the expression of injected power depending the quantity produced and the value of demand side. That mean that the prosumer, as knowing his demand side of energy, can answer his consumption by combining the both energies (PV E_{pv} or from grid $E_{\bar{G}}$) or each one of them and by the way managing his consumption from the provider or the injected PV energy into the grid.

In this paper, each prosumer has the choice to define his own production capacity based on the coverage rate he seeks to ensure through his own production unit.

So that, we find that:

$$q_i : q_1 \neq q_2 \neq \ldots \neq q_n, i = \{1; 2; \ldots.; n\} \in N \quad (7)$$

2.2 Costs Model

This model represents a set of costs related to the establishment of the PV unit, the conventional energy consumption costs $(E_{\bar{G}})$ as well as the savings related to the planning of this consumption by ensuring a minimal dynamic pricing. In addition, the integration of E_{pv} in the daily consumption cycle (outside night period) can introduce some economy on the energy bill through the withdrawal of the amount related to the purchase of the quantities of energy injected (REFIT: Renewable energy feed-in-tariff) [13, 14].

Investment Costs:
The investment cost represents all the expenses relating to the setting up of a photo-voltaic power generation unit, the size of which must be well dimensioned in order to define the rate of coverage of the quantity produced for the immediate demand in internal consumption. So that, like any productive facility, the costs are divided into two categories:

$$\vartheta_i(q_i) = q_i * (v_i + f_i), \quad i = \{1; 2; \ldots.; n\} \in N \quad (8)$$

q_i represent the Produced power of the PV unit
v_i represent the $\sum$ *variable costs*
f_i represent the $\sum$ *fixed costs*.

This explains that for each prosumer i, the variable costs are related to the infrastructure dimension necessary to produce the quantity PV energy $E_{pv}(q_i)$ compatible with the energy consumption and production profile chosen by the concerned prosumer, e.g. the number of PV platforms that will respond to the load profile. The expression of the fixed costs represents the investments which corresponds to the infrastructure by installed power (electrical installation, internal management equipment, civil engineering ...).

Consumption Costs function:
In this model, the consumption costs only represent the bill related to the absorbed energy pricing from the electricity grid. According to a pricing policy specific to the electricity grid operator, static (uniform in relation to the threshold of the quantity consumed or time slot) or dynamic (subject to a billing per regulated slice by the consumption threshold and/or the time slot during or outside peak periods [13] the expression of consumption expenditure G_i is:

$$G_i = \bar{p} * d_i^{\bar{G}} = \bar{p} * (D_i - q_i^i), \quad i = \{1; 2; .....; n\} \in N \tag{9}$$

$\bar{p}$ is cost unit of energy consumption from the electricity grid.

In this paper, the value of $\bar{p}$ expresses the Current Value for the non-discriminatory energy term of the Last Resource Tariff [9] to simplify the calculations in the following sections.

Injection Price function:
This function represents the value of unitary price of each unity of energy E_{pv} that influenced by the total quantity q_T^G injected into the grid by N player or the unitary price of the PV energy market.

We note:

$$P(Q_T^G) = (b * \bar{p}) - \frac{1}{\alpha} * \left(\sum_j^n q_j^G \right), i = \{1; 2; .....; n\} \in N \tag{10}$$

When α represents the price sensitivity of the unit of energy $\langle q_i^G \rangle$ injected into the Grid which corresponds to the final average price of the total demand on the wholesale market of electricity.

The constant **b** represents the exogenous variable such as income and wealth, prices of substitutes and complements expectations of future prices... [15]

3   Utility Function

After discussing the different elements characterizing the model, we consider a market with N prosumers (players) such that $i = \{1; 2; .....; n\} \in N$. The Smart Grid Structure represents a perfectly competitive market, where each individual seeks to maximize their market share by maximizing their incomes. We call $\pi_i(q_i^G)$ the Profit function of each self-consumer is therefore:

$$\pi_i\left(q^G\right) = P\left(\sum_j^n q_j^G\right) * q_i^G - C_i\left(q_i, q_i^i, D_i, \bar{p}\right) \tag{11}$$

where $P\left(\sum_j^n q_j^G\right)$ is the price set by the Market E_{pv} energy injected into the Grid, and $C_i\left(q_i, q_i^G, D_i, \bar{p}\right)$ is the cost function which can be written:

$$C_i\left(q_i, q_i^G, D_i, \bar{p}\right) = \vartheta_i(q_i) + G_i\left(q_i^i, D_i, \bar{p}\right), i = \{1; 2; \ldots; n\} \in N \tag{12}$$

In this work, we consider that a self-consumer profile seeks to maximize its market share through the quantity of energy E_{pv} to be injected taking into consideration a selling price set by the energy network manager.

3.1 Analysis of the Market Game

In the rest of this paper, we will proceed to the analysis of the perfect market (existence of the competition) for Photovoltaic energy, and therefore the product marketed is identical for all A_i^c. The objective of this paper is to represent a fair marketing model of the concept of self-consumption through the incentive of LV customers to the benefits generated by participation in the process of liberalization of the energy sector through the decentralization of photovoltaic production.

This model is considered by:

- A non-cooperative market game in PV energy.
- The system of strategies is pure and continuous.
- Each player knows the strategy of games of/or other competitors.
- The decision is simultaneous between players.

So that, it is then necessary to specify the appropriate combination (equilibrium point), based on the injected quantity, which will consequently have an impact on the purchased price of E_{pv} and of course on the final income $U_i\left(q^G\right)$.

3.2 Cournot-Nash Equilibrium

On this section, we are going to study the game environment with introduction the quantity of PV energy injected into the grid, which going to drive the system to an equilibrium point.

We consider a strategic form of game of N players $\Gamma = \{Q_1, \ldots, Q_N, U_1, \ldots, U_N\}$, Q_i represents the strategy of quantity of the i players and U_i is the function of utility of players.

A Nash equilibrium [16] in pure strategies of a game in normal form $\langle N, (s_i)_{i \in N}, (u_i)_{i \in N} \rangle$ is a profile of actions $s^* = \left(s_1^*, s_2^*, \ldots, s_n^*\right) \in S$, such that the action of each player is a better answer to the actions chosen by the other players.

Definition: The Cournot-Nash equilibrium specifies the strategy $q_i^{G*} \in Q_i$ for each player i, $i = \{1; 2; \ldots; N\}$ so that:

$$u_i\left(q_i^{G*}, q_{-i}^{G*}\right) \geq u_i\left(q_j^{G*}, q_{-i}^{G*}\right), \forall q_{i,j} \in Q_i, \forall i,j \in N \tag{13}$$

Where q_i^{G*} represents the quantity of PV energy injected by each player i while maximizing its utility.

In words, a Nash equilibrium specifies a strategy, that may yield for each player (taking into account his chosen strategy) at least as high a payoff as any other strategy of the principal player, given the strategies of the other players and vice to that.

For that, the analysis of the competitive injection quantity of prosumer contributes to maximize their profit. To do so, we will show the existence and uniqueness of the balance of play between the prosumers, and we are going to calculate the equilibrium point. So that, the researching for the Cournot-Nash equilibrium will depend on the proper combination of the injected E_{pv} vector by fixing the price of a unit of energy.

4 PV Energy Market Game

4.1 Study of Cournot-Nash Definition Equilibrium

In this model, the players (prosumers) are looking for a maximization of revenues by maintaining the equilibrium of the system through the injection of the amount of equilibrium PV energy. Hence the strategy vector:

$$q^G = \left(q_1^G, \ldots, q_i^G, \ldots, q_n^G\right) \in S, i = \{1; 2; \ldots ; N\} \tag{14}$$

Since the following model is static (only one decision is made), we can consider that:

The information is perfect, each player knows the cost function of the others (this function represents the function of income at the moment of decision on the amount of injection chosen by the player). And the player A_i^c **decides simultaneously.**

Each strategy decision represents a quantity of $E_{pv}: s_i\left(q_i^G\right)$ that may satisfy Nash equilibrium conditions through the maximum of profit function:

$$\pi_i\left(q^G\right) = \left[(b*\bar{p}) - \frac{1}{\alpha}*\left(\sum_j^n q_j^G\right)\right]*q_i^G - \left[q_i*(v_i+f_i)+\bar{p}*\left(D_i - q_i^i\right)\right] \tag{15}$$

Assumption 1: The quantity decided by each player take into account the profile of internal consumption, when the conditions of each combined energy consumption situation is given in **PV production and Demand Model** section when $0 \leq q_i^G \leq q_i$.

The Eq. (15) represent that the utility of a user is affected by the other user's strategy. Let $s_{-i} = \{s_1, \ldots, s_{i-1}, \ldots, s_{i+1}, \ldots, s_N\}$ denote the set of strategies adopted by all users except i, and $s = s_{-i} \cup \{s_i\}$. Then user's best-response function is given by:

$$BR_i(q^G_{-i}) = \arg max_{q_i} U_i(q^G_i, q^G_{-i}); \ i = \{1; 2; \ldots; n\} \in N \tag{16}$$

The best strategy set of all the users that run-in connection with maximum of profit is $q^{G^*} = \{q^{G*}_1, \ldots, q^{G*}_N\}$, then construct the Nash equilibrium:

$$q^{G*}_i = \max(0, BR_i(q^{G*})); i = \{1; 2; \ldots; n\} \in N \tag{17}$$

Lemma 1 (*Existence*): Consider the E_{pv} quantity game which arises when the price parameter is fixed for all prosumers, there exists in less one quantity-based Nash equilibrium q^{G*} of the A^cs players.

Proof: The Eqs. (18) and (19) represent respectively the derivative and second derivative of utility function (15) w.r.t the E_{pv} quantity:

$$\frac{\partial \pi_i(q^G)}{\partial q^G_i} = (b * \bar{p}) - \frac{1}{\alpha}\left(2q^G_i + \sum_{j \neq i}^{n-1} q^G_j\right) - (v_i + f_i + \bar{p}) \tag{18}$$

$$\frac{\partial^2 \pi_i(q^G)}{\partial q^{G2}_i} = -\frac{2}{\alpha} \leq 0 \tag{19}$$

The second derivative of the function of profit is negative, then the utility function is thus concave and the existence of one in less of Nash equilibrium of injected quantity of PV energy [17] is proven.

Lemma 2 (*Uniqueness*): Regarding the Moulin's condition and Rosen's condition [17] the uniqueness of Nash equilibrium referred to the next condition:

$$-\frac{\partial^2 \pi_i(q^G)}{\partial q^{G\,2}_i} - \sum_{j,j \neq i}\left|\frac{\partial^2 \pi_i(q^G)}{\partial q^G_i \partial q^G_j}\right| \geq 0 \tag{20}$$

Proof: The mixed partial is written as:

$$\frac{\partial^2 \pi_i(q^G)}{\partial q^G_i \partial q^G_j} = -\frac{1}{\alpha} \tag{21}$$

$$-\frac{\partial^2 \pi_i(q^G)}{\partial q^{G\,2}_i} - \sum_{j,j \neq i}\left|\frac{\partial^2 \pi_i(q^G)}{\partial q^G_i \partial q^G_j}\right| = \frac{1}{\alpha} \geq 0 \tag{22}$$

Regarding the results from the Lemma 1 and 2, and according the continuity of utility function (profit) (last function profit) and regarding the Assumption 1, for $0 \leq q^G_i \leq q_i$ the profit Function ins strictly concave in each $\{q^G_i\}^N_{i=1}$, and jointly concave as well. A strictly concave function must be a quasi-concavity one. So, we can conclude that a Cournot-Nash equilibrium does exist in this case of the market game.

4.2 Computation of Nash Equilibrium

The definition of Cournot-Nash Equilibrium is depending to resolve the vector of Best Response (BR) of injected energy q^{G*}. From the Eq. (18) we can solve the expression of BR when:

$$\frac{\partial \pi_i(q^G)}{\partial q_i^G} = 0, i = \{1; 2; \ldots; N\} \tag{23}$$

That's mean:

$$2q_i^G + \sum_j^n q_j^G = \alpha * ((b * \bar{p}) - (v_i + f_i + \bar{p})) \tag{24}$$

From this expression we can extract the expression of the Injected Grid Quantity equilibrium vector $\langle q_i^{G*} \rangle_{i=1}^N$:

$$q_i^{G*} = \begin{pmatrix} \frac{1}{2} & \cdots & \frac{-1}{(n+1)} \\ \vdots & \ddots & \vdots \\ \frac{-1}{(n+1)} & \cdots & \frac{n}{(n+1)} \end{pmatrix}^{-1} * \begin{pmatrix} ((b * \bar{p}) - (v_1 + f_1 + \check{p})) * \alpha \\ \vdots \\ ((b * \bar{p}) - (v_n + f_n + \check{p})) * \alpha \end{pmatrix} \tag{25}$$

Finally, the equilibrium value represented in the expression represent the reaction of each player to inject a quantity of PV energy which going to maximize their profit. But, and unknowing the market demand, the global quantity injected into the market can be upper than the demand of users, when the price can go down to.

5 Conclusion

In this paper we present a non-cooperative game for a market share game. Each prosumer A^C and according his strategy, act to deploy and/or to inject into the market a part or a total quantity of E_{pv} in order to maximize his own revenues. This presented case study integrate the Cournot Oligopoly market approach with playing the quantity of energy PV injected with fixed price by the market or government. This first introduction takes in consideration a perfect environment that proof some system efficacity in founding the Nash equilibrium of the game, but he is waiting for us to explore the system with others constraints to satisfy the attended of the market in this field of research.

References

1. Tahri, M., Hakdaoui, M., Maanan, M.: The evaluation of solar farm locations applying geographic information system and multi-criteria decision-making methods: case study in southern Morocco. Renew. Sustain. Energy Rev. **51**, 1354–1362 (2015)
2. Hoff, T.E., Perez, R., Margolis, R.M.: Maximizing the value of customer-sited PV systems using storage and controls. Sol. Energy **81**(7), 940–945 (2007)
3. Rehman, S., Bader, M.A., Al-Moallem, S.A.: Cost of solar energy generated using PV panels. Renew. Sustain. Energy Rev. **11**(8), 1843–1857 (2007)
4. Evans, A., Strezov, V., Evans, T.J.: Assessment of sustainability indicators for renewable energy technologies. Renew. Sustain. Energy Rev. **13**(5), 1082–1088 (2009)
5. Rand, B.P., Genoe, J., Heremans, P., Poortmans, J.: Solar cells utilizing small molecular weight organic semiconductors. Prog. Photovolt Res. Appl. **35**(February 2013), 659–676 (2007)
6. Nguyen, K.Q.: Alternatives to grid extension for rural electrification: Decentralized renewable energy technologies in Vietnam. Energy Policy **35**(4), 2579–2589 (2007)
7. Eltawil, M.A., Zhao, Z.: Grid-connected photovoltaic power systems: technical and potential problems-a review. Renew. Sustain. Energy Rev. **14**(1), 112–129 (2010)
8. Moraes, O., Oliveira, D.: Distributed photovoltaic generation and energy storage systems : a review ^ nia So, **14**, 506–511 (2010)
9. Colmenar-Santos, A., Campíñez-Romero, S., Pérez-Molina, C., Castro-Gil, M.: Profitability analysis of grid-connected photovoltaic facilities for household electricity self-sufficiency. Energy Policy **51**, 749–764 (2012)
10. Luthander, R., Widén, J., Nilsson, D., Palm, J.: Photovoltaic self-consumption in buildings: a review. Appl. Energy **142**, 80–94 (2015)
11. Castillo-Cagigal, M., et al.: PV self-consumption optimization with storage and active DSM for the residential sector. Sol. Energy **85**(9), 2338–2348 (2011)
12. Thiam, D.R.: An energy pricing scheme for the diffusion of decentralized renewable technology investment in developing countries. Energy Policy **39**(7), 4284–4297 (2011)
13. Caron, S., Kesidis, G.: Incentive-based energy consumption scheduling algorithms for the smart grid. In: 2010 First IEEE Int. Conf. Smart Grid Commun., pp. 391–396 (2010)
14. Balcombe, P., Rigby, D., Azapagic, A.: Energy self-sufficiency, grid demand variability and consumer costs: integrating solar PV, stirling engine CHP and battery storage. Appl. Energy **155**, 393–408 (2015)
15. Afonso, O., Vasconcelos, P.B.: Computational Economics: A Concise Introduction. Boca Raton, Numerical (2016)
16. National Academy of Sciences of the United States of America: Equilibrium points in n-person games Author (s): John, F.: Nash Source: Proceedings of the National Academy of Sciences of the United States of America. National Academy of Sciences Stable, vol. 36, no. 1, pp. 48–49 (2013). http://www.jstor.org/stable/88031
17. TE Society.: Existence and Uniqueness of Equilibrium Points for Concave N-Person Games Author (s): Rosen, J.B.: Published by: The Econometric Society Stable. References Linked references are available on JSTOR for this arti, vol. 33, no. 3, pp. 520–534 (2016). http://www.jstor.org/stable/1911749

"SmartParking": Toward an Intelligent Parking System Management in Casablanca

Sofia Belkhala[1,2(✉)] and Hicham Medromi[1]

[1] System Architecture Team, Engineering Research Laboratory,
National and High School of Electricity and Mechanic (ENSEM),
HASSAN II University, Casablanca, Morocco
Belk.sophia@gmail.com, Hmedromi@yahoo.fr
[2] Research Foundation for Development and Innovation in Science
and Engineering, Casablanca, Morocco

Abstract. Cities are the economic and social progress for nations, but the speed with which they grow up creates many problems, especially in terms of mobility. In reality, finding a parking space in the city of Casablanca in Morocco in working hours is an almost impossible mission. This search for parking space results in waste of time, fuels, and traffic jams. In order to resolve these issues and reduce the problems caused by inefficient and classic parking system, we proposed a solution to contribute to the good management of traffic, reduce the search time of free parking spaces and improve the profitability of the parking by regulating rates.

Keywords: Smart parking · Urban mobility · WSN · IoT
Parking management · Cloud

1 Introduction and Related Works

The amount of time spent cruising for parking creates issues on both social and individual levels. At the personal plane, it consumes much fuel and time. From the point of view of the society, cruising for parking creates a surprising amount of traffic and therefore increases the level of environmental pollution.

In order to diminish and solve those problems, cities seek to implement both traditional and modern communication infrastructures to increase efficiency and sustainability level and to improve the overall quality of life. For optimal long-term efficiency, such measures need to be accompanied by good management plans of the city's natural resources at the institutional level [1].

In fact, a significant improvement of the transport infrastructure can be done through the concept of the Internet Of Things (IoT). IoT is defined as a variety of connected devices communicating and collaborating together through specific schemes aimed at meeting specific needs. Among those facilities, radio frequency identification (RFID) tags, sensors, actuators and mobile phones play an important role in diminishing the time spent cruising for parking [2]. Through them, information from transport systems is continuously collected, and this information is further stored,

© Springer Nature Switzerland AG 2018
N. Boudriga et al. (Eds.): UNet 2018, LNCS 11277, pp. 241–246, 2018.
https://doi.org/10.1007/978-3-030-02849-7_21

transferred and processed in real time, providing users as well as traffic operators with real time information aimed at improving traffic conditions and common transportation.

Smart parking is considered one major strategy for solving most of the problems related to urban traffic, so several systems have been proposed for helping citizens search for and find a free parking place by exploring their availability within the urban infrastructure. San Francisco's SFpark, and Los Angeles' LA Express Parkin are considered amongst the most successful smart parking systems in the world to date [3, 4].

Other solutions around the world have subsequently emerged, such as in Abu Dhabi [5], where researchers have developed a system called MAWAQIF that help users to identify which Mall has available free parking before arriving, and this influences their decision whether or not to visit a specific place. Sadhukhan [6] proposed a parking prototype called E-Parking for several urban areas in which the available parking time for each user is estimated through a slide called Parcmeter. This system also offers users the option of smart payment through automatically collecting parking fees. Mainetti et al. [7] have made a hybrid detection network based on wireless sensor network (WSN) and RFID technology which exploits the communication capability of the WSN and combines it with the identification systems of RFID.

The approaches above are mostly based on the WSN, but there are also solutions based on crowd-sourcing, which consist in collecting information concerning the state of car parking occupancy from the smartphone of users. For example, the solution proposed by Yans et al. [8] takes into consideration the location of vehicles and, based on the different patterns of behavior while searching for a parking place, it suggests to the user possible trajectories based on parameters specified previously. By using system-learning algorithms, it classifies the trajectory according to two categories: The Parking Lot (PL) and the Parking Zone (PZ).

In this paper we present a system to address these issues. First, we describe the architecture of our system, detailing the main actors and the flow of information. Then we discuss the services that this system offers, explain the part our proposed web application plays in the system, and finally discuss security implications.

2   Architecture System

At Casablanca, users still find a problem to have a parking space, because of the exponential growth in the number of vehicles, buses, and other modes of transport. In fact, finding a parking space at Casablanca's trendy neighborhood is an almost impossible mission due to several factors, including poor management or the lack of an infrastructure dedicated to parking.

As a result, we proposed a solution that will allow drivers to check in real time the free parking spaces, be guides from their current location until they reach the place that has been assigned by the system.

Our system aims to simplify the parking process for everyone involved, while allowing all parties concerned to communicate with each other and seek help from the system operator.

Before discussing the functional part and the architecture of the proposed solution, we start by presenting the different actors:

- **User:** he interacts with the web application, after authentication or registration the user can perform several actions such as checking the parking status (if there is a place available for parking) pay his subscription, reserve his place beforehand, present a claim...etc. a use case diagram shows user's interaction with the system (see Fig. 1).

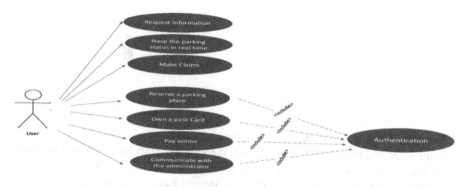

Fig. 1. Use case diagram

- **Web administrator:** he has a visibility on the whole system, he manages the users and must make sure that the database of the application is updated.
  Note that for users there are two main categories:
- **Subscribers:** they use the car park almost daily, they have a weekly, monthly or even annual subscription card. the drivers who take advantage of our services with an average of 7–10 times a month have a rechargeable card, every time they use the parking the amount subtracts from the main balance.
- **Visitor:** A user who consults the application without registering and he can use the parking with payment on the spot.

All these users can benefit from the features of the application with different privileges, nevertheless a traveler who does not have access to the application can also use the car park and he will be treated like a visitor during the payment.

The proposed technical architecture is based on the three-tier cloud architecture. There are three layers: The Application Tier, the Cloud Tier, and the Parking Tier. Each of the three layers was assigned a reusable portion of code with a specific function. These layers also interact with the other ones to achieve assigned goals within the system (see Fig. 2).

Cloud Tier can be instantiated in a 3-tiered cloud setup with separated, rather than integrated layers. This system has separate pools of web servers and application servers connected via load balancers. The application server has access to databases and information about the parking systems.

In fact, the information that feeds our application comes mainly from two resources:

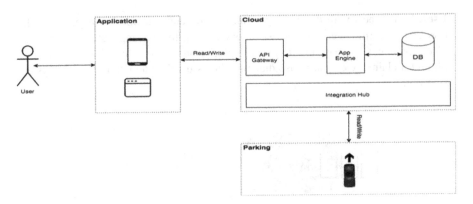

Fig. 2. Architecture system

- **Wireless Sensor Network WSN:** it used to display the state of our car park (number of free/busy places) in real time, the location of the free places, Incoming vehicles/drivers using Radio Frequency Identification RFID and cameras.
- **Users:** payment made online, reservations, current balance, claims ...etc.

After the collection, the data processing takes place, it helps to determine the areas that contain the free/busy places, the drivers who parked badly, the amount to be paid according to the types of drivers, grant or refuse a new parking request...etc.

All these informations and more, will be communicated later via the internet to drivers, to show them the status of parking in real time and benefit from other services. And on the other hand, the system administrator receives an updated parking status.

3   Services and Platform

When a driver is looking for a parking space, he can visit the web application to check the current status of the parking (the number of occupied and free places), if he decides to use it, the trajectory is determined from its current location to the parking.

In addition to that, drivers with an account, have additional services, such as paying their subscription or check parking fees, send/receive message to the system administrator. Further, we thought to include a service to book a parking place. The booking is made, by indicating entrance and exit time and the car number plate. When the user makes a reservation, the administrator checks the availability and sends him a confirmation/cancellation e-mail. The services discussed previously are simple to use and easily accessible in the web application, it represents the services, prices, etc. The user can submit a complaint, register or log in to his account (see Fig. 3).

The web application shows users the number of available space, as well as offering them the option to get the parking route from their location (see Fig. 4).

User can have the trajectory to the parking. If the driver is registered, he could reserve his place before reaching the parking (see Fig. 5).

Fig. 3. Home page of the web application

Fig. 4. Parking current status

After authentication the website the user can make the payment of his subscription or recharge his account, plan his future journey by making a reservation or change his profile information (this change must be approved by the administrator) (see Fig. 6).

Fig. 5. Parking itinerary

Fig. 6. Reservation interface

As for the administrator he deals with the management of users, reservations, respond to messages, it also has a general view of the state of parking in real time.

In addition to its features, we opted for a responsive application with a design that makes it easy to use.

4 Control and Security

For security reasons, a system is set up to control the site, it allows to monitor the parking, and trigger alerts when an incident happens to act as quickly as possible.

In reality, there is different type of equipment that cooperates to control what's going on at the parking. A screen is located at the entrance for users to check if there is a place available, if there is not, entrance barrier will be closed. And before entering double identification takes place: the identification of the person and the car by the RFID system and the video surveillance system. After entering our system guide user to the available parking spaces by displaying the number of the place and its location on the screens.

However; the parking sensors will not be enough to guarantee improved parking conditions, in this perspective we opted for the analysis of the video stream to identify the presence of a car and its license plate (to store it in our database), as well as the free places, this analysis will also make possible to detect if a car is badly parked: it occupies two places or it blocks the traffic for example.

5   Conclusion

With the advancement of technology, services related to urban mobility can be improved, drivers will have an accessible and easy service that will save them time and frustration. Several solutions have been proposed over the years, with different methodologies and differing implementation environment. The proposed parking solution based on the WSN, implement a system that does not allow drivers to have the parking offer in real time and easily find a free place. As a perspective, plus the improvement of our system, we are working on a prediction algorithm based on machine learning that will allow users to plan their journey in advance.

References

1. Caragliu, A., Del Bo, C., Nijkamp, P.: Smart cities in Europe. Serie Research Memoranda 0048 (VU University Amsterdam, Faculty of Economics, Business Administration and Econometrics) (2009)
2. Atzori, L., Iera, A., Morabito, F.: The internet of things: a survey. Comput. Netw. **54**(15), 2787–2805 (2010)
3. SFPark: http://sfpark.org/how-it-works/applications/. Accessed 18 Oct 2016
4. LA Express Parkin: http://www.laexpresspark.org/. Accessed 20 Dec 2017
5. Alkheder, S.A., Al Rajab, M., Alzoubi, K.: Parking problems in Abu Dhabi, UAE toward an intelligent parking management system "ADIP: Abu Dhabi intelligent parking". Alex. Eng. J. **55**(3), 2679–2687 (2016)
6. Sadhukhan, P.: An IoT-based E-Parking system for smart cities). In: International Conference on Advances in Computing, Communications and Informatics (ICACCI) 2017. IEEE, Udupi, India (2017)
7. Mainetti, L., Patrono, L., Stefanizzi, M.: A smart parking system based on IoT protocols and emerging enabling technologies. In: IEEE 2nd World Forum on Internet of Things (WF-IoT). IEEE (2015)
8. Yans, B., Fantini, N., Jensen, C.S.: iPark: identifying parking spaces from trajectories. In: Proceedings of the 16th International Conference on Extending Database Technology, Genoa, Italy, pp. 705–708 (2013)

Improving Cross-Layer Routing in Wireless Sensor Networks

Fouzi Semchedine[(✉)] and Naima Bouandas[(✉)]

Institute of Optics and Precision Mechanics (IOMP) and Computer Science
Department, University of Setif, Setif, Algeria
fouzi.jams@gmail.com, naima.prog@gmail.com

Abstract. Researches in the field of wireless sensor networks set as a main objective the development of algorithms and protocols to ensure the minimum of energy consumption. Most of the proposed solutions are based on a single-layer approach of the OSI model. Recently, works tend to use several layers at the aim of optimizing the energy consumption. We proposed in this paper an energy-aware protocol based on the Cross-Layer mechanism for wireless sensor networks and that considers the physical layer, the MAC layer and the network layer to route the sensed data. The new variant of the proposed protocol Energy Efficient Cross-layer Protocol (EECP) tries to improve the algorithm of relay nodes selection in order to avoid loops and delaying the packet delivery. We simulate the new variant and we compare it with CLEEP in terms of residual energy, packet delivery ratio and load balancing metric.

1 Introduction

The need of information and the rapid evolution of the micro-electronic technology allowed the creation of small devices with low cost and limited resources able to collect and to process information in an autonomous and a flexible manner. These devices, called wireless sensors, can be deployed in different areas and form a Wireless Sensor Network (WSN).

WSN's are conceived to cooperate in order to deliver the collected data to the base station (the sink). Due to the limited resources of the sensors and the hostile nature of the sensed area, the WSN must operate as long as possible. Thus, the energy is the first factor that must be considered. On the other hand, some WSN applications are event-driven. In such applications, the sensors operate in the active mode and listen to the channel until a event occurs. So, the sensors consume unnecessarily energy by waiting an event. Thus, a sleep/active mode is used by a combination of the different network layers [2,3]. In this mode of interaction, the sensors are synchronized to switch between the sleep and the active mode to preserve the energy of the sensors. However, the synchronization may cause loss of packets when the sensors switch to the sleep mode and the event occurs.

Recently, different cross-layer protocols [4–10] have been proposed. The existing literature works show that CLEEP [8] don't consider synchronization and it is

© Springer Nature Switzerland AG 2018
N. Boudriga et al. (Eds.): UNet 2018, LNCS 11277, pp. 247–256, 2018.
https://doi.org/10.1007/978-3-030-02849-7_22

the unique protocol that uses the wake-up mechanism to switch between the sleep and the active mode which avoids missing events. However, CLEEP presents some limits witch motivate the proposition of the Energy Efficient Cross-layer Protocol (EECP) [1]. EECP tries to vary the routing paths in order to balance the energy of sensors and, extends the sleep mode at the MAC layer by considering the duty-cycle property. However, EECP is still suffering in the routing process.

In this paper, we propose an improvement of EECP by addressing its limits. In fact, EECP presents two major limits: (i) EECP don't consider the case where two or more sensors have the same routing cost. In this case, the rely node will be randomly chosen and could be the farthest one from the sink; (ii) EECP can choose the source node as a relay which could cause loops in the network. The new variant of EECP tries to address these limits by improving the routing mechanism. On the other hand, authors in [1] have considered a comparative analysis (without simulation) between EECP and CLEEP to show the improvements of the protocols. Thus, in this paper, we simulate the two protocols and we compare their performance in terms of residual energy, packet delivery ratio and load balancing metric.

The rest of the paper is organized as follows: Sect. 3 presents the design of the new routing protocol which addresses the limits of EECP and avoids the collisions, the overhearing and the idle listening. In Sect. 4, we show the effectiveness of the new variant by simulation and we conclude the paper in Sect. 5.

2   Energy Aware Protocol Based on the Cross-Layer Mechanism

The protocol CLEEP [8] shown an energy efficiency by using a wake up mechanism at the difference with the recalled protocols which use the synchronization mechanism. CLEEP wakes up just the nodes belonging to the routing path. However, it suffers from different drawbacks. In fact, CLEEP, when selecting the node, wakes up this last before the ideal moment. Further, the mechanism used to construct the routing table seems to be very costly in energy; mostly, in dense networks. Finally, CLEEP does not balance the energy of the sensors since it could use the same path to route the data due to the static routing table.

Based on these analysis, a new protocol has been proposed and called: Energy Efficient Cross-layer Protocol (EECP) [1], and which interacts between the different layers: physical, MAC and network, at the aim of:

- Maximizing the sleep time of the nodes that do not participate in the routing process;
- Avoiding the energy exhaustion caused by the idle listening and the overhearing;
- Avoiding using the same path to route the packets;
- Avoiding waking up a node before the ideal moment of its participation in the communication;
- Reducing the collisions.

However, EECP still presents two major limits:

1. In EECP, the source selects the rely node with a low cost of the routing function. Thus, a case is not considered where two or more relay nodes are found with the same cost. So, if the choice is made randomly, the protocol risks to selects the farthest relay nodes and the packet could not reach the sink. Hence, as an improvement, we propose to select the nearest node to the sink.
2. Based on the routing function, EECP may select the source node and the routing process could loop. Thus, to remedy this case, we propose to eliminate the node that sent the packet from the routing choices. So, the node estimates the cost of its neighbors except that of the source node.

3   Protocol Conception

The proposed variant of EECP considers the same assumptions and the same setup phases as EECP [1] at the difference of the routing process. In EECP, each node has an identifier (i.e. the sequence number, the MAC address, etc). EECP is a reactive protocol where routes are built dynamically at each transmission. In EECP, the communication is started by a source node and each node maintains a neighboring table. Like CLEEP, EECP considers that each node has two radios: one for signaling (wake up), and another for data communication.

EECP bases on the Received Signal Strength Indicator (RSSI) signal [12] to construct the routing table and to route the data to the sink. So, the sink broadcasts a packet to all the nodes of the network. Each node received the packet, calculates and saves its local RSSI (in dB). At the end of this phase, all the nodes of the network have their initialized RSSI (we note: $Local\_RSSI$).

Further, each node broadcasts a signal to its neighbors. So, each node calculates and saves based on the RSSI the distances to its neighbors. Then, each node calculates its average distance as follows:

$$D_{avg} = \sum_{i=1}^{N} D_i/N$$

where:
D_i: is the distance between the node and its neighbor;
N: is the total number of neighbors.

Each node broadcasts a packet containing: its address, the address of the destination, the $Local\_RSSI$, the D_{avg} and its energy level. Each node received such packet, saves/updates the information in the routing table. At the end of this phase, each node creates its routing table relative to the exchanged information. Further, all the nodes of the network transit to the sleep mode.

When an event occurs, the source node starts the routing process. So, the node selects the next hop that must be waked up using the following cost function:

$$cost = Local\_RSSI_{neighbor} * (\frac{1}{RE_{neighbor}}) \tag{1}$$

where:

$RE_{neighbor}$: is the residual energy of the neighbor.

The source selects, from its neighbors, the next hop (relay node) with a low cost. This means that the source chooses the neighbor that has the maximum of residual energy and close to the sink.

In the case where two or more rely nodes have the same cost, the new variant of EECP uses the distance and selects the nearest node to the sink. This avoids delaying the packet delivery.

On the other hand, the new variant of EECP eliminates the source node from the routing choices. This avoids loops in the network.

When the source node sends the packet to the selected next hop, all its neighbors receive the signal. Thus, each neighbor node updates the residual energy of the source for further communications using the following formula:

$$E_{estimate} = E_{send} + E_{reception} + E_{cp} + E_{trans} \tag{2}$$

where:

E_{send}: is the emission energy. This energy is calculated by using the average distance of the node with respect to its neighbors.

$E_{reception}$: is the reception energy.

E_{cp}: is the energy of receiving a control packet.

E_{trans}: is the energy of the sleep/active mode transition.

The EECP protocol uses at the MAC layer a wake up mechanism to prevent the overhearing. The wake up is sent to the node selected from the neighboring table. The idea is to wake up just the next node that will participate in the routing process and put it in the sleep mode at the end of the communication. So, once the next node is selected, the source wakes it up and sends the data. Once the packet is acknowledged, the source goes into the sleep mode. Each node that receives the data do the same until the packet reaches the sink (see Fig. 1).

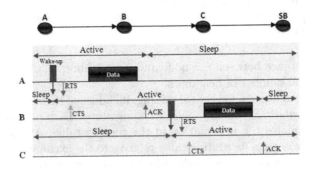

Fig. 1. Medium access and communication process.

4   Simulations and Results

With the development of the wireless sensor networks, different simulators were proposed. Network Simulator 2 (NS2), GloMoSim, OPNET and TOSIM are currently the most efficient and suitable platforms of simulation. However, most of these simulators don't have existing implementations of the routing protocols. This motives us to opt for discrete event simulations to validate the proposed protocols. In fact, we implemented the algorithms of EECP and CLEEP on a discrete event simulator developed in Java [14]. The simulator represents an agriculture application. The sensors are used to sense different environmental information like: the temperature, the pressure and the CO_2 rate. So, the system considers an agriculture field of 10 ha of surface that comprises 80 greenhouses partitioned into 9 zones. In each zone, there is 9 greenhouses where each greenhouse contains one sensor. The parameters of simulation considered and inspired from some reference works [15–17] are resumed in the Table 1.

Table 1. Simulation parameters

Constant definition	Constant name	Initial value	Type	Measure unit
Initial energy of the sink	E_{0SB}	Unlimited	Real	Joule
Initial energy of the sensor	E_{0ca}	1	Real	Joule
Amplification energy	E_{amp}	10	Integer	$pJ/bit/m^2$
Electrical energy	E_{elec}	50	Integer	nJ/bit
Energy of transaction (Sleep/Active mode)	E_{trans}	42.3	Real	$\mu Joule$
Energy of idle mode	E_{idle}	1.035	Real	$\mu Joule$
Sink position	(X,Y)	(0,0)	Integer	–
Maximum number of sensors	C_{max}	80	Integer	–
Message length	M	256	Integer	Bit
Time of simulation	T_{max}	50	Integer	Day
Arrival rate	Lambda	20	Real	Requests/Day

The different metrics which we consider to evaluate the performance of the two protocols are:

Average residual energy of the network: represents the average of the residual energies of the sensors at each event. This metric is used to compare the consumed energy of the protocols.

Network lifetime: represents the time between the moment of deployment and the moment of disconnection of the network. For ease of analysis, we consider, the disconnection of the network, the moment when one sensor exhausts totally its energy.

Packet delivery ratio: represents the ratio of packets successfully received by the sink.

Load balancing: allows to show the efficiency of the protocols in balancing the energies of the sensors.

Discussions: Figure 2 shows the simulation results of the protocols in terms of average residual energy.

We can see that the CLEEP curve decreases until the number of events equal to 2012, and remains stable until the end of the simulation. This means that the average residual energy of the network decreases and the protocol stops at the event 2012 (one sensor exhausts totally its energy). The EECP protocol maintains the average residual energy of the network until the event 46000. This explains the advantage of the protocol in using the cost function and waking up the sensor nodes that must participate in the routing process at the perfect moment.

Table 2 shows the results for the network lifetime of EECP and CLEEP. The network lifetime of CLEEP is estimated at: 01 day, 9 h and 32 min while that of EECP is estimated at: 32 days, 2 h and 48 min. We note that EECP prolongs the network lifetime since it preserves the energy of the sensors (Fig. 2). Consequently, more the energy is preserved, more the network lifetime is prolonged and vice versa.

Table 2. Network lifetime of CLEEP vs. EECP

Protocol	Network lifetime
CLEEP	01 Days 9 h 32 min
EECP	32 Days 2 h 48 min

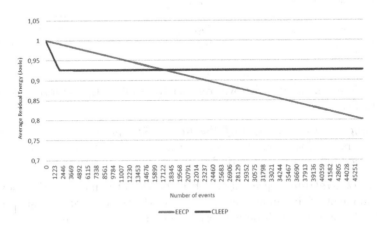

Fig. 2. Average residual energy of the network.

Figure 3 shows the simulation results of the protocols in terms of packet delivery ratio.

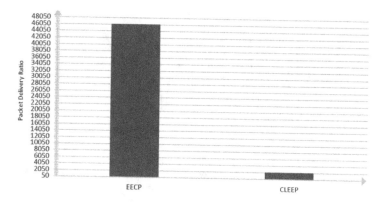

Fig. 3. Packet delivery ratio.

From Fig. 3, we note that the packet delivery ratio for EECP is better than CLEEP. In fact, we show that EECP ensures delivering a large number of packets to the sink. This is due to the strategy of EECP in preserving the energy of the sensors and prolonging the network lifetime by diversifying the routing paths. However, CLEEP chooses practically the same routing paths which accelerates the energy exhaustion of the sensors and causes a network disconnection.

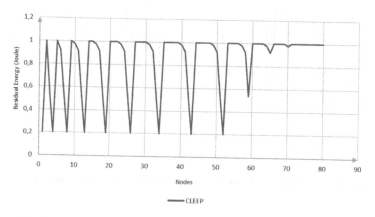

Fig. 4. Load balancing in terms of energy for CLEEP.

Figures 4 and 5 show the load balancing in terms of energy for the protocols. We note from the figures that there is a balance in the energy consumption of nodes for the EECP protocol. This means that the majority of nodes participate in the routing process. However, in CLEEP, some nodes participate frequently in the routing process while other remain in the sleep mode. Indeed, we can see from Fig. 4, that there are several nodes which have never participated in the routing process (their residual energy remain equal to 1 J).

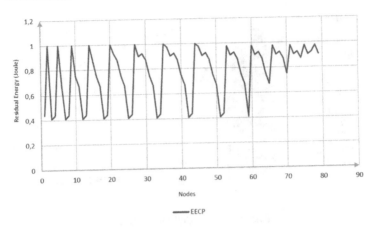

Fig. 5. Load balancing in terms of energy for EECP.

To more show the effectiveness of EECP compared to CLEEP in terms of balancing the network load, we set the number of sources equal to 1 (one and the same source node that senses and sends the data to the sink).

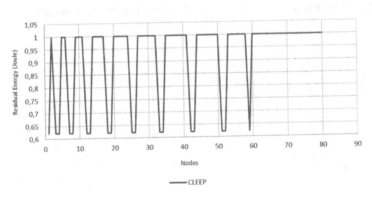

Fig. 6. Load balancing in terms of energy for CLEEP using one source.

We can see from Figs. 6 and 7 that CLEEP don't ensure a load balancing in terms of sensors' energy. This is explained by the fact that CLEEP, when routing the packets, uses always the same path. Thus, the energy of the sensors belonging to the path exhausts while the others remain with the initial energy. On the other hand, EECP diversifies the paths by using the cost function which balances the energy of the sensors.

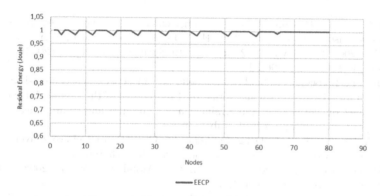

Fig. 7. Load balancing in terms of energy for EECP using one source.

5 Conclusion

In this paper, we have proposed a new variant of the routing protocol Energy Efficient Cross-layer Protocol (EECP) for wireless sensor networks. EECP takes into account the energy consumption at three layers: physical, MAC and network.

EECP addresses different sources of energy dissipation: the consumed energy of the routing path, the collisions, the idle listening and the overhearing. In addition, EECP balances the energy of the sensors and allows participating the majority of sensors in the routing process which consequently, prolongs the network lifetime and ensures delivering a large number of packets.

As a future work, we plan to improve the variant by considering the case where the choice of the next hop is limited to a node that does not have a relay to the sink. In this case, the packet will never reaches the sink. In addition, an implementation of the variant on a standard simulator can be envisaged to consider congestion situations, the overhearing and the idle listening.

References

1. Semchedine, F., Oukachbi, W., Zaichi, N., Bouallouche, L.: EECP: a new cross-layer protocol for routing in wireless sensor networks. In: The International Conference on Advanced Wireless, Information, and Communication Technologies (AWICT 2015), Tunis (2015)
2. Srivastava, V., Motani, M.: Cross-layer design: a survey and the road ahead. Commun. Mag. IEEE **43**(12), 112–119 (2005)
3. Raisinghani, V.T., Iyer, S.: Cross-layer design optimizations in wireless protocol stacks. Comput. Commun. **27**(8), 720–724 (2004)
4. Škraba, P., Aghajan, H., Bahai, A.: Cross-layer optimization for high density sensor networks: distributed passive routing decisions. In: Nikolaidis, I., Barbeau, M., Kranakis, E. (eds.) ADHOC-NOW 2004. LNCS, vol. 3158, pp. 266–279. Springer, Heidelberg (2004). https://doi.org/10.1007/978-3-540-28634-9_21
5. Wang, X., Yin, J., Zhang, Q., Agrawal, D.P.: A cross-layer approach for efficient flooding in wireless sensor networks. In: Wireless Communications and Networking Conference 2005 IEEE, vol. 3, pp. 1812–1817. IEEE, March 2005

6. Suh, C., Ko, Y.-B., Son, D.-M.: An energy efficient cross-layer MAC protocol for wireless sensor networks. In: Shen, H.T., Li, J., Li, M., Ni, J., Wang, W. (eds.) APWeb 2006. LNCS, vol. 3842, pp. 410–419. Springer, Heidelberg (2006). https://doi.org/10.1007/11610496_54

7. Kechar, B., Louazani, A., Sekhri, L., Khelfi, M.F.: Energy efficient cross-layer MAC protocol for wireless sensor networks. In: Proceedings of the Second International Conference on Verification and Evaluation of Computer and Communication Systems (VECoS 2008), pp. 61–71, July 2008

8. Liu, S., Bai, Y., Sha, M., Deng, Q., Qian, D.: CLEEP: a novel cross-layer energy-efficient protocol for wireless sensor networks. In: 4th International Conference on Wireless Communications, Networking and Mobile Computing, 2008. WiCOM 2008, pp. 1–4. IEEE, October 2008

9. Kim, J., Lee, J., Kim, S.: An enhanced cross-layer protocol for energy efficiency in wireless sensor networks. In: Third International Conference on Sensor Technologies and Applications, 2009. SENSORCOMM 2009, pp. 657–664. IEEE, June 2009

10. Surekha, K.B., Basavaraju, T.G.: Energy efficient cross layer routing protocol with adaptive dynamic retransmission for wireless sensor networks. IJCNWC $4(2)$ (2014)

11. Ye, W., Heidemann, J., Estrin, D.: An energy-efficient MAC protocol for wireless sensor networks. In: Proceedings IEEE Twenty-First Annual Joint Conference of the IEEE Computer and Communications Societies. INFOCOM 2002, vol. 3, pp. 1567–1576. IEEE (2002)

12. Awad, A., Frunzke, T., Dressler, F.: Adaptive distance estimation and localization in WSN using RSSI measures. In: 10th Euromicro Conference on Digital System Design Architectures, Methods and Tools 2007. DSD 2007, pp. 471–478. IEEE, August 2007

13. Xing, G., Lu, C., Zhang, Y., Huang, Q., Pless, R.: Minimum power configuration in wireless sensor networks. In: Proceedings of the 6th ACM International Symposium on Mobile ad Hoc Networking and Computing, pp. 390–401. ACM, May 2005

14. Semchedine, F., Bouallouche, L., Zaddi, M., Ayane, D.: A new variant of directed diffusion for routing in wireless sensor networks. In: International Conference on Advanced Communications Systems and Signal Processing, Tlemcen, Algeria (2015)

15. Heinzelman, W.R., Chandrakasan, A., Balakrishnan, H.: Energy-efficient communication protocol for wireless microsensor networks. In: Proceedings of the 33rd Annual Hawaii International Conference on System Sciences 2000, pp. 10–pp. IEEE, January 2000

16. Lindsay, S., Raghavendra, C. S., Sivalingam, K.M.: Data gathering in sensor networks using the energy delay metric. In: Proceedings of the 15th International Parallel and Distributed Processing Symposium, p. 188. IEEE Computer Society, April 2001

17. Jurdak, R., Ruzzelli, A.G., O'Hare, G.M.: Radio sleep mode optimization in wireless sensor networks. IEEE Tran. Mobile Comput. $9(7)$, 955–968 (2010)

Hierarchical Availability in Flying Radio Access Networks as a Cournot Duopoly

Sara Handouf$^{(\boxtimes)}$, Essaid Sabir, and Mohammed Sadik

NEST Research Group, ENSEM, Hassan II University of Casablanca,
Casablanca, Morocco
{sara.handouf,e.sabir,m.sadik}@ensem.ac.ma

Abstract. Nowadays, unmanned aerial vehicles (UAVs) as flying base stations have attracted significant interest in telecommunications service field; Thanks to their low-cost, high maneuverability, flexible deployment and mobility advantages, they have become a main stream solution, to provide wireless communication in exceptional scenarios such as hard to reach areas or massive-attended events. Because UAVs are energy budget constrained, optimal availability control for energy efficiency is proposed in this paper. Within such a situation, the most important objective of a UAVs operator is to provide a service with acceptable availability and cost effective, so that, to realize a satisfactory benefit. The conducted study provides a non-cooperative duopoly game where UAVs Service Providers (SP) are competing to serve a geographical area. We focus on the scheduling of beaconing periods as an efficient mean of energy consumption optimization that results in temporary unavailability of network connectivity. A tractable comparative analysis for the game's equilibrium, in terms of both Cournot and stackelberg frameworks is derived. We show that the benefit when adopting the leadership model is exhibiting some additional properties compared to the Cournot (anarchic) game. Some extensive simulations are given to confirm our proposal.

Keywords: Unmanned aerial vehicles (UAV) · Cournot
Best response · Nash equilibrium · Stackelberg

1 Introduction

Drones or remotely piloted aircrafts, commonly known as unmanned aerial vehicles (UAVs), are promising to provide cost-effective wireless connectivity and ubiquitous usability for scenarios without infrastructure coverage [1].

Although the historical UAVs monopoly by the military, they are gaining approval and usage for civilian, scientific and commercial purposes. Compared to terrestrial communications or those based on wireless base stations, unmanned aerial vehicles (UAVs) present new and exciting tools. Indeed, they present in general faster and lower cost deployment, high maneuverability and flexible reconfiguration.

© Springer Nature Switzerland AG 2018
N. Boudriga et al. (Eds.): UNet 2018, LNCS 11277, pp. 257–266, 2018.
https://doi.org/10.1007/978-3-030-02849-7_23

The important improvements in the UAVs efficient on demand telecommunication, mobility [2] and also continuous cost reduction, along with their availability for scientific and easy accessibility for the public has resulted in a wide range of technological advantages.

Furthermore, due to their possibility of sensing the surrounding environment (see paper [3]), UAVs are now a key technology for boundless applications; these applications include: recognition, search, inspection tasks, surveillance, public services, and so on. Another key feature of UAVs is the Internet of Things (IoT), which is a technological revolution that has made the leap from conceptual to actual (see [4] and [5]). IoT enables devices to exchange data and interoperate within the internet infrastructure, which affords ubiquitous connectivity while reducing the transmission cost and providing extended range for low-power communication. Technically, UAVs play an important role in the Internet of Things (IoT) vision, it offers flexible deployability and reprogramming in mission possibilities to deliver solutions and services that give the ground IoT clients and partners numerous operating advantages.

Among the numerous applications enabled by UAVs, their use as aerial base stations has been reported as a promising approach that can boost the capacity and coverage performance of existing wireless networks. In fact, UAVs-aided wireless coverage could support and provide wireless communication in exceptional scenarios such as rural or disaster-affected areas, emergency situations and festivals or sporting events where the terrestrial base stations installation may be too expensive. Thanks to their high mobility, a main concern is that, UAVs are likely to have better communication channel since the UAV-ground link is more likely to have line-of-sight (LoS) links (see [6] and [7]).

While deploying drones as flying base stations offers various coverage and energy-effective advantages, still a number of economic and technical challenges arise. These challenges comprise not only deployment and pricing issues, but also effective energy and activity management features [8]. Yet, for UAVs service providers to overcome these relevant challenges, availability scheduling becomes a very important but largely unexplored topic. In this context, a comprehensive modeling and performance analysis of UAVs setups is extremely attractive.

Because UAVs are battery empowered and given their limited battery capacity and recharging requirements, we provide in this paper a UAVs strategic availability setting. Yet, optimal periodic beaconing (sending signals that advertise existence of a UAV) is an important but challenging task that needs to be addressed. In this context, we construct a UAVs duopoly model to capture the adversarial behavior of service providers in terms of their availability.

The UAVs are belonging to different operators and deployed as aerial mobile base stations to provide wireless service for the IoT ground users. Thus, the ultimate goal of a UAVs operator is to provide a service with acceptable availability and cost effective, so that to absorb an important market share allowing satisfactory benefits.

The proposed computational scenario deals with the concept of non-cooperative game theory which is a formal, branch of applied mathematics for modeling and analyzing interactions among intelligent rational players. Game theory may be useful with significant success for solving problems in many disciplines, from psychology, economics, political science, psychology, marketing and trade, to wireless telecommunication. A such mathematical methodology, allows us to study how rational UAVs (players) in competitive environment, constrained with scarce (battery capacity)and common resources (market share) can interact among themselves to achieve an optimal behavior.

Comparisons between simultaneous and sequential move games is a crucial step to assimilate the properties and efficiency aspects of this proposal.

In this paper, the game formulation is divided into classical (anarchic) distributed game where UAV operators chose their strategies simultaneously, and leadership framework defined as a sequential game.

We primarily involve the Cournot-duopoly framework, and define the best-replay function. We also compute the Nash equilibrium which have a considerable impact on the game's usefulness. After that, we assume a hierarchical approach namely stackelberg game, we further calculate the leader and follower equilibrium. Our discussion proceeds to more specific aspects and compare the obtained equilibrium to those of cournot model.

Extensive numerical simulations are provided to highlight the impact availability as a decision parameters and provide thereby some important insights/heuristics on how the game parameters may be adjusted to control the duopoly game.

1.1   Organization of the Paper

The remainder of this paper is organized as follows. In Sect. 2 we give an overview of the proposed UAVs duopoly system model and strategic Availability. In Sect. 3 we present the Cournot-Availability game analysis, NE solution and also define the best replay function. Stackelberg game analysis is provided in Sect. 4. And finally, Sect. 5 concludes the paper.

2   System Model and Problem Formulation

In our setting we assume a duopoly telecommunication market where just two UAVs Service Providers compete against one another and offering a homogeneous services. This minimizes mathematical complication but still allows us to analyze many of the important features of Operators strategies. Consider a circular geographical area with a radius R within which, a set of two UAVs moving randomly according to a Random Way-point mobility model, are used as aerial mobile base stations to provide wireless service for the ground IoT devices (see Fig. 1). The drones belong to different operators and are engaged to provide an effective coverage for mobile IoT users. In this setting the drones are assuming to have the same characteristics such as altitude h, total available bandwidth and maximum transmit power. Thus, the coverage radius. Because UAVs have a limited battery capacity and given the recharging battery requirements, a very important but challenging solution is to allow switching their radio modules to sleep mode in order to extend battery lifetime. Within such a situation, each UAV will send periodic beacon advertising his availability for IoT users on the ground during a fixed period of duration. The UAVs are strategically adjusting their beaconing duration in order to avoid battery depletion resulting from maintaining useless beacon, This strategic behaviour results in temporary unavailability of the wireless access network while providing an acceptable availability and cost effective service.

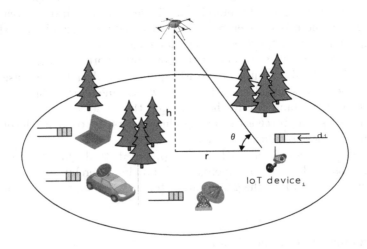

Fig. 1. Duopoly system model.

Figure 2 describes the periodic availability for two competing UAVs. The beacon/sleep cycle is periodically repeated every T slot. The beaconing period duration for a UAV i is $\tau_i \in [0; T]$.

Drones need to independently choose their optimal availability duration so that to realize a good market share and satisfactory benefits. These lead to a rational behavior with conflicting self-interests which falls within the non cooperative game theory.

3   UAVs Behavior Within a Cournot Oligopoly Problem

For a duopolist, revenues depend on both its own strategy and the other operator's strategy. In the proposed model, the two operators are competing by setting an end user (uplink/downlink) service each UAV i with some QoS_i and a fee f_i. Of course, increasing market share is the ultimate goal of each operator. For this UAVs need to offer a wireless coverage service with adequate QoS determined by the availability parameter and also effective cost.

Based on this two parameters policy, each ground customer decides to register to one of the two UAVs or to stay at no subscription state. The Cournot problem

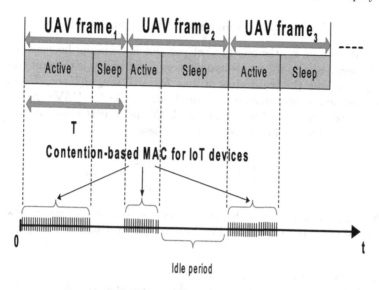

Fig. 2. Periodic availability periods.

[9] is to determine the optimal values of variables of interest, that are QoS (τ_1 and τ_2) and service prices (f_1 and f_2) for each UAV service provider that affect directly the experienced demand. Notice that, because the UAVs services are homogeneous, we assume, $f_i = f_j = f^*$ in equilibrium if both Service providers are to participate.

We assume a linear demand function:

$$d_i = (\alpha_i^i.\tau_i + \alpha_i^j.\tau_j), \tag{1}$$

Let $D = d_i + d_j$ be the total experienced demand, f_{max} is the maximum allowable price by the authorities and $\alpha_i^i \geq 0$ and $\alpha_i^j \leq 0$ are the sensibility parameters that control the market share. α_i^i represents UAV is changing availability (QoS) effect on it's experienced demand, whereas α_i^j is representing the sensitivity of the UAV i to availability parameter of his competitor. In other word it indicates what effect of changing the QoS of UAV j compared to UAV i on the consumer intention to subscribe to the given UAV service provider. Because we are also interested in studying how costs especially in term of energy affect the market, we will assume that costs are positive and the SP is total cost equation is

$$C_i = E_i.d_i. \qquad E_i > 0 \tag{2}$$

In terms of notation, E_i is the unit dissipated energy of serving ground users. It is explained as follows:

$$E_i = \left([1 - \prod_{i \in \mathcal{R}_i} (1 - p_u)] \right).\epsilon_r + \sum_{u \in \mathcal{R}_i} \theta_{u,i} \epsilon_{Ack} + \epsilon_b.\tau_i + \epsilon_s \tag{3}$$

Here $\theta_{u,i} = p_u \prod_{k \neq u} (1 - p_k)$ is the normalized throughput of user u served by a UAV$_i$. We denote by ϵ_b, the energy cost per slot for sending beacons, ϵ_r is the reception energy, ϵ_{Ack} is the transmission energy cost and ϵ_s is the unit energy for remaining switching the transceiver status. $\mathcal{R}_i = (User_u, d(User_u, UAV_i) \leq r)$ is the set of ground users served by a given drone i. Since the UAVs are belonging to different operators it is likely that one UAV has a cost advantage over the other one, as an assumption we set $\varepsilon_i \leq \varepsilon_j$, where

$$\varepsilon_i = \left([1 - \prod_{i \in \mathcal{R}_i} (1 - p_u)] \right) . \epsilon_r + \sum_{u \in \mathcal{R}_i} \theta_{u,i} \epsilon_{Ack} + \epsilon_s \qquad (4)$$

Each SPs goal is to choose the level of service that maximizes profits, given the service of the other Operator. The formal characteristics of the game are as follows.

- Players: UAVs Service Providers i and j.
- Strategic parameter: Each Operator i plays non-negative values of availability action τ_i.
- Operator's payoffs are the difference between profits and costs,

$$U_i = d_i f_i - E_i d_i \qquad (5)$$

At the Cournot equilibrium, each UAV must behave optimally to maximize its utility function assuming that its rival is doing the same. Another way of saying this, is that each UAV maximizes profits and calculates its best response or reply to the expected best-reply behavior of the other UAV. For this reason, the Cournot-Nash equilibrium may be described as a mutual best reply. Mathematically, the revenue maximizing problem takes the following form:

$$BR_i = \underset{\tau_i}{\mathrm{argmax}} U_i(\tau_i, \tau_j). \qquad (6)$$

The optimal strategy of each UAV is embedded in the following first-order conditions:

$$\frac{\partial U_i}{\partial \tau_i} = 2\alpha_i^i(\eta - E_b)\tau_i + (\alpha_i^i \eta + \alpha_i^j \eta - \alpha_i^j E_b)\tau_j - \alpha_i^i \varepsilon_i \qquad (7)$$

$$\frac{\partial U_j}{\partial \tau_j} = 2\alpha_j^j(\eta - \epsilon_b)\tau_j + (\alpha_j^j \eta + \alpha_j^i \eta - \alpha_j^i \epsilon_b)\tau_i - \alpha_j^j \varepsilon_j \qquad (8)$$

Solving the above equations system produces the following Cournot equilibrium:

$$\tau_j^* = \frac{(f - \varepsilon_i)(\alpha_i^i \alpha_j^i) - (f - \varepsilon_j)(2\alpha_i^i \alpha_j^j)}{\epsilon_b(\alpha_i^j \alpha_j^i - 4\alpha_i^i \alpha_j^j)} \qquad (9)$$

$$\tau_i^* = \frac{(f - \varepsilon_j)(\alpha_j^j \alpha_i^j) - (f - \varepsilon_i)(2\alpha_j^j \alpha_i^i)}{\epsilon_b(\alpha_j^i \alpha_i^j - 4\alpha_j^j \alpha_i^i)} \qquad (10)$$

Symmetry will typically occur when the two UAVs have the same cost functions and sensibility parameters values. It is easy to verify that the Cournot service revenues level increases with a decrease in marginal cost (dissipated energy for both UAVs) and an increase in cost (directly affected by ϵ_b). However when deciding the price, it may increase with respect to the marginal cost and demand. The key insight gained by studying this scenario is that UAV is realized revenues and market share are proportional to competitors' energy costs. Thus more competitors energy costs increase (ε_j in this setting) more U_i and d_i increase.

Because the calculated Cournot-equilibrium strategies and profits can be so important to UAVs service providers for taking strategical decisions, we also want to analyze it graphically. For this, we first describe the equilibrium in terms of best-response function which is derived again by solving each UAV's first-order conditions for τ_i.

$$BR_i : \tau_i = \frac{f - E_i'}{2E_b} - \frac{\alpha_i^j \tau_j}{2\alpha_i^i} \tag{11}$$

$$BR_j : \tau_i = \frac{f\alpha_j^j - E_j'\alpha_j^j - 2E_b\alpha_j^j \tau_j}{E_b\alpha_j^i} \tag{12}$$

Thanks to the Eqs. (11) and (12) we calculate the optimal availability for each service provider, this results exactly in the Cournot-equilibrium state. We depict in Fig. 3 the best response of the two adversarial service providers with respect to their availability strategies, while setting the same price. The parameters values are chosen as follows: $T = 1$, $\alpha_i^i = \alpha_j^j = 0.2$, $\alpha_i^j = \alpha_j^i = -0.1$ and $f = 0.6$ and $\varepsilon_i = 0.42$ and $\varepsilon_j = 0.4$ we set $0.1 \leq \epsilon_b \leq \epsilon_b^{max} = 1$. The intersection between the two graphs represents the Cournot-Nash equilibrium point of the game. This point represent a mutual best replay, and no UAV service provider has an incentive to deviate from this equilibrium. Notice, however, that each UAV can earn higher profits in other conditions if they both change some choice parameters, an issue that will be discussed later. Through several simulations, we always obtained a unique Nash equilibrium. Another flagrant feature is that the availability strategies evolve in the opposite direction of the beaconing energy cost. In other words, the end availability strategy increases as the beaconing cost decreases.

So far we have assumed decisions simultaneity, which does not mean that actions are made at the same time, but rather service providers cannot observe each other's availability strategies before making their own. Next, we move from simultaneous move games to sequential move ones. A lot of economics papers, argue that this reallocation of firms' decisions will increase the quality of service and benefit.

4   UAVs Behavior Within a Stackelberg Oligopoly Problem

Stackelberg games [9] are promising tools for modeling the telecommunication market competition. They are non-symmetric games where one player, being the

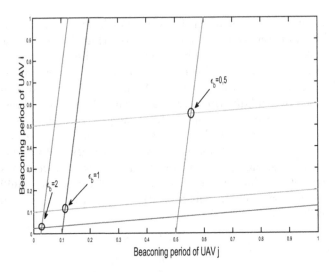

Fig. 3. Best responses for both UAVs providers for different values of ϵ_b.

leader, has the privilege position and can make strategical decision before the other called follower. This way, the leader plays first, but using backward induction, it anticipates the resulting strategy of it's competitor who actually make the last move. Such situations were firstly studied by the German Economist H. von Stackelberg (1934).

Conceptually, with this approach we consider a duopoly leadership game where a UAVs' operator is the leaders and his competitor is the follower.

While modeling UAVs operators' interactions within Stackelberg framework, we use the same market conditions that we used in Cournot. This allows us to provide a comparative analysis of the two models properties.

Lets Consider UAV j as a stackelberg leader, thus, it's the one who make the first move to set its availability parameter τ_j.

We define the following relevant characteristics of the game:

- Players: Service Providers i and j.
- Strategic parameter: Operator j plays first non-negative value of action τ_j, then, operator 2 plays τ_i.
- Operator's payoffs are the difference between profits and costs (same expression but not necessarily the same value as in Cournot model).

From the leader's perspective, before making a strategical decision, it considers it's competitor's reaction function. Since we consider the same conditions assumed in Cournot's model, the reaction function is already defined in Eq. (11). By plugging this reaction into the utility function we obtain the following UAV j's payoff:

$$U_j = (\alpha_j^j \tau_j + \alpha_j^i [\frac{f - E_i'}{2E_b} - \frac{\alpha_i^j \tau_j}{2\alpha_i^i}])(f - E_j' - E_b \tau_j) \tag{13}$$

The optimal market share strategy is obtained at U_i^{max}, thus, it is embedded in the following first-order condition:

$$\frac{\partial U_j}{\partial \tau_j} = \alpha_j^j f - \alpha_j^j \varepsilon_j - 2\alpha_j^j \epsilon_b \tau_j - \frac{\alpha_j^j \alpha_i^j f}{2\alpha_i^i} + \frac{\alpha_j^j \alpha_i^i \varepsilon_j}{2\alpha_i^i} - \frac{\alpha_j^i(f - \varepsilon_i)}{2} + \frac{\alpha_j^i \alpha_j^i}{\alpha_i^i}\epsilon_b \tau_j = 0;$$
(14)

Then, Stackelberg equilibrium strategies are given below:

$$\tau_j^* = \frac{f - \varepsilon_j}{2E_b} + \frac{\alpha_j^i(f - \varepsilon_i)}{2(-2\alpha_j^j \alpha_i^i + \alpha_j^i \alpha_i^j)E_b}$$
(15)

$$\tau_i^* = \frac{f - \varepsilon_i}{2\epsilon_b}(1 - \frac{\alpha_j^i \alpha_i^j}{(-2\alpha_j^j \alpha_i^i + \alpha_j^i \alpha_i^j)2\alpha_i^i}) - \frac{\alpha_i^j(f - \varepsilon_j)}{4\alpha_i^i \epsilon_b}$$
(16)

Contrary to Cournot game, UAVs Stackelberg equilibrium strategies are non-symmetric. When calculating the UAVs equilibrium payoffs for both proposed approaches (cournot and stackelberg), we notice that, in stackelber game, the leader makes a higher profit to that of Cournot-Nash, however the profit of the follower is considerably lower than Cournot's payoff.

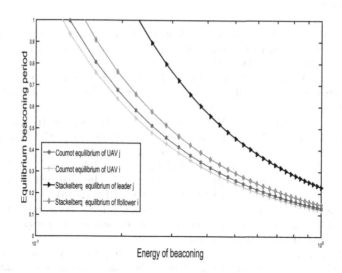

Fig. 4. Equilibrium availability for UAVs providers within both Cournot and Stackelberg models.

Our finding is clearly illustrated in Fig. 4, when we plot the UAVs equilibrium status for both Cournot and Stackelberg models with respect to the beaconing energy ϵ_b.

It is clear from the graphs that, the benefit of the stackelberg leader is much better than that when adopting a Cournot approach. As regards the follower, the profit is better in the Cournot game. Another important result is that as the ϵ_b increases as the equilibrium value decreases. This is quite intuitive since it means for a service provider to realize a considerable benefit it should optimize more and more it's availability strategy.

5   Conclusion

In this paper, we dealt with the activity scheduling of unmanned aerial vehicles acting as mobile aerial base stations. We considered a UAVs duopoly network scenario based on non-cooperative game theory. The interactions and equilibrium strategies for each UAV, are characterize both in Cournot (anarchic) and stackelberg (hierarchical) approaches. We have shown with both mathematical analysis and extensive simulations that the equilibrium state, that allows UAVs to optimize their energy consumption while optimizing theyfffir availability exists. Furthermore, we have compared the two proposed solutions. As a future work, we are generalizing our proposal while considering an oligopoly model and heterogeneous mobility motions.

References

1. Mozaffari, M., Saad, W., Bennis, M., Debbah, M.: Mobile unmanned aerial vehicles (UAVs) for energy-efficient internet of things communications. IEEE Trans. Wirel. Commun. **16**(11), 7574–7589 (2017)
2. Bouachir, O., Abrassart, A., Garcia, F., Larrieu, N.: A mobility model for UAV ad Hoc network. In: 2014 International Conference on Unmanned Aircraft Systems (ICUAS), pp. 383–388. IEEE (2014)
3. Kuester, D.G., Jacobs, R.T., Ma, Y., Coder, J.B.: Testing spectrum sensing networks by UAV. In: 2016 United States National Committee of URSI National Radio Science Meeting (USNC-URSI NRSM), pp. 1–2. IEEE (2016)
4. Mozaffari, M., Saad, W., Bennis, M., Debbah, M.: Mobile Internet of Things: can UAVs provide an energy-efficient mobile architecture? In: 2016 IEEE Global Communications Conference (GLOBECOM), pp. 1–6. IEEE (2016)
5. Motlagh, N.H., Taleb, T., Arouk, O.: Low-altitude unmanned aerial vehicles-based Internet of Things services: comprehensive survey and future perspectives. IEEE Internet Things J. **3**(6), 899–922 (2016)
6. Zhang, J., Zeng, Y., Zhang, R.: Spectrum and energy efficiency maximization in UAV-enabled mobile relaying. In: 2017 IEEE International Conference on Communications (ICC), pp. 1–6. IEEE (2017)
7. Chandhar, P., Danev, D., Larsson, E.G.: Massive MIMO for communications with drone swarms. IEEE Trans. Wirel. Commun. **17**(3), 1604–1629 (2018)
8. Liu, Y.D., Ziarek, L.: Toward energy-aware programming for unmanned aerial vehicles. In: Proceedings of the 3rd International Workshop on Software Engineering for Smart Cyber-Physical Systems, pp. 30–33. IEEE Press (2017)
9. Vives, X.: Duopoly information equilibrium: cournot and bertrand. J. Econ. Theory **34**(1), 71–94 (1984)

Homography and Morphological Detection-Based Virtual Shooting Range

Wilbert G. Aguilar[1,2(✉)], Patricio Castro[1], Jessica Caballeros[1],
and David Segarra[1]

[1] CICTE Research Center, Universidad de las Fuerzas Armadas ESPE,
Sangolquí, Ecuador
wgaguilar@espe.edu.ec
[2] GREC Research Group, Universitat Politècnica de Catalunya,
Barcelona, Spain

Abstract. The purpose of this paper is to describe the development and present the results of the design and implementation of a laser shooting simulator based on computer vision. Our proposal is to develop a virtual environment through a simulation platform to project it on a surface and combine it with computer vision to interact with created targets. Two main stages haven been structured: adjustment and calibration of the camera in the environment and integration of the laser in the simulation.

Keywords: Laser tracking · Virtual reality · Shooting simulator

1 Introduction

Virtual reality has become a very useful tool for training simulation since it allows professionals prepare for real situations. Virtual reality [1–3] helps train machinery operators [4, 5], doctors [6, 7], pilots [8–10], and it even enables firearm training [11–13].

Different methods have been used so that a person can interact directly with virtual environments [14], however thanks to computer vision, the sensation of immersion has increased due to high precision delivered by images obtained by cameras [13, 15–17].

In the field of vision by computer, algorithms are incorporated that perform geometric transformations 2D [18–22]. They do not change the image content but deform the pixel grid. Allowing a better perspective of the image for a simpler processing. Mathematical concepts such as gradient and timing [23–27] are commonly used in image processing, allowing an in-depth analysis of each pixel set.

In institutions such as the army or the police, firing training is conducted to improve the performance of its members in which real firearms and real targets are used. However, this represents a great loss of resources, in terms of cost, due to the amount of ammunition that is used during training. To solve this problem virtual environments have been created enabling real firing simulations with laser guns.

Our proposal is to work with a laser gun in a complete virtual environment which, likewise, has virtual targets to recreate a shooting practice, providing a real-time and low-cost evaluation.

© Springer Nature Switzerland AG 2018
N. Boudriga et al. (Eds.): UNet 2018, LNCS 11277, pp. 267–272, 2018.
https://doi.org/10.1007/978-3-030-02849-7_24

2   Our Approach

A complete virtual reproduction of a shooting range is created based on laser flashes recognition which simulate the firing of a weapon. Initially, a digital environment with several targets is created to be displayed on a specific surface, subsequently, the user shoots a laser gun on the projection. A camera identifies the exact location of the shot to finally digitize its position and assign a score according to the target reached by the laser shot. Figure 1 represents a general system schema.

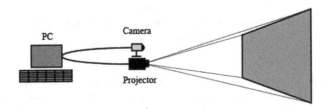

Fig. 1. General prototype schema.

During the calibration process four points of interest have been integrated (P1, P2, P3, P4). These points allow the selection of the vertices of the quadrangle that represents the work of area, forming the matrix IA. Figure 2 shows the selection of the work area.

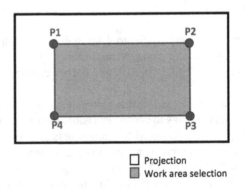

Fig. 2. Selection of the work area.

In order to obtain the position of the laser firing, the central moment of the flash produced by the laser shot must be found. As a result, the center of gravity of the laser flash is obtained providing us with the laser shot coordinates.

The laser device produces a red flash, hence the red channel of the image is considered for processing, then the image is binarized in values to prevent the detection of false positives.

In Fig. 3a shows how the laser image is obtained inside the matrix of work (IW). Then, image binarization is performed to determine the contour of the laser flash among other objects within the field of view (Fig. 3b). Next, the central moment (mu) of the image contour is obtained from a vector containing all its points.

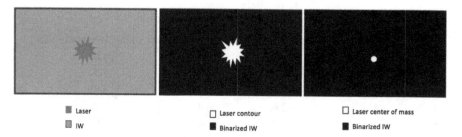

Fig. 3. (a) Camera laser capture (b) laser contour (c) laser center of mass (Color figure online)

Finally, when transferring the position of the laser to the virtual environment, a comparison of its position with the digital targets is performed, therefore, it is possible to assess performance and assign a score according to the exact location of the shot and the target reached by the laser shot.

3 Results and Discussion

The prototype has different scenarios which simulate a wild environment, an urban environment, and a real shooting range facility as it is shown in Fig. 4. Several tests were conducted to determine the error that exists when transferring the *L point* to the virtual environment. To obtain the error, a camera calibration was performed 5 times within each scenario. Additionally, in every calibration 5 laser shots were registered. Each one of these shots were measured.

Fig. 4. Virtual environments.

An average of the error was calculated based on all the measurements of the laser shots in each calibration. Likewise, an average percentage of the error generated by the camera in each calibration was obtained considering the entire field of view. Table 1 presents these values.

Table 1. Laser shot measurement results

Calibration	Width error (mm)	Width error (%)	Height error (mm)	Height error (%)
1	7	3.68	6	4.62
2	8	4.21	2	1.54
3	4	2.11	5	3.85
4	5	2.63	4	3.08
5	8	4.21	4	3.08

4 Conclusions and Future Works

We conclude that because its minimum response time and low error percentage, the virtual shooting range exceeds expectations. Hence, the virtual shooting range could be used effectively to train arm forces members.

For future works, we propose to incorporate artificial intelligence into the system to enable virtual interaction. Likewise, through the creation of virtual characters, obstacles or moving targets the user would enjoy a real shooting practice experience.

References

1. Aguilar, W.G., Rodríguez, G.A., Álvarez, L., Sandoval, S., Quisaguano, F., Limaico, A.: Visual SLAM with a RGB-D camera on a quadrotor UAV using on-board processing. In: Rojas, I., Joya, G., Catala, A. (eds.) IWANN 2017. LNCS, vol. 10306, pp. 596–606. Springer, Cham (2017). https://doi.org/10.1007/978-3-319-59147-6_51
2. Aguilar, W.G., Rodríguez, G.A., Álvarez, L., Sandoval, S., Quisaguano, F., Limaico, A.: Real-time 3D modeling with a RGB-D camera and on-board processing. In: De Paolis, L.T., Bourdot, P., Mongelli, A. (eds.) AVR 2017. LNCS, vol. 10325, pp. 410–419. Springer, Cham (2017). https://doi.org/10.1007/978-3-319-60928-7_35
3. Aguilar, W.G., Rodríguez, G.A., Álvarez, L., Sandoval, S., Quisaguano, F., Limaico, A.: On-board visual SLAM on a UGV using a RGB-D camera. In: Huang, Y., Wu, H., Liu, H., Yin, Z. (eds.) ICIRA 2017. LNCS (LNAI), vol. 10464, pp. 298–308. Springer, Cham (2017). https://doi.org/10.1007/978-3-319-65298-6_28
4. Champagne, R., Dessaint, L.A., Fortin-Blanchette, H., Sybille, G.: Analysis and validation of a real-time AC drive simulator. IEEE Trans. Power Electron. **19**(2), 336–345 (2004). https://doi.org/10.1109/TPEL.2003.823242
5. Lee, W.-S., Kim, J.-H., Cho, J.-H.: A driving simulator as a virtual reality tool. In: Proceedings IEEE International Conference on Robotics and Automation, pp. 71–76, May 1998. https://doi.org/10.1109/ROBOT.1998.676264

6. Korzeniowski, P., Brown, D.C., Sodergren, M.H., Barrow, A., Bello, F.: Validation of NOViSE. Surg. Innov. **24**(1), 55–65 (2017). https://doi.org/10.1177/1553350616669896
7. Sugand, K., Akhtar, K., Khatri, C., Cobb, J., Gupte, C.: Training effect of a virtual reality haptics-enabled dynamic hip screw simulator. Acta Orthop. **86**(6), 695–701 (2015). https://doi.org/10.3109/17453674.2015.1071111
8. Aslandere, T., Dreyer, D., Pankratz, F.: Virtual hand-button interaction in a generic virtual reality flight simulator. In: IEEE Aerospace Conference Proceedings, June (2015). https://doi.org/10.1109/AERO.2015.7118876
9. Aguilar, W.G., Morales, S.G.: 3D environment mapping using the Kinect V2 and path planning based on RRT algorithms. Electronics **5**(4), 70 (2016)
10. Aguilar, W.G., Morales, S., Ruiz, H., Abad, V.: RRT* GL based optimal path planning for real-time navigation of UAVs. In: Rojas, I., Joya, G., Catala, A. (eds.) IWANN 2017. LNCS, vol. 10306, pp. 585–595. Springer, Cham (2017). https://doi.org/10.1007/978-3-319-59147-6_50
11. Smith-miles, K., Smith-miles, K.: Vision Assisted Safety Enhanced Shooting Range Simulator, January 2010
12. Soetedjo, A., Nurcahyo, E.: Developing of low cost vision-based shooting range simulator. IJCSNS Int. J. Comput. Sci. Netw. Secur. **11**(2), 109–113 (2011)
13. Bhagat, K.K., Liou, W.K., Chang, C.Y.: A cost-effective interactive 3D virtual reality system applied to military live firing training. Virtual Real. **20**(2), 127–140 (2016). https://doi.org/10.1007/s10055-016-0284-x
14. Kiploks, J., Vjaters, J.: Shooting Simulator structure. Sci. J. RTU Power Electr. Eng. **22**, 118–126 (2008)
15. Fraser, C.S.: Automatic camera calibration in close range photogrammetry. Photogramm. Eng. Remote. Sens. **79**(4), 381–388 (2013). https://doi.org/10.14358/PERS.79.4.381
16. Aguilar, W.G., et al.: Pedestrian detection for UAVs using cascade classifiers and saliency maps. In: Rojas, I., Joya, G., Catala, A. (eds.) IWANN 2017. LNCS, vol. 10306, pp. 563–574. Springer, Cham (2017). https://doi.org/10.1007/978-3-319-59147-6_48
17. Aguilar, W.G., et al.: Cascade classifiers and saliency maps based people detection. In: De Paolis, L.T., Bourdot, P., Mongelli, A. (eds.) AVR 2017. LNCS, vol. 10325, pp. 501–510. Springer, Cham (2017). https://doi.org/10.1007/978-3-319-60928-7_42
18. Mizutani, H., Yamamoto, D., Takahashi, N.: A Geometric Transformation Method for Preventing Focuses from Overlapping in a Focus + Glue + Context Map (n.d.)
19. Sonka, M., Hlavac, V., Boyle, R.: Image Processing, Analysis, and Machine Vision. Cengage Learning, Boston (2014)
20. Aguilar, W.G., Salcedo, V.S., Sandoval, D.S., Cobeña, B.: Developing of a video-based model for UAV autonomous navigation. In: Barone, D.A.C., Teles, E.O., Brackmann, C.P. (eds.) LAWCN 2017. CCIS, vol. 720, pp. 94–105. Springer, Cham (2017). https://doi.org/10.1007/978-3-319-71011-2_8
21. Aguilar, W.G., Casaiglla, V.P., Pólit, J.L.: Obstacle avoidance based-visual navigation for micro aerial vehicles. Electronics **6**(1), 10 (2017)
22. Aguilar, W.G., Casaiglla, V.P., Pólit, J.L., Abad, V., Ruiz, H.: Obstacle avoidance for flight safety on unmanned aerial vehicles. In: Rojas, I., Joya, G., Catala, A. (eds.) IWANN 2017. LNCS, vol. 10306, pp. 575–584. Springer, Cham (2017). https://doi.org/10.1007/978-3-319-59147-6_49
23. Xue, W., Zhang, L., Mou, X., Bovik, A.C.: Gradient magnitude similarity deviation: a highly efficient perceptual image quality index. IEEE Trans. Image Process. **23**(2), 668–695 (2014). https://doi.org/10.1109/TIP.2013.2293423

24. Vassou, S.A., Amanatiadis, A., Christodoulou, K., Chatzichristoos, S.A.: CoMo: a compact composite moment-based descriptor for image retrieval. In: Proceedings of the 15th International Workshop on Content-Based Multimedia Indexing. CBMI 2017, vol. 5, no. 17, pp. 1–5 (2017). https://doi.org/10.1145/3095713.3095744

25. Chen, B., Shu, H., Zhang, H., Chen, G., Luo, L., Quaternions, A.: Color image analysis by quaternion Zernike moments, no. 7, pp. 7–10 (2010). https://doi.org/10.1109/ICPR.2010.158

26. Aguilar, W.G., Angulo, C.: Real-time model-based video stabilization for microaerial vehicles. Neural Process. Lett. **43**(2), 459–477 (2016)

27. Aguilar, W.G., Angulo, C.: Real-time video stabilization without phantom movements for micro aerial vehicles. EURASIP J. Image Video Process. **2014**(1), 46 (2014)

RRT Path Planning and Morphological Segmentation Based Navigation for a Tetrapod Robot

Wilbert G. Aguilar[1,2($\boxtimes$)], Jessica Caballeros[1], David Segarra[1],
and Patricio Castro[1]

[1] CICTE Research Center, Universidad de las Fuerzas Armadas ESPE,
Sangolquí, Ecuador
wgaguilar@espe.edu.ec
[2] GREC Research Group, Universitat Politècnica de Catalunya,
Barcelona, Spain

Abstract. This article will establish the physical design of a tetrapod robot, highlighting its own characteristics of low-level three-dimensional movement to move from one point to another. The navigation system was also examined in environments not defined from a top-down perspective, making the analysis and processing of the images with the purpose of avoiding collisions between the robot and static obstacles, and using probabilistic techniques and partial information on the environment, RRT generate paths that are less artificial.

Keywords: Quadruped robot · Path planning · RRT · Obstacle avoidance

1 Introduction

Currently, one of the main objectives of robotics is to develop robust methods of autonomous trajectory planning [1]. Many applications require the use of robots capable of moving to achieve their objectives, this being where the articulated robots take importance. The use of robots with wheels is complicated when it comes to moving in irregular areas and developing autonomously [2].

Avoiding obstacles in dynamic environments is one of the most significant and most fascinating problems in the field of mobile robotics [3–6]. Route planning methods are found in automatic routes without collisions, while obstacle avoidance methods consist in avoiding obstacles that arise in the path of the robot, while achieving the objective, in which the of decisions is made according to the information captured from the environment in which the robot is [7]. The RRT (Rapidly-exploring Random Tree) is based on the creation of branches of a tree in space, which iteratively samples new states and then directs the existing node that is closer to each sample to a new sample and thus forming a tree with ramifications [8].

All mobile robots have some kind of collision prevention, ranging from primitive algorithms that detect an obstacle and stop the robot to avoid a collision, to sophisticated algorithms, which allow the robot to deflect obstacles. Once they have been

© Springer Nature Switzerland AG 2018
N. Boudriga et al. (Eds.): UNet 2018, LNCS 11277, pp. 273–280, 2018.
https://doi.org/10.1007/978-3-030-02849-7_25

determined, the obstacle avoidance algorithm needs to steer the robot around the obstacle and resume movement towards the original target [9].

For [10] the main purpose of road planning is to create algorithms that allow paths to be established considering restrictions in the movements of mobile robots. The Path Planning applications are oriented to different tasks that interact with the human being in different areas: (i) health: because it allows the support of robots in tasks for the elderly and people with paraplegia, (ii) military: because it is focused on the supervision [11–14] of remote-controlled robots, autonomous and intelligent weapons, (iii) industrial: monitoring of robots with artificial intelligence through the use of mobile robots [15].

2 Related Works

The robots that are based on locomotion with legs are characterized by having a great relationship with the ground. The main advantages of this type of robots are that they have great adaptability and maneuverability in terrains that are irregular [16].

An example of a quadruped robot is the (LAVA) [17] developed at the Robotics Research Center, NTU, Singapore. To decrease the weight and increase the energy production of each servomotor, each leg with its 3° of freedom is driven through a reverse differential gear. Two engines are located in the hip section and the third is in the knee section.

Computer vision is a tool that is used in electronic systems to similarly simulate the vision that man has by replacing the human eye with a camera and the brain of the person with a processor. An example of this is in its use on Mars in the 2004 MER mission, in which two identical rovers, Spirit and Opportunity, landed to search for geologic clues about whether part of Mars had previously wet enough environments to be hospitable. for life [18], in this work computer vision algorithms were used for odometry, stereoscopic vision and for mobile navigation and tracking characteristics for the estimation of horizontal speed for landing.

There are some ways to position the camera and be able to give vision to the robot that you want to control, one of them is with a zenith perspective, that is, with the camera placed perpendicularly to the plane of the ground, to the plane of movement of the robot, this perspective was used by the work done by [19] in which the position of mobile robots and a ball in a game called robot soccer was defined; Here, the color patterns were distinguished by the camera, but before that, the algorithm created first was a circle detection. As in the previous case, this work will control an autonomous robot, a tetrapod, using a camera with overhead perspective, which will use computer vision to navigate in chaotic environments.

Now we turn our attention to the cognitive level of the robot. Cognition generally represents decision-making to achieve your objectives of higher order. Navigation includes the ability of the robot to act on its knowledge to achieve the position of the target in the most efficient and reliable way possible. Several techniques have been devised, for example, exact cellular decomposition [20], approximate cell decomposition [21], retraction in a network of one-dimensional curves [22]. The local approach consists of looking for a grid placed in the configuration space of the robot [23].

3 Tetrapod Robot

Robot control unit is based on technology of ATMega328. Each leg was commanded by microcontroller. PWM signal from outputs of Microcontroller board is transmitted over connector board to servo motors. Totally, robot has 12 motors of them belong to legs. The block diagram of the system can be expressed as shown in Fig. 1.

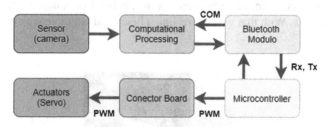

Fig. 1. Block diagram

The locomotion is provided by entering commands into the mobile phone. The command was transmitted over Bluetooth link to microcontroller, and then the mechanism runs. The mechanical part of Spider Robot is composed of ABS plastic that was used to print it in 3D, the four legs of it are also made of this material. The axes and the form of movement of each joint are shown in Fig. 2.

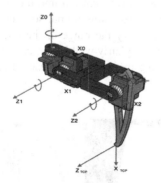

Fig. 2. Motion axes of each leg.

4 Mapping

In this work an autonomous robot, a tetrapod, will be controlled by means of a camera with a zenith perspective, which will be used by computer vision to navigate in chaotic environments, that is to avoid collisions between a quadruped robot and static obstacles that have a specific shape.

The decision making is based on the information captured from the environment in which the robot is located through the camera as the visual sensor, from a zenith perspective, for the analysis and processing of images for the evasion of obstacles will be used OpenCV software, designed for computational efficiency, which provides a simplified use of its infrastructure for computer vision and which is available for Python whose development is based on open source libraries; this last tool will be used as a basis for the computational development of the method of evasion objects and with this information the mobile robot performs a determined task.

Threshold is essential for computer vision and image processing whereby we replace each pixel in an image with a binary value, either 1 or 0, depending if that pixel meets some criteria. With that we are creating a black and white version of the original image.

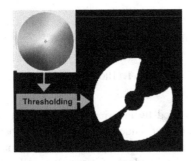

Fig. 3. Threshold frame with hue range of 220 to 260 (Color figure online)

In Fig. 3 the white areas are pixels that fall into the color range that was set. You can see that the parts of circle in red show up but so does a lot of other warm colors, like orange and yellow. As we vary the range of the hue can improve the detection conditions and as our robot will be fairly well-lit, we can remove the darker areas from the masked image by increasing the minimum threshold and we can get very precise color detection (see Fig. 4).

Fig. 4. Threshold frame (Color figure online)

5 Rapidly-Exploring Random Trees

The rapid-scan random tree route planners (RRTs) have been shown to be suitable for solving various high-dimensional route planning problems. While they share many of the beneficial properties of existing random planning techniques [24].

The RRT algorithm presented in [24] is shown in Algorithm 1. The tree grows from the adjacent neighbor in the tree, xnear, to a configuration that was created at random, xrand. The length of the step described in this work should be a small distance.

Algorithm 1. Basic RRT expansion method.

For i=1 ... K do
    Xrand = random configuration
    Xnear = nearest neighbor in tree τ to Xrand
    Xnew = extend Xnear toward Xrand for step length
    If (Xnew can connect to Xnear along valid edge) then
        τ.AddVertex(Xnew). T.AddEdge(Xnew,Xnear)
    end if
  end for
  return τ

---

6 Experimentation and Results

The goal is to get the fastest time to find the solution path and to be distant enough between each point that makes up the route, allowing the robot to move easily. For this we vary the Delta constant between the following values: delta equal to 40, 20, and finally 10, the tests were performed in iterations of 10 times each and calculating the average of the time that is delayed in tracing the route.

In Fig. 5, we observe the results obtained for a Delta equal to 40 and the time in finding the route towards the objective, while decreasing the value of Delta as shown in Fig. 6, the time to find the route Is considerably reduced, but as the Delta value continues to decrease, the mean time begins to elapse as shown in Fig. 7.

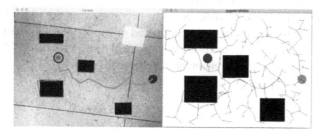

Fig. 5. Test delta = 40, average time to find the route equal 19.45 s.

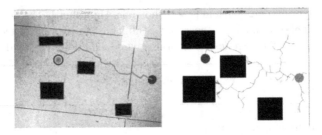

Fig. 6. Test delta = 20, average time to find the route equal 12.74 s.

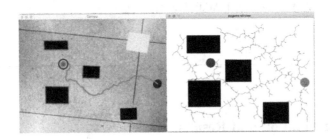

Fig. 7. Test delta = 10, average time to find the route equal 21.41 s.

7 Conclusions and Future Work

The rapidly exploring random tree RRT method for path planning, allows to determine with relative speed the way between an initial and final position, in an environment with obstacles detected with morphological segmentation, that allow the autonomous movement of the Spider Robot.

Based on the experiments performed, lighting should be considered as a determining factor for optimal software performance since a low amount of light affects the recognition of both colors and objects.

As a future work, a PID controller could be implemented to better track the path by receiving the angle of rotation in the spider instead of left or right commands. Likewise, you can perform an RRT in an unknown environment using a Kinect [25–29] mounted on a large structure and get the planning of trajectories.

References

1. Menéndez, C.: Navegación de robots autónomos en entronos dinámicos (2012)
2. Fernández, J.F., Barrientos, T.A.: Análisis, desarrollo y evaluación de modos de marcha para un robot hexápodo (2016)
3. Bertozzi, M., Broggi, A., Fascioli, A.: A stereo vision system for real-time automotive obstacle detection. In: International Conference on Image Processing, vol. 1, pp. 681–684 (1996). https://doi.org/10.1109/icip.1996.560970

4. Aguilar, W.G., Salcedo, V.S., Sandoval, D.S., Cobeña, B.: Developing of a video-based model for UAV autonomous navigation. In: Barone, D.A.C., Teles, E.O., Brackmann, C. P. (eds.) LAWCN 2017. CCIS, vol. 720, pp. 94–105. Springer, Cham (2017). https://doi.org/10.1007/978-3-319-71011-2_8

5. Aguilar, W.G., Casaliglla, V.P., Pólit, J.L.: Obstacle avoidance based-visual navigation for micro aerial vehicles. Electronics 6(1), 10 (2017)

6. Aguilar, W.G., Casaliglla, V.P., Pólit, J.L., Abad, V., Ruiz, H.: Obstacle avoidance for flight safety on unmanned aerial vehicles. In: Rojas, I., Joya, G., Catala, A. (eds.) IWANN 2017. LNCS, vol. 10306, pp. 575–584. Springer, Cham (2017). https://doi.org/10.1007/978-3-319-59147-6_49

7. Alvarez, P.Q., Antonio, J., Estrada, R., Fernández, A.A., Torres, J.G.R.: Técnicas para evasión de obstáculos en Robótica Móvil. 1 (2010)

8. Karaman, S., Frazzoli, E.: Optimal kinodynamic motion planning using incremental sampling-based methods. In: Proceedings of the IEEE Conference Decision Control, pp. 7681–7687 (2010). https://doi.org/10.1109/cdc.2010.5717430

9. Borenstein, J., Koren, Y.: The vector field histogram: fast obstacle avoidance for mobile robots. IEEE Trans. Robot. Autom. 7, 278–288 (1991). https://doi.org/10.1109/70.88137

10. Barraquand, J., Kavraki, L., Latombe, J.-C., Motwani, R., Li, T.-Y., Raghavan, P.: A random sampling scheme for planning 16, 759–774 (1997)

11. Aguilar, W.G., Angulo, C.: Real-time video stabilization without phantom movements for micro aerial vehicles. EURASIP J. Image Video Process. 2014(1), 46 (2014)

12. Aguilar, W.G., Angulo, C.: Real-time model-based video stabilization for microaerial vehicles. Neural Process. Lett. 43(2), 459–477 (2016)

13. Aguilar, W.G., et al.: Pedestrian detection for UAVs using cascade classifiers and saliency maps. In: Rojas, I., Joya, G., Catala, A. (eds.) IWANN 2017. LNCS, vol. 10306, pp. 563–574. Springer, Cham (2017). https://doi.org/10.1007/978-3-319-59147-6_48

14. Aguilar, W.G., et al.: Cascade classifiers and saliency maps based people detection. In: De Paolis, L.T., Bourdot, P., Mongelli, A. (eds.) AVR 2017. LNCS, vol. 10325, pp. 501–510. Springer, Cham (2017). https://doi.org/10.1007/978-3-319-60928-7_42

15. Ortiz, O., Santana, A.: Planificación de caminos para Robots en Realidad Virtual (2017)

16. Siegwart, R., Nourbakhsh, I.R.: Introduction to Autonomous Mobile Robots. MIT Press, Cambridge (2004)

17. Zielinska, T., Heng, J.: Mechanical design of multifunctional quadruped. Mech. Mach. Theory 38, 463–478 (2003). https://doi.org/10.1016/S0094-114X(03)00004-1

18. Matthies, L., et al.: Computer vision on Mars. Int. J. Comput. Vis. 75, 67–92 (2007). https://doi.org/10.1007/s11263-007-0046-z

19. Antipov, V., Kokovkina, V., Kirnos, V., Priorov, A.: Computer vision system for recognition and detection of color patterns in real-time task of robot control. In: 2017 Systems of Signal Synchronization, Generating and Processing in Telecommunications Sink 2017 (2017). https://doi.org/10.1109/sinkhroinfo.2017.7997496

20. Schwartz, J.T., Sharir, M.: On the "piano movers" problem. II. General techniques for computing topological properties of real algebraic manifolds. Adv. Appl. Math. 4, 298–351 (1983). https://doi.org/10.1016/0196-8858(83)90014-3

21. Brooks, R.A., Lozano-Pérez, T.: A subdivision algorithm in configuration space for findpath with rotation. IEEE Trans. Syst. Man. Cybern. SMC-15, 224–233 (1985). https://doi.org/10.1109/tsmc.1985.6313352

22. Dúnlaing, C., Sharir, M., Yap, C.K.: Retraction: a new approach to motion-planning. In: Proceedings of the Fifteenth Annual ACM Symposium on Theory of Computing, pp. 207–220. ACM, New York (1983)

23. Donald, B.R.: A search algorithm for motion planning with six degrees of freedom. Artif. Intell. **31**, 295–353 (1987). https://doi.org/10.1016/0004-3702(87)90069-5

24. LaValle, S.M.: Rapidly-exploring random trees: a new tool for path planning. In: vol. 129, pp. 98–11 (1998). 10.1.1.35.1853

25. Aguilar, W.G., Rodríguez, G.A., Álvarez, L., Sandoval, S., Quisaguano, F., Limaico, A.: Visual SLAM with a RGB-D camera on a quadrotor UAV using on-board processing. In: Rojas, I., Joya, G., Catala, A. (eds.) IWANN 2017. LNCS, vol. 10306, pp. 596–606. Springer, Cham (2017). https://doi.org/10.1007/978-3-319-59147-6_51

26. Aguilar, W.G., Rodríguez, G.A., Álvarez, L., Sandoval, S., Quisaguano, F., Limaico, A.: Real-time 3D modeling with a RGB-D camera and on-board processing. In: De Paolis, L.T., Bourdot, P., Mongelli, A. (eds.) AVR 2017. LNCS, vol. 10325, pp. 410–419. Springer, Cham (2017). https://doi.org/10.1007/978-3-319-60928-7_35

27. Aguilar, W.G., Rodríguez, G.A., Álvarez, L., Sandoval, S., Quisaguano, F., Limaico, A.: On-board visual SLAM on a UGV using a RGB-D camera. In: Huang, Y., Wu, H., Liu, H., Yin, Z. (eds.) ICIRA 2017. LNCS (LNAI), vol. 10464, pp. 298–308. Springer, Cham (2017). https://doi.org/10.1007/978-3-319-65298-6_28

28. Aguilar, W.G., Morales, S.G.: 3D environment mapping using the Kinect V2 and path planning based on RRT algorithms. Electronics **5**(4), 70 (2016)

29. Aguilar, W.G., Morales, S., Ruiz, H., Abad, V.: RRT* GL based optimal path planning for real-time navigation of UAVs. In: Rojas, I., Joya, G., Catala, A. (eds.) IWANN 2017. LNCS, vol. 10306, pp. 585–595. Springer, Cham (2017). https://doi.org/10.1007/978-3-319-59147-6_50

Cyber Security for Ubiquitous Communications

Methodology for the Implementation of QoS in Li-Fi Networks in 5th Generation Environments

Jesús Manuel Paternina Durán[1], Octavio José Salcedo Parra[1,2(✉)], and José de Jesús Paternina Anaya[1]

[1] Faculty of Engineering, Universidad Distrital "Francisco José de Caldas", Bogotá D.C., Colombia
{jmpaterninad, osalcedo, jjpaterninaa}@udistrital.edu.co
[2] Department of Systems and Industrial Engineering, Faculty of Engineering, Universidad Nacional de Colombia, Bogotá D.C., Colombia
ojsalcedop@unal.edu.co

Abstract. The present document discusses a methodology for the implementation of services that require QoS in 5G Li-Fi networks. It takes into account the inherent characteristics of these technologies and the necessary requirements for their implementation.

Keywords: Methodology · Li-Fi · 5G · QoS · NS-2

1 Introduction

This article is the result of a research in which the approach, analysis and implementation of a service quality algorithm was carried out that allowed to improve the performance in UDP traffic in a simulated Li-Fi network with the NS-2 tool. Special emphasis was placed on the MAC layer and physical characteristics of the Li-fi networks to obtain similar conditions to the real ones. The results were compared with three research documents that allowed establishing the viability of the proposed algorithm.

2 Background

With respect to the quality of service in communications networks, IntServ (Integrated Services) has been known since 1990, supporting this feature for end-to-end services. The resources were pre-reserved while traffic was transferred between the two nodes. The resources were reserved according to priorities for each new session. The packets had to be processed in each intermediate node to locate the corresponding resources [1].

Differentiated services (Diffserv) were introduced to provide greater efficiency and less complexity in the systems for extensive networks. Diffserv applies packet classification in the autonomous computers of the network. It provides QoS end-to-end, which is based on aggregation of PHB (per-hob behavior) traffic. Traffic is categorized

© Springer Nature Switzerland AG 2018
N. Boudriga et al. (Eds.): UNet 2018, LNCS 11277, pp. 283–294, 2018.
https://doi.org/10.1007/978-3-030-02849-7_26

into flows to which a codepoint is assigned according to the way in which the resources of the system will interconnect with the routing equipment.

The Diffserv architecture includes classification, marking, metric-related and scheduling processes. The first interaction with the incoming packets is presented in the classification. The classification rules are specified according to several parameters. The classifier marks the packets according to the specified rules. In the marking process, the traffic is differentiated in terms of whether the profile has been assigned or not. The marking is done with DS codepoints in the IP packet header.

In the process of the metric the decisions are made according to modification or discarding of packets. Here we store data like the current rat, the size of the buffer, etc.; and also, it is checked if the traffic obtained an appropriate profile.

Once the package has been classified and marked, it is sent to the corresponding queue. The transmission of the package into the media is scheduled [1]. This background-related feature in network traffic treatment for QoS is an essential part of the present work.

3   Definition of Simulation Criteria and Tools Selection

In this section, the simulation criteria established to implement QoS in 5G Li-Fi networks will be analyzed. Taking into account that the methodology was oriented solely towards the quality of service in terms of Li-Fi networks, it was necessary to delimit the observation framework in items to relate this optical network with 5th generation environments. Methodology

The summary of the proposed methodology is presented in Fig. 1. The first phase of the project consisted in determining the metrics and QoS services. Within the Li-Fi environment, a fundamental aspect should be included, such as the 802.15.7 standard, corresponding to short-range wireless optical communications through the use of visible light. The importance of the physical layers (PHY) and control of access to the medium (MAC) of the standard, is that these layers determine the maximum transmission speed of audio and video that can be achieved while the lighting characteristics are not affected.

As the main objective of this work was oriented towards QoS in Li-Fi networks, it was important to recognize algorithms and protocols that could be applied to this type of

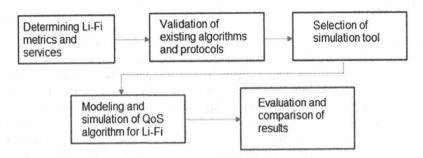

Fig. 1. Proposed QoS methodology for Li-Fi.

technology and are susceptible to improvement. This was part of the second phase of the project. Since the Li-Fi networks are so recent from the point of view of implementation, this work was carried out in simulated environments, based on the tool selected in the previous section. As mentioned in the process of selecting the tool, it had to include certain features that would allow the complete integration of the protocols and algorithms that could be necessary for Li-Fi networks. This possibility of modification of modules (Present in the selected tool, NS-2) was fundamental to determine a model and its applicability in the QoS parameters object of this study. The third phase was due to the modeling and simulation of the algorithm that allows the implementation of QoS in Li-Fi networks including the characteristics of the 5th generation environments and finally, an evaluation and comparison of the results is carried out comparing them with three articles that approach to the objectives set in this project.

4 Definition of QoS Metrics and Services

The metrics chosen for the analysis, according to the specific objectives, were the following: Latency, packet loss and bandwidth.

The QoS services that were validated in the development of the project should be those that require greater network characteristics for the end users. These are undoubtedly real-time traffic services, Voice over IP, video and streaming. For purposes of the work, the traffic of video streaming through UDP packets was specifically analyzed, because many of the entertainment applications use this service to broadcast content.

The general QoS application algorithm for Li-Fi networks is shown in Fig. 2, taking into account the specific policies of load management and queue management.

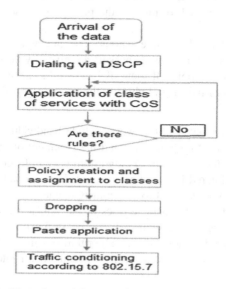

Fig. 2. Flow chart of the general QoS application algorithm.

This decision is oriented to that thanks to the high speeds that are handled in optical communications, it is possible to increase the processes of quality of service that will obviously result in increases in processing times, however this will be compensated with the high transmission speeds.

5 Algorithm Design

Starting from the flow diagram of the previous section, we proceeded to design a new algorithm that would allow to establish QoS on optical media, in this case Li-Fi networks, this with respect to the latency, packet loss and bandwidth metrics.

This new algorithm relied on the development of mathematical modeling based on the interaction of each of the components involved in the communication process.

It is important to bear in mind that one of the main differences between the simplified algorithm of the previous section and this algorithm proposal, lies in the processes carried out in the stages of policy identification, Dropping and queuing. This difference is based on the specific needs of the environment that are fundamental in these stages. The visible light spectrum for Li-Fi networks should also be taken into account, which is between 400 and 800 THz, in addition to the characteristics specified in the IEEE 802.15.7 standard.

For modeling, the following considerations were taken into account:

- Components: Transmitter, receiver and medium. All these elements are optical and open air, respectively.
- Descriptive variables: Latency, packet loss and bandwidth (QoS metrics).
- Identification of interaction rules: Packets must pass a marking and classification process to prioritize services. Privilege processing rules should be assigned according to the identified service. Subsequently, Policing, Dropping and Queuing processes must be executed to improve the perception of services in real time by end users.
- Descriptive parameters of the interactions: The interactions between the aforementioned processes and the marked packets are given by the characteristics of the Li-Fi network, from the point of view of bandwidth, latency and packet loss, in addition to the layer of liaison and physics, the latter described in detail in standard 802.15.7.

The metrics to be evaluated in this work include bandwidth, a parameter directly related to the throughput of the interfaces and the treatment of the service packets in real time. In particular, the Token Bucket algorithm used in LLQ was identified at the moment when the configured bandwidth is exceeded and packet discarding is necessary, prioritizing the traffic destined to the Priority queue.

In the work carried out, the characteristics of the Token Bucket algorithm and its improvement possibilities were established to process the traffic destined to a Li-Fi network. The reason for the choice of this algorithm lies in its robustness for Traffic Shaping from the point of view of the controls required for latency and bandwidth control [2].

The basic expression of the algorithm allows assigning a single token for each service class, thus compromising multiple connections. Thus, it was not possible to differentiate connections for the same classes of service and therefore, the transmission speed was compromised [2].

Other algorithm proposals made the tokens approve the transmission of an entire packet and not a defined volume of data, leading to different packet sizes resulting in different transmission speeds if the token speed was the same.

On the other hand, there were also algorithms that made a token approve a single package, generating high processing and in general terms, an inefficient system.

Finally, there is a algorithm that has two token buckets. The first token bucket monitors the minimum reservation rate for traffic and the second reinforces the maximum rate of sustained traffic. Only when the first bucket is empty, the tokens are removed from the second bucket. The capacity of the token buckets is determined by the maximum latency of the system.

In this way, the need to improve the existing token bucket algorithms to apply them to Li-Fi networks was reached. Specifically, the feature of this algorithm would apply to the bandwidth metric with respect to the requirements of standard 802.15.7.

The proposed algorithm, which is a variation of LLQ (will be called Optical Low Latency Queuing - OLLQ) for Li-Fi network environments, modifies the token bucket mechanism for the treatment of real-time traffic in inclusive conditions for the standard 802.15.7. The flowchart of this algorithm is shown in Fig. 3.

According to the limitations expressed in the previous sections, this algorithm allowed a better management of real-time service traffic for Li-Fi networks.

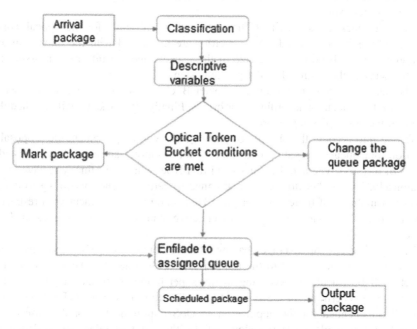

Fig. 3. OLLA algorithm with optical Token Bucket proposal

A comparison of the proposed algorithm with the conventional results of Token Bucket with two token storage containers was carried out. The variation lies mainly in the treatment of the packets before assigning the corresponding token. One of the most important achievements in the development of Token bucket for QoS had been the implementation of a low priority traffic allocation in high priority queues based on the availability of space, this without affecting the performance of the routing elements, improving in this way the loss of packets [3].

Two physical buckets are proposed, taking into account that a greater number of containers would increase the level of processing, but the main innovation lies in the fact that apart from making an evaluation of space in the bucket and the tail according to the present traffic in a dynamic way, the optical characteristics of Li-Fi networks are included in the analysis, which demand agile procedures.

As there is currently no specific standard for Li-Fi, it is important to mention that the proposed algorithm (OLLQ) is based on the general needs to provide QoS in communications networks.

Initially, in the classification process, the kind of service that could be treated should be taken into account. Very probably, in the standard that will be socialized at the end of 2017 by the IEEE with respect to the modifications of IEEE 802.15.7, it will be necessary to specify the classes of service for the traffic of applications in real time, this for packets and arrivals of the same in variable and constant sizes and times. The treatment of the packets must also be included with respect to the best applicable effort. Additionally, due to the variation of the traffic pattern, parameters must be taken into account that define the minimum transfer rate that is required for the applications to remain functional, in addition to the maximum rate that should not be exceeded for the defined time intervals.

Once the package is classified, the metrics that will apply for the optical Token Bucket process are calculated. These metrics are associated with the maximum and minimum average bandwidth, the size of the packets and the information associated with the service class defined in the previous step.

The decisions made in the optical Token Bucket process will make the packets marked for their queuing according to priorities. Finally, the package will be scheduled to exit to the corresponding interface.

Taking into account that 4 types of packet flows will be presented, the proposal is based on four queues for data processing. As the resources are limited, we worked 2 queues of physical type and 4 queues of virtual type, which will finally receive traffic dynamically. The packet flow will be assigned to certain queues according to conditions of availability of buffers and queues. This adaptive management with respect to changing data flow conditions will allow effective management of resources for Li-Fi networks.

The parameters of average bandwidth minimum (BWMN) and maximum (BWMX), are closely related to the transfer rate of the buckets. The size of the two buckets will be calculated according to the super-frame established in the standard 802.15.7. The superframe of the standard has a few timeslots called GTS (Guaranteed Time Slots) intended for the application of QoS requirements. For the case of the proposal of this work, these timeslots will be the point of reference to define the maximum tolerable latency and in turn, will allow to determine the size of the buckets.

Each Token of the buckets allows the transmission of a byte. The first Bucket monitors the average minimum bandwidth (BWMN) of each connection and the second Bucket reinforces the maximum bandwidth according to the information obtained from the behavior of the queues and interfaces. The Tokens are taken initially from the first Bucket and only after this Bucket is empty do they begin to take from the second Bucket. The transfer rate of the first Bucket is equal to BWMN and the difference between BWMX and BWMN is calculated to determine the transfer rate of the second Bucket. The proposed algorithm is illustrated in Fig. 4.

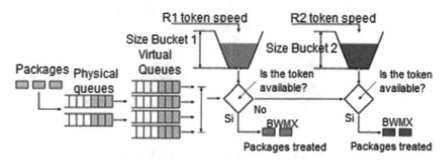

Fig. 4. Optical Bucket Token algorithm.

6 State Transition

To establish the mathematical correspondences of the proposed algorithm, the Markov state chain model was used. This model has been present in modeling phases similar to the one proposed in [4]. A discrete chain is used to represent the possible states present in the solution. The state of the Markov chain is described by a random variable $q(t)$. This variable has a behavior that changes with respect to a given timeslot. The variable $q(t)$ responds to the state of the queues. The value of this variable changes according to the following:

- The variable $q(t) = 0$ if the queues are free, therefore the BWMN value is the base value of the transmission rats of the buckets.
- The variable $q(t) = 1$ if the queues have packets with defined priorities without the need to generate overflow processes. Priority queues can process packets without inconvenience. The BWMN value starts to fluctuate with respect to the amount of traffic that is being processed in the queues.
- The variable $q(t) = 2$ if the queues have packets on which their priorities should be modified to improve the use of resources. It is possible but not mandatory that in this state, the tokens of the first Bucket have been terminated and the tokens of the second Bucket begin to be used. The BWMN value approaches the limit of the maximum bandwidth value of the interfaces.
- The variable $q(t) = 3$ if the queues have packets with better effort classifications in which the system should not perform any additional process to allow the flow of

packets. No packets are presented in the system with defined priorities and they can take any route as they come from any of the system's predefined queues.

According to the mentioned states in which the process of each one of the tails is described and the treatment thereof in the optical Bucket Token, the transition of these states is illustrated in Fig. 5.

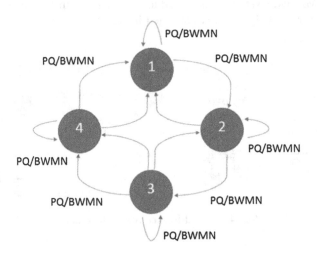

Fig. 5. Graph of transition of states.

7   Algorithm Simulation

Before starting the simulation process on the NS-2 tool, matlab tests and processing of the states raised in the previous section were made in Matlab with respect to the optical Bucket Token, the latter being the main object of code analysis and the starting point for further development, this also because Li-fi technology is so recent that the real data for comparison are extremely scarce.

7.1   Simulation in MATLAB

Initially, a validation of the traditional Bucket token was performed with a single tail of fixed size (200 packets). Packets with arrivals and random sizes were selected, which would be transmitted after a token arrived at the Bucket. If the bucket rate is fixed, the result of the simulation for different iterations is illustrated in Fig. 6.

As the number of iterations increases in the traditional Bucket token simulations (with a single Bucket and a fixed size queue), there is an evident tendency of an increasing number of packets in terms of the size of the queue. This makes the fixed system unviable for implementation in dynamic networks such as Li-Fi. Figure 7 shows the results for two Buckets and four queues according to the proposed algorithm.

With regard to the simulation of 50 iterations with the conventional Bucket token algorithm, it is observed that the buffer packets are significantly reduced if the number

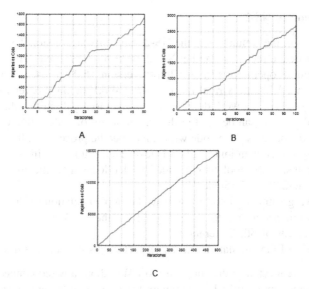

Fig. 6. Traditional Bucket Token with A. 50 Iterations, B. 100 Iterations, C. 500 iterations.

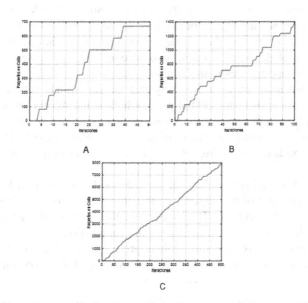

Fig. 7. Optical Token Bucket with A. 50 Iterations, B. 100 Iterations, C. 500 iterations.

of elements involved in the process is modified, that is, if the storage queues and buckets increase of tokens. The results of the optical bucket token in Matlab show that it is agile, since each Bucket token handles shorter times in terms of generating the necessary tokens for the processes of transmission of the packets to the optical medium.

7.2   Simulation in NS-2

For the purposes of the simulation in the NS-2 tool, software version 2.35 of November 2011, downloaded directly from the NS 2 website, was used. The software was implemented on an operating system Ubuntu version 16.04 of 64 bits, which in turn was installed on a VMware virtual machine type Workstation Pro version 12.5.0.

For the purposes of the work done, it is important to highlight that the ns-2 tool has native protocols, which can be used in the development of a algorithm or, failing that, can be modified from its source code with some specific procedures. It started from the need to modify the conventional Token Bucket algorithm, identified as TBF (Token Bucket Filter) inside the tool in the "adc" folder located in the following route: / home/ns-allinone-2.35/ns-2.35/adc.

The following simulation corresponds to the implementation of the Token Bucket Optical algorithm according to the proposal of the work with a Li-Fi scenario, responding to needs of 5th Generation.

The scenario of the simulation and its respective justification are described below:

– Five nodes are located in the space (n0 to n4) without a wired connection. Four of these elements represent Li-Fi users, with the remaining being the access point (or LED lamp). In this simulation scenario, five elements are established by the effects of conventional disposition in a determined enclosure. The relevance in the connectivity lies in the line of sight of the devices and light power of the central node. The number of nodes and their arrangement in the space is due to the electrical characteristics of the devices, taking into account VLC type communications and possible smart applications in the remaining devices.
– The nodes are arranged in such a way that all the packets between them must necessarily pass through the central node, which is the Access Point of the Li-Fi network. This arrangement of the elements around the central device is based on the VLC facilities, the basis for this work of Li-Fi communications. The differences between the packet flows in this node will be crucial to determine the success of the proposal.
– Modify the characteristics of the netif variables with respect to the bandwidth and MAC characteristics of the network so that this wireless network has the characteristics of a Li-Fi network. This is done in this way to take advantage of the algorithms developed in the simulator by the community.
– Initially, a simulation is performed without preferential treatment of data. With this, a point of reference with respect to the performance of the proposed algorithm is sought.

In the following simulation, the data with optical bucket token is sent on nodes 1 and 3 to compare the differences with respect to the initial traffic treatment.

The results will be discussed in the following section.

The scenario of the simulation is shown in Fig. 8.

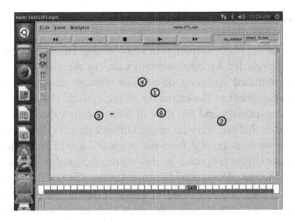

Fig. 8. Simulated Li-Fi network in NS-2.

8   Results Analysis

In [3], the first reference article; the results focus on the fact that the number of discarded packets is reduced by performing dynamic queue handling. Additionally, special emphasis is placed on the fact that the discarded packets identified with Codepoint 21 correspond to the queue with the lowest priority, thus demonstrating an improvement in the use of resources since, with the static distribution, the packets identified with the Codepoint 20 that belong to the queue with the highest priority were those discarded. However, a single device is being evaluated here, concluding that in total the performance of the administration of the queue would be given by the rate of delivery of the packets to the interface, in this case it would be equal to **number of compatible packets/total number of packets** = 675/762 = 88.5%. Regarding the simulation performed in this work clearly identifies the excellent performance of the algorithm, since 46539 packets sent only were discarded 57, i.e. the rate of delivery of packets at the interface it is given by number of **delivered packets/total number of packets = 46539/46596 = 99.8%**. Also taking into account that the amount of packets sent in the simulation exceeds the traffic of the reference simulation by an amount 61 times greater. Additionally, it is possible to show that the treatment of the tails was done correctly through the algorithm of the proposed bucket token. This is concluded because there are no queued packets in the results.

With respect to the results of [5], the second reference article; it is observed that the performance of the network is in the order of 60% with respect to the total of the speed rate that is 256 kbps, that is, in the specific case of the article, the performance of the network is 153 kbps.

9 Conclusions

Li-Fi networks allow the implementation of complex algorithms that guarantee QoS as a Bucket token, disregarded by other networks due to the time they require for processing. The differentiated handling of packets through duplicated Token Bucket, allows a better management of the resources of the system, since the packets will not remain longer than necessary and the flow of them through the Li-Fi interfaces compensates for the times that are invested in the Diffserv process. While it is true that the performance of the network is 38% from the point of view of the network bandwidth, with the quality assurance proposed in this work, the quality of the link increases because the packet failure disappears due to collision effects. The packet loss for the proposed solution is very low, allowing to obtain a packet delivery rate to the 99.8% interface, taking into account the administration of congestion in an appropriate way ensuring the correct management of resources within the elements of the network.

References

1. Kulhari, A., Pandey, A., Shukla, D.: Implementing and testing priority scheduler and token bucket policer in differentiated service. Int. J. Comput. Appl. **101**(13) (2014)
2. Richter, V.: Accurate traffic shaping algorithms for IEEE 802.16-2012 based WiMAX networks. Deutsche Telekom Chair Communication Networks. Technische Universitat Dresden, Dresden, Germany. IEEE (2016)
3. Kulhari, A. Pandey, A.: Traffic shaping at differentiated services enabled edge router using adaptative packet allocation to router input queue. In: Second International Conference on Computational Intelligence and Communication Technology (2016)
4. Shams, P., Erol-Kantarci, M., Uysal, M.: MAC layer performance of the IEEE 802.15.7 visible light communication standard. Trans. Emerg. Telecommun. Technol. **27**, 662–674 (2016)

A Context-Based Model for Validating the Ability of Cyber Systems to Defend Against Attacks

Yosra Lakhdhar[(✉)], Slim Rekhis, and Noureddine Boudriga

Communication Networks and Security Research Lab., University of Carthage,
Tunis, Tunisia
lakhdhar.yosra@gmail.com

Abstract. Deploying security solutions to defend against known security attacks could fail not only due to policy, design, or implementation flaws in the designed solutions, but also due to lack of data regarding the environment under which the attack is executed, or the security solution supervising the malicious behavior. To this end, we develop in this paper a new cyber defense system that assesses the efficiency of a cyber security solution when faced to attack scenarios occurring under different contexts (the configuration and location of distributed security solutions, called observer agents, the used reaction system, and the information visibility of attacks). The work also considers the development of a model for describing the concept of global, local and observable executable scenarios, which allows to observe step by step the execution of an attack scenario, and the observer agents' behavior and their reactions to the attack execution. The model allows also to identify the step at which an attack scenario can be blocked. A case study is presented to exemplify the proposal.

Keywords: Cyber defense · Contextual attack execution
Distributed monitoring system

1 Introduction

Ensuring system security regardless of the released cyber attacks is a big issue. In fact, the recent cyber attacks are characterized by their ability to cause catastrophic damages to different cyber systems. This can be noticed in the last released cyber attacks (e.g. NotPetya[1], WannaCry [1]) that caused the disruption of many services (financial, healthcare, transport) in different countries (e.g. US, UK, Ukraine)[2]. The main issue is that, even by knowing the attack scenario and deploying a set of security solutions, the attack can still take place [2], which can be explained by two major points. First, the security solution may

---

[1] CERTbe, Petya/NotPetya Malware Report on worldwide infection, June 2017.
[2] Symantec Internet Security Threat Report ISTR, Ransomware 2017, July 2017.

© Springer Nature Switzerland AG 2018
N. Boudriga et al. (Eds.): UNet 2018, LNCS 11277, pp. 295–307, 2018.
https://doi.org/10.1007/978-3-030-02849-7_27

not detect the attack due to lack of data about what is occurring in the system as these solutions are characterized by their inability to completely observe, collect and analyse all the system assets because of technological constraints or visibility problems (i.e., inaccurate data interpretation or a difficulty to observe events). Second, whereas the attack may impact different system components located everywhere, a security reaction can be ineffective as it affects only a specific component in a particular emplacement. To this end, we need to test the resilience of the supervised system to different attack executions under diverse contexts and using a set of distributed security solutions.

Many works were developed to analyze the system' security state. For example, in [3], researchers studied the Vulnerability Assessment and Penetration Testing (VAPT) tool which consists of two tasks which are the vulnerability assessment and the penetration tests. In another work [4], researchers proposed a graph-based active cyber defense model, developed analytics to describe the supervised systems and the deployed security solutions, and studied the effectiveness of the adopted defense techniques when faced to threats and vulnerability rate increase. The majority of the developed cyber defense models are centralized. For example, in [5], researchers presented an observation-based technique ensuring the detection of cyber attacks on femtocells. In fact, they deployed a set of observer agents on smartphones to monitor, collect, and send detected events to a centralized server where the data will be analyzed. Moreover, in [6], researchers developed a centralized intrusion detection system for cloud based environment. The proposed model consists of a set of collaborative SHIDS (Smart Host Intrusion Detection System) deployed in the virtual machines in the cloud ensuring intrusions detection and alerts exchange with a central agent. Also, in [7], researchers deployed a set of agents to supervise the networked system and send their observations to a central agent to be analyzed. The latter decides about the security state of the system, and the appropriate reaction will be chosen based on a set of heuristics. The problem with these systems is that they have a Single Point Of Failure (SPOF) [8] as if the central agent is affected, the system becomes inefficient.

From these works, we can deduce the need to develop a distributed cyber defense model to assess the effectiveness of the deployed security solutions faced to known attack executions. Thus, we propose a context-based cyber defense model for validating the ability of cyber system to defend against attacks by executing them under a predefined context. Our model consists in: (a) defining a library containing the different intruder actions part of known attack scenarios. Using a correlation rule, the possible attack scenarios will be automatically generated; (b) deploying a set of distributed agents to monitor the different system parameters. Each agent is characterized by its observation function, defense domain and reaction database; (c) developing the concept of attack execution context describing the security environment in which the attack takes place; (d) developing a model for describing the concept of global, local and observed executable scenarios which allow to observe the step-by-step execution of an attack scenario, and the observer agents' behavior and reactions to this attack execution. The model allows also identifying the step at which this attack scenario can be blocked.

Our contribution is four-fold. First, we develop a cyber defense model that allows to generate a set of observed local attack scenarios from global executable ones by executing the latter under diverse contexts. Second, we develop a model to assess the efficiency of the deployed security solutions faced to different attack executions. Third, we model the context under which the attack scenario is executed. Fourth, we develop a distributed monitoring system to supervise different system parameters and thus to generate a novel layered attack scenarios' execution model.

The remaining part of this paper is organized as follows. In Sect. 2, we present the requirements of a context-based cyber defense model to validate the system's resilience to different attack scenario executions. Section 3 illustrates the concept and usage of Global Executable Scenario and Local Executable Scenario. Section 4 defines the context concept, the observation-based system and the Observed Local Scenario. In Sect. 5, we present the methodology that we follow to apply our approach. Before concluding our work, we test, in Sect. 6, our approach against the Wannacry attack [9].

2   Requirements

A context-based cyber defense model for validating the cyber system resilience to different attacks execution should fulfill the subsequent requirements:

Modeling the Attack Execution Context: The attack scenario execution and its impact differ from one system to another. In fact, an attack scenario can target one/many systems containing distributely deployed security solutions that have different configurations. The latter may/may not observe the attack scenario and defend against it. Thus, introducing the attack execution context (the security environment of the supervised system) becomes important.

Modeling Security Solution and Incompleteness of Data Observation: As the deployed security solutions are unable to observe a complete information about what is occurring in the networked system, it is needed to develop a novel technique that models the system reactivity based on incomplete collected data. This model describes the observations generated by a set of distributed and autonomous security solutions and presents how and when the system reacts.

Modeling the Actual Attack Scenario Execution: To accurately analyze the effectiveness of the security solutions in defending the networked system, it is necessary to model the real scenario execution that can be obtained by considering the distributed security solutions, their partial observability to the scenario execution, their defense domains, and the reaction that they may execute.

Modeling the Reaction System: It is needed to provide a formal definition of system security reactions. In fact, defining the reactions that can be executed on the system and the conditions related to their execution is important to well defend the networked system against released cyber attacks. Also, a formal definition of security reactions will ensure the description of a wide class of them.

Developing a Virtual Execution Technique: It is important to develop a technique that allows to verify the system resilience to the execution of different known attack scenarios. This technique can be used to identify the system weaknesses, help modifying the adopted defense strategies, and updating the security techniques to ensure a better system security.

3   Attack Modeling

In this section, we will illustrate the concept of Global Executable Scenario (GES) and Local Executable Scenario (LES), in addition to the initialization steps of the actions library used to generate these two types of scenarios.

3.1   Global Executable Scenario

An attack scenario is a set of actions that the intruder executes to reach his objective. Each action execution moves the system from its actual state to the next one until the state where the damage occurs, is reached. A state in our model is the valuation of the variables used to model the system. Let $V = \{v_1, v_2, ..., v_n\}$ be the set of variables that model the system. A state s is modeled as $s = <||v_1||, ||v_2||, ..., ||v_n||>_s$ where $||v_i||_s$ presents the value taken by the variable v_i in the state s, and n is the number of variables used to model the system.

In our model, we define an actions library Lib that contains the different actions (legitimate and malicious) part of known attack scenarios. Each action, say A, in Lib provides modifications on the set of global variables V, and is defined by two parameters:

- Action Preconditions (Pre): Logical predicates presenting the information needed to execute the action (i.e., predicates that once satisfied in the actual system state, the action can be executed).
- A Relation between two system states "$A(s_i) = s_{i+1}$": If the preconditions of the action A are satisfied in the state s_i (i.e., $Pre(A)_{s_i} = True$), the action can be executed and the system will move to the next state s_{i+1}.

From Lib we can automatically generate all possible attack scenarios using the following correlation rule. Let A_i and A_j two actions contained in Lib, A_i and A_j will be correlated iff there exist two states s_{i-1} and s_i such that: (a) $A_i(s_{i-1}) = s_i$ and (b) $Pre(A_j)_{s_i} = True$.

We assume that all the scenarios contained in Lib are finite scenarios, or can be transformed to finite ones by using generation heuristics (e.g., an action will be considered as terminated if it is executed more than a predefined number of times even if it is still enabled). We define a Global Executable Scenario (GES) S as $S = <s_0, A_0, s_1, ..., A_{m-1}, s_m>$, where a state s_i provides a valuation of all the variables used to model the networked system and an action A_i can modify one or many of variables in V.

3.2 Local Executable Scenario

The variables $V = \{v_1, v_2, ..., v_n\}$ used to model the supervised system can be divided according to a chosen feature to a set of groups. This feature can be the security solution placement in the networked system, the nature of the system resources or any other one. Based on the selected feature, the system can be divided into a set of layers $L = \{L_1, L_2, ..., L_m\}$. Each layer L_i is defined by a set of local variables $V_i \in V$. For example, if we choose the nature of the supervised system resources, the system can be divided into three layers which are the physical layer, the network layer and the software layer. Consequently, an action A_i executed in the system and moving it from the state s_i to the next state s_{i+1}, is in reality a set of subactions A_i^j, $i \in \{1, .., n\}$ (n is the number of actions composing a known scenario S) and $j \in \{1, ..m\}$ (m is the number of system layers), that are executed in parallel and in an atomic manner (i.e., either all occur, or nothing occurs). Indeed, the execution of the global action A_i is conditioned by the successful execution of all the subactions A_i^j, thus an action A_i will be modeled as: $A_i = A_i^1 | A_i^2 | .... | A_i^m$, where A_i^j is the local action part of the global action A_i which impacts only the values of the variables belonging to the system layer j. Hence, the subaction A_i^j will move the subsystem j from the substate s_i^j (i.e., the valuation of the variables belonging to this layer) to another one s_{i+1}^j. As a result, the GES is a set of Local Executable Scenarios (LES) S^j that we model as $S^j = <s_0^j, A_0^j, s_1^j, ..., s_n^j, A_n^j>$. If the execution of an action A_i does not modify the variables belonging to the layer j, the subaction A_i^j part of A_i will be replaced by the action "identity" Id. So, if $S^j = <s_0^j, A_0^j, s_1^j, ..., s_n^j, A_n^j>$ and $A_0^j = Id$, this means that $s_0^j = s_1^j$. To clarify the concept of LES, we present the example shown in Fig. 1, where the GES $S = < s_0, A_0, s_1, A_1, s_2, A_2, s_3 >$ is divided into three LESs as the system was decomposed into three layers based on the supervised system resources nature (physical layer (L_1), network layer (L_2), software layer (L_3)): L_1: $S^1 = <s_0^1, A_0^1, s_1^1, A_1^1, s_2^1, A_2^1, s_3^1>$, L_2: $S^2 = <s_0^2, A_0^2, s_1^2, Id, s_2^2, A_2^2, s_3^2>$ and L_3: $S^3 = <s_0^3, A_0^3, s_1^3, A_1^3, s_2^3, A_2^3, s_3^3>$. The action A_1 has no impact on the network layer as its execution does not modify the substate s_1^2, thus the action $A_1^2 = Id$. Moreover, each global action is a set of subactions according to the layer in which the action is observed. For example, the global action $A_0 = \{A_0^1, A_0^2, A_0^3\}$, where A_0^1 is the impact of the execution of A_0 on the physical layer, A_0^2 is the impact of the execution of A_0 on the Network layer, and A_0^3 is the impact of the execution of A_0 on the software layer.

4 Context Modeling

In this section, we will define the attack execution context and the observations-based system.

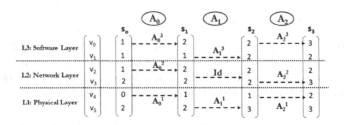

Fig. 1. Local Executable Scenario

4.1   Context Definition

The execution of cyber attack scenarios differs from one system to another based on the security environment of the latter. In this work, we define an attack execution context C as a three tuple information $<OA, obs(), Rdb>$, where:

OA: the network of distributed Observer Agents (OA) deployed on the supervised system to monitor a set of system parameters. The OA network' role consists in monitoring a set of variables modeling the layer to which they belong.

obs(): the observation function characterizing each OA.

Rdb: the reactions databases, where each one will be assigned to an OA.

4.2   Observer Agent Role and Configuration

An observer agent OA denotes a security solution used to monitor a set of variables belonging to a specific system layer. The Agents are supposed to be protected against flooding attacks that overwhelm them with a huge amount of traffic. It is modeled as: $OA(L, DD, obs(), Rdb)$:

- L: Each OA is deployed at some layer L which limits its ability to supervise any type of resources.
- DD: Each OA has a Defense Domain DD which defines the set of variables V in the layer L that is able to observe. Indeed, the DD provides the set of local variables whose values can be used to deduce if an action was executed and whether such an action is malicious.
- Rdb: To each OA, we assign a local reactions database Rdb which defines the countermeasures that this agent can execute based on a predefined predicates that will be computed over the values of the variables belonging to the DD.
- $obs()$: Each OA is characterized by its observation function $obs()$ that describes how it observes the variable values modification in each system state. In fact, $obs()$ is a function that associates to each variable $v \in V$ of the DD its observed value in a given system state s, denoted by $||v||_s$. If, in a given state s, the value of the variable v becomes invisible, we have $||v||_s = \varepsilon$.

4.3   Reactions Database Rdb

In our model, we assign a reactions database Rdb to each OA representing the countermeasures that it can execute. Each reaction R in Rdb is modeled by two parameters $(Pred, Act)$, where $Pred$ is a predicate that will be computed over the observations O obtained by the observer (such an observation was computed over the variables belonging to the DD), and Act is the action to be executed once $Pred = True$. In this work, we model five possible actions:

Alert: if $R.Pred(O) = True$, an alert $Alt(O)$ will be generated.

Alert&Block: if $R.Pred(O) = True$, an alert $Alt(O)$ will be generated, and the scenario execution will be blocked.

Reconfigure obs(): if $R.Pred(O) = True$, $ReConf(Agents, Rconf)$ will be executed, so for the OA designed in the parameter 'Agents', their observation functions will be reconfigured based on the functions defined in '$Rconf$'. This reaction will enhance the system observability, as for certain variables that are invisible unless a set of variable values exceed certain thresholds, the adjustment of the latter will enhance the system visibility.

Activate OA: if $R.Pred(O) = True$, $Activate(Agents)$ will be executed, so that asleep OA denoted by the parameter 'gents' will be activated. We suppose that initially not all the agents are activated to reduce resources overhead. Activating asleep observers will increase the system observability.

Activate Rules: if $R.Pred(O) = True$, $Activate(R)$ will be executed, so the deactivated security rules defined in Rdb will be activated. In fact, we assume that in each Rdb, a set of reactions will be deactivated to reduce the processing time and complexity. Based on a set of predefined predicates, the OA can decide to activate them and use them in the remaining part of the scenario execution.

To prevent the reactions from interfering, we define the following rule: The reaction rules in each database Rdb should be ordered, so that, the first enabled reaction (i.e., its predicate becomes true) is the one that will be executed and the subsequent ones are ignored.

4.4 Observed Local Scenario

As we said before, a GES is decomposed into a set of LESs. The latter will not be totally visible. In fact, the LES can be totally observed by a set of OA, partially observed by other ones and invisible by the rest. Also, in each step of the scenario execution, a security reaction can be executed where the latter can be: (a) blocking the considered subaction which results in blocking the global action, and therefore, the scenario execution, (b) activating new agents, and/or reactions rules or (c) modifying the configurations of some OA (see previous subsection). The reactions' impact on the local attack scenario execution needs to be considered to deduce the actual executable scenario. From this perspective, we define the concept of Observed Local Scenario (OLS) which describes the observed part of the generated LES and the OA' behavior and reaction to each step of its execution. In fact, in each step of the scenario execution, each OA will generate a set of observations. Based on the latter, a set of reactions can be executed and thus, considered in the remaining part of the attack executions (a list of alerts will be updated each time an alert is generated, the new activated agents and/or rules will contribute in detecting and reacting to the next execution steps) until a blocking reaction is executed. At this stage, the system

---

Algorithm 1. Observed Local Scenario Generation

$AltTrails = \{\emptyset\}$: list of generated alerts
$SysEnd = False$: once the scenario execution is blocked $SysEnd = True$

- **For** each scenario S in Lib,
    1. let s be the initial state of S
    2. **Repeat until** (all states in S are tested or $SysEnd = True$)
        (a) **For** each system layer L_i
            i. Compute obs(s^i)
            - **For** each OA
                * Compute the set of enabled reaction $R' = \bigcup\{R \in \Re / Pred(R) = True\}$
                * If $R' \neq \{\emptyset\}$ Then set $r \leftarrow Head(R')$ // execute the first reaction
                    · If $r.Act = Alert$ Then $AltTrails = \{Alt(O)\}$;
                    · If $r.Act = Alert\&Block$ Then $AltTrails\{Alt(O)\}$ & $SysEnd = True$;
                    · If $r.Act = Reconf(Agents, Rconf())$ Then
                      For each $OA \in Agents$ **Do** $OA.obs() \leftarrow Rconf()$;
                    · If $r.Act = Activate(Agents)$ Then $OAlist = \{OAlist, Agents\}$;
                    · If $r.Act = Activate(R)$ Then $R_{init} = \{R_{init}, R\}/R \in R_d$;
                * End
            - **End**
        (b) **End**
    3. Execute $A/\ Pred(A)_s = True$ & $A(s) = t$
    4. $s \leftarrow t$
    5. **End**
- **End**

---

will verify whether the state where the damage occurs has been reached or not to conclude whether the security solution is efficient in reacting to the attacks under the current context.

5 Methodology

In this section, we will detail our approach. First, we define the actions library and configure it so that all the possible scenarios will be automatically generated. Then, the variables that will be used to model the supervised system have to be chosen and divided into groups based on the system layers. From these groups, the variables that will be monitored by the OA network need to be specified and the OA need to be configured. Our methodology is presented in Algorithm 1 that takes as input the set of reactions $\Re = \{R_{init}, R_d\}$, where R_{init} and R_d are the subsets of initially activated and deactivated reactions, respectively, and $OAlist$ is the list of initially activated agents.

To exemplify our approach, let's refer to the example presented in Fig. 2. The system is divided into three layers according to the nature of the supervised system resources: S (Software Layer), N (Network Layer), Ph (Physical Layer) and it will be modeled by six parameters$\{v_0, v_1, v_2, v_3, v_4, v_5\}$. We deploy three OA configured as follows:

OA1: (S, $\{v_0, v_1\}$, $obs_1()$, Rdb_1) where $obs_1() = \{obs(v_1, s) = ||v_1||_s$ if $v_1 \geq$ 1 else ε; $obs(v_0, s) = ||v_0||_s$ if $v_0 \geq 1$ else $\varepsilon\}$ and $Rdb_1 = \{(v_0 > 2, Alert);$ $(v_1 \geq 5, Alert\&Block)\}$

OA2: (N, $\{v_2\}$, $obs_2()$, Rdb_2) where $obs_2() = \{obs(v_2, s) = ||v_2||_s$ if $v_2 >$ 0, else $\varepsilon\}$ and $Rdb_2 = \{(v_2 \geq 3, Alert\&Block)\}$

OA3: (Ph, $\{v_4\}$, $obs_3()$, Rdb_3) where $obs_3() = \{obs(v_4, s) = ||v_4||_s$ if $v_4 \geq$ 0, else $\varepsilon\}$ and $Rdb_3 = \{(v_4 = 5, Alert)\}$

We define the damage state as the state where the predicate "Damage : $v_3 \overset{\triangle}{=} 4$" is equal to True. We start by computing $obs(s_0^k)$ where $k \in \{1, 2, 3\}$ and, in each execution step, we verify whether a reaction will be executed by the OA network. As it is presented in Fig. 2a, no security reaction was launched and the action A_0 will be executed. Similarly, we repeat the same tasks for the next scenario execution steps. We notice that by computing $obs(s_3^3)$, an alert was generated by $OA1$ as $v_0 > 2$, and the scenario execution was blocked in the state s_4 by the $OA2$ as $v_2 \geq 3$. Also, even if OA_2 noticed that the damage occurred in state s_2^2 ("$v_3 = 4$"=$True$), it can only react in the substate s_4^2 by blocking the attack scenario execution. By changing the attack execution context as follows: $C\{\{OA_1, OA_2, OA_3, OA_4\}, \{obs_1(), obs_2(), obs_3(), obs_4() = \{obs(v_3, s) = ||v_3||_s$ if $v_3 > 1,$ else $\varepsilon\}\}$ and $\{Rdb_1, Rdb_2, Rdb_3, Rdb_4 = \{(v_3 \geq 3, Alert\&Block)\}\}$ (see Fig. 2b), the attack execution will be blocked from sate s_2 which shows the importance of considering the attack execution context to verify the system resilience to different attack executions.

Compared to machine learning-based mechanisms, our proposed approach does not require a learning phase and it allows to test the execution of the same attack scenario under diverse contexts.

6   Case Study

To show the effectiveness of our approach, we consider the "WannaCry" attack that took place in May 2017 and affected more than 300000 computers all over the world. This ransomware spreads over the internet by exploiting a vulnerability in Windows operating systems. After gaining access to these systems, the users data will be encrypted, and a message will be displayed informing the victim that he needs to pay a ransom (between 300\$ and 600\$) to get his data back. The WannaCry attack consists of a set of actions which are: Spear Phishing, Gaining access, Thread creation, Scanning over 445, Exploiting EternalBlue, Installing DOUBLEPULSAR Backdoor, Communication to C2 server, Installing Ransomware, Changing the file access permission, Terminating processes and Encrypting Files. We divide the supervised system to three layers based on the system resources nature as follows:

Software Layer: To monitor this layer, five parameters are used:

v_1 = File-access-control-violation: Initially $v_1 = 0$ and once a violation of at least one of the file access control policy is detected, its value changes to 1.

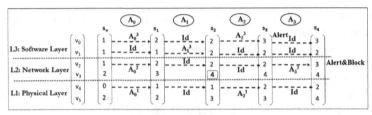

(a) First Configuration

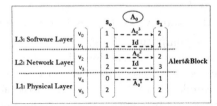

(b) Second Configuration

Fig. 2. Observed local scenario generations

v_2 = Important-services-availability = [DB-service, file-sharing service, email-service]: It informs about the state of three important services which are DB-service, file-sharing service, and email-service. Initially $v_2 = 1$, but once one of them is terminated/cannot be executed normally, its value changes to 0.

v_3 = Installed-suspect-programs: Initially $v_3 = 0$ and once a suspect program is detected in the supervised asset, its value changes to 1.

v_4 = Unusual-asset-activities: Initially $v_4 = 0$ and its value changes to 1 once an unusual activity in the supervised asset is detected.

v_5= Gained-privileges: Initially $v_5 = 0$ (no access is gained) and it changes to 1 once a user access is gained and to 2 if a root access is gained.

Network Layer: To monitor this layer, two parameters are used:

v_6 = Network-traffic-amount: v_6 supervises the network traffic volume. We configure it to take one of three values: τ_1 if an usual network traffic volume is detected, τ_2 once an acceptable increased rate of the network traffic volume is noticed, and τ_3 if an unusual volume of the network traffic is identified.

v_7 = Unusual-traffic-connection: Initially, $v_7 = 0$ and, once an internal agent connects to an unauthorized external asset, its value changes to 1.

Physical Layer: To monitor this layer, two parameters are used:

v_8 = System-performance-degradation: Initially, $v_8 = 0$ and, once a degradation in system performance is detected, its valuechanges to 1.

v_9 = System-availability: Initially, the system is available and $v_9 = 1$, but once it becomes unavailable the value of v_9 changes to 0.

After modeling each system layer, we configure the OA network. In this case study, three OA will be deployed and configured as follows:

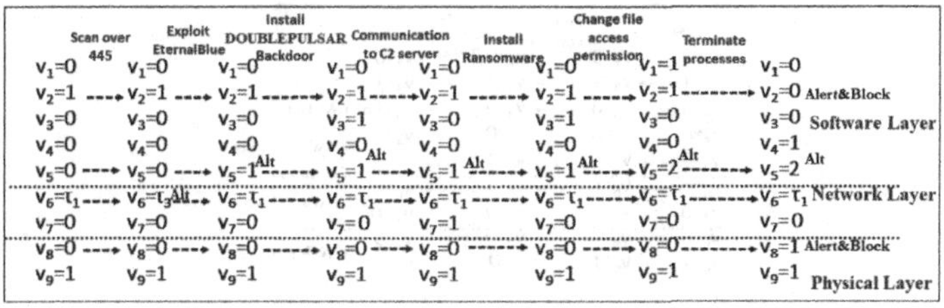

	Scan over 445	Exploit EternalBlue	Install DOUBLEPULSAR Backdoor	Communication to C2 server	Install Ransomware	Change file access permission	Terminate processes	
$v_1=0$	$v_1=0$	$v_1=0$	$v_1=0$	$v_1=0$	$v_1=0$	$v_1=0$	$v_1=0$	
$v_2=1$	$v_2=1$	$v_2=1$	$v_2=1$	$v_2=1$	$v_2=1$	$v_2=1$	$v_2=0$	Alert&Block
$v_3=0$	$v_3=0$	$v_3=0$	$v_3=1$	$v_3=0$	$v_3=1$	$v_3=0$	$v_3=0$	Software Layer
$v_4=0$	$v_4=0$	$v_4=0$	$v_4=0_{Alt}$	$v_4=0$	$v_4=0$	$v_4=0_{Alt}$	$v_4=1$	
$v_5=0$	$v_5=0$	$v_5=1^{Alt}$	$v_5=1$	$v_5=1^{Alt}$	$v_5=1^{Alt}$	$v_5=2$	$v_5=2$	Alt
$v_6=\tau_1$	$v_6=\tau_3^{Alt}$	$v_6=\tau_1$	$v_6=\tau_1$	$v_6=\tau_1$	$v_6=\tau_1$	$v_6=\tau_1$	$v_6=\tau_1$	Network Layer
$v_7=0$	$v_7=0$	$v_7=0$	$v_7=0$	$v_7=1$	$v_7=0$	$v_7=0$	$v_7=0$	
$v_8=0$	$v_8=0$	$v_8=0$	$v_8=0$	$v_8=0$	$v_8=0$	$v_8=0$	$v_8=1$	Alert&Block
$v_9=1$	$v_9=1$	$v_9=1$	$v_9=1$	$v_9=1$	$v_9=1$	$v_9=1$	$v_9=1$	Physical Layer

Fig. 3. Wannacry scenario execution

OA1: $(S, \{v_2, v_5\}, obs_1(), Rdb_1)$; $obs_1() = \{obs(v_2, s) = \|v_2\|_s$ if $v_2 \geq 1$ else ε; $obs(v_5, s) = \|v_5\|_s$ if $v_5 \geq 0$ else $\varepsilon\}$ and $Rdb_1 = \{(v_2 \neq 1, Alert\& Block); (v_5 \geq 1, Alert)\}$.

OA2: $(N, \{v_6\}, obs_2(), Rdb_2)$; $obs_2() = \{obs(v_6, s) = \|v_6\|_s$ if $v_6 \geq \tau_1$, else $\varepsilon\}$ and $Rdb_2 = \{(v_6 \geq \tau_2, Alert)\}$.

OA3: $(Ph, \{v_8\}, obs_3(), Rdb_3)$; $obs_3() = \{obs(v_8, s) = \|v_8\|_s$ if $v_8 \geq 0$, else $\varepsilon\}$ and $Rdb_3 = \{(v_8 = 1, Alert\& Block)\}$.

To assess the efficiency of the deployed security solutions faced to Wannacry attack execution, we start by computing the observations of its initial state s_0 w.r.t. each system layer: $obs(s_0^1) = \{v_2 = 1, v_5 = 0\}$, $obs(s_0^2) = \{v_6 = \tau_1\}$ and $obs(s_0^3) = \{v_8 = 0\}$, and in each layer we verify whether a security reaction will be executed. As none of the predicates on which the reactions execution depends is equal to true, no reaction was enabled and thus, "Scan over 445" will be executed. By computing $obs(s_1^k)$ where $k \in \{1, 2, 3\}$, we notice that the network traffic amount increases ($v_6 = \tau_3$) (see Fig. 3), and an alert was generated by the OA2. "Scan over 445" action did not modify the substates s_0^1 and s_0^3, thus, this action is equal to the Id action. After that, "exploit EternalBlue" will be executed. Even if OA1 sees this action as a suspicious one, and generates an alert ($v_5 = 1$), this action did not modify the values of the observed variables in both the network and the physical layer. The actions will be executed, the observations over the different substates will be computed and the enabled reactions will be launched until the scenario execution is either blocked or terminated. In this case, the scenario was blocked after the "termination processes" action as the OA1 blocks the sub-action indicating that one or more of the important services are unexpectedly terminated ($obs(s_7^1) = \{v_2=0\}$) and the OA2 blocks the sub-action that informs about a degradation in the system performance ($obs(s_7^3) = \{v_8=1\}$).

Even thought the scenario was blocked in this state, we can get a much better result by modifying the execution context as follows:

$C\{\{OA_1, OA_2, OA_3\}, \{obs_1(), obs_2(), obs_3()\}, \{Rdb_1, Rdb_2, Rdb_3\}; obs_1() = \{\{obs(v_2) = \|v_2\|_s$ if $v_2 \geq 1$, else ε; $obs(v_5) = \|v_5\|_s$ if $v_5 \geq 0$ else ε; $obs(v_3) = \|v_3\|_s$ if $v_3 \geq 0$ else $\varepsilon\}$ and $Rdb_1 = \{(v_2 \neq 1, Alert\& Block); (v_5 \geq 1, Alert); (v_3 = 1, Alert\& Block)\}$. In fact, we added the variable v_3 to OA1' DD. We re-execute the WannaCry attack scenario (Fig. 4). The scenario execution was blocked from the "Install DOUBLEPULSAR Backdoor" action as the OA1 detects the installation of a malicious program in the supervised asset.

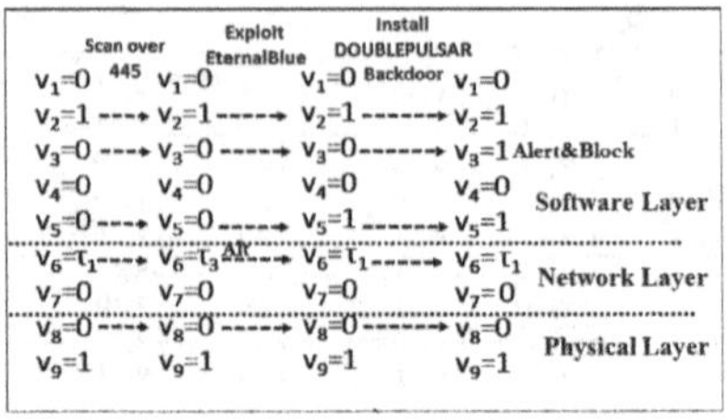

Fig. 4. WannaCry scenario execution under a changed context

7 Conclusion

In this paper, we developed a context-based cyber defense model for validating the ability of cyber systems to defend against cyber attacks execution. In fact, we implemented a distributed observer agents network to monitor the supervised system, where each observer has a partial observation to the cyber system, a defense domain, and a reaction database. In addition, we developed a model ensuring the generation of a set of observed local attack scenarios from a global executable one by executing that scenario under different contexts describing the security environment in which the attacks take place. The developed model ensures a detailed description and an observation of the step-by-step execution of the attack scenario, and the identification of the step at which the scenario can be blocked. In a future work, we will deploy a cooperative OA network and extend the defense model to take into consideration the processing time of actions and its impact on the undertaken reactions.

References

1. Mohurle, S., Patil, M.: A brief study of wannacry threat: ransomware attack 2017. Int. J. Adv. Res. Comput. Sci. **8**(5) (2017)
2. Razzaq, A., Hur, A., Ahmad, H.F., Masood, M.: Cyber security: threats, reasons, challenges, methodologies and state of the art solutions for industrial applications. In: IEEE Eleventh International Symposium on Autonomous Decentralized Systems (ISADS), Mexico, 06–08 March 2013
3. Shinde, P.S., Ardhapurkar, S.B.: Cyber security analysis using vulnerability assessment and penetration testing. In: IEEE Sponsored World Conference on Futuristic Trends in Research and Innovation for Social Welfare (2016)
4. Lakhdhar, Y., Rekhis, S., Boudriga, N.: An approach to a graph-based active cyber defense model. In: The 14th International Conference on Advances in Mobile Computing & Multimedia (MoMM 2016), Singapore, 28–30 November 2016
5. Guezguez, M.J., Rekhis, S., Boudriga, N.: Observation-based detection of femtocell attacks in wireless mobile networks. In: Proceedings of the Symposium on Applied Computing, Morocco, 03–07 April 2017
6. Derfouf, M., Eleuldj, M., Enniari, S., Diouri, O.: Smart intrusion detection model for the cloud computing. In: Rocha, Á., Serrhini, M., Felgueiras, C. (eds.) Europe and MENA Cooperation Advances in Information and Communication Technologies, vol. 520, pp. 411–421. Springer, Heidelberg (2017). https://doi.org/10.1007/978-3-319-46568-5_42

7. Lakhdhar, Y., Rekhis, S., Boudriga, N.: Proactive damage assessment of cyber attacks using mobile observer agents. In: The 15th International Conference on Advances in Mobile Computing & Multimedia (MoMM 2017), Salzburg, Austria, 04–06 December 2017
8. Vasilomanolakis, E., Karuppayah, S., Mühlhäuser, M., Fischer, M.: Taxonomy and survey of collaborative intrusion detection. ACM Comput. Surv. (CSUR) 47(4), 55 (2015)
9. Ganame, K., Allaire, M.A., Zagdene, G., Boudar, O.: Network behavioral analysis for zero-day malware detection-a case study. In: Proceedings of International Conference on Intelligent, Secure, and Dependable Systems in Distributed and Cloud Environments (2017)

MIMO Beamforming Anti-jamming Scheme for Mobile Smallcell Networks

Meriem Salhi[✉] and Noureddine Boudriga

Communication Networks and Security (CNAS) Research Laboratory,
University of Carthage, Tunis, Tunisia
mariem.slh@gmail.com

Abstract. Contrary to interference which is unintended, jamming is intentionally created by an adversary in order to prevent the receiver from properly decoding the legitimate signal. It can cause severe denial of service by targeting channels carrying critical information. In this paper, we use multiple-input multiple-output (MIMO) technology to eliminate the jamming signal in mobile smallcells. To achieve this, we combine spectral diversity together with beamforming. The receiver is equipped with two antennas receiving at two different frequencies, while the transmitter uses two uniform linear antennas arrays (ULA) each transmitting the signal at one of those frequencies. Based on a pre-calculated ratio of the jammer's channels sensed by the receiver, jamming is suppressed from the output signal. In fact, beamforming weights associated to each antenna array are adequately adjusted in order to constructively combine the received signals. Conducted simulations prove the efficiency of the solution in mitigating the attack by achieving satisfying bit-error-rates (BER).

1 Introduction

The research on jamming attack mitigation in next generation wireless networks is of a great interest. In fact, the transmission reliability in these networks is very important due to the higher requirements of the carried services as well as the scarcity of frequency resources. In the meantime, jammers' capabilities are increasing due to software defined networking advancements. Until today, the most popular anti-jamming methods consist in channel hopping. Several works have been proposed in this way [1–3]. However this technique degrades the spectral efficiency. Furthermore, it is inefficient when the whole bandwidth is being jammed, or when the jammer have enough cognitive radio capability to rapidly switch to the used frequency. A promising category, nowadays, includes Multiple Input Multiple Output (MIMO) based techniques. In fact, in addition to its promising feature in enhancing the wireless system capability by boosting the achievable throughputs, MIMO enables efficient interference cancellation (IC) [4–6]. Similarly, it can be exploited for jamming signal suppression, which has recently inspired several researchers to propose MIMO-based techniques for jamming attack mitigation [7–9]. In [7] authors consider the case of a reactive

© Springer Nature Switzerland AG 2018
N. Boudriga et al. (Eds.): UNet 2018, LNCS 11277, pp. 308–319, 2018.
https://doi.org/10.1007/978-3-030-02849-7_28

jammer in Orthogonal Frequency Division Multiplexing (OFDM) communication. Their defense scheme works by adjusting the legitimate signal direction to be orthogonal to that of the jammer through signal rotation enabled by MIMO. Eventhough, the jamming can be efficiently mitigated, the measures and calculs required to track the jammer's channel in this scheme are very costly. In [9], authors use two antennas at the reception to eliminate the jamming signal using a pre-calculated ratio of the jammer channel coefficient, and their scheme can be applied for constant and reactive jammers. Authors of [8] propose to optimize the transmission strategy of a MIMO-OFDM communication according to the jammer status while reducing energy consumption. Another sub-category of multiple antenna based techniques consists in beamforming schemes. Beamforming can be applied at the transmission or the reception sides, known respectively as transmit beamforming and receive beamforming. In the literature, the most used approach, among the two, is receive beamforming [10] (also known as spatial filtering). It permits to enhance the signal-to-interference-plus-noise ratio (SINR) at the direction of arrival of the intended signal and nulls signal coming from the direction of the jammer. Several works have been proposed in this way [11–14]. However, the main inconvenient of these schemes is that the receiver should have strong capabilities to perform the necessary processing. In addition, they necessitate knowledge about the jammer's position, which further increases their complexity.

The aim of this work is to propose a jamming attack supression scheme suitable to mobile smallcells based on transmit beamforming and double channel ratio (DCR). The anti-jamming scheme presented in this paper is limited to the case of a constant jammer. Nevertheless, we note that it can be extended to a reactive jammer scenario through the use of preamble exchange. The contributions are three-fold:

1. First, we propose a jamming mitigation startegy based on a collaboration between the transmitter and the receiver. In fact, the communication cycle is divided into three periods, namely: DCR sensing period by the receiver, beamforming weight adaptation period by the transmitter, and transmission period.
2. Second, we combine spectral and spatial diversity by subdividing the antenna array into two sub-arrays each performing transmit beamforming at a distinct frequency. The jamming elimination is performed thanks to the used spectral diversity and the pre-calculated DCR.
3. Third, we adequately adjust the beamforming weights in a way that constructively combines the received signals. The desired signal is then efficiently recovered.

The remainder of this paper is organized as follows. Section 2 presents the system model considered for this framework. Then, in Sect. 3, the proposed jamming mitigation scheme is described. After that, simulations are presented in Sect. 4. Finally, Sect. 5 concludes the work.

2   System Model

2.1   General System Architecture

As illustrated in Fig. 1, we consider a network architecture composed of fixed SmallCells (each denoted fSC) deployed at the edge of a road, and mobile Small-Cell nodes (denoted mSC) deployed at the exterior roof of vehicles and are served by the fSCs. The road is composed of two ways of opposite directions, and jammer is located at the edge of the road. In our architecture, each fSC is equipped with a vector of multiple antennas for downlink transmission. This vector is designed to create beams towards the targeted served mSCs. The latter, on the other hand are equipped each by a vector of only two antennas for reception. In fact, we assume that the fSC uses, for each served mSC, two frequencies to carry the downlink signal. Thus, the mSC should receive two versions for the same signal each on separate frequency.

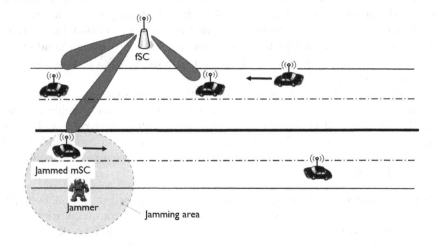

Fig. 1. General network architecture.

2.2   Jamming Model

The jammer considered in our architecture is immobile and assumed to be located at the edge of the road. We assume that it is equipped with multiple antennas in a way that it transmits the jamming signal on multiple sub-channels simultaneously. The worst case would be when he transmits on all the available sub-channels. It is clear that in this case channel hopping cannot be applied to countermeasure the attack.

2.3 Transmit/Receive Model

At the fSC level, we are interested in a rectangular antenna array composed of L parallel uniform linear arrays each of which is composed of N-elements. Uniformity of ULA arrays is related to the fact that all the antenna elements have the same radiation pattern (assumed to be omnidirectional) and are equispaced with d the distance between two consecutive elements. For each mSC node a linear sub-array is used to create a beam towards it. These L vectors are parallel to each other with a distance e between each two consecutive ones. The illustration of the transmitting antenna design at the fSC is depicted in Fig. 2. The antenna array at the fSC base station is supposed to be parallel to the ground with an altitude h. Le o be the projection of the first antenna element to the ground. We consider the coordinates system (X, Y, Z) having as origin the point o and where (oZ) is the line passing through the first antenna element of the array, (oY) is parallel to the trajectory of the vehicle which is supposed to be a straight line, and (oX) the perpendicular to (oZ, oY). A depicted in Fig. 2, the position of the targeted mSC m according to these coordinates is given by its elevation angle θ and its azimuth angle ϕ and its distance l_m to the origin o.

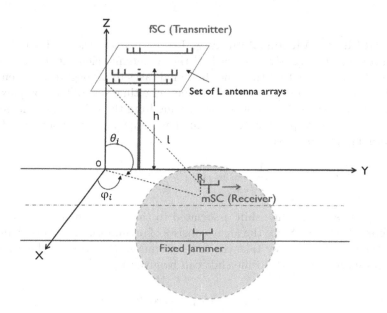

Fig. 2. Transmitting antenna design at the fixed smallcell node.

Channel Model. The available bandwidth is divided into multiple sub-channels. The channel model characterizing each of these sub-channels is affected by three phenomena, namely, small scale fading including channel fading and Doppler shift effect, and large scale fading including pathloss.

Channel fading: We consider slow fading channel model related to shadowing so that the channel fading matrix H is constant over a time period of m symbols. The entries of H are assumed to be independent and identically distributed (i.i.d).

Doppler shift effect: The Doppler shift effect is a phenomenon related to mobility. In fact, the transmitted signal is subject to a shift f_D in the carrier frequency given by:

$$f_D = \frac{v \cos \psi}{\lambda}$$

where ψ is the angle of arrival of the signal to the receiving antenna relatively to the direction of motion. The Doppler shift f_D is positive if the vehicle is moving towards the transmitting fSC, and it is negative otherwise.

Pathloss: We adopt a free-space pathloss model. For an omnidirection antenna elements, it is expressed in function of the distance l of the mSC to the fSC as follows:

$$PL\left(l\right) = \frac{(4\pi l)^2}{\lambda^2}$$

Received Signal Without Jamming. Let $x\left(t\right)$ denote the modulated signal transmitted simultaneously from each of the N antenna elements of the fSC at time slot t. We assume that the time the signal takes to propagate is low enough that the receiving antenna receives it at the same time slot t. The complex representation of the signal component originating from the kth antenna element of the fSC array i (corresponding to transmission frequency i), without considering beamforming, is expressed by [15]:

$$x_k\left(t\right) = \frac{1}{\sqrt{PL\left(l_{k,i}\right)}} h_{k,i}\left(t\right) e^{j2\pi\left(f_{c,i}+f_{D,i}\right)\left(t+\tau_{k,i}\right)} x\left(t\right) \tag{1}$$

where $\tau_{k,i}$ refers to the time shift associated to the kth antenna respectively to the reference antenna. Since the array consists of an uniform linear array aligned within the y-axis, and if we take the first antenna in the array as the reference as illustrated in 2, then this time shift can be given by [16]:

$$\tau_{k,i} = \frac{d}{c}\left(l_{k,i} - 1\right)\cos\theta_i \tag{2}$$

Thus the complex representation of the received signal at the ith antenna element of the mSC without considering jamming is expressed as follows:

$$y_{i,free}\left(t\right) = \sum_{k=1}^{k=N} \omega_{k,i} \frac{1}{\sqrt{PL\left(l_{k,i}\right)}} x\left(t\right) h_{k,i}\left(t\right) e^{j2\pi\left(f_{c,i}+f_{D,i}\right)\left(t+\tau_{k,i}\right)} \tag{3}$$

where ω_k is the beamforming weight applied to antenna k.

Received Signal with Jamming. We denote by $j(t)$ the jamming signal transmitted by the jammer at time slot t, $h_{J,i}(t)$ the channel coefficient between the jammer and the receiving antenna i. The complex representation of the received signal at he i^{th} antenna element of the mSC subject to jamming at time slot t is expressed as follows:

$$y_{i,jammed}(t) = y_{i,free} + \frac{1}{\sqrt{PL(l_{J,i})}} j(t) \, h_{J,i}(t) \, e^{j2\pi(f_{c,i}+f_{D,i,J})t} \qquad (4)$$

Signal-to-noise Ratio. The signal to noise ratio is the ratio between the received signal power and the power of noise. Let $N_i(t)$ be the noise perceived by the receiving antenna i at time slot t. The signal-to-noise ratio expressions for antenna i at time slot t without jamming and with jamming, are respectively given by:

$$SNR_{i,free}(t) = \frac{|y_i(t)|^2}{|N_i(t)|^2}$$

and

$$SNR_{i,jammed}(t) = \frac{|y_{i,jammed}(t)|^2}{|N_i(t)|^2}$$

3 Proposed Jamming Mitigation Approach

3.1 Jamming Detection

The mSC detects the jamming based on the perceived signal-to-noise ratio. We assume that the fSC transmits with a constant transmit power. At each time slot the mSc estimates the SNR without jamming, denoted $S\tilde{N}R_{i,free}(t)$. Then, the power of jamming signal is estimated based on the difference between the received SNR and the estimated one.

$$\tilde{P}_{jamming}(t) = SNR_{i,jammed}(t) - S\tilde{N}R_{i,free}(t)$$

If the estimated jamming power is higher than a certain threshold value Γ_{th} ($\tilde{P}_{jamming}(t) \geq \Gamma_{th}$), then there is jamming, otherwise no jamming is detected and the calculated value $\tilde{P}_{jamming}(t)$ is considered to be the estimation error.

3.2 Jamming Elimination

Once jamming detection is successful, the mSC informs the fSC of it and the jamming elimination mechanism is launched between the mSC and the serving fSC. Communication between the fSC and the mSC is based on communication cycles as illustrated in Fig. 3. Each communication cycle t is constituted of a total of m mini times slots which is the period during which the channel fading is assumed to be quasi-constant, and it includes three periods:

Period 1: Sensing or DCR Calculation. This period is of length n such that $n < m$. During this period, the fSC doesn't transmit any signal to the mSC. In fact, this period is used to let the mSC sense the jamming signal received at each antenna element, and have an updated channel coefficient at each communication cycle to calculate the DCR value. In fact, for a time slot t in the sensing period of a given communication cycle, the received signal during sensing at antenna i of the mSCis expressed as follows:

$$y_{i,sensing}(t) = \frac{1}{\sqrt{PL(l_{J,i})}} j(t) h_{J,i}(t) e^{j2\pi(f_{c,i}+f_{D,i,J})t} \tag{5}$$

Thus the jamming channels ratio (DCR) for each time slot t in the communication cycle in question is given by:

$$\varphi(t) = \frac{y_{1,sensing}(t)}{y_{2,sensing}(t)} = \left(\frac{\sqrt{PL(l_{J,2})}}{\sqrt{PL(l_{J,1})}} e^{j2\pi(f_{c,1}+f_{D,1,J}-f_{c,2}-f_{D,2,J})t} \right) \frac{h_{J,1}(t)}{h_{J,2}(t)} \tag{6}$$

Thus:

$$h_{J,1}(t) = \varphi(t) \left(\frac{\sqrt{PL(l_{J,1})}}{\sqrt{PL(l_{J,2})}} e^{j2\pi(f_{c,2}+f_{D,2,J}-f_{c,1}-f_{D,1,J})t} \right) h_{J,2}(t) \tag{7}$$

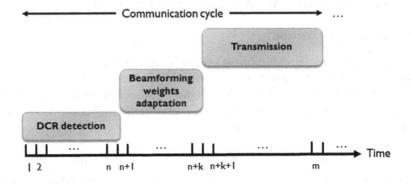

Fig. 3. Communication cycle periods

Period 2: Beamforming Weights Adaptation. The beamforming weights adaptation period is a short period following the DCR calculation. During this period, the mSC informs the fSC about the value of φin order to adjust the beamforming weights accordingly. For this purpose, the maximum ratio transmission (MRT) beamforming is used and the beamforming weights are adjusted according to new channel coefficients as it will be explained in the next paragraph (see Eqs. 10 and 11). The fSC is assumed to have knowledge about the channel coefficients based on channel state information.

Period 3: Transmission. During the transmission period, the fSC transmits the useful signal to the mSC in the two carrier frequencies using beamforming. At the mSc level, the received signals at each antenna include a useful signal component and a jamming component. They are combined based on the already calculated jamming signals ratio in a way to eliminate jamming.

In fact, based on the received $y_{1,jammed}(t)$, $y_{2,jammed}(t)$, and the pre-calculated $\varphi(t)$, the mSC computes a new output signal $y_{new}(t)$:

$$y_{new}(t) = y_{y1,jammed}(t) - \varphi(t) y_{2,jammed}(t) \tag{8}$$

For simplification, the pathloss from each transmitting antenna to each receiving antenna can be assumed to be equal. This is because the distance between elements in the antenna arrays are negligible compared to the distance between the transmitter and the receiver. We denote by $PL(t)$ the pathloss at time slot t.

Furthermore, given the symmetry between the two transmitting antenna arrays, we have $\tau_{k,2} = \tau_{k,1} = \tau_k$ for each two equivalent elements of indice k in arrays 1 and 2. Thus, $e^{j2\pi(f_{c,1}+f_{D,1})(t+\tau_{k,1})}$ can be expressed as follows:

$$e^{j2\pi(f_{c,1}+f_{D,1})(t+\tau_{k,1})} = \gamma e^{j2\pi(f_{c,2}+f_{D,2})(t+\tau_k)}$$

where $\gamma_k = e^{j2\pi(\Delta f_c + \Delta f_D)(t+\tau_k)}$.

In order to combine the two incoming signals, the mSC performs frequency modulation operation on $y_{y1,jammed}(t)$ to modulate it over the carrier frequency $f_{c,2}$. Then, the two signals are combined and the output signal can be expressed as follows:

$$y_{new}(t) = \frac{1}{\sqrt{PL(t)}} \sum_{k=1}^{k=N} \left(\gamma_k h_{k,1}(t) \omega_{k,1} - \varphi(t) h_{k,2}(t) \omega_{k,2} \right) e^{j2\pi \left(f_{c,2}+f_{D,2} \right)(t+\tau_k)} x(t) \tag{9}$$

This signal can be treated as being coming from the second antenna array after using adjusted beamforming. $\gamma_k h_{k,1}(t) \omega_{k,1} - \varphi(t) h_{k,2}(t) \omega_{k,2}$ can be seen as the concatenation of two weighted channels. In fact, for each antenna element k, the two new channel coefficients at communication cycle t from the first and the second array are: $\tilde{h}_{k,1}(t) = \gamma_k h_{k,1}(t)$ and $\tilde{h}_{k,2}(t) = -\varphi(t) h_{k,2}(t)$. Using the maximum channel transmission beamforming, the adjusted beamforming weights for array 1 and array 2 are respectively given by:

$$\hat{\omega}_{k,1}(t) = \frac{\overline{\gamma_k h_{k,1}(t)}}{\|\gamma_k h_{k,1}(t)\|} \tag{10}$$

$$\hat{\omega}_{k,2}(t) = \frac{\overline{-\varphi(t) h_{k,2}(t)}}{\|\varphi(t) h_{k,2}(t)\|} \tag{11}$$

4   Simulation Results

We evaluate the performance of the proposed beamforming based de-jamming scheme performed when a jamming attack is detected. The simulation model can be described as follows. A transmission period of 10^4 symbol times is considered. The used carrier frequencies values are 1800 GHz and 1800 MHz for $f_{c,1}$ and $f_{c,2}$ respectively, and a Rayleigh fading channel model is considered. We assume that the receiving mSC follows a linear trajectory with a constant velocity v taken equal to 90 Km/h throughout the simulation. The legitimate fSC and the jammer are deployed at the either sides of the road, and they are equi-distant to the mSC. This distance is initialized to 500 m at start of the simulation.

We define the de-jamming efficiency as the percentage of achieving a BER less or equal to a given BER threshold BER_{th} after jamming suppression. The DCR detection period refers to the number of samples n used for averaging the DCR value that will be used for jamming suppression when both the transmitter and the jammer are transmitting. In Fig. 4 the de-jamming efficiency is evaluated as function of the length of this period for both BPSK and QPSK modulations. And it is compared for two values of BER threshold (BER_{th}) 10^{-5} and 10^{-6}. The number of antenna elements in each antenna array is fixed to 15 elements and the jammer's power is considered to be equal to half the transmitter's power (in Watts). We remark that the more the detection length is increased the better is the de-jamming efficiency. This is because the channel coefficients change slightly over time. This change becomes more relevant when both the jammer and the transmitter are using the channel simultaneously [9]. So it is important to accurately estimate the value of φ by averaging on multiple samples. For BPSK, after a certain DCR detection period n, the de-jamming efficiency reaches 100%. As depicted in the figure, the efficiency in eliminating the jamming effect varies according to the applied modulation. In fact, QPSK gives less efficiency than BPSK. This is because it is characterized by a denser constellation which makes successful decoding of symbols under jamming more difficult.

In Fig. 5 we vary the jammer-to-transmitter power ratio and evaluate its impact on the de-jamming efficiency for two BER_{th}: 10^{-5} and 10^{-6}, the DCR detection period to 30 mini times slots, and the number of antenna elements per transmitting array to 15. We note that the power ratio is considered for values of powers expressed in Watt. As expected, the de-jamming is at its highest efficiency for low levels of jamming power. In fact, in the case of BPSK it stays acceptable (higher than 90%) when the power ratio is lower than 0.4. However, after this point the anti-jamming capability of the scheme decreases dramatically until becoming null from 0.8 and 0.9 for $BER_{th} = 10^{-6}$ and $BER_{th} = 10^{-5}$, respectively. The same behaviour is noticed in QPSK with a more rapid decrease starting from a power ratio of 0.3. For this type of modulation, the efficiency becomes null from a ratio of 0.6.

Figure 6 illustrates the variation of the average BER in function of the number of transmitting antennas for different values of jammer-to-transmitter power ratio (0.5, 0.6, 0.7 and 0.8). Here the DCR detection period is fixed to 30. The values of the x-axis refers to the total number of antenna elements at the

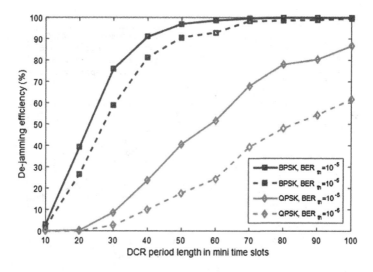

Fig. 4. De-jamming efficiency in function of the length of the DCR detection period

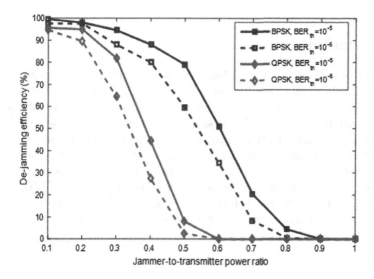

Fig. 5. De-jamming efficiency in function of the jammer-to-transmitter power ratio

transmitter side, which is varied from 6 to 42 with a step of 6. The BER decreases linearly as the number of antennas increases. It goes below 10^{-6} for 42 antenna elements and power ratio of 0.5. The obtained curves prove that the more we increase the number of antennas used for beamforming, the better is the signal recovered at the receiver. We can say that increasing the number of antennas used for beamforming helps enhancing the resilience of the receiver to the jamming attack under the same power transmission conditions.

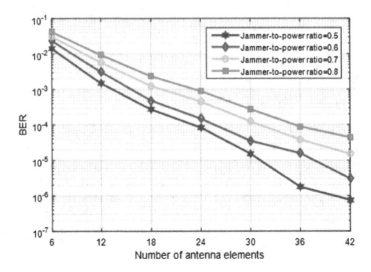

Fig. 6. BER in function of the total number of antenna elements using BPSK modulation

5   Conclusion

This paper presents a new MIMO beamforming based framework that permits to mobile smallcells to efficiently receive the useful signal in a presence of a constant jammer. The jamming elimination scheme exploits spectral diversity together with transmit beamforming. It works in three steps starting by calculating a jammer channel ratio, then communicating it to the serving node to adjust its beamforming weights, and finally transmitting the adequately beamformed signals. Simulations, prove that the scheme can efficiently eliminate the jamming signal for a sufficient number of transmitting antennas as well as DCR detection period length. The presented solution can be extended for a reactive jammer as well as multiple jammers scenarios, which can be the subjects of future works.

References

1. Lazos, L., Liu, S., Krunz, M.: Mitigating control-channel jamming attacks in multi-channel ad hoc networks. In: Proceedings of the Second ACM Conference on Wireless Network Security, WiSec 2009, New York, NY, USA, pp. 169–180. ACM (2009)
2. Djuraev, S., Choi, J.G., Sohn, K.S., Nam, S.Y.: Channel hopping scheme to mitigate jamming attacks in wireless LANs. EURASIP J. Wirel. Commun. Netw. **2017**(1), 11 (2017)
3. Chang, G.Y., Wang, S.Y., Liu, Y.X.: A jamming-resistant channel hopping scheme for cognitive radio networks. IEEE Trans. Wirel. Commun. **16**(10), 6712–6725 (2017)
4. Gollakota, S., Perli, S.D., Katabi, D.: Interference alignment and cancellation. In: Proceedings of the ACM SIGCOMM 2009 Conference on Data Communication, SIGCOMM 2009, New York, NY, USA, pp. 159–170. ACM (2009)

5. Lin, K.C.J., Gollakota, S., Katabi, D.: Random access heterogeneous MIMO networks. In: Proceedings of the ACM SIGCOMM 2011 Conference, SIGCOMM 2011, New York, NY, USA, pp. 146–157. ACM (2011)
6. Xu, T., Ma, L., Sternberg, G.: Practical interference alignment and cancellation for MIMO underlay cognitive radio networks with multiple secondary users. In: 2013 IEEE Global Communications Conference (GLOBECOM), pp. 1009–1014, December 2013
7. Yan, Q., Zeng, H., Jiang, T., Li, M., Lou, W., Hou, Y.T.: Jamming resilient communication using MIMO interference cancellation. IEEE Trans. Inf. Forensics Secur. **11**(7), 1486–1499 (2016)
8. Sani, S.S., Yaqub, A.: MIMO-OFDM energy efficient cognitive system with intelligent anti-jam capability. Wirel. Pers. Commun. **98**(2), 2291–2317 (2018)
9. Shen, W., Ning, P., He, X., Dai, H., Liu, Y.: MCR decoding: a MIMO approach for defending against wireless jamming attacks. In: 2014 IEEE Conference on Communications and Network Security, pp. 133–138, October 2014
10. Veen, B.D.V., Buckley, K.M.: Beamforming: a versatile approach to spatial filtering. IEEE ASSP Mag. **5**(2), 4–24 (1988)
11. Tao, Y., Zhang, G., Zhang, Y.: Spatial filter measurement matrix design for interference/jamming suppression in colocated compressive sensing MIMO radars. Electron. Lett. **52**(11), 956–958 (2016)
12. Li, Q., Wang, W., Xu, D., Wang, X.: A robust anti-jamming navigation receiver with antenna array and GPS/SINS. IEEE Commun. Lett. **18**(3), 467–470 (2014)
13. Hurley, P., Simeoni, M.: Flexibeam: analytic spatial filtering by beamforming. In: 2016 IEEE International Conference on Acoustics, Speech and Signal Processing (ICASSP), pp. 2877–2880, March 2016
14. Bhunia, S., Behzadan, V., Regis, P.A., Sengupta, S.: Adaptive beam nulling in multihop ad hoc networks against a jammer in motion. Comput. Netw. **109**, 50–66 (2016). Special issue on Recent Advances in Physical-Layer Security
15. Goldsmith, A.: Wireless Communications. Cambridge University Press, Cambridge (2005)
16. Godara, L.C.: Application of antenna arrays to mobile communications. ii. beamforming and direction-of-arrival considerations. Proc. IEEE **85**(8), 1195–1245 (1997)

A Critical Analysis of the Application of Data Mining Methods to Detect Healthcare Claim Fraud in the Medical Billing Process

Nnaemeka Obodoekwe and Dustin Terence van der Haar[(✉)]

Academy of Computer Science and Software Engineering, University of Johannesburg, Cnr Kingsway and University Road, Johannesburg 2092, Gauteng, South Africa
nnaemekaobodo@gmail.com, dvanderhaar@uj.ac.za

Abstract. The healthcare industry has become a very important pillar in modern society but has witnessed an increase in fraudulent activities. Traditional fraud detection methods have been used to detect potential fraud, but in certain cases, they have been insufficient and time-consuming. Data mining which has emerged as a very important process in knowledge discovery has been successfully applied in the health insurance claims fraud detection. We performed an analysis of studies that used data mining techniques for detecting healthcare fraud and abuse using the supervised and unsupervised data mining methods. Each of these methods has their own strengths and weaknesses. This article attempts to highlight these areas, along with trends and propose recommendations relevant for deployment. We identified the need for the use of more computationally efficient models that can easily adapt and identify the novel fraud patterns generated by the perpetrators of healthcare claims fraud.

Keywords: Healthcare · Fraud detection · Assessment
Supervised learning · Unsupervised leanring

1 Introduction

According to Maslow's hierarchy of needs, the most basic need of every individual is the physiological need. The physiological needs of individuals consist of basic needs such as food, water, and good health [1]. For the full functioning of any individual, the individual first needs to be in good health. To be in good health one needs to have access to the adequate medical treatment when needed. The continuous rise in the cost of the medical care makes it more of a luxury than a basic need in recent times. Health insurance was introduced to help manage this cost and make healthcare more affordable for everyone. Health insurance is a contract between a group of individuals or person with an insurer stating that an individual pays an agreed premium for a specified health insurance cover [2].

© Springer Nature Switzerland AG 2018
N. Boudriga et al. (Eds.): UNet 2018, LNCS 11277, pp. 320–330, 2018.
https://doi.org/10.1007/978-3-030-02849-7_29

Health insurance relates to an insurance type that covers medical and surgical expenses of a member.

The health insurance system has been impacted by fraudulent activities with several parties involved trying to gain illegal benefits [3]. The impact of fraud in the health insurance system results in loss of revenue, excessive time spent on reviewing these claims by the insurance service provider thereby leading to delayed feedback on reimbursements. We start by analyzing the medical billing process in Sect. 2 to gain a better understanding of problem background. In Sect. 3, we see how data mining can be applied to healthcare claims fraud and current work. Section 4 defines an assessment framework which we apply to the current work discussed in Sect. 3.2 to derive the results in Sect. 5. Based on the results, we make recommendations for further improvements in Sect. 6 and conclude in Sect. 7.

2   The Medical Billing Process

In this section, we analyze the healthcare system to understand how it functions and the different role players involved. An understanding of the healthcare process forms a base for the further exploration of how fraud can occur in the healthcare claims process.

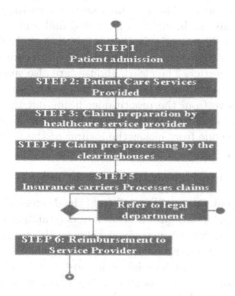

Fig. 1. A summary of the medical billing process flow (as visualized by the author)

The purpose of the health insurance claim process is for the service providers to receive reimbursements for the services they offered. The reimbursements can be paid to patients or the service providers. Figure 1 shows the flow of activities in the health insurance claim process.

2.1   Steps in the Health Insurance Claims Process

There are several steps involved in processing a health insurance claim. A brief review of the steps involved in the medical insurance claim process involves a patient receiving care from the licensed practitioner. The practitioner records the services provided to the patient and the relevant International Classification of Diseases (ICD) codes if diagnoses were made or Current Procedural Terminology (CPT) codes if the patient was treated [4]. The patient's data along with the patient's insurance information are also captured and added to the bill for claim processing.

Now the claim has been sent through, the next step is processing the claim. Processing these claims involves taking the details on the claim form and then lining it up to a policy and then ensuring that these claims correspond to a rule set out in the policy. Technologies such as Optical Character Recognition have been employed to improve the speed and accuracy of claim processing. Software systems have been employed to capture health insurance claim, thereby reducing the possibility of unreadable information and reduce the risk of error in retrieving the information on the claim form. Optical Character Recognition equipment has also been used to process hard copy claims for efficiency and more accuracy [4].

Now, these claims have been processed, the next phase is the clearinghouses which serve as the third-party or intermediate between the healthcare providers and the insurance providers. The clearinghouses act as the central hub where all the insurance claims are brought to be sorted and sent through to the various insurance carriers. The clearinghouses are necessary because the number of claims that provider needs to submit daily can be quite enormous and all these claims go to different carrier. The clearinghouses are also susceptible to error or fraudulent activities, so the process can go wrong at this stage [4]. The entire process described above from the practitioner filling out the claim form to the insurer receiving the claim can be exposed to various fraudulent activities and can lead to loss of revenue from either the insurer or the healthcare provider.

2.2   The Definition of Health Insurance Fraud

Fraud has affected many facets of life and from the discussion above, the Healthcare sector is no stranger. To gain a clearer understanding of what healthcare fraud is, a distinctive comparison is given between the terms fraud, waste and abuse as these terms are sometimes used interchangeably.

Health insurance waste in healthcare is most times unrelated to fraud as it mainly the provision of unnecessary health services without the intention of defrauding the system [3]. Waste can only be fraud and abuse when the act is intentional. Waste can occur when services are over-utilized and then results in unnecessary expenditure [5].

Health insurance abuse describes the billings of practices that either directly or indirectly, is not consistent with the goals of providing patients with services that are medically necessary, meet professionally recognized standards, and are fairly priced [5]. Abuse occurs when the practices of the service provider are not in line with sound business practices.

Health insurance fraud is purposely billing for services that were never performed and or supplies not provided, medically unnecessary services and altering claims to receive higher reimbursement than the service produced [5]. Fraud is when healthcare is paid for by the insurance subscriber but not provided or a situation whereby reimbursements are paid to the service provider while no such services were provided.

Now we have discussed the differences between waste, abuse, and fraud. The next section discusses the role data mining plays in reducing or eliminating fraud in the healthcare billing process. We look at the drivers for fraud in the healthcare industry and how these factors have affected the health insurance industry.

3   Data Mining in Health Insurance

Technology has played a major role in the Health insurance industry. The impact of advances in technology can be seen in the various aspects of health insurance and the medical billing process is no exception. In the past, the medical billing and coding process was carried out with a paper and pen, then submitted via mail but today the professionals in the insurance field have found their workspace in the virtual and electronic world [6].

Data mining techniques have in recent times been applied in the health insurance domain to detect these fraudulent claims. Data mining involves extracting, discovering or mining knowledge from a large amount of data. The availability of data and the advancement in technology allows for the design of data mining systems that can extract previously unknown knowledge and insight from the available data [7].

3.1   Data Mining (DM), Knowledge Discovery from Databases (KDD)

The terms data mining and knowledge discovery are used interchangeably. It is the nontrivial extraction of implicit, previously unknown and potentially useful information from data in a repository [8]. Data mining enables us to filter through immense volume of data to find unknown or hidden patterns that can give new perceptions [9]. Although the terms data mining and knowledge discovery in the databases are synonyms, data mining forms a part of the knowledge discovery system as can be seen from the figure below. The data mining process starts with first understanding and collecting the required data. Preprocessing is done on the dataset to get it to the most desirable state. Data transformation is then applied which may involve feature extraction and selection. The features derived from the transformation process are then fed into the machine learning model to gain insights on the data. In the context of this research, we are going to use the terms knowledge discovery in database and data mining interchangeably (Fig. 2).

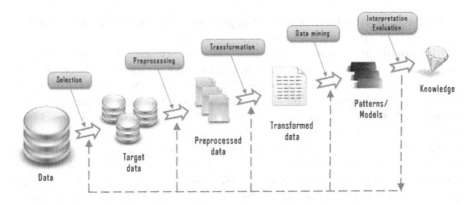

Fig. 2. Diagram illustrating the processes in the data mining system adapted from [10]

3.2 Current Work

Electronic fraud detection is a relatively new field and grew in popularity with the advent of larger databases. Data mining, used in electronic fraud detection became a reality now as cloud services, data warehouse, and big data have now become a commonplace. Advances in the field of information technology, digitalization of the medical billing process and the vast amount of research on healthcare fraud have created an avenue for the use of data mining and machine learning to fight fraudulent activities [11]. Data mining has gained popularity in researchers as a potential tool to combat health care fraud.

There are several works that have been done in using data mining for fraud detection and this section would be exploring some of those systems. Literature has categorized data mining and machine learning techniques into supervised, unsupervised or hybrid methods. The supervised methods require labelling of data to build a training set, the unsupervised methods, on the other hand, deals with data statistical detection of outlier behaviour. In the following subsections, we discuss several systems that make use of data mining to detect health insurance fraud.

Systems Based on Supervised Learning. In this subsection, we discuss the systems that make use of the supervised data mining learning algorithms to solve the problem of health insurance fraud. The systems are reviewed in a chronological order according to the date of publication to see the progression of methods used.

In the National Health Institute (NHI) Taiwan, Wan-Shiou, and San-Yih developed a process-mining framework which detected healthcare fraud [12]. They made use of data from a regional hospital that is a service provider of the NHI program. They created two datasets by filtering out noisy data, identifying medical activities using domain knowledge, identifying fraudulent instances and non-fraudulent instances with the help of domain experts. They made use of the filter model for feature selection as the filter model algorithm does not need to search through the entire space for feature subsets. It is very efficient for domains with many features such as the health insurance domain.

Liou et al. in Taiwan made use of supervised data mining methods to analyze claims for diabetic outpatients that were submitted to National Health Insurance Taiwan [13]. The data used in validating the model was from a random sample of diabetes patients' health insurance claims. The fraudulent claims in the dataset were identified by the termination of claim contract. The fraud detection model was built by selecting nine expense related variables and a comparison of these variables was done in two groups of fraudulent and non-fraudulent claims. The expense related input variables used include average drug cost, average drug cost per day, average consultation and treatment fee, average diagnosis fee, average days of drug dispense, average claim amount, average medical expenditure per day and average dispensing service fee.

Shin et al. created a scoring model to detect abusive patterns in health insurance using the 3705 Korean internal medical clinics [14]. They made use of data from the Health Insurance Review and Assessment Services (HIRA). They examined the relationship between the intervention listed by HIRA and the indicating factors to get the data to a manageable size. They extracted 38 indicators which were further validated by HIRA domain experts. The 38 features extracted were used for identifying fraudulent claims using a simple definition of anomaly score.

Now we have seen the systems that used supervised learning algorithms in the data mining process to detect fraud in healthcare. The next sets of systems we look at are the systems that use unsupervised learning methods.

Systems Based on Unsupervised Learning. Supervised methods work well when used with labelled data. Sometimes the healthcare claim dataset does not have a clear distinction between the records that are fraudulent and those that are not. In this subsection, we discuss the several approaches that used unsupervised learning to detect fraud and abuse in healthcare.

In Canada, Fletcher Lu et al. built an adaptive fraud detection system using Benford's law. Adaptive Benford's law specifies the probabilistic distribution of digits for many repeating phenomena, notwithstanding incomplete records [15]. The data used was retrieved from Ernst and Young which contained already audited claims data. Their approach created a new fraud discovery approach by combining digital analysis with reinforcement learning technique.

Lin et al. in the work they did on detecting fraud in the Nation health insurance Taiwan general physicians' practice data, they made use of unsupervised clustering methods [16]. The applied PCA feature compression for dimensionality reduction of the feature space. They made use of 10 features in the clustering of physicians' data. The indicators used include number of cases, average treatment fee per case, average fee per case, amount of fee, average consultation fee per case, percentage of antibiotic prescriptions, number of visits per case, percentage of injection prescriptions, average drug fee per case, amount of prescription days and percentage of injection prescriptions.

4   Assessment Framework

One aspect that is highly important in implementing a data mining model is to critically evaluate and analyze the proposed model. The analysis of a system helps highlight the strengths and the weaknesses of the solution. To compare the similar systems discussed in Sect. 3.2, we defined criteria for the evaluation of the system.

We consider criteria that enable us to gain insights into the system. Some of the criteria considered are highlighted below:

Robustness: Given noisy data or data with missing values, a robust system will still be able to make predictions correctly [17]. The data preprocessing step in the system design is responsible for cleaning up the data before machine learning methods can be applied to it. A system that cannot handle noisy or incomplete data will not be suitable for deployment as data in the real world is dirty as a result data can be incomplete, noisy and inconsistent.

Scalability: In developing a data mining system for healthcare claims fraud detection, the volume of available data needs to be considered. The systems need to be designed in such a way that given the large volume of data, they should be able to function effectively [18]. The scalability of the system is assessed using a series of data sets of increasing size.

Interpretability: The interpretability of the model refers to the level of insights and understanding that is generated by the model. Interpretability is subjective, hence it is not so easy to assess. The more insights a system can provide, the more useful it is to the problem it is trying to solve.

Algorithm efficiency: The efficiency of an algorithm mainly depends on the time and space usage. Algorithm efficiency relates to the number of computational resources used by the model. To maximize efficiency, we must minimize resource usage. The efficiency of the systems refers to the cost of computation incurred when generating and using the system [18]. An efficient data mining system will make use of minimal computational resources thereby increasing the speed of operations and reducing the memory usage [17].

Properties of data used: Two very important properties of data we consider are variety and volume. These characteristics of data influence the results generated. The more data used the more inferences can be made. The higher the variety of data the more the deductions can be generalized [17].

Accuracy: Accuracy is a measure of the overall correctness of the model. To compute the accuracy of model, there are four additional terms that form the building block for calculating several evaluation measures: true positives (TP), true negatives (TN), false positives FP) and false negatives (FN) [18]. The TP refers to the positive tuples that were correctly identified by the classifier. The TN refers to the negative tuples that were correctly identified by the classifier. Accuracy is the ratio of the sum of the TP and TF to the total predictions. Accuracy is useful in inferring the correctness of the system [18]. Accuracy involves testing a generated model against an already calibrated data that contains output. The aim is to build models that have high accuracy.

Error rate or misclassification rate: This is the ratio of the sum of false positives and false negatives to the total predictions. It can also be calculated by subtraction the accuracy from 1. A good model will have a very low error rate which implies a high accuracy [18].

5   Results

In this section, we discuss how the different criteria in the previous section apply to the systems considered in Sect. 3.2. The systems are analyzed from a structural point of view and then a discussion on the methods used by the system is given. The end goal of the systems discussed is to detect fraudulent claims. We discuss how the systems achieved this goal and to what extent did they solve the intended problem.

The healthcare fraud detection process mining framework defined by Wan-Shiou and San-Yih made use of clinical pathways which are defined as multidisciplinary care plan which diagnosis and therapeutic intervention are performed. In simple terms, it means the order which a physician is supposed to take when carrying out a treatment. They mined frequent patterns from clinical instances and systematically identified practices that deviated from the pathway and flagged them as fraudulent. The approach was evaluated with a real-world dataset retrieved from NHI Taiwan. The results showed that the proposed model could capture and identify several fraudulent and abusive cases that cannot be detected manually [12].

Liou et al. used three data mining techniques including logistic regression, neural networks and classification tree for the fraud detection model [13]. They compared the three data mining techniques and discovered that all three were accurate, but the classification tree method had the best performance as it recorded a 99% accuracy in the overall identification rate. The model had a limitation in the sample data used. The sample data used only consisted three fraudulent service providers whose contracts were cancelled by BNHI. The dataset did not include fraudulent service providers that padded claims but didn't face any penalty such as contract termination. This caused some data limitation and hence result cannot be generalized [13].

The model created by Shin et al. comprised two aspects: scoring to rate the degree of abusiveness and a second part which is identifying the problematic providers by performing segmentation and finding similar utilization patterns. They made use of a decision tree in classifying the providers.

The model performed well when presented with different payment arrangements in detecting abusive patterns. The system made use of the scoring model to alert payers of a potential fraudulent billing pattern [14]. The scoring model provides information on the attributes most dissimilar from the norm. Fraud keeps growing in sophistication and the patterns identified for fraudulent and non-fraudulent behaviour quickly become outdated. The model proposed by Shin et al. is scalable, flexible, easy to use and update. The use of decision trees in the model improved the level of complexity in creating the model as preparing decision trees especially the ones with numerous branches can be difficult and time-consuming.

The adaptive fraud detection system built by Fletcher Fu et al. made use of the Benford's distribution to benchmark the unsupervised machine learning method used to discover new cases of fraudulent activities [15]. When this technique was applied to several records of naturally occurring events, the fraud detection system finds the deviations from expected Benford's law distributions showing an anomaly in the behaviour indicating a strong possibility of fraud. The system then searches for the root cause of the anomalous behaviour by identifying the underlying attributes causing the anomaly. The model proposed by Shan et al. made use of association rules to mine medical specialist billing pattern. Association rule can be described as statements in the form of antecedents and consequences [19]. For example, if a patient is diagnosed with A then the physician would prescribe drug B and C with a likelihood of 95%. 215 of the association rules were identified Using these predetermined association rules, the model could pick out the physicians who broke these rules and were flagged with a high likelihood of fraud. The study introduced the mining of negative and positive association rules and not just positive rules only, as found in previous models.

Lin et al. used expert opinions to determine the impact of some of these features on the health expenditure. The opinions of the experts were then used to identify and rank critical clusters. The model successfully integrated the data mining process with the segmentation of the GP's practice patterns [16]. The GP's practice pattern detected by applying clustering methods using the features of expenditures of the GP. The final step was then to illustrate managerial guidance based on these expert opinions. The model was benchmarked against real-world data and the results show that the model can effectively and accurately identify fraudulent abuse and behaviours in healthcare [16].

6   Recommendations

The works we have examined in the review paper clearly demonstrates that machine learning and data mining methods can be applied successfully in the health insurance claims fraud detection. However, the review of this literature also shows that there are several gaps that need to be addressed in applying data mining and machine learning methods to effectively detect healthcare claim fraud. Section 7 highlights these gaps and suggests possible ways to address these gaps.

An observation that can be made from the systems reviewed is that less attention was paid to the efficiency of the algorithms and methods used. Even with the abundance of computational resource, we need still need to build systems that not only solve the problem at hand, but we must ensure that we make use of computationally efficient methods.

The practical implementation parameters and the deployment of the proposed model were not discussed by most literature. More research needs to include the deployment and practical implementation of the proposed system in the actual environment to understand what the deployment constraints are and any anomalies that may occur.

The healthcare ecosystem consists of several role players who can be involved in fraud. More research needs to be done to detect fraud that can arise from other roles in the medical billing process. Studies need to be carried out on the potentials of applying data mining methods to detect the insurer fraud.

An interesting observation is the unavailability of literature for the application of data mining methods to detect healthcare fraud different contexts, such as third world countries. The lack of electronic systems for data capturing and auditing could be the major cause. However, where data is available the use of machine learning methods can be used to detect fraudulent activities that may be going unnoticed in the healthcare process.

Finally, the perpetrators that carry out health insurance claims fraud always find new ways to circumvent measures in place to detect fraudulent claims, therefore making it very important for the fraud detection systems to keep up with the novel forms of fraud. The process of making improvements to systems, such as retraining classification models or gearing implementation parameters can be an expensive exercise especially in the supervised methods where dataset needs to be labelled. One area that can be explored is the use of semi-supervised online machine learning model that can regularly update itself with the new data and then be able to detect novel fraudulent claims pattern leveraging the strengths of unsupervised machine learning.

7 Conclusion

This paper presents an analysis of the literature on the application of data mining methods to health insurance claims fraud detection. Several of the literature reviewed show that the healthcare claims system is highly prone to fraudulent activities which can occur at the different stages of the medical billing process. The adoption of electronic health systems and availability of medical claims data have created an avenue for the application of data mining methods to detect fraud in the healthcare claims process. Data mining methods have been successfully applied to detect these fraudulent activities.

However, each of these data mining methods has their own strengths and weaknesses. In this article, we highlighted the areas, along with trends and propose recommendations relevant for deployment. We identified that there is a need for attention to be paid to the computational efficiency of methods used even with the abundance of the resource. The review of the current data mining solutions to healthcare fraud also highlights the need for data of large volume and variety to be able to improve accuracy and generalize findings.

The development of practical implementation guides that contain details about deployment as well as implementation parameters may improve the adoption and usage of data mining methods to prevent possible claim fraud and misuse of techniques.

Finally, both supervised and unsupervised techniques have important merits in discovering different fraud strategies and schemes. However, to keep the model updated with the latest trends and patterns used by the perpetrators in healthcare claims fraud we suggest exploring a cost-saving model which uses semi-supervised learning to reduce the cost of retraining classification models and subsequently improves the level of accuracy and currency of the model.

References

1. McLeod, S.: Maslow's hierarchy of needs. Simply Psychol. **1**, 1–2 (2007)
2. Jinhee Kim, B.B., Williams, A.D.: Understanding health insurance literacy:a literature review. Fam. Consum. Sci. Res. **42**(1), 3–13 (2013)
3. Centers for Medicare & Medicaid Services, et al.: Medicare fraud & abuse: prevention, detection, and reporting (2015)
4. Ferenc, D.P.: Understanding Hospital Billing and Coding, pp. 89–95. Elsevier Health Sciences, London (2014)
5. Coustasse, J.B.S.T.V.: Medicare fraud, waste and abuse. In: Business and Health Administration Association Annual Conference (2017)
6. Farzandipour, M., Sheikhtaheri, A., Sadoughi, F.: Effective factors on accuracy of principal diagnosis coding based on International Classification of Diseases, the 10th revision (ICD-10). Int. J. Inf. Manag. **30**(1), 78–84 (2010)
7. Kirlidog, M., Asuk, C.: A fraud detection approach with data mining in health insurance. Procedia - Soc. Behav. Sci. **62**, 989–994 (2012)
8. Fayyad, U., Piatetsky-Shapiro, G., Smyth, P.: From data mining to knowledge discovery in databases. AI Mag. **17**(3), 37 (1996)
9. Bhowmik, R.: Data mining techniques in fraud detection. J. Digit. Forensics Secur. Law JDFSL **3**(2), 35 (2008)
10. Julio, P.: Data Mining and Knowledge Discovery in Real Life Applications, pp. 15–20. Sciyo.com, SL (2009)
11. Rawte, V., Anuradha, G.: Fraud detection in health insurance using data mining techniques. In: 2015 International Conference on Communication, Information & Computing Technology (ICCICT), pp. 1–5. IEEE (2015)
12. Yang, W.S., Hwang, S.Y.: A process-mining framework for the detection of healthcare fraud and abuse. Expert Syst. Appl. **31**(1), 56–68 (2006)
13. Liou, F.M., Tang, Y.C., Chen, J.Y.: Detecting hospital fraud and claim abuse through diabetic outpatient services. Health Care Manag. Sci. **11**(4), 353–358 (2008)
14. Shin, H., Park, H., Lee, J., Jhee, W.C.: A scoring model to detect abusive billing patterns in health insurance claims. Expert Syst. Appl. **39**(8), 7441–7450 (2012)
15. Lu, F., Boritz, J.E., Covvey, D.: Adaptive fraud detection using Benford's law. In: Lamontagne, L., Marchand, M. (eds.) AI 2006. LNCS (LNAI), vol. 4013, pp. 347–358. Springer, Heidelberg (2006). https://doi.org/10.1007/11766247_30
16. Lin, C., Lin, C.M., Li, S.T., Kuo, S.C.: Intelligent physician segmentation and management based on KDD approach. Expert Syst. Appl. **34**(3), 1963–1973 (2008)
17. Sint, R., Stroka, S., Schaffert, S., Ferstl, R.: Combining unstructured, fully structured and semi-structured information in semantic wikis. In: SemWiki, vol. 464 (2009)
18. Han, J., Pei, J., Kamber, M.: Data Mining: Concepts and Techniques. Elsevier, Amsterdam (2011)
19. Shan, Y., Jeacocke, D., Murray, D.W., Sutinen, A.: Mining medical specialist billing patterns for health service management. In: Proceedings of the 7th Australasian Data Mining Conference, vol. 87, pp. 105–110. Australian Computer Society, Inc. (2008)

Ubiquitous Networks, Ubiquitous Sensors: Issues of Security, Reliability and Privacy in the Internet of Things

Michael Losavio[1]([⊠]) [iD], Adel Elmaghraby[1] [iD],
and Antonio Losavio[2] [iD]

[1] University of Louisville, Louisville, KY, USA
michael.losavio@louisville.edu
[2] University of Central Florida, Orlando, FL, USA

Abstract. The growth of ubiquitous networks moves ever more personal data into collectible and computational opportunities. This changes assumptions based on past latency and limits on data analysis and brings challenges to the reliability of data acquisition principles and practices and their proper use in societies. System engineers must consider outcomes and related regulation in the design and use of these systems. It also cautions us as to overreaching. We examine the general legal sphere within which ubiquitous networks and associated data exist, mapping some technological outcomes to legal consequences. We consider the impact and legal decisions regarding ubiquitous networks in the United States as an indicator of future direction and legal entanglements of these technological systems. In particular, we consider security and privacy principles that may regulate computational use through ubiquitous networks, and the competing interests/benefits/detriments in their use. This informs as to possible future regulation that may be needed or required and offer guidance with the growing data sphere and ubiquitous networking, and advises that the engineering of such systems should be flexible enough to accommodate new regulatory regimes as to deployment, access and use.

Keywords: Internet of Things · Ubiquitous networking · Privacy
Security

1 Introduction

Ubiquitous networking brings things together. The faster the network, the quicker the information is usable. These changes in the facts of data have led to changes in the law as to the impact of data and information on people and societies.

Matched with data sensing and computational analytics, this impacts privacy and security. This creates a need for network designs and principles for their protection. Massive personal, computational data sets may be used for a broad range of purposes, from illegal and criminal activity to state security investigations and personal self-protection. The design and use of these systems must be sensitive to risks and conflicts in light of what powerful computation using ubiquitous networks can reveal.

For example, a "personal credit information system" under development aims for nationwide implementation by 2020 to monitor citizen conduct. [1] It uses multiple

N. Boudriga et al. (Eds.): UNet 2018, LNCS 11277, pp. 331–343, 2018.
https://doi.org/10.1007/978-3-030-02849-7_30

data collections to examine a citizen's financial and social activities and to direct, via algorithmic analysis, the services they may access. The goal is to "build sincerity" into the social life of the citizens, promoting "moral" behavior.

Al-Ameen et al., examined the risks to medical devices linked to networks. Risks are due to the wide amount of personal information that is imbedded in networked medical devices, including location, medical status changes, and dependency on networks for functionality. These are exploited through active and passive attacks. These risks have led some countries to require enhanced security through encrypted data for such devices, including the United States, and the authors feel more laws are needed to address this [2].

Kargl et al., examined security, privacy and legal issues in health systems and noted the impact of various statutes, including the National Information Infrastructure Act of 1996 (US), the Electronic Communications Privacy Act (US) and its Sect. 18 USC 2511 (2) g (i). They note it is permissible to access an electronic communication system that is configured so that electronic communication is accessible to the general public. The authors proposed a model of such systems to discuss threats and attacks, address security requirements and give guidelines for security mechanisms. They note the especially contentious issues of privacy of medical data and the challenges presented through the ubiquitous deployment of home health monitoring systems and their accompanying networks [3].

Chen et al., proposed goals for security in sensor networks with implicit collaboration with lawmaking. Security compromises may be from both external and internal sources. Beyond integrating security goals, (confidentiality, availability, integrity, non-repudiation, authorization, freshness, forward secrecy and backward secrecy), security measures should also have a system of evaluation based on resilience, resistance, scalability, robustness, energy efficiency and assurance. This can form the criteria that informs how regulatory laws are created, which commensurately requires flexibility in network engineering to comply with those regulations as they evolve [4].

The privacy versus security debate may place privacy and security in opposing positions where legal regulation balances between them. Ethical concerns may also mediate. The opposition and balance of this model within a polity is seen in Fig. 1:

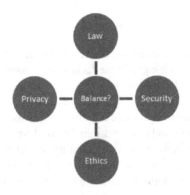

Fig. 1. Privacy balanced against security via law and ethics

But this may be a misleading dichotomy as privacy and security are not mutually antagonistic, but interrelated. Privacy is a key attribute that security protects. Privacy reflects legal rights and protections that are part of a system of information security and those objects for which protection is sought.

Security shielding personal rights of individuals must consider the role of states or others in providing security for the rights of others, individually and collectively. This is true whether for a statist model within which citizen rights are subordinate to state needs or that of functional constitutional states, such as the United States, that place significant limits on state action and assure foundational protections for individuals. Adapting regulation to this new evolving area of data for citizens everywhere will be a political and ethical challenge for everyone, from technologists to citizens to leaders.

The different nodes of data on the lives of people reflect risk elements, especially the Internet of Things and the Smart City. Figure 2 outlines centers of activity and services that generate key information about the lives that then can be exchanged, collected and analyzed:

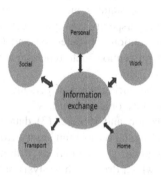

Fig. 2. Exchange nodes of activities and services

The power to profile the life of each and every person mandates an examination of the legal context for the regulation of conduct within the ubiquitously networked data sphere.

2 Design and Implementation for Security and Privacy in the Ubiquitous Networked World

Use of information derived from ubiquitous networking is subject to high-level mapping of technical functions to legal/social rules, algorithms in their own right. The design, implementation and use of technical systems are constrained by them. Failure in this may lead to severe sanctions, including financial penalties and the loss of liberty and reputation. Well-designed flexible systems compliant with clearly defined regulations may mitigate this.

Figure 3 reflects this perspective of integrated and over-lapping interests between different rights within the security shell of a polity:

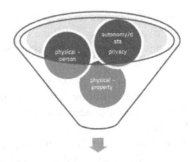

Fig. 3. Ordered personal life within a security shell

Confidentiality and data integrity are core components of privacy rights and information security. This consonance in values forms a foundation for regulatory design. Security is the shell within which the rights and interests of people are protected, including those within the "right" of privacy, whether under common-law of Anglo-American jurisdictions or statutes and regulations of world legal systems. Stallings [5] submits a realistic perspective on cyber security requires a focus on three principal subdomains: (1) prevention, (2) detection and (3) recovery. These map to public security principles of prevention, deterrence and incapacitation, investigation and arrest, and restoration to victims.

Civil law restrictions on the infringement of personal autonomy may be based on constitutional provisions, statutes or common-law practices. General foci for data regulation are (1) data collection and storage, (2) data analytics and analysis, and (3) data use and disclosure. Regulation to limit injury from these systems may limit these activities and define granular sub-regulations within them. But the use of data analytics and the algorithms which drive such analysis has generally not been deeply scrutinized except where outputs produce clearly discriminatory results which may conflict with other regulations.

There are concerns about the inherent dangers of discriminatory programming, whether intentional or unintentional, that may produce inappropriate output. This is connected to the final rendition and representation of the data analysis. From this flows the issue of who uses that analysis, how they use it or how they might disclose it to others along with any underlying data associated with it.

The United States does not have a general, comprehensive statutory scheme for the protection of privacy and security, so common law principles form a floor of protection, supplemented by domain specific statutes. The protected interests relate to the appropriation of a person's identity, improper publicity over or intrusion into private affairs, and misrepresentation relating to a person's identity and autonomy. [6] These legal protections are supplemented by statutes for selected areas, including healthcare, finance and education and for breach notification. These map from the technology to the injuries caused, as seen in Table 1:

Table 1. Technical operations leading to privacy violations

Sensed and networked data	→	Improper publicity
Analytics against the networked and collected data	→	Intrusion into private affairs
Incomplete data, network gaps and flawed analytics	→	Mis-inference

Data collected across ubiquitous networks can reveal intensely private facts that should remain private. Revelation from such data might give improper and illegal publicity to private facts and identity. Error-ridden algorithms and partial data may lead to mis-inference and error in conclusions. These may wrongly injure the related data subjects. This leads to basic legal regulation and protection of the data corpus of a citizen, supplemented by statutory protections, of which the most powerful are those incorporated into the constitutional law of the country.

Yet many were formulated under a regime where physical intrusion was the prevalent state invasion of the privacy of the citizen. Both constitutional case law and statutory law have evolved to deal with invasions due to data interception, but is only now beginning to address how the analytics of crowd-sensed data sphere may bypass all of these protections yet still reveal that which should be protected.

Regulation of privacy invasions via statute reflect this under the European Union, structured in reference to EU and national laws relating to security and police power. The protections of individuals and their rights of privacy, person and autonomy in the United States are not absolute but also weighed against the security and police power of the nation.

The General Data Protection Regulation (GDPR) [7] more comprehensively provides data protection for those within the European Union. It provides control over personal data, heightening recognition of personal autonomy within the growing data world. It applies to all that collect and process data on citizens of the European Union, regardless of location. Rights of data subjects include the right to access to collected data and information on its processing, purposes, sharing and acquisition. Obligations of those collecting and transmitting data include extensive security systems to protect the data and limit its processing to specific purposes. This may include local encryption of data and key control within the network.

In all of these areas of the ubiquitously networked data sphere presents another, significant contribution to the data corpus on a living person that enable analytical revelation that may injure the data subject. Properly engineered systems and practices can limit and avoid unnecessary injuries to the innocent.

3 Case-Based Analysis: Legal Analysis and Ubiquitous Networks

Case-based judicial analysis in the United States of ubiquitous networks begins in 1977 with discussion of how legal standards for professional services (medicine) moved from local standards ("locality rule") to national standards due to the impact of ubiquitous national communication networks. [8] This reasoning, adopted by other courts in the United States, shows the impact on the law and its development of ubiquitous data networks. That impact will be seen in other domains as use of ubiquitous networks engenders legal conflicts over that use.

Case analysis of US judicial rulings relating to ubiquitous networking shows increasing concern with their use and their impact. From sporadic legal discussion of legal conflicts relating to networks, issues with ubiquitous networks now appear regularly. The subject matter relating to the ubiquitous networks has expanded from beneficial growth and access to information to regulatory and technical concerns, included monopoly effects. Subject matter content issues expand to use, IP attribution, financial and banking services, and the near-impossibility of limiting Internet access by online criminal offenders.

Figure 4 and Table 2 detail the frequency and expansion of juridical analysis of ubiquitous networks over 40 years in the United States, noting the increasing frequency of juridical reference to issues of ubiquitous networks:

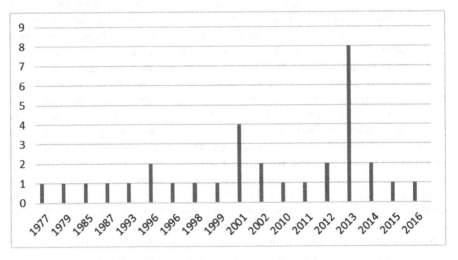

Fig. 4. Case discussion frequency distribution for "ubiquitous networks"

The outlier count for year 2013 is due to a consolidation of multiple copyright infringement cases where IP attribution was challenged due to ubiquity of home wireless networks. That for year 2001 reflects legal issues for new competitive network access. Though an outlier, it shows the impact of ubiquitous networks used to expand alleged misconduct such as copyright infringement.

Review of jurisdictional and context issues for this time span show the growth in frequency and subject matter diversity in the impact of ubiquitous networks, such as where electronic financial networks create "... An endless lattice of financial and other services that will eventually be part of the information superhighway." The growth of ubiquitous home wireless networks makes attribution strictly via the IP address more difficult; this has required additional information to justify legal claims regarding use of

Table 2. Case discussion-ubiquitous networks

Year	Court	Discussion relating to ubiquitous networks
1977	Federal appellate	Impact of ubiquitous national communication networks on the locality rule
1979	State appellate	Impact of ubiquitous national communication networks on the locality rule
1985	State appellate	Impact of ubiquitous national communication networks on the locality rule
1987	Federal trial	Comment on ubiquity of telephone local exchange networks
1993	State appellate	Impact of ubiquitous national communication networks on licensing standards
1996	Federal appellate	Impact of ubiquitous financial network and monopoly power
1996	Federal trial	Comment on ubiquity of small and local area networks
1998	Federal trial	Regulatory encouragement of ubiquitous telephone networks
1999	Federal trial	Comment on high cost of duplicating ubiquitous local exchange networks
2001	Federal trial	Comment on anticompetitive conduct through monopoly control of ubiquitous telecommunications network
2001	State appellate	Comment on directory services needed for ubiquitous telecommunications networks to function
2001	Federal trial	Monopoly power in ubiquitous telecommunications networks
2001	Federal appellate	Discussion of technical needs in ubiquitous satellite networks
2002	Federal trial	Law relating to access to networks
2002	State trial	Balancing of local powers with state powers to regulate deployment of ubiquitous telecommunications networks
2010	Federal trial	Value of a strategic, operational ubiquitous network
2011	Federal trial	Value of electronic ubiquitous financial network
2012	Federal appellate	Value and portals to electronic ubiquitous financial network
2012	Federal trial	Impact of ubiquitous wireless home networks on IP attribution
2013	Federal trial	Comment on provision of ubiquitous networking services
2013	Federal appellate	Patent issue relating to ubiquitous banking networks
2013	Federal trial	Debit card networks and monopoly
2013	Federal trial	59 defendants-impact of ubiquitous home wireless networks on IP attribution and increase in risk of false positives via BitTorrent)
2013	Related above	194 defendants; 152 defendants; 104 defendants; 18 defendants
2013	Federal trial	Need for expert on antitrust market definitions where there are ubiquitous wired networks
2014	As above 2013 copyright cases	Dismissal of infringement claims for failure of attribution beyond IPs for ubiquitous networks
2014	As above	194 defendants-dismissal as above
2015	State appellate	Comment on social network Facebook's ubiquity
2016	Federal trial	Bail denied - "wireless networks are ubiquitous and Internet-capable devices are easy to obtain." Internet access remains a risk

the BitTorrent peer-to-peer network, a significant change from earlier practice. This is seen in Table 2, listing by year the increase in frequency of discussions relating to ubiquitous networks and the expansion in the subject matter of those discussions relating to such networks:

The *facts* of ubiquitous networks continue to impact legal principles in a wide variety of social domains, from medicine to crime. Their impact on privacy and security must be anticipated and engineered in preparation for future regulation.

4 Ubiquitous Networks, Police Power, Security, Privacy

4.1 Quantitative/Qualitative Legal Data and Ubiquitous Networks

The progression in judicial decisions relating to ubiquitous networks shows greater and greater scrutiny of the impact of those networks at the citizen level. The 2012/2013 cases show the impact of ubiquitous networks on facilitating alleged consumer-level misconduct. The 2016 Federal Trial Court decision denying bail due to the ubiquity of wireless networks and the accompanying risk to public security of an Internet offender using them confronts the security risks of ubiquitous networking and their impact on the law. [9] This demonstrates the expansion of the potential of ubiquitous networks for facilitating misconduct. The growth in such misconduct can motivate legal responses to limit such activity, such as legislative efforts in the United States to limit or repeal immunity for online service providers for user posted conduct.

Yet ubiquitous networking and associated data systems are widely used by police in pursuit of public security. In 2011, 88% of respondent US police departments used personal data tools, primarily social media, for a variety of purposes. [10] The exercise of the police power of the state in such a densely networked data space raises issues as to data collection, transmission and analysis for purposes ranging from investigation to police-citizen relations. [11] Rapid release of information on suspects via online networks enabled rapid identification, whether for terrorism or street crime, but may produce false positives. [12–15] Police have begun training and policy development on the use of evidence from data systems, including social media and local sensing networks. [16, 17] This shows the benefits for public security from ubiquitous networking and the need to continue their expansion and use.

The benefits of ubiquitous networking, the Internet of Things, the Smart City and other data paradigms clearly come with risks, as these show. The ability to exchange and develop information can degrade public security through criminal activity, ranging from burglary of dwellings whose occupants are elsewhere to physical violence against those identified as vulnerable. It is vital that systems be in place for the protection misuse of the systems, beginning with their very engineering and continuing through to oversight investigation their proper use.

4.2 Particular Case-Based Analysis of Judicial Decisions

Beyond this quantitative and qualitative data there is case-based analysis of possible impacts from use of geospatial locational, time and other data show the need for a structured, ethical model for implementation and use. [18] Key geospatial and time information may guide someone, tell friends where to meet or give one's timeline to others. The "when" and "where" of physical and cyber interactions are powerful data for analytical purposes. Computational geospatial and temporal analysis may direct public safety resources with greater efficiency and effectiveness. The growth of more and newer data classes that can be aggregated for analysis give more precise and granular modeling and prediction of behavior, good and bad.

This creates significant challenges in law, ethics and public policy as the data from people's lives grows in volume, variety, velocity and veracity. [19] These challenges may impact the use of geospatial analytics, both as to their direct use in law enforcement and collateral obligations for authentication, validation and protection of this data. With more modeling and analysis, the predictive ability and behavioral inferences have increased, posing different legal and privacy concerns.

The US Supreme Court justices in *United States v. Jones* [20] addressed the impact on data privacy and security from new ways of computational data collection, analysis and use. One judge's concern was the implication of this system of inexpensive GIS for people could "alter the relationship between citizen and government in a way that is inimical to democratic society." The potential for that lies in the power of GPS data monitoring, aggregation and analysis that are fundamental to GIS crime analysis to detail the activities of a person's life. Another listed the instrumented devices contributing data to the geospatial corpus: CCTV, automated tolling systems, automobile automatic notifications systems, cellular telephones and other wireless devices. He suggested that long-term monitoring would be an illegal invasion of a citizen's reasonable expectation of privacy. The Supreme Court in *Riley v. California* expanded privacy protections to mobile data devices due to their unprecedented ability to store information. [21] Lower federal courts have found themselves in conflict over the propriety of forced decryption of locally stored data.

The US Supreme Court is currently reviewing whether data transmitted and stored through extraterritorial transnational networks can be ordered produced by any government in which the custodian has a legal presence. [22] This will resolve a conflict between federal appellate courts where one found such an order was improper but another found it to be so.

Paralleling the evolution of a legal regime for information misconduct by the state is that for injury cause by private parties. While markets have punished commercial organizations for failure to adequately protect their data, civil liability for such failures is increasingly a subject of legal sanctions from both state and private actions.

We may anticipate judicial regulation from an analysis of risk nodes mapped to privacy and security attributes. These may indicate the need for engineering design flexibility and legal regulation. The Smart City paradigm suggested by IBM of instrumented, interconnectedness and intelligent (computable) [23] offers one way to define risks and remediation. Table 3 presents another aspect of matching/mapping risk nodes to vulnerabilities and their technical results:

Ubiquitous sensors on the network risk intrusion into personal affairs in unprecedented and unanticipated ways, damaging personal autonomy and compromising security. Keyed to powerful analytics even more inferential revelations may result. Mis-inferences causing injuries may result from flawed analytical algorithms. This turmoil in US courts is a harbinger of problems and issues for the future of ubiquitous data systems. If we look at the consequences of injury from various risk nodes within ubiquitous networking, it is only a matter of time before these must face legal reckoning.

Table 3. Risk nodes mapped to privacy and security

Risk Node	Privacy	Security
Ubiquitous sensors	Intrusion into personal space, personal affairs	Hijacked/spoofed instrumentation, or erroneous data
Ubiquitous networking	Transfer beyond areas of personal control	Interception, masquerade, hostile injection
Powerful analytics	Revelation, direct and inferential of private facts, mis-inference	Mis-inference, false negatives, false positives, political backlash

For ubiquitous networks this may manifest in regulations of input into the network, network transmission controls and output from the network. Under the EU GDPR transmission across borders and to entities may be limited, prohibited or subject to the control of state data regulators or by the data subject herself.

The US Supreme Court in *Jones* detailed significant concerns with how this new huge data space, connected everywhere will affect fundamental civil values. The data rich world of ubiquitous networking must contend with the topology of bringing a motivated offender into immediate proximity to a vulnerable target victim, without the protection of any kind of guardian as a shield. The sexual exploitation of children via social media has been an ongoing scourge that has taken new twists. The suicides of four adult British men were attributed by Britain's National Crime Agency to "sextortion" from online conduct in a growing criminal phenomenon. [24] The use of the power of ubiquitous networks will not be allowed to freely injure other people, as detailed in Table 3. Regulation will require limitations of the technology.

Security needs must be balanced against the regulation of systems built upon these ubiquitous networks and data systems. Yet it is vital that such regulation does not produce unintended consequences through the unexamined use of these systems. Security and privacy are so intertwined that limitations on one it may lead to damage to the other, intended or not.

Access, use and deployment regulation relating to data use extend to the use of ubiquitous networks. With this common core of concern as to rights of privacy and autonomy, technical systems must attend to regulatory mandates and be structured to fit them in order to avoid sanctions. Table 4 demonstrates how high-level systems can be mapped to particular regulatory features that, in turn, protect particular rights in privacy and personal autonomy; system engineering must be able to accommodate such regulation quickly and inexpensively:

Table 4. Technical operations mapped to privacy-protecting regulations

Systems	Regulatory controls	Injuries mitigated
Sensed and networked data →	Use limitations and filters, controls over transmission →	Improper publicity
Analytics against the networked and → collected data	Data limits, bi-directional network limits, use limits. →	Intrusion into private affairs
Incomplete data, network gaps and → flawed analytics	Assurance criteria for data, vetted algorithms →	Mis-Inference

These can do a great deal of damage to people. It can break up social relations between people and, rather than engendering trust, destroy it. This damages the very opportunities these data systems offer for bringing people together for common cause and common good.

The commensurate regulatory controls may mitigate those risks. Controls on the networks themselves can provide content filtering and control to limit misuse; indeed, they may provide a key protective component at nodes to block propagation of hostile actions at user in points. In this manner systems for providing security and privacy using the network itself reflect real-world public security solutions to limiting misconduct. They may be most effective means for the centralized component of information security; nations may implement backbone filtering and monitoring to alert end-users to hostile payloads and anomalous activity that may indicate attacks against the security and privacy of systems. The engineering must be able to respond and not be locked into a single paradigm or protocol that cannot be changed.

Use limitations may be the most malleable to soft solutions, where they are deemed insufficient in mitigating the risk of misuse. As in the *Fitzhugh* pretrial release denial, they may lead to access and deployment limitations. These, in turn, may place a greater burden on system designers, vendors and service providers to comply. But failure to comply creates both potential criminal liability for violation of statutory limits and civil liability for the injuries done in the failure of the systems to protect others from system misuse on the network. The legal uncertainties and turmoil seen in digital investigations can spill over into networked systems as governments may seek to require compliance with surveillance and data recovery operations to prevent misconduct and discovery and prove such misconduct [25, 26].

5   Conclusion

Ubiquitous networks have had an impact on the law for decades, changing the facts relating to access to information as to increase accountability for the use of that information. Extrapolating from case frequency and case decisions relating to computational systems generally and ubiquitous networks in particular, we predict potential liability for the use of ubiquitous networks to broadly create injuries and risk of injuries to others. For ubiquitous networks this may manifest in regulations of input into the network, network transmission controls and output filtering from the network.

Ubiquitous networks increasingly support the threat of misconduct, including invasion of privacy and the personal autonomy of individuals, their families and communities as to disrupt traditional relations. A profiling bonanza for law enforcement or merchants may become a person's personal nightmare. The increasing legal struggles by courts and legislatures to define rights and obligations in the outcomes for the use and deployment of ubiquitous networks portend associated obligations by system designers and operators. The engineering of these systems must anticipate these changes and be flexible enough to accommodate them. These privacy and security issues will only become more and more of a challenge for a democratic polity trying to deal with public security threats both internal and external. We must be prepared to meet them.

Acknowledgments. The authors thank the National Institute of Justice (US) and the International Association for Crime Analysts for the opportunity to develop these ideas.

References

1. Chin, J, Wong, G.: China's new tool: a social credit score. Wall Str. J. (US) 1 (2016)
2. Al Ameen, M., Liu, J., Kwak, K.: Security and privacy issues in wireless sensor networks for healthcare applications. J. Med. Syst. **36**(1), 93–101 (2012)
3. Kargl, F., Lawrence, E., Fischer, M., Lim, Y.Y.: Security, privacy and legal issues in pervasive ehealth monitoring systems. In: 2008 7th International Conference on Mobile Business. ICMB 2008, pp. 296–304. IEEE, July 2008
4. Chen, X., Makki, K., Yen, K., Pissinou, N.: Sensor network security: a survey. IEEE Commun. Surv. Tutor. **11**(2), 52–73 (2009)
5. Stallings, W., Brown, L.: Computer Security: Principles and Practice, 3rd edn. Pearson Publishing, Upper Saddle River (2008)
6. Restatement (Second) of Torts, (Am. Law Inst. 1965) (US)
7. General Data Privacy Regulation (EU) 2016/679 Regulation (EU) 2016/679 of the European Parliament and of the Council of 27 April 2016 on the protection of the natural persons with regard to the processing of personal data and on the free movement of such data, and repealing Directive 95/46/EC (Gen. Data Protection Regulation), Official Journal of the European Union, vol. L119, pp. 1–88, 4 May 2016
8. Robbins v. Footer, 553 F.2d 123 (DC Cir. 1977)
9. United States v. Fitzhugh, 2016 U.S. Dist. LEXIS 122953 (USDC ED MI)
10. International Association of Chiefs of Police: 2011 Survey of Law Enforcement's Use of Social Media Tools (2011)
11. Losavio, J., Losavio, M.: Prosecution and social media. In: Chapter 11. Higgins and Marcum (eds.) Social Networking as a Criminal Enterprise (2014)
12. CBS News: Social media and the search for the Boston bombing suspects, 20 April 2013
13. Bensinger, K., Chang, A.: Boston bombings: social media spirals out of control. Los Angeles Times, 20 April 2013
14. Dyer, J.: Social media and the Boston bombings. BBC Radio, 27 April 2013
15. NBC Connecticut: Police use Facebook to ID waterford robbery suspects, 2 January 2013

16. Stuart, R.: Social media: establishing criteria for law enforcement use. FBI Law Enforcement: Bulletin, February 2013
17. United States Department of Justice Global Justice Information Sharing Initiative Federal Advisory Committee. https://www.it.ojp.gov/global. Accessed 8 Apr 2018
18. Agnar, A., Enric, P.: Case-based reasoning: foundational issues, methodological variations, and system approaches. Artif. Intell. Commun. 7(1), 39–52 (1994)
19. IBM: Info graphic: the four V's of big data. http://www.ibmbigdatahub.com/infographic/four-vs-big-data. Accessed 8 Apr 2018
20. United States v. Jones 132 S. Ct. 945 (2012)
21. Riley v. California, 134 S.Ct. 2473 (US) (2014)
22. United States, Petitioner v. Microsoft Corporation, Case number 17-2, on writ of certiorari to the United States Court of Appeals for the Second Circuit, Supreme Court of the United States
23. IBM: IBM builds a smarter planet. https://www.ibm.com/smarterplanet/us/en/. Accessed 8 Apr 2018
24. Burillo, D.: Four suicides linked to webcam "sextortion" and blackmail. The Descrier, 30 November 2016
25. Losavio, M., Chow, K.P., Koltay, A., James, J.: The internet of things and the smart city: legal challenges with digital forensics, privacy and information security. Secur. Priv. (2018). https://doi.org/10.1002/spy2.23
26. Elmaghraby, A., Losavio, M.: Cyber security challenges in smart cities: safety, security and privacy. J. Adv. Res. 5(4), 491–497 (2014)

Special Session on Wireless Networking, Applications and Enabling Technologies for Unmanned Aerial Vehicles

Generating Dubins Path for Fixed Wing UAVs in Search Missions

Adiel Ismail$^{(\boxtimes)}$, Emmanuel Tuyishimire, and Antoine Bagula

University of the Western Cape, Bellville, South Africa
aismail@uwc.ac.za

Abstract. Finding the shortest path from source to target is key to efficient search missions of unmanned aerial vehicles (UAVs). For fixed wing UAVs, Dubins curves can be used to find the shortest path. For successive visits to targets during a single mission, the direction of flight of the UAV at each target is not of any significance. In such cases Dubins curves can be simplified to two instead of three constituent components. This paper proposes an algorithm derived using elementary geometry that generates Dubins curves for multiple target search missions. The algorithm proposed is tested and results reported for a search and rescue mission indicate that the path generator is fairly robust.

Keywords: Dubins curves · Multi UAVs · Task allocation
Simultaneous prosecution

1 Introduction

Unmanned aerial vehicles are often used for target search, widely used in missions that involve rescue [1,2], monitoring [3] or destruction [4,5]. UAVs can also be used to complement a ground sensor network in data collection missions where the sensor readings are collected and ferried to specified delivery points to provide data muling services in applications such as smart parking [6,7], drought mitigation [8] and many other applications. In such missions, the UAV has to visit several targets in succession before returning to the UAV base. As suggested in [9], the ground sensor network may be organized into a service-aware clustered topology where these targets play the role of collection points for the readings while the UAV base plays the role of gateway where the sensor readings are stored, analyzed and processed. Since a UAV's battery life limits the time spent on a mission, the time saved by traversing a minimal path length to a target will enable a UAV to visit potentially more targets during a mission. It is therefore critical to minimise the path length to targets to improve efficiency in UAV search missions.

Dubins in [10] presented a solution for the shortest path between two positions given a car's direction or heading at both positions. His solutions consist of all combinations of arcs of minimal turning radius of the car and a straight line segment joining the two arcs. The shortest path solution provided by Reeds

© Springer Nature Switzerland AG 2018
N. Boudriga et al. (Eds.): UNet 2018, LNCS 11277, pp. 347–358, 2018.
https://doi.org/10.1007/978-3-030-02849-7_31

and Shepp [11] included both, forward and backward movement of the vehicle. Svestka *et al.* [12] constructed a probabilistic road map of all feasible paths between source and target, the path with lowest cost was then selected as a solution. Nelson [13] replaced circular arc segments with polar polynomials and used cartesian-polynomials for lane change maneuvres for path planning of mobile robots. Komoriya and Tanie [14] used B-spline curves that passed through specified points in their path planning solution.

In [15] a swarm of UAVs with airborne sensors cooperate in path planning by using Dubins curves in conjunction with splinegons, which are generalizations of polygons with sides of constant curvature, to detect the boundaries of contaminant clouds in order to model and track its movement. A path generator is proposed in [16] that finds the shortest path for a fixed wing UAV from its current position and direction of flight to a new position and direction. The generated path was traversed using their Lyapunov path-following approach. In [17] a path planning approach for mobile robots is modeled as an optimisation problem with the objective of achieving a smooth path linking several waypoints by using 5-th order Bézier curves. Dubins curves have been used in fixed wing UAVs in [19–24].

This paper presents an algorithm that generates a Dubins path that consists of only two components, i.e. an arc and a straight line for a UAV that visits a number of targets in succession during a mission.

The Dubins curves are described and computed in Sect. 2. The problem is described in Sect. 3. Experiments are described and results reported in Sect. 4. The paper is concluded in Sect. 5.

2   Calculating Dubins Longest Path

Dubins curves can be used to calculate the shortest path to a target for a fixed wing UAV. A Dubins curve consists of all combinations of arcs of minimal turning radius and a straight line segment that joins the two arcs. Six possible configurations were considered, namely LSL, LSR, RSL, RSR, RLR, LRL, where L and R represent a left and right turn, respectively and S a straight line segment. In many search missions, fixed wing UAVs require only to fly a circular path followed by a straight line path to reach a target. No second arc is required. Hence, the original Dubins curves that consist of three components can be reduced to a curve with two components, in which case only two possible cases need to be considered, i.e. LS and RS.

Given a drone's current position and a target, two types of Dubins paths can be traversed to reach the target, i.e. Dubins shortest path (DSP) and Dubins longest path (DLP), denoted by DSP and DLP, respectively in the diagrams in Fig. 1a. A target may lie either to the left or to the right of the straight line path of a UAV. In the case of DSP, the UAV performs a turn in the same direction as the direction of the target relative to the UAVs straight line path of flight. In the case of DLP, the UAV turns in the opposite direction of the direction of the target relative to a UAVs position.

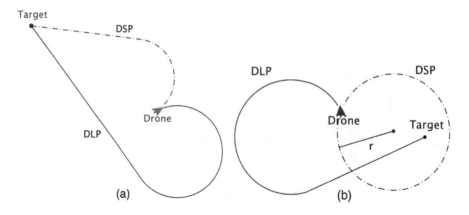

Fig. 1. Dubins shortest and longest paths

When the distance between the UAV and the target is smaller than the minimum turning radius of the UAV, then the target cannot be reached using Dubins shortest path as shown in Fig. 1b. With Dubins longest path, this problem does not exist.

To calculate the distance of Dubins longest path, the following two cases are considered,

1. the target lies to the right of the straight line path of the UAV
2. the target lies to the left of the straight line path of the UAV

In case (1), the UAV has to turn left or counterclockwise, while in case (2) the UAV has to turn right or clockwise to reach the target.

An approach to calculate the Dubins longest path is proposed next. If the UAV's initial position, (x_i, y_i), the angle of flight of the UAV, α, the target's position (x_t, y_t) and the minimum turning radius of the UAV, r_{min}, are provided, then the distance of the circular path and the straight line path of Dubins longest path can be calculated based on; (1) the centre of the circular path of the UAV, (2) the exit point of the UAV from the circular path and (3) the central angle traversed by the UAV while turning.

The values referred to above are calculated in the next three subsections.

2.1 Calculating the Coordinates of the Centre of the Circle

Based on the diagrams in Fig. 2 the centre of the circle is calculated below.

$$x_c = x_i - s \cdot r \cdot \sin \alpha \tag{1}$$
$$y_c = y_i + s \cdot r \cdot \cos \alpha \tag{2}$$

where $s = 1$ if the target lies to the right of the straight line path of the UAV, else if the target lies to the left of the straight line path of the UAV then $s = -1$.

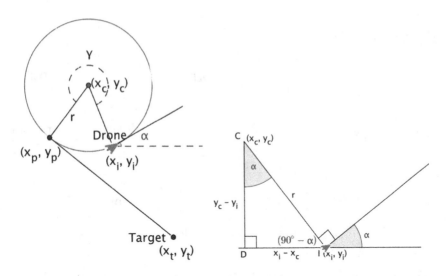

Fig. 2. Calculating the centre of the circle

2.2 Calculating the UAVs Exit Point on the Arc

In Fig. 3, line L_3 is perpendicular to line L_2, m_3 and m_2 are the gradients of lines L_3 and L_2, respectively. The point of tangency or the exit point of the UAV from the circular path is the intersection of lines L_2 and L_3 and is calculated as,

$$(x_p, y_p) = \left(\frac{y_c - m_3 \cdot x_c - c_2}{m_2 - m_3}, m_2 \cdot x_p + c_2\right) \tag{3}$$

2.3 Calculating the Angle Traversed by the UAV While Turning

If L_0 denotes the line that joins the UAVs initial position, (x_i, y_i), with the centre of the circle, (x_c, y_c), and L_3, the line that joins the exit position of the UAV on the arc, (x_p, y_p), with the centre of the circle, then the angle traversed by the UAV is the angle measured from line L_0 to line L_3 in the same direction as that of the UAVs circular direction of flight. In Fig. 4, α_0 and α_3 denote the angles formed between the x-axis and lines L_0 and L_3, respectively. The size of the angle traversed by the UAV for the circular path is the angle measured from L_0 to L_3 as shown in the diagrams in Figs. 4 and 5.

The central angle is calculated as indicated in Algorithm 1.

Finally, the distance of the Dubins longest path, d, is the distance measured along the arc from the UAVs initial position to the exit point on the circular path, plus the distance of the straight line path from the exit point to the target's position, i.e.

$$d = \omega \cdot r_{min} + \sqrt{(x_t - x_p)^2 + (y_t - y_p)^2} \tag{4}$$

This concludes the discussion on the calculation of Dubins longest path based on elementary geometry.

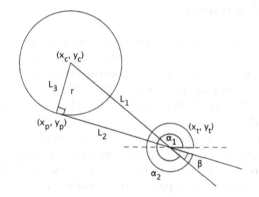

Fig. 3. Target lies to the right of the UAVs straight line path

Fig. 4. UAV flies counterclockwise

Fig. 5. UAV flies clockwise

Algorithm 1. Calculating central angle, ω

---

if (UAV turns left) **then**
    if ($\alpha_3 > \alpha_0$) **then**
        $\omega \leftarrow \alpha_3 - \alpha_0$
    else
        $\omega \leftarrow 360° + (\alpha_3 - \alpha_0)$
    end if
else
    if (UAV turns right) **then**
        if ($\alpha_0 > \alpha_3$) **then**
            $\omega \leftarrow \alpha_0 - \alpha_3$
        else
            $\omega \leftarrow 360° + (\alpha_0 - \alpha_3)$
        end if
    else
        $\omega \leftarrow 0°$
    end if
end if

---

3   Problem Statement

A number of fixed wing UAVs are required to search and prosecute a number of targets. Each target requires a specific number of different types of resources to be prosecuted completely, while each UAV carries the same type of resources as that of the target but often in different quantities. The positions of the targets are not known to the UAVs. The UAVs fly in search of the targets and can only detect a target once the distance to the target from the UAV is equal or less than the UAVs sensor range. All UAVs can communicate with each other. Once a target is detected a single member coalition or multiple member coalition can potentially be formed to prosecute the target using Dubins longest path. After prosecuting a target, the UAVs that formed part of the coalition are released and continue to search for the remaining targets and may participate in further coalitions if they have any resources remaining. The objective of coalition formation is to complete a mission in minimum time, by forming a coalition for each target that (a) reaches its target in minimum time, (b) uses a minimum number of UAVs and (c) prosecutes the target simultaneously for effective prosecution.

Instead of initiating a mission that may not end in success, one can establish if the combined resources of all UAVs in a mission are adequate to prosecute all targets successfully before commencing a mission. This was the case for the data used in the experiments reported in this paper.

If the targets are dynamic and moving all the time one could understand the need for searching for its positions. But if the targets are fixed and static then the actual positions of the targets can be communicated to the UAVs at the start of the mission. This is a more realistic representation of problems that involve targets at fixed positions. The Polynomial Time Coalition Formation Algorithm (PTCFA) solution proposed by Manathara et al. in [18] where targets are searched for, can easily be remodeled as a solution where the positions of the targets are known to the UAVs at the start of the execution of the algorithm by ensuring that the sensor range is large enough to cover the entire fly zone. Fitting the UAVs with sensors with sensor range 1500 m will ensure that the entire square search area with each side 1000 m is covered and that all targets are detected by the UAVs sensors when the coalition formation algorithm is executed.

Coalition formation incorporating Dubins paths is applied to PTCFA, proposed by Manathara et al. [18]. In the algorithm it is assumed that all UAVs fly at a constant speed and at a constant altitude. A short description of the PTCFA algorithm appears below.

PTCFA
The PTCFA consists of two parts. In the first part each UAV is in search of a target and is equipped with a sensor with limited range capability. As soon as a target is detected, its position and resource requirements are communicated to all UAVs. The UAV that detects the target is referred to as the coalition leader. All UAVs that are not in a coalition and that contain any of the resources required by the target calculate their estimated time of arrival (ETA) or cost and

communicates this information together with the amount of resources on board the UAV to the coalition leader. The coalition leader sorts all the ETAs received into ascending order. The coalition leader starts by adding the UAV closest to the target to the potential coalition and accumulates its resources. If the accumulated resources do not meet the target's resource requirements then the next closest UAV is also included in the coalition and its resources accumulated too. This process of adding a UAV with the next smallest ETA to the potential coalition continues until the resources accrued satisfy the resource requirements of the target. The second part of PTCFA is then executed. The coalition leader sorts the ETAs of the UAVs in the coalition again in ascending order. Again starting with the UAV closest to the target, the coalition leader removes the resources of this UAV from the resources accumulated. If the remaining accumulated resources after removal still satisfy the target's resource requirements then the UAV under consideration is removed from the potential coalition, otherwise its resources are added back to the accumulated resources. The UAV removed is redundant since its resources are not required for prosecution. The removal from the coalition of the next closest UAV is then considered. This process ends after all UAVs in the coalition have been considered for removal. The coalition leader then informs all remaining coalition members of, (a) their inclusion in the coalition and (b) the ETA of the UAV furthest from the target. Coalition members then calculate a revised radii that increase their ETAs at the target to match the ETA of the UAV furthest from the target.

4   Experiments and Results

For the PTCFA algorithm, 100 simulations were performed on a square search area with sides of length 1000 m. To restrict the UAVs to the search area and to allow sufficient space for turning around within the search area, a strip of width 100 m around the boundary of the search area was deemed out of place for placing the targets. Targets were randomly placed at positions within the 800 m × 800 m area inside the search area. The UAVs were restricted to fly inside this smaller area. The UAVs were also initially placed at random positions inside the fly zone with an angle of direction of flight generated randomly. All UAVs had a minimum turning radius of 50 m. A UAV that flies outside the fly zone will immediately turn around and can comfortably return inside the 100 m strip without leaving the search space. All UAVs were flying at a constant speed of 10 m/s. It is assumed that all UAVs fly at the same constant speed at the same altitude during the entire mission.

The resource quantity for each target was generated as a random integer value in the range 0 to 3. The resources for the UAVs were randomly generated with values ranging from 0 to the (number-of-targets/2) and stored only if, for each type of resource, the total sum of quantities of the resources of all UAVs was equal to or greater than the total sum of quantities of the specific resource of all the targets. This was done to ensure that all missions would lead to the successful prosecution of all targets.

4.1 Effect of Increased Sensor Range

If the positions of the targets are not known to the UAVs then the UAVs must first spend time to search and find a target before they can form a coalition. A large sensor range that covers the entire search area enables a UAV to detect the positions of all the targets immediately at the start of the mission.

In the first set of experiments the sensor range of the UAVs was gradually increased from 100 m to 1100 m in increments of 200 m. Noting that targets are placed inside a square with each side 800 m long. A sensor range of 1100 m effectively covers a total distance of 2×radius (=2200 m) which is the diameter of the circle of the area covered by a sensor with sensor range 1100 m. A distance of 1100 m should cover almost the full distance of 1131 m between any two corners positioned diagonally opposite each other in the fly zone. A sensor range of 1100 m should enable the sensor of a UAV to detect almost all the targets. A hundred simulations were performed with each sensor range value. Results are reported in Figs. 6, 7 and 8.

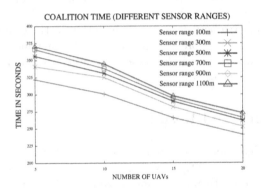

Fig. 6. Coalition times for various sensor ranges

Plots in Fig. 6 indicate that coalition time increases with an increase in sensor range. Mission time consists of time spent on searching for the targets plus time spent on executing coalitions. During execution of a coalition the UAVs traverse the Dubins longest paths to reach the target, with each radii of the participating UAVs increased to ensure that the path lengths of all UAVs are equal for simultaneous arrival at the target. With a smaller sensor range, targets are only detected once they are within this smaller sensor range of a UAV. With a larger sensor range, less time is spent and wasted on searching for targets and coalitions are formed earlier which lead to reduced mission times. Plots in Fig. 7 confirm that mission time also decreases with an increase in sensor range and that mission time decreases with an increase in the number of UAVs.

Simulation time decreases with an increase in sensor range as reflected in Fig. 8. A sensor range of 500 m forms a circle with corresponding diameter of 1000 m which covers a large part of the square fly zone. Plots in Fig. 8 indicate

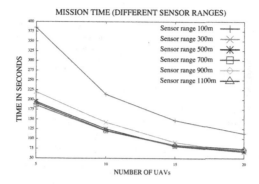

Fig. 7. Mission time for various sensor ranges

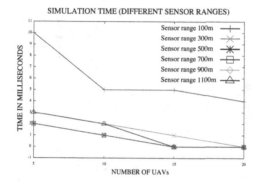

Fig. 8. Simulation time for various sensor ranges

that sensor ranges 500 m and 700 m produce identical simulation times which on face value implies that PTCFA did not benefit at all from the larger sensor range. However, Fig. 7 confirms that sensor range 700 m produced smaller mission times than sensor range 500 m. Similar simulation times are reported also for sensor ranges 500 m, 700 m and 900 m in the case of 15 and 20 UAVs.

4.2 Effect of Increased Number of Types of Resources

Another set of experiments was conducted to investigate the effect of an increased number of types of resources on the mission, w.r.t. coalition time, mission completion time and simulation time. The number of types of resources was increased from 3 to 11 in increments of 2. Configurations comprising 15 targets and UAVs varying from 5 to 20 in increments of 5 were considered. For each configuration a hundred simulations were performed and the average for each of the characteristics referred to above were recorded. Results are reported in Figs. 9, 10 and 11. Plots in Fig. 9 indicate that the coalition time increases with an increase in the number of types of resources and that the coalition time decreases with an increase in the number of UAVs.

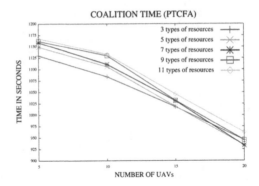

Fig. 9. Coalition times for various number of types of resources for 15 targets

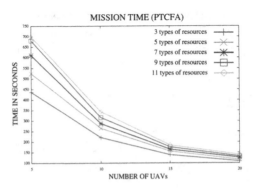

Fig. 10. Mission time for various number of types of resources

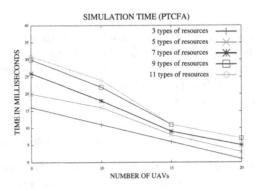

Fig. 11. Simulation time for various number of types of resources

Plots in Fig. 10 indicate that the mission time increases with an increase in the number of types of resources. For a fixed number of types of resources the mission time decreases with an increase in the number of UAVs.

Graphs in Fig. 11 indicate that simulation time also increases with an increase in the number of type of resources.

5   Conclusion

Dubins longest path can be used to map the shortest path traversed by a fixed wing unmanned aerial vehicle (UAV) in pursuit of a target. This paper provides an approach that calculates Dubins longest path using elementary geometry. Experiments were conducted where Dubins longest path was applied to the Polynomial Time Coalition Formation Algorithm. Results show that an increase in the sensor range produced an increase in coalition time with a corresponding reduction in mission times. Results also indicate that an increase in the number of type of resources lead to an increase in coalition time and to an increase in mission time. Future investigations will study the effect of wind on the Dubins path and search missions using constraints such as time and energy.

References

1. Asadpour, M., Giustiniano, D., Hummel, K., Egli, S.: UAV networks in rescue missions. In: Proceedings of the 8th ACM International Workshop on Wireless Network Testbeds, Experimental Evaluation & Characterization, pp. 91–92 (2013)
2. Pólka, M., Ptak, S., Kuziora, L.: The use of UAVs for search and rescue operations. In: TRANSCOM 2017, 12th International Scientific Conference on Sustainable, Modern and Safe Transport, vol. 192, pp. 748–752 (2017)
3. Gonzalez, L.F., Montes, G.A., Puig, E., Johnson, S., Mengersen, K., Gaston, K.J.: Unmanned aerial vehicles (UAVs) and artificial intelligence revolutionizing wildlife monitoring and conservation. Sensors 16(1), 97 (2016)
4. Erdelj, M., Natalizio, E., Chowdhury, K.R., Akyildiz, I.F.: Help from the sky: leveraging UAVs for disaster management. IEEE Pervasive Comput. 16(1), 24–32 (2017)
5. Hartmann, K., Steup, C.: The vulnerability of UAVs to cyber attacks - an approach to the risk assessment. In: Podins, K., Stinissen, J., Maybaum, M. (eds.) 5th International Conference on Cyber Conflict, CYCON, pp. 1–23 (2013)
6. Bagula, A., Castelli, L., Zennaro, M.: On the design of smart parking networks in the smart cities: an optimal sensor placement model. Sensors 15(7), 15443–15467 (2015)
7. Mouatez Karbab, E., Djenouri, D., Boulkaboul, S., Bagula, A.: Car park management with networked wireless sensors and active RFID. In: 2015 IEEE International Conference on Electro/Information Technology (EIT), pp. 373–378 (2015)
8. Masinde, M., Bagula, A.: A framework for predicting droughts in developing countries using sensor networks and mobile phones. In: Proceedings of the 2010 Annual Research Conference of the South African Institute of Computer Scientists and Information Technologists, pp. 390–393. ACM (2010)
9. Bagula, A., Abidoye, A.P., Zodi, L.: Service-aware clustering: an energy-efficient model for the internet-of-things. Sensors 16(1), 9 (2016). https://doi.org/10.3390/s16010009
10. Dubins, L.E.: On curves of minimal length with a constraint on average curvature. Am. J. Math. 79(3), 497–516 (1957)

11. Reeds, J.A., Shepp, L.A.: Optimal paths for a car that goes both forwards and backwards. Pac. J. Math. **145**(2), 367–393 (1990)

12. Kavraki, L.E., Svestka, P., Latombe, J.-C., Overmars, M.H.: Probabilistic roadmaps for path planning in high-dimensional configuration spaces. IEEE Trans. Robot. Autom. **12**(4), 566–580 (1996)

13. Nelson, W.L.: Continuous-curvature paths for autonomous vehicles. In: IEEE International Conference on Robotics and Automation, Scottsdale, AZ, US, vol. 3, pp. 1260–1264, May 1989

14. Komoriya, K., Tanie, K.: Trajectory design and control of a wheel-type mobile robot using B-spline curve. In: IEEE/RSJ International Conference on Intelligent Robots and Systems, Tsukuba, Japan, pp. 398–405 (1989)

15. Subchan, S., White, B.A., Tsourdos, A., Shanmugavel, M., Żbikowski, R.: Dubins path planning of multiple UAVs for tracking contaminant cloud. In: 17th World Congress International Federation of Automatic Control (lFAC), vol. 41, no. 2, pp. 5718–5723 (2008)

16. Lugo-Cárdenas, I., Flores, G., Salazar, S., Lozano, R.: Dubins path generation for a fixed wing UAV. In: 2014 International Conference on Unmanned Aircraft Systems (ICUAS), Orlando, FL, USA, 27–30 May 2014

17. Costanzi, R., Fanelli, F., Meli, E., Ridolfi, A., Allotta, B.: Generic path planning algorithm for mobile robots based on Bézier curves. In: 9th IFAC Symposium on Intelligent Autonomous Vehicles IAV 2016, Leipzig, Germany, vol. 49, no. 15, pp. 145–150 (2016)

18. Manathara, J.G., Surit, P.B., Beard, R.W.: Multiple UAV coalitions for a search and prosecute mission. J. Intell. Robot. Syst. **62**(1), 125–158 (2011)

19. Hwangbo, M., Kuffner, J., Kanade, T.: Efficient two-phase 3D motion planning for small fixed-wing UAVs. In: Proceedings - IEEE International Conference on Robotics and Automation, pp. 1035–1041, April 2007

20. Oh, H., Turchi, D., Kim, S., Tsourdos, A., Pollini, L., White, B.: Coordinated standoff tracking using path shaping for multiple UAVs. IEEE Trans. Aerosp. Electron. Syst. **50**(1), 348–363 (2014)

21. Wang, Z., Li, Y., Li, W.: An approximation path planning algorithm for fixed-wing UAVs in stationary obstacle environment. In: 2014 33rd Chinese Control Conference (CCC), pp. 664–669, July 2014

22. Owen, M., Beard, R., McLain, T.: Implementing Dubins airplane paths on fixed-wing UAVs*. In: Valavanis, K., Vachtsevanos, G. (eds.) Handbook of Unmanned Aerial Vehicles, pp. 1677–1701. Springer, Dordrecht (2015). https://doi.org/10.1007/978-90-481-9707-1_120

23. Darbari, V., Gupta, S., Verma, O.: Dynamic motion planning for aerial surveillance on a fixed-wing UAV. In: 2017 International Conference on Unmanned Aircraft Systems (ICUAS), pp. 488–497, June 2017

24. Song, X., Hu, S.: 2D path planning with dubins-path-based A* algorithm for a fixed-wing UAV. In: 2017 3rd IEEE International Conference on Control Science and Systems Engineering (ICCSSE), pp. 69–73, August 2017

Optimal Clustering for Efficient Data Muling in the Internet-of-Things in Motion

Emmanuel Tuyishimire$^{(\boxtimes)}$, B. Antoine Bagula, and Adiel Ismail

University of the Western Cape, Cape Town, South Africa
tuyinuel@gmail.com

Abstract. Recent studies have revealed the benefit of capitalising on the interplay between Unmanned Aerial Vehicles (UAVs) and ground sensors, for the efficient data muling from locations of interest to back-end infrastructures where, it is analysed and processed for further decision making. However, such studies have not considered minimizing the energy spent by a UAV for moving from one location to another; a requirement that can help maximize the lifetime of the resulting hybrid network infrastructure before recharging. This paper proposes an optimal clustering model for a case where, an Unmanned Aerial Vehicle (UAV) is to monitor an area of interest, to collect data captured by a terrestrial sensor network. The proposed clustering algorithm minimises a combination of the energy for routing data in the terrestrial network and the energy used by the UAV to collect data from cluster heads and report to a back-end infrastructure. We formally calculate the optimal number of clusters in a uniformly distributed sensor network, to support existing k-clustering schemes, and for general networks, a general clustering algorithm is proposed. Performance evaluation reveals relevance of accurately modelling the hybrid networks underlying the"Internet-of-Things in Motion".

Keywords: Hybrid network · Clustering · Restricted network

1 Introduction

Recent studies [1–6] have revealed that capitalising on the interplay between UAVs and ground sensors can be a very efficient way of collecting data from locations of interest and delivering the data to back-end infrastructures where it is analysed and processed for further decision making. Such an interplay is at the heart of Internet-of-Things (IoT) called "Internet-of-Things in Motion" where hybrid networks are built by using teams of UAVs as airborne sensor networks and sets of sensors scattered on the ground as terrestrial sensor networks. Potential applications of these networks include using UAVs to extend the reach of city mesh networks for smart parking [7] and pollution monitoring [8] or using UAVs to extend the reach of community sensor networks in rural settings

© Springer Nature Switzerland AG 2018
N. Boudriga et al. (Eds.): UNet 2018, LNCS 11277, pp. 359–371, 2018.
https://doi.org/10.1007/978-3-030-02849-7_32

for drought mitigation [9,10] and healthcare [11,12]. However, designing such hybrid networks is a challenging task that may lead to complex optimization models with multiple competing objectives such as optimizing the lifetime of both airborne and terrestrial sensor networks to meet traffic engineering constraints while achieving a minimal coverage to meet application and network engineering constraints. Furthermore, optimizing the lifetime of the airborne sensor network may require minimizing the number of data collection points by the airborne sensor network while ensuring that ground sensor data is collected from all the nodes of the terrestrial sensor network and transported efficiently to the UAVs' collection points. Sensor network clustering can solve this problem by enabling an m-to-n communication model where the terrestrial sensor network is engineered as a multi-sink network where data is collected from m edge nodes and sent to n sink nodes designed as UAV collection points. In such a network deployment, the terrestrial sensor network is subdivided into n clusters with n UAV collection points referred to as cluster-heads while the other nodes are considered as cluster-members which have usually a direct link to one of the cluster-heads.

The three main challenges raised by hybrid terrestrial/airborne sensor network engineering include (1) finding the optimal number of clusters that optimize a defined objective function (2) selection of the optimal cluster heads to be used as UAV data collection points and (3) performing a cluster member association through a policy that should meet some optimization constraints. Note that, while similar challenges are involved in all clustering techniques, they are worsened by the introduction of airborne data collection agents such as UAVs.

The optimal clustering for terrestrial sensor networks has been a subject of high interest in the literature. An analytical approach for determining the optimum number of clusters by minimizing the communication-energy consumption in a highly dense SN is proposed in [13]. The work in [13] was motivated by the two research outputs revealing that (1) the number of clusters increases with the minimization of the energy usage [14] and (2) finding an optimal number of clusters is an important parameter upon which the efficiency of cluster-based sensor networks depends [15]. In [16], the optimal number of cluster heads and their locations has been analytically computed by adopting the cluster-head selection method in [17], which is based on the calculated probability of a node to be a cluster head. However, all these clustering schemes assumed a static network model suitable for only terrestrial sensor networks, discounting data collection agents such as UAVs or other mobile data collector devices.

A model of clustering UAVs as moving nodes/agents was proposed in [18] where mobility attributes enabling UAVs-motion predictions were used for clusters' predictions. In [19], the UAVs were also clustered to discover the optimal route while in [20], a clustering scheme was proposed to provide internet connectivity, using a mobile sink (UAV). To the best of our knowledge, these are the first clustering schemes that considered different positions of a UAV (path). However, these works did not consider minimizing the energy spent by the UAV while moving from one position to another; a requirement that allows the UAV to collect as much data as possible prior to battery recharging.

1.1 Motivation and Contribution

This paper revisits the problem of clustering in hybrid terrestrial/airborne sensor networks by considering both the efficient sensor network communication and the efficient cluster heads visitation by a UAV. We first define the clustering problem for a hybrid network (UAV routes and the communication-based SN). Thereafter, the optimal number of clusters in the situation of uniform and dense distribution is rigorously computed. Finally, a heuristic clustering algorithm is proposed for general networks which takes care of the situation explained above.

The rest of this paper, is organised as follows. The problem is mathematically formulated in Sect. 2, and the proposed algorithmic solution is described in Sect. 3. The performance evaluation of the proposed solution is presented in Sect. 4 while Sect. 5 concludes the paper.

2 Problem Modelling

The network considered in this paper is denoted by $\mathcal{H}(\mathcal{N}, \mathcal{P}_g, \mathcal{P}_a, E_g, E_a)$, where $\mathcal{N}$ is the set of sensor nodes and the UAVs base stations locations, $\mathcal{P}_g$ is the set of paths expressing possible sensors communication pathways in the ground-based terrestrial network, $\mathcal{P}_a$ the set of paths in the airborne network consisting of possible routes followed by the UAVs to collect data delivered by the ground-based sensor network, and the energy consumed by the set of paths $\mathcal{P}_g$ and $\mathcal{P}_a$ is respectively represented by E_g and E_a. Note that the network $\mathcal{H}$ is a hybrid of the ground sensor network denoted by H_g and the aerial network denoted by H_a.

2.1 The Energy Models

As suggested earlier, this paper considers an energy-efficient model where the energy consumption is described below.

$$E_g = E_t + E_r, \tag{1}$$
$$E_a = \beta E_c + \gamma E_u \tag{2}$$

where, the constants β and γ are proportionality constants corresponding to E_c and E_u, respectively and the energy components E_r, E_t, E_c and E_u are defined below.

– **Energy for sensors data reception** (E_r). It is the energy spent by cluster heads due to its topological, environmental, the physical/electronic properties of the receiving node, and the nature of messages to be received. We assume that all possible cluster heads are in the same and good conditions and hence they require the same quantity of energy to receive a message.

- **Energy for data transmission among sensors** (E_t). It is the total energy required to move the captured data from each cluster node to its corresponding cluster head. This form of energy is directly proportional to the distance separating the two communicating sensors. We assume one hop inter-cluster communication and hence the considered distance is the Euclidean length of links. All nodes of the network are assumed to require the same quantity of energy for message transmissions.
- **Energy for UAV data transport** (E_u). It refers to the expected energy required for a UAV to visit cluster heads. This energy depends on the number of cluster heads in the H_g network and the distance between these nodes (the expected link length).
- **Energy for UAV data collection** (Ec). It is the energy spent by the UAV to collect data from the sensor nodes (cluster heads).

From Eqs. 1 and 2, the overall energy for data dissemination in the terrestrial ground-based sensor network to cluster heads and data muling by the UAV can be expressed by the weighted sum of energy consumption in both ground and airborne networks as expressed by

$$E_h = \alpha E_g + \beta E_c + \gamma E_u. \tag{3}$$

2.2   The Terrestrial Network Energy Consumption: E_g

Let L^2 be the area (in square meters) of the field where sensors are distributed and needs to be partitioned into k clusters. It follows that one cluster's area is $\sqrt{L^2/k} \times \sqrt{L^2/k}$, based on Voronoi diagram (see [21]). It has been shown in [16], that the total energy E for data gathering in the network of type $H1$ is expressed as follows.

$$E_g = (2n - 2k + ak)E_e + nE_p + (n - k)e_f \frac{L^2}{3k} + ake_m \frac{4L^4}{9}, \tag{4}$$

where, E_e denotes the energy for driving the electronics, E_p is the energy for data processing, n the number of all sensors in the field and the constants e_f and e_m represent the coefficient corresponding the effects of the clusters intra-distances and inter-distances and a with $0 < a \leq 1$, denotes the data compression ratio: k bits are compressed to ak.

The considered case in this paper assumes that there is no inter-cluster communication and thus,

$$e_m = 0.$$

This is why the gathering energy E_g is computed as follows.

$$E_g = (2n - 2k + ak)E_e + nE_p + (n - k)e_f \frac{L^2}{3k}. \tag{5}$$

2.3   Energy for UAV Transportation: E_u

The transportation energy E_t depends on the length of the used path which gets longer as the number of clusters increases. We assume that the UAV moves from one node to another, using the Dijkstra's algorithm [22] on the network of type H_a. This will enable us to evaluate the goodness of a node to be in a particular cluster or even being a cluster head.

Since the UAV-transportation energy is directly proportional to the length of the used path, it is directly proportional to the number of cluster heads. It is also proportional to the average distance from one cluster head to another and hence the distance D to travel from one node to another. So, E_u is computed as follows,

$$E_u = kD. \tag{6}$$

where, $D = E(E_j(d))$ is the expected value of the average length of shortest paths d from each sensor node j to others.

2.4   The Data Collection Energy Consumption: E_c

The total energy for data collection from cluster heads by a UAV. Let 1, 2, ..., k be the indices corresponding to k cluster heads. If E_i is the energy required by the UAV to receive data from the cluster head i (with $1 \leq i \leq k$) and e_i is the energy required by cluster head to forward the gathered data to the UAV, then the total energy E_c for data collection is expressed as follows.

$$E_c = \sum_{i=1}^{k} E_i + e_i = \frac{k}{k} \sum_{i=1}^{k} (E_i + e_i) \tag{7}$$

Hence,

$$E_c = k(\overline{E} + \overline{e}), \tag{8}$$

where, $\overline{E}$ and $\overline{e}$ are the expected value of the energy required to receive and forward data, respectively.

It follows from Eqs. 3, 5, 8 and 6 that the total energy used in data collection is expressed as follows.

$$E_h(k) = \alpha[-\frac{L^2 e_f(k-n)}{3k} + (ak - 2k + 2n)E_e + nE_p] + \beta kD + \gamma k(\overline{E} + \overline{e}). \tag{9}$$

2.5   Problem Definition

Given a hybrid network $\mathcal{H}$, the problem consists of finding the smallest nodes' partition $\mathcal{P}(N)$ to minimise the total energy E_h (see Eq. 3), such that, each partition (cluster) is connected and its optimum head is known. The energy E_h is refereed to as the clustering cost. The network design consists of finding a network configuration that minimizes the clustering cost function subject to node selection and topology constraints with the objective of partitioning the network into two sets: a dominating set of UAV collection points and a dominated set of cluster members forming the edge of the network. Mathematically formulated, the design process consists of finding a network partition C derived from the graph of type $\mathcal{H}$ explained in Sect. 2 such that $\mathcal{N}$ is divided into disjoint clusters, where the cluster head is communicatively connected with all its cluster mates.

$$\min E_h = \alpha E_g + \beta E_u + \gamma E_c \tag{10}$$

Subject to
(10.1) $\forall c \in C, \exists x \in c, \forall y \in c, (x, y) \in P_g$
(10.2) $c_1, c_2 \in C, c_1 \vee c_2 = \emptyset$
(10.3) $\bigcup\limits_{c \in C} c = N$

where, constraints 10.1 shows the dominating set property of the set of cluster heads, 10.2 and 10.3 represent the network partitioning properties.

3   The Optimal Clustering Model

The main issues involved in the optimal clustering model considered in this paper are (i) finding the optimal number of clusters, (ii) selection of the optimal cluster heads/sinks and (iii) associating the cluster members to the sinks. These issues can be solved by three algorithmic solutions: (a) a myopic k-mean clustering algorithm where the optimal number of clusters $k = \mathcal{K}_{opt}$ is computed and the classical K-means algorithm is applied with $k = \mathcal{K}_{opt}$, (b) an optimized k-mean clustering algorithm where the optimal number of clusters $k = \mathcal{K}_{opt}$ is computed and the $\mathcal{K}_{opt}$ best cluster heads are selected and fed to the k-means algorithm to guide the clustering process and (c) a multi-step clustering algorithm where a sequence of cluster head selection and cluster member association is performed on the network until all the nodes are assigned a cluster head or member status. Note that while the k-means algorithm can be applied to a dense and uniform network where each sensor node is able to communicate to its neighbours, the multi-step algorithm is more suitable to general networks where the connectivity property may not be met.

3.1   Optimal Number of Clusters

We express the total energy required for data transport in terms of the number k of clusters in the hybrid network (see Sect. 2). Calculus basics are used to compute the value of the number k which could minimise the energy required for data collection in case of uniformly distributed networks.

The equation of energy expressed by 9 can be derived with relation to the number of clusters k to obtain its optimal value. Differentiating the equation of the energy expressed by 9 leads to the Eq. 11 below

$$\frac{\partial E_h}{\partial k} = \alpha(E_e(a-2) + \frac{L^2 e_f(k-n)}{3\,k^2} - \frac{L^2 e_f}{3\,k}) + \beta D + \gamma(\overline{E} + \overline{e}) \tag{11}$$

By solving the equation $\frac{\partial E_h}{\partial k} = 0$, where, $k \geq 1$, we obtain the optimal value of E_h for

$$K_{opt} = \sqrt{\frac{L^2 e_f n}{3(E_e(a-2) + bD + \overline{E} + \overline{e})}} \tag{12}$$

Notice that the second derivative is

$$\frac{\partial^2 E_h}{\partial k^2} = -\frac{2 L^2 e_f (k-n)}{3 k^3} + \frac{2 L^2 e_f}{3 k^2}. \tag{13}$$

We know that all observables in the Eq. 13 are positively valued. Furthermore, the difference $k-n$ is always negative (the number of cluster heads can not exceed the number of all existing nodes). It follows that,

$$\frac{\partial^2 E_h}{\partial k^2} \geq 0. \tag{14}$$

This confirms that the the total energy $E_h(k)$ is minimum at K_{opt} as shown in Eq. 12.

Since the optimal number of clusters has to be a positive integer, the optimal number of clusters is denoted by K and it is calculated as follows.

$$K = \begin{cases} \lceil k \rceil & \text{if } E(\lceil k \rceil) \leq E(\lfloor k \rfloor) \\ \lfloor k \rfloor & \text{else where.} \end{cases} \tag{15}$$

3.2 The Clustering Algorithm

The multi-steps clustering has been designed based on a multi-steps algorithm using the following cluster head selection assumptions:

- *Density-aware selection policy* where nodes are assigned the cluster head identity based on their node density $deg(i)$. While leading to the UAV collecting data collection points with high volume of data, this policy might lead to the UAV flying longer distances for collecting this data and hence depleting its energy during its inbound journey.
- *Distance-aware selection policy* where nodes are elected cluster heads based on their distance to the UAV base D_i. This policy aims at minimizing the energy usage of the airborne sensor network but might lead to the UAV to be tasked to collect data at collection points with very few data.
- *Hybrid policy* that combines features from density and distance aware cluster head selection by combining both parameters into a weighted sum metric expressed by

$$P_i = \lambda \, deg(i) + \psi \frac{1}{D_i}. \tag{16}$$

Here, $deg(i)$ represents the number of available neighbours (of node i) in the network of type H_g whereas D_i is the average distance from node i to all nodes in the network of type H_a. λ and ψ are coefficients corresponding to the node degree in H_g and average distance in H_a, respectively.

Input: The graph of type $H(H_1, H_2)$
Output: A dictionary of cluster heads and their cluster mates

---

Algorithm 1: Optimal clustering.

---

1 $L \longleftarrow$ set of the lengths of links in L_g
2 $Dp \longleftarrow$ dictionary of nodes (keys) and their expected length of shortest path to each sensor
    node in H_a (values).
3 $E_{min} \longleftarrow \infty$
4 $C_{min} = \{\}$
5 **for** $Radius \in L$ **do**
6 $\quad$ $N_{rad} \longleftarrow$ dictionary of nodes (keys) and a list of their available neighbours at distance
    $\quad$ $dist \leq Radius$
7 $\quad$ Order N_{rad} in terms of the decreasing order of the value of the price P of the keys
    $\quad$ (cluster heads)
8 $\quad$ Ch $\longleftarrow$ List of N_{rad} ordered keys (cluster heads)
9 $\quad$ Cv $\longleftarrow$ List of $Nrad$ ordered values (cluster mates)
10 $\quad$ C $\longleftarrow$ empty dictionary which will contain clusters
11 $\quad$ **while** $Ch \neq \emptyset$ **do**
12 $\quad\quad$ $C_{Ch_0} \longleftarrow Cv_0$
13 $\quad\quad$ Remove Ch_0 and all nodes in Cv_0 from Ch.
14 $\quad\quad$ $N_{rad} \longleftarrow$ dictionary of nodes in Ch (keys) and a list of their neighbours Not in any
    $\quad\quad$ formed clusters
15 $\quad\quad$ Order N_{rad} in terms of the value of the price P of the keys (cluster heads)
16 $\quad\quad$ Ch $\longleftarrow$ List of N_{rad} ordered keys (cluster heads)
17 $\quad\quad$ Cv $\longleftarrow$ List of $Nrad$ ordered values (cluster mates)
18 $\quad$ Calculate the price $P(C)$ using Equation 3
19 $\quad$ **if** $P(C) < E_{min}$ **then**
20 $\quad\quad$ $C_{min} \longleftarrow C$
21 $\quad\quad$ $E_{min} \longleftarrow P(C)$
22 Return C_{min}

In Algorithm 1, the first steps consist of computing a list L of all link lengths
in the SN (Network of type H_g), and the dictionary D_P whose keys is the sensor
labels and the corresponding values consists of the average distance to each node
in the restricted network (network of type H_a). The minimum coverage energy
E_{min} is initialised to infinity. The network clustering is expressed in the form of
a dictionary whose keys are the cluster heads and the values correspond to the
clusters members. The clusters dictionary C is initially set to empty (Line 4).
The cluster dictionary is assumed to have the cluster head as keys and the their
corresponding values are the list of nodes each cluster head is to support.

From Line 5 on, each link length (Euclidean distance between two connected
nodes) is used as the clustering radius (maximum distance of nodes and cluster
heads), to form a corresponding clustering C.

Clustering is done using a dictionary N_{rad}, consisting of nodes and their H_g
neighbours at a distance less or equal to the chosen radius. Note that the radius
is only chosen from a list of lengths of the H_g links and it is assumed to be the
same for all clusters to be formed. This dictionary gets formed (Line 6), and
using the pricing shown by Eq. 16, it is decreasingly ordered (Line 7).

Let Ch be a list of ordered N_{rad} keys (list of potential cluster heads), Cv be
the list of the corresponding keys (possible cluster members). To form the first
cluster we take first element of the list Ch to be the cluster head and the first
list in Cv constitutes the corresponding cluster mates.

N_{rad} is then updated to contain the remaining possible cluster heads and their neighbours which are the nodes not in any of the formed clusters.

The process of using the available nodes in the list N_{rad} to make one cluster is repeated (Lines 11–16) until no more cluster head is available. In this case, one clustering is done and its price is computed using Eq. 3 (Line 17).

Each new clustering related price is compared to the existing minimum price to check the possibility of updating the best cluster C_{min} and the corresponding cost E_{min}.

4   Results and Discussion

In this section, we report on the experimental results on the effect of introducing the energy spent by the UAV. This is achieved by running our solution for different values of weighting constants in Eq. 3 to evaluate their impacts on cost, which is the energy in joule (j), number of clusters, and the corresponding radius as Algorithm 1 evolves.

4.1   Case Study

We considered the public safety network consisting of Cape Town (South Africa) police stations as collection points of a ground sensor network used for example for city safety or traffic control. Cape Town police stations are labelled in terms of integers in interval $[1, 49]$ and their GPS coordinates are used as their positions (Figs. 1 and 2). The Radio Mobile software was used to create the hybrid network: the ground communication network was obtained by considering the link margin greater than 50 dB, and the links corresponding to the UAV paths correspond to the link margin between 30 and 50 dB.

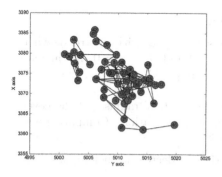

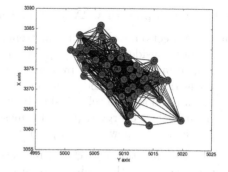

Fig. 1.   Considered   communication network.

Fig. 2. Considered UAV paths network.

4.2　The impact of the weighting parameters on performance

Figure 3 shows that if the length of cluster radius is increased, the coverage cost (total coverage energy), the number of clusters expectedly decreases until it converges. Note that the convergence point is not the optimal one. This is justified by the fact that there is a radius which corresponds to the case where every clusters consists of just the cluster head. Increasing the radius, will give the same results. However this has been motivated not to be an optimal solution for a UAV.

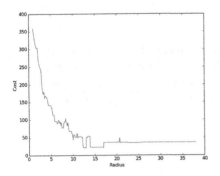

Fig. 3. Radius-cost.　　　　　　　　　**Fig. 4.** Coverage cost against the number of clusters.

Figure 4 reveals that the number of clusters is positively and highly correlated with the coverage cost. This justifies the results found in Fig. 3. So, a big number of clusters corresponds to a high transportation cost. The better clustering would correspond to the radius which minimises the number of clusters, and hence the transportation cost as shown by Fig. 4.

4.3　The Impact of UAV on Clustering

In this subsection, we compare the trends observed so far with the trends when, we do not consider the UAV's presence $\alpha = 10$ and $\beta = \gamma = 0$. In this case the clustering is done only by considering the required energy for the ground messages transmission and receptions.

Figure 5 shows the relationship between the clusters' radius and the coverage related cost (energy required for messages transportation). Comparing with Fig. 3, the figure shows two major differences.

1. The cost function expectedly increases (it was decreasing before) until the convergence, as the radius increases.
2. The cost gets smaller values (less than 1.0 joules), whereas previously, it ranges between 20 and 370 joules.

Figure 6 shows that fewer number of clusters are expected to correspond to lower energy. However the relationship is not linear unlike the case were the UAV influence is considered (see Fig. 4). So the correlation gets negative and smaller.

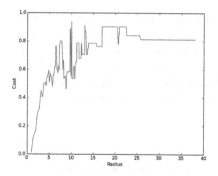

Fig. 5. Radius-cost.   **Fig. 6.** Communication network.

4.4   Efficiency of the Proposed Solution

We compare our proposed algorithm with the Distance-based Crowdedness Clustering (DCC) which does not take care of the presence of the UAV. We consider the experiment where, both positions and links for both networks were generated randomly. The total number of considered nodes is 48 and the positions were generated by randomly selecting the coordinates from a normal distribution of mean = 500 and standard deviation of 300 ($\mathcal{N}(500, 300)$).

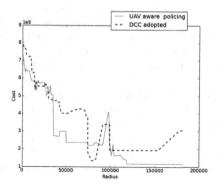

Fig. 7. comparison

Figure 7 shows that in most of the values of the radius, the DCC has higher cost and also converges to a higher cost.

5   Conclusion

In this paper, a model for optimal sensor network design has been provided where a multi-sink ground-based terrestrial sensor network is expanded by an airborne network using a UAV to ferry the sensor data from the sinks of the terrestrial sensor network to the gateway where the data is to be processed. The coverage problem has been mathematically formulated as an optimisation problem aiming at finding the optimal number of clusters to achieve an energy efficient hybrid terrestrial/airborne sensor network using an UAV as mobile gateway. It has been shown that the energy spent by the UAV data muling has a big impact on the change in the energy consumed by the whole process of data transport.

References

1. Bagula, A., Ismail, A., Tuyishimire, E.: Generating Dubins path for fixed wing UAVs in search missions. In: International Symposium on Ubiquitous Networking. Springer, Heidelberg (2018)
2. Tuyishimire, E., Bagula, A., Rekhis, S., Boudriga, N.: Cooperative data muling from ground sensors to base stations using UAVs. In: 2017 IEEE Symposium on Computers and Communications (ISCC), pp. 35–41. IEEE (2017)
3. Las Fargeas, J., Kabamba, P., Girard, A.: Cooperative surveillance and pursuit using unmanned aerial vehicles and unattended ground sensors. Sensors 15(1), 1365–1388 (2015)
4. Boudriga, N., Hadj, S.B., Rekhis, S., Bagula, A.: A cloud of UAVs for the delivery of a sink as a service to terrestrial WSNs. In: 2016 International Conference on Unmanned Aircraft Systems (ICUAS). IEEE (2016)
5. Bagula, A., Tuyishimire, E., Wadepoel, J., Boudriga, N., Rekhis, S.: Internet-of-things in motion: a cooperative data muling model for public safety. In: 2016 Intl IEEE Conferences Ubiquitous Intelligence & Computing, Advanced and Trusted Computing, Scalable Computing and Communications, Cloud and Big Data Computing, Internet of People, and Smart World Congress (UIC/ATC/ScalCom/CBDCom/IoP/SmartWorld), pp. 17–24. IEEE (2016)
6. Tuyishimire, E., Adiel, I., Rekhis, S., Bagula, B.A., Boudriga, N.: Internet of things in motion: a cooperative data muling model under revisit constraints. In: 2016 Intl IEEE Conferences Ubiquitous Intelligence & Computing, Advanced and Trusted Computing, Scalable Computing and Communications, Cloud and Big Data Computing, Internet of People, and Smart World Congress (UIC/ATC/ScalCom/CBDCom/IoP/SmartWorld), pp. 1123–1130. IEEE (2016)
7. Bagula, A., Castelli, L., Zennaro, M.: On the design of smart parking networks in the smart cities: an optimal sensor placement model. Sensors 15(7), 15443–15467 (2015)
8. Bagula, A., Zennaro, M., Inggs, G., Scott, S., Gascon, D.: Ubiquitous sensor networking for development (USN4D): an application to pollution monitoring. Sensors 12(7), 391–414 (2012). ISSN 1424-8220
9. Masinde. M.,Bagula, A.: A framework for predicting droughts in developing countries using sensor networks and mobile phones. In: Proceedings of the 2010 Annual Research Conference of the South African Institute of Computer Scientists and Information Technologists, pp. 390–393. ACM (2010)
10. Masinde, M., Bagula, A., Mthama, T.N.: The role of ICTs in downscaling and up-scaling integrated weather forecasts for farmers in sub-Saharan Africa. In: In proceedings of ICTD 1202, pp. 122–129. ACM (2012)
11. Mandava, M., Lubamba, C., Ismail, A., Bagula, H., Bagula, A.: Cyber-healthcare for public healthcare in the developing world. In: Proceedings of the 2016 IEEE Symposium on Computers and Communication (ISCC), pp. 14–19. IEEE (2016)

12. Bagula, A., Lubamba, C., Mandava, M., Bagula, H., Zennaro, M., Pietrosemoli, E.: Cloud based patient prioritization as service in public health care. In: Proceedings of the ITU Kaleidoscope 2016, 14–16 November, Bangkok, Thailand. IEEE (2016)
13. Wang, L.-C., Wang, C.-W., Liu, C.-M.: Optimal number of clusters in dense wireless sensor networks: a cross-layer approach. IEEE Trans. Veh. Technol. **58**(2), 966–976 (2009)
14. Duarte-Melo, E.J., Liu, M.: Energy efficiency of many-to-one communications in wireless networks. In: The 2002 45th Midwest Symposium on Circuits and Systems, MWSCAS-2002, vol. 1, pp. I-615. IEEE (2002)
15. Chen, G., Nocetti, F.B., Gonzalez, J.S., Stojmenovic, I.: Connectivity based k-hop clustering in wireless networks. In: 2002 Proceedings of the 35th Annual Hawaii International Conference on System Sciences, HICSS, pp. 2450–2459. IEEE (2002)
16. Gu, Y., Wu, Q., Rao, N.S.V.: Optimizing cluster heads for energy efficiency in large-scale heterogeneous wireless sensor networks. Int. J. Distrib. Sens. Netw. **6**, 961591 (2010)
17. Yang, H., Sikdar, B.: Optimal cluster head selection in the leach architecture. In: 2007 IEEE International Performance, Computing, and Communications Conference, IPCCC 2007, pp. 93–100. IEEE (2007)
18. Zang, C., Zang, S.: Mobility prediction clustering algorithm for UAV networking. In: 2011 IEEE GLOBECOM Workshops (GC Wkshps), pp. 1158–1161. IEEE (2011)
19. Shi, N., Luo, X.: A novel cluster-based location-aided routing protocol for UAV fleet networks. Int. J. Digit. Content Technol. Appl. **6**(18), 376 (2012)
20. Okcu, H., Soyturk, M.: Distributed clustering approach for UAV integrated wireless sensor networks. Int. J. Ad Hoc Ubiquitous Comput. **15**(1–3), 106–120 (2014)
21. Aurenhammer, F., Klein, R., Lee, D.-T.: Voronoi Diagrams and Delaunay Triangulations, vol. 8. World Scientific, Singapore (2013)
22. Skiena, S.: Dijkstra's algorithm. In: Implementing Discrete Mathematics: Combinatorics and Graph Theory with Mathematica, Reading, MA, pp. 225–227. Addison-Wesley (1990)

Air-to-Ground Channel Modeling for UAV Communications Using 3D Building Footprints

Hajar El Hammouti[1](✉) and Mounir Ghogho[1,2](✉)

[1] FIL, TICLab, International University of Rabat, Rabat, Morocco
{hajar.elhammouti,mounir.ghogho}@uir.ac.ma
[2] School of IEEE, University of Leeds, Leeds, UK

Abstract. Unmanned aerial vehicles (UAV) deployment and emerging air-to-ground wireless services have been a topic of great interest in the last few years. The main virtue of UAV networks is that they provide on demand connectivity. However, the design of such networks is intrinsically dependent on the air-to-ground propagation conditions. In order to construct a reliable air-to-ground channel model that takes into account the nature of the surrounding environment, we propose to exploit the information provided by building footprints. The obtained results are compared with existing statistical air-to-ground channel models. It is shown that both the the path loss exponent and the variance of the shadow fading are dependent on the distance on the ground between the UAV and the user and the drone's altitude. The proposed channel modeling method is then used to estimate the coverage probability over the studied area.

Keywords: UAV · Air-to-ground channel · Real building footprints
Shadowing · Coverage probability · Meta-distribution of SNR

1 Introduction

In the last few years, unmanned aerial vehicles (UAV) have gained interest among industrial and research communities as a rapidly deployable network that provides on-demand connectivity. By contrast to terrestrial infrastructures, both expensive and time-consuming in terms of deployment, UAV can be seen as a rapid and efficient support for a short-fall in network capacity after a natural disaster or during a temporary mass event. Additionally, in the wide Internet of things (IoT) ecosystem, UAV can also be used as mobile base stations that move towards IoT devices, provide connectivity, collect and relay data to terrestrial gateways or out-of-range receivers.

While UAV networks use cases are numerous [14], their deployment, however, is associated with several technical challenges that need to be addressed. Many issues related to network architecture [7], energy consumption [16], interference management [18,19], coverage and movement optimization [12,15], and

© Springer Nature Switzerland AG 2018
N. Boudriga et al. (Eds.): UNet 2018, LNCS 11277, pp. 372–383, 2018.
https://doi.org/10.1007/978-3-030-02849-7_33

air-to-ground channel modeling [2] have been presented in the literature. These challenges, commonly discussed for ground-to-ground communications, need to be addressed from an air-to-ground communication perspective. This is because the air-to ground propagation conditions are different from the terrestrial ones. For example, a drone's coverage is tightly related to its position, in particular its altitude. Indeed, improving a drone's altitude has a double-edged sword effect: it provides a stronger link with a higher probability of line-of-sight, but at the same time, it results in an important path loss. This tradeoff has been the subject of many research papers that aim to optimize the drone's altitude while maximizing its coverage. In [15], authors show the concavity of the coverage probability with respect to a single drone's altitude. In [10], authors investigate the optimal altitude by taking into account different antenna's gain patterns and a multipath fading channel. Interference is considered in [18] where the authors derive the probability of coverage using a dominant interferer approach. Additional interferences, resulting from coexistence with device-to-device communications (D2D), are characterized in [17] which provides a closed-form expression of the coverage probability.

Despite the large amount of existing works that address UAV coverage from a theoretical perspective, the experimental validation of these results is still in its infancy. In general, the air-to-ground channel is represented by an average path loss model obtained by assuming both LOS and non-LOS links [4,5,11]. Although this statistical model provides a good baseline for the network performance on average, it may not predict accurately the coverage for a *specific* urban area. Alternatively, the radio channel can be estimated with high precision using ray-tracing softwares. However, the problem with ray-tracing is that it involves expensive softwares requiring very high load and execution time as well as very accurate 3D map of the urban area including type of building materials. The idea behind our work is to propose a hybrid approach that uses the 3D buildings footprints to estimate the shadowing component, and employs statistical models for the small-scale fading. The proposed channel modeling is then used to estimate the coverage probability as a function of the UAV's position. In this paper, the 3D building footprints from Paris city is used as a use case.

The contributions and organization of the paper are as follows.

1. A comprehensive description of the system model, the studied area, and the realistic channel model that takes into account buildings blockages is provided (see Sect. 2).
2. A simplified method to determine the channel models in terms of LOS probability, and shadowing mean and variance, by using real building footprints is proposed. Our results show that the path loss exponent and the shadowing variance are dependent on both the UAV altitude and the distance on the ground between the UAV and the user (see Sect. 3).
3. To evaluate the coverage, two performance metrics are considered: coverage probability and the meta-distribution of signal-to-noise-ratio (SNR) (see Sect. 4).

4. Simulation results that estimate the coverage probability are discussed (see Sect. 5), and concluding remarks are provided (see Sect. 6).

2   System Model

In this section, we present the studied area and explain the data extraction process. We also provide a comprehensive description of the adopted air-to-ground channel model.

2.1   Area Under Study

In order to capture the effect of buildings obstructions, we consider an urban area from the 16ème arrondissement of Paris. Specifically, we are interested in an area $\mathcal{A}$ of 1055×990 m^2 located at the eastern part of the district as described in Fig. 1. In addition of being a prestigious residential neighborhood, the area of study hosts a large number of companies (PSA Peugeot Citroen, Lafarge ..) and includes a concentration of museums and touristic sites (Guimet museum, Trocadéro place ..) which makes it an interesting case of study (as a dense and diverse area). Data related to area $\mathcal{A}$ is available in [1]. It mainly contains buildings footprints that describe the buildings shapes in 2D (in a shape file) and the number of levels per building (in an excel file) of all Paris city. Since the exact heights of the buildings are not provided, we use, instead, the number of levels per building times the average height per level (2.9 m for Paris). Even though this approximation is not perfectly accurate, it provides good insights on the impact of buildings elevation on coverage. A summary of the characteristics of the studied area is given in Table 1.

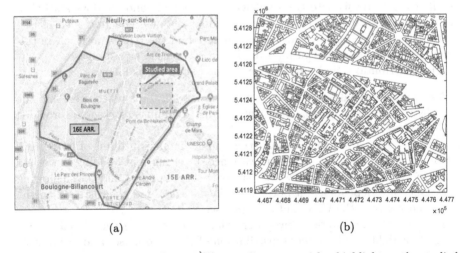

(a)   (b)

Fig. 1. A Google map view of the 16ème arrondissement with a highlight on the studied area, (b) The entire area under analysis with base stations locations, x and y axis express distances in meters

Table 1. A summary of the region under analysis

Location	Area (m × m)	Center location (longitude, latitude)	Density of Buildings	Average number of levels
Paris (16ème)	1055 × 990	(2.27978, 48.86185)	47%	4.13

To extract desirable data from raw data provided by [1], we proceed as follows.

1. A master file that contains all the building footprints of Paris city is downloaded from [1].
2. Data related to the studied area are extracted using Quantum Geographic Information System software (QGIS) [13]. The resulted file is uploaded to Matlab using the mapping toolbox.
3. Users positions are generated in the 2D plane according to a circular grid. The choice of the circular grid provides an easy way for probability of line of sight computation (more details are provided in Sect. 3.1).
4. For the sake of comparison with existing statistical models that assume outdoor users, we remove all points inside building polygons.
5. The UAV is located at the center of the area with fixed x_0 and y_0 coordinates, and a variable altitude h.

2.2 Blockage Model

In an urban type environment, the distortion of the signal due to shadowing is intrinsically dependent on the number of buildings between the UAV and the ground user. In order to capture the effect of obstructions caused by buildings, we adopt the shadowing model proposed in [6].

Assume that N_i is the number of intersected buildings between user i and the UAV. To reach the user, the transmitted signal has to penetrate N_i buildings that cause, for each, a propagation loss of K_b, where $K_b \in [0, 1]$ is the penetration loss related to building b. For the sake of simplicity, we assume that $K_b = K$ is the same for all buildings. As a consequence, the shadowing attenuation h_i between user i and the UAV is given by

$$\zeta_i = K^{N_i}. \tag{1}$$

Note that, when no shadowing is considered, i.e. there is a line-of-sight between the UAV and the ground user, $N_i = 0$ and thus $\zeta_i = 1$.

2.3 Free Space Path Loss Model

We use the standard power-law path loss model where the path loss attenuation between user i and the UAV separated by distance $(r_i^2 + h^2)^2$ is given by $(r_i^2 + h^2)^{\frac{-\alpha_1}{2}}$, with α_1 being the path loss exponent, and r_i is the distance between user i and the projection of the UAV on the 2D plane.

2.4   Small-Scale Fading

We adopt the commonly used Rayleigh fading. We also assume that the Rayleigh channel gains are independent and identically distributed (i.i.d). Hence, the channel power gain g_i between user i and the UAV is a random variable that follows a standard exponential distribution.

3   Simplified Air-To-Ground Channel Model

In this section, we provide a general method to evaluate LOS probability and shadowing mean and variance by using real 3D building footprints.

3.1   Line of Sight Probability

The probability of LOS is a key element when modeling the air-to-ground channel. It is particularly useful to identify straight paths between the UAV and the ground user. In order to compute such probability, we generate outdoor users according to a circular grid centered on the projected position of the UAV on the ground (x_0, y_0). For each circle $\mathcal{C}_j(x_0, y_0, r_j)$ of radius r_j, we identify the number of outdoor users that have a LOS with the UAV. The probability of LOS at a radius $r = r_j$ and an altitude h is estimated as the percentage of outdoor users on the circle that have a LOS with UAV.

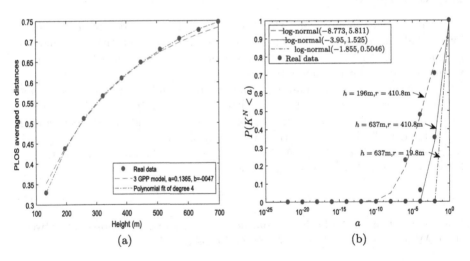

Fig. 2. (a) Average LOS probability, (b) Cumulative distribution function of shadowing, $K = -20\,\mathrm{dB}$

In Fig. 2(a), we compare the actual LOS probability with the following existing statistical model [15]

$$p_{LOS}(r,h) = \frac{1}{1 + a \exp\left(-b\left(\frac{180}{\pi} \arctan\frac{r}{h} - a\right)\right)} \tag{2}$$

where the environmental-dependent variables a and b are obtained by performing a non-linear least square data fitting.

Figure 2(a) plots the probability of LOS as a function of the UAV's altitude. These results are obtained by averaging over 100 distances. We observe a good agreement between the fit of the statistical model and actual data ($R^2 = 0.88$). This fit can be slightly improved by using a polynomial function of degree 4 ($R^2 = 0.9$). As intuitively expected, the probability of LOS is improved when the drone increases its altitude. This is justified by a significant reduction of intersected buildings as the UAV moves up.

3.2 Shadowing

The shadowing accounts for random losses caused by obstructions along the propagation link. In general, the random behavior of shadow fading is modeled by a log-normal variable, with constant mean and variance, that reflects the multiplicative penetration loss caused by buildings [8].

Shadowing CDF. In Fig. 2(a), the cumulative distribution function (CDF) of the adopted shadowing model is plotted. As depicted in the figure, the actual model is compatible with the log-normal shadowing widely adopted in the literature. However, these observations show that the parameters of the log-normal fading are both distance and altitude-dependent. This is corroborated by the next findings regarding the mean and variance of the adopted shadowing model.

Shadowing Mean. To study the shadowing distribution caused by buildings, a good understanding of the mean and variance structure is required. In fact, the shadowing mean with respect to the distance r and height h, $\mu(r,h)$, can be written

$$\mu(r,h) = \sum_{n=0}^{+\infty} \mathbb{P}(N_i(r,h) = n)K^n, \tag{3}$$

where $N_i(r,h)$ denotes the number of intersected buildings for a given distance r and altitude h, and $\mathbb{P}(N_i(r,h) = n)$ is the probability that n buildings are intersected at distance r and altitude h.

The shadowing mean for $r = 311.85$ is plotted in Fig. 3(a). As shown in the figure, the mean value increases with altitude. Moreover, it can be noticed from the same figure that the shadowing mean can be approximated, with a good fit, by a power law function. The shadowing mean is therefore estimated as follows

$$\mu(r,h) \approx (r^2 + h^2)^{-\alpha_2(r,h)/2}. \tag{4}$$

In Fig. 3(b), we plot an approximation of $\alpha_2(r, h)$ for the same distance ($r = 311.85$ m) versus the UAV's height. α_2 is then estimated as follows

$$\alpha_2(r, h) = a_0 r^{b_0} h^{-c_0} - d_0 h + e_0, \tag{5}$$

where a_0, b_0, c_0, d_0 are a non negative parameters to be determined, with the parameter e_0, through curve-fitting.

The proposed fit provides a good estimation of real data, the resulted $R^2 = 0.93, 0.9, 0.88$ for $K = -3$ dB, -10 dB, -20 dB respectively. Moreover, it can be noticed from Eq. (5) and Fig. 3(b) that the shadowing mean exponent, α_2, decays with the drone's height. This is attributed to the fact that the number of intersected buildings decreases as the UAV moves up. These findings are in line with conclusions of works in [20] and [3] where authors show that the path loss exponent decreases with altitude. On the other side, α_2 increases with distance as additional penetration loss will be accumulated for an increasing distance (and fixed height).

Another more intuitive finding is that the shadowing mean estimation is tightly related to buildings penetration loss. In particular the shadow mean increases as the penetration loss increases. This is intuitively expected as additional penetration loss will result in higher shadowing values.

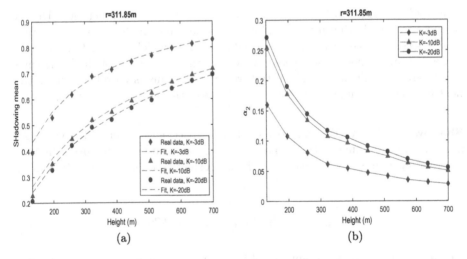

Fig. 3. (a) The mean of the shadowing for distance $r = 361.35$ m, (b) Exponent of the shadowing mean $r = 311.85$ m

Shadowing Variance. The results in Fig. 4(a) show the height-dependency of the shadowing variations for $r = 311.85$ m. In fact, the estimated variance increases as the UAV improves its altitude until a maximal value before it decreases with height. The existence of a height that maximizes the variance depends on the penetration loss. Indeed, when the penetration loss is low, the shadowing variance monotonically decreases with height. Furthermore, the figure shows that the shadowing variance is reduced when the penetration loss is lower. This is attributed to the fact that a building with a lower penetration loss will cause a lower signal distortion. The figure proposes also a simplified expression to estimate the variance by using the following polynomial fit

$$\sigma^2(r, h) \approx \sum_{i=0}^{i=4} \sum_{j=0}^{j=4} a_{ij} r^i h^j, \tag{6}$$

where a_{ij} are determined through curve-fitting. The proposed variance fit results in $R^2 = 0.86, 0.75, 0.75$ for $K = -3\,\text{dB}, -10\,\text{dB}, -20\,\text{dB}$ respectively.

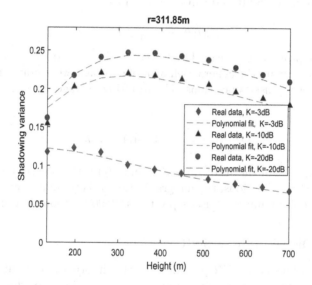

Fig. 4. Variance of the shadowing for distance $r = 311.85\,\text{m}$

It is worth mentioning that the proposed simplified shadowing model does not include correlation. An accurate model should capture spatial correlation between neighboring users. This has been left as part of future work.

4   Performance Metrics

In order to evaluate the effects of shadowing on coverage, we consider two performance metrics: average coverage probability and the meta-distribution of SNR.

4.1   Average Coverage Probability

We consider downlink communication. Hence, when a frame is transmitted by the UAV with power P, it is received at the ground user t with the power $Pg_t K_t^N (r_t^2 + h^2)^{-\alpha_1}$. The quality of the wireless link is measured in terms of SNR γ_t, which is defined as

$$\gamma_t = \frac{Pg_t K_t^N (r_t^2 + h^2)^{-\alpha_1}}{\sigma^2}, \tag{7}$$

where σ^2 represents the power of an additive Gaussian noise.

We are interested in coverage probability for a given user t, which is the probability that the SNR of that user is above a given threshold θ. This probability can also be seen as the complementary cumulative distribution function (CCDF) of the user's SNR and can be written as

$$P_c(t; \theta) = \mathbb{P}(\gamma_t > \theta), \tag{8}$$

Note that this probability is calculated over small-scale fading.

In order to evaluate the general behavior of coverage, we average the coverage probability over the user's positions. The resulting average coverage probability is defined as

$$\tilde{P}_c(\theta) = \frac{1}{|\mathcal{A}|} \int_{\mathcal{A}} \mathbb{P}(\gamma(t) > \theta) dt, \tag{9}$$

with $|\mathcal{A}|$ the surface of the studied area $\mathcal{A}$, and $\gamma(t)$ is the SNR of a ground user at position t. For simulations, the integral in Eq. (9) is computed numerically by considering a finite number of user's positions (2890 positions in our case).

4.2   Meta-Distribution of SNR

The meta-distribution of SNR provides a better information about the performance of the coverage probability. It answers the question 'to what extend the coverage is good?' [9]. For a given threshold θ, and a fixed position of UAV, the meta-distribution is given by the percentage of users that achieve a coverage performance higher than a threshold x. This can be formulated as follows

$$P_m(x, \theta) = \mathbb{P}(P_c(t; \theta) > x), \tag{10}$$

with $x \in [0, 1]$.

5   Coverage Experiments

In this section, we present simulation experiments for coverage performance. Details about simulation settings are provided in Table 2.

Figure 5(a) shows the average coverage probability versus the UAV altitude. Here, it can be seen that for a given desired coverage, there exists an optimal

Table 2. Simulation settings

Parameter	Value
Number of user positions	2890
Monte Carlo simulations	1000
Path loss exponent	$\{2, 3.4\}$
Noise power	$-100\,\text{dBm}$
BS power	$1\,\text{mW}$
Penetration loss	$\{-20, -10, -3\}\,\text{dB}$
Small-scale fading	Rayleigh with parameter 1

altitude at which the average coverage is at its maximum. This optimal altitude is achieved at $700\,\text{m}$ when the path loss exponent $\alpha_1 = 2$, and is equal to $448\,\text{m}$ for $\alpha_1 = 3.4$. Furthermore, the results show that the average coverage probability can be predicted approximately using statistical fits (provided in Sect. 3). The accuracy of such approximation could be improved when spatial correlation is included in the shadowing modeling. In Fig. 5(b), the average meta-distribution

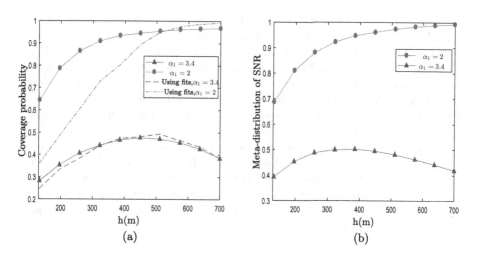

Fig. 5. (a) Average coverage probability, (b) Average of the meta-distribution of coverage. $K = -20\,\text{dB}$, $\theta = -20\,\text{dB}$.

of SNR (average on θ and x) is plotted versus the drone's altitude. Once again, we observe the same trend as for the coverage probability. Moreover, it can be noticed from Fig. 6 that the meta-distribution of SNR decreases when the thresholds θ and x increase as intuitively expected.

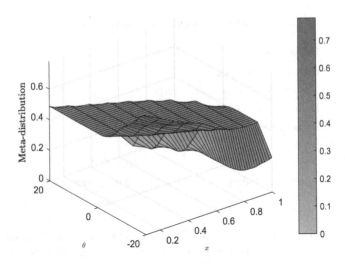

Fig. 6. A 3D illustration of the meta-distribution, $h = 322\,\mathrm{m}$, $K = -20\,\mathrm{dB}$

6   Conclusion

In this paper, we presented a general framework to model the air-to-ground channel model using 3D building footprints. More specifically, we proposed to use 3D building maps to estimate the line-of-sight probability, the CDF of the shadowing and its mean and variance. Our findings show that it is important to include distance and altitude-dependent parameters for the air-to-ground channel modeling. Particularly, we showed that the path loss exponent decreases with UAV's altitude and increases with the distance on the ground between the UAV and the user. We also showed that the shadow fading variance is reduced for higher altitudes. Furthermore, our proposed method allows for a tractable way of estimating the wireless coverage of urban areas. Indeed, instead of using sophisticated ray-tracing techniques that are both expensive and time-consuming, only 3D maps are needed in order to provide a reliable channel modeling. In ongoing work, we are investigating the effect of the spatial shadow correlation, and interfering UAVs on coverage performance.

References

1. https://opendata.paris.fr/explore/dataset/volumesbatisparis2011/ (2017)
2. Al-Hourani, A., Kandeepan, S., Jamalipour, A.: Modeling air-to-ground path loss for low altitude platforms in urban environments. In: IEEE Global Communications Conference (GLOBECOM), Austin, USA, pp. 2898–2904, December 2014
3. Amorim, R., Nguyen, H., Mogensen, P., Kovács, I.Z., Wigard, J., Sørensen, T.B.: Radio channel modeling for UAV communication over cellular networks. IEEE Wirel. Commun. Lett. **6**(4), 514–517 (2017)

4. Azari, M.M., Murillo, Y., Amin, O., Rosas, F., Alouini, M.S., Pollin, S.: Coverage maximization for a poisson field of drone cells. arXiv preprint arXiv:1708.06598 (2017)
5. Azari, M.M., Rosas, F., Chiumento, A., Pollin, S.: Coexistence of terrestrial and aerial users in cellular networks. arXiv preprint arXiv:1710.03103 (2017)
6. Baccelli, F., Zhang, X.: A correlated shadowing model for urban wireless networks. In: 2015 IEEE Conference on Computer Communications (INFOCOM), pp. 801–809 (2015)
7. Bucaille, I., Héthuin, S., Munari, A., Hermenier, R., Rasheed, T., Allsopp, S.: Rapidly deployable network for tactical applications: aerial base station with opportunistic links for unattended and temporary events absolute example. In: IEEE Military Communications Conference (MILCOM), San Diego, USA, pp. 1116–1120, November 2013
8. Coulson, A.J., Williamson, A.G., Vaughan, R.G.: A statistical basis for lognormal shadowing effects in multipath fading channels. IEEE Trans. Commun. 46(4), 494–502 (1998)
9. Haenggi, M.: The meta distribution of the SIR in poisson bipolar and cellular networks. IEEE Trans. Wirel. Commun. 15(4), 2577–2589 (2016)
10. Hayajneh, A.M., Zaidi, S.A.R., McLernon, D.C., Ghogho, M.: Optimal dimensioning and performance analysis of drone-based wireless communications. In: IEEE Globecom Workshops (GC Wkshps), pp. 1–6 (2016)
11. Kalantari, E., Yanikomeroglu, H., Yongacoglu, A.: On the number and 3D placement of drone base stations in wireless cellular networks. In: IEEE Vehicular Technology Conference (VTC-Fall), pp. 1–6 (2016)
12. Lee, G., Saad, W., Bennis, M., Mehbodniya, A., Adachi, F.: Online ski rental for scheduling self-powered, energy harvesting small base stations. In: IEEE International Conference on Communications (ICC), Kuala Lumpur, Malaysia, pp. 1–6, May 2016
13. Q Software Manual. http://www.qgis.org/en/site/ (2017)
14. Motlagh, N.H., Taleb, T., Arouk, O.: Low-altitude unmanned aerial vehicles-based internet of things services: comprehensive survey and future perspectives. IEEE Internet Things J. PP(99), 1–27 (2016)
15. Mozaffari, M., Saad, W., Bennis, M., Debbah, M.: Drone small cells in the clouds: design, deployment and performance analysis. In: IEEE Global Communications Conference (GLOBECOM), San Francisco, USA, pp. 1–6, December 2015
16. Mozaffari, M., Saad, W., Bennis, M., Debbah, M.: Efficient deployment of multiple unmanned aerial vehicles for optimal wireless coverage. arXiv preprint arXiv:1606.01962 (2016)
17. Mozaffari, M., Saad, W., Bennis, M., Debbah, M.: Unmanned aerial vehicle with underlaid device-to-device communications: performance and tradeoffs. IEEE Trans. Wirel. Commun. 15(6), 3949–3963 (2016)
18. Ravi, V.V.C., Dhillon, H.: Downlink coverage probability in a finite network of unmanned aerial vehicle (UAV) base stations. In: IEEE International Workshop on Signal Processing Advances in Wireless Communications (SPAWC), Edinburgh, United Kingdom, pp. 1–5, July 2016
19. Rohde, S., Wietfeld, C.: Interference aware positioning of aerial relays for cell overload and outage compensation. In: IEEE Vehicular Technology Conference (VTC Fall), Quebec, Canada, pp. 1–5, September 2012
20. Sallouha, H., Azari, M.M., Chiumento, A., Pollin, S.: Aerial anchors positioning for reliable RSS-based outdoor localization in urban environments. IEEE Wirel. Commun. Lett. PP(99) (2017)

On-Board Target Virtualization Using Image Features for UAV Autonomous Tracking

Vinicio S. Salcedo[1], Wilbert G. Aguilar[1,2(✉)], Bryan Cobeña[1],
Jorge A. Pardo[3], and Zahira Proaño[3]

[1] CICTE Research Center, Universidad de Las Fuerzas Armadas ESPE,
Sangolquí, Ecuador
wgaguilar@espe.edu.ec
[2] GREC Research Group, Universitat Politècnica de Catalunya,
Barcelona, Spain
[3] UGT Department, Universidad de Las Fuerzas Armadas ESPE,
Latacunga, Ecuador

Abstract. This paper describes a proposal of solution for target visual loss in autonomous navigation of UAVs by using artificial. Tests of target maintenance and position recovery have been included along with the sequence of images that verify the method performance.

Keywords: UAV · Target location · Geometric transform · Motion estimation

1 Introduction

The use of unmanned aerial vehicles (UAV) has been a great advance in civil applications such as event detection, object recognition, cultivation soils, vehicular traffic, 3D modeling and others [1]. Human operation of aerial vehicles has several drawbacks [9, 40] and decreases the effectiveness and speed of the proposed routines, so there is the need to develop algorithms that support the navigation in micro or macro scale UAVs. Some applications can perform using its size and capabilities with innovative systems for its control as shown in [3], control through Google glass, brain computer interface or large distance remote control, but still susceptible to climate change that restrict their use [4, 21].

UAVs main on-board resources for data acquisition are: the camera, IMU and GPS, however, there are environments where GPS does not work or there is IMU problems [5] leaving only camera images as position and navigation feedback. For this cases it is necessary a good image capture [6] and a reliable and robust image processing with an undesired effects reduction [7] to ensure the correct navigation and target location.

In navigation and target location, the system is expected to be robust for different environment changes. The use of image features allows the target discrimination despite visualization changes. Events such as drone flight disturbances or advanced flight speeds cause the sudden target loss [19], so that many jobs related to drone navigation opt for different methods for this, such as continuous mapping, for example [12] where the SLAM algorithm is applied to perform the mapping and subsequent

© Springer Nature Switzerland AG 2018
N. Boudriga et al. (Eds.): UNet 2018, LNCS 11277, pp. 384–391, 2018.
https://doi.org/10.1007/978-3-030-02849-7_34

navigation control, or in [15] through scenario reconstructions with SLAM, other proposals opt for reliability on image capture and other sensors, when target is loss of sight maintains search algorithms or specific routines [6, 8, 21]. However performing the continuous mapping for target localization and monitoring means a high computational cost and a response speed reduction compared with image features.

This work includes Random Sample Consensus (RANSAC) [23] to remove outliers followed by the estimation of the target position based on inter-frame motion.

2 Related Works

Multiple proposal for UAV autonomous navigation are based on two main components: Perception, Visual SLAM system with monocular cameras [12, 15, 41] or cameras RGB-D [42–44] for real-time mapping, and an Extended Kalman filter for sensor data fusion and UAV state estimation. Trajectory Tracking, A map-based trajectory planner probabilistic or search trees [45, 46] and a PID control for tracking trajectory.

These methods are implemented in [12] where continuous scene constructions are made with monocular SLAM for visual perception, altitude and depth data is obtained by ultrasonic and barometer sensors, then the motion parameters are clearly extract. In [15] the 3D scene reconstruction with SLAM is achieved with great efficiency thanks to the use of omnidirectional cameras, making the orientation and location more accurate with environment.

Although the use of these methods allows great autonomy and a robust target location, the use of SLAM with monocular cameras makes the procedure more expensive computationally, some approaches overcome this problem as in [47] where the use of multiple MAVs allow perception with visual SLAM and real-time mapping.

In addition [38–40] monocular SLAM is used to improve the positioning of a low cost quadcopter achieving errors of few centimeters and making it unnecessary to use GPS or artificial reference points, giving room to unknown environments.

We have decided to work with the Bebop mini drone of the brand Parrot, an UAV to the micro scale in the VI classification according to [3, 4] which is easy to assemble and with ten minutes of autonomy in the air, it also has a powerful built-in computer, flight and video stability algorithms. This drone has a 14-megapixel front facing fisheye camera with 180° and video stabilization algorithms.

3 Image Features

Once the image extraction process has been made from the vision device on board the micro UAV, the next step is processing them to obtain its features, which must comply in being enough, compact, invariant and congruent [25, 26].

The image feature types can vary in a large number of possibilities such as edges, interest points, blobs, corners, textures and colors that set the beginning of the process of finding similarities between images [26].

Among the most famous keypoint detection algorithms, there are Harris detectors [27] that have a high invariance to rotational changes of characteristic points and robustness to intensity changes, then there are SIFT(Scale Invariant Feature Transform) detectors [28–30] and Speeded Up Robust Features(SURF), the first ones are very efficient when it comes to images that have scale variations and are perfect for noisy environments, the second ones present a speed ten times higher than SIFT based on an approximation of the Hessian matrix for its obtainment [31].

In spite of SIFT and SURF detectors good performance, the ORB (Oriented FAST and Rotated BRIEF [32–34]) detection and description algorithms work very efficiently when it comes to on board cameras and agile processing, this is because the ORB keypoint detection uses the Features from Accelerated Segment Test (FAST) algorithm with a set of descriptors from Binary Robust Independent Elementary Features (BRIEF).

4 Target Detection and Location

The process called matching is responsible of finding correspondences between the images, based on the measurement of the descriptor vectors of each one as a distance vector that is matched as the error that differs the least between points of each frame.

To increase the quality of inter-frame feature detection and matching, the algorithm RANSAC (Random Sample Consensus) [23] has been used, which consist in the decrease in differences of the gray level and allows the removal of correspondences that do not adjust to the model, in a determined amount of iterative repetitions.

When a fixed target is used as processing and matching reference, there is a loss of keypoints with the motion and light changes, besides the correspondent blur, in such a way that the uncertainty in target detection is increased.

In spite of algorithms that look for system robustness such as ORB and RANSAC for the matching, a decrease in the target image matches is denoted.

One solution to avoid the loss of correspondences and outlier generation is to make the matching process frame to frame, in this way the change in lightning intensity, rotation and scaling do not differ in a great way from a descriptor vector to another.

The geometric transformations used in this work serve mainly to relate 3D geometry from the drone navigation space with the on board camera and the 2D images captured. The three dimensional space in E^3 denote that each frame would be represented by a point to point relation of a R^3 set with the Euclidean space E^3 [35].

This transformations allows the motion parameter estimation in the interval of frame capturing to be made. The analyzed frames motion can be expressed as:

$$X_{sp} = H_t X_t \tag{1}$$

Where a set of X_t points are converted to X_{sp}, the behavior of this conversion depends on the H_t transformation matrix that can vary between the three most common models, translation model, affine model and perspective model [36, 37].

In this work the latter transformation has been chosen, the perspective that integrates three rotations and translations needed to be completed, its transformation matrix

H is the one responsible to give the pertinent parameters to the change in perspective given between the compared frame and the set point frame denoted by the Eq. (2).

$$H_t = \begin{bmatrix} h_{11} & h_{12} & h_{13} \\ h_{21} & h_{22} & h_{23} \\ h_{31} & h_{32} & 1 \end{bmatrix} \tag{2}$$

Finally, an encapsulation has been done, to follow the target in the drone motion sequence by applying the perspective transformation that transfers the target image frame, to a frame with the correspondent one as shown in Fig. 1:

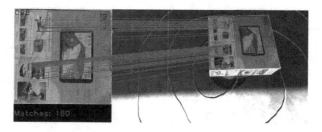

Fig. 1. Target encapsulation with a bounding frame.

5   Target Virtual Position

The target loss of sight causes it to no longer be able to follow the trajectory or come close thereof. To solve this problem a target bounding box virtual position refreshment has been done with a frame to frame matching algorithm by applying the perspective transformation of said frame by moving the box to where the image has moved in regard to the previous frame, which allows us to obtain the target virtual position without the need of watching it directly. Figure 2 shows the procedure that is performed to maintain the position of a target as virtual.

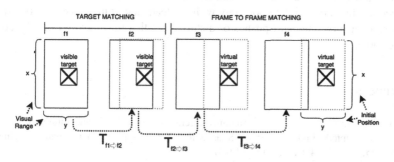

Fig. 2. Virtual target represented by transforms frame to frame.

It can be appreciated that the operation $T_{f1 \to f2}$ represents the geometric transformation of the $f1$ frame in perspective to the $f2$ frame where this transformation is applied to the Eq. 1 in the target points that originally where in $f1$ to move them to a new position in $f2$.

6 Experimentation, Conclusions and Future Works

It can be seen in Fig. 3 the application of algorithm in a controlled sequence of movements allowing an estimation of target position to remain keeping it out of sight.

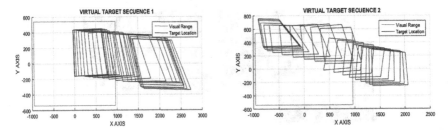

Fig. 3. Maintenance of virtual target position in four sequences of predefined movements.

The predefined sequences of movements are defined as follows:

1. Target recognition and take it out of camera vision (to the right)
2. Recovery of target visibility (bottom).

An optimal solution has been presented to detect and maintain targets that can be lost from sight by spatial disorientation, visualization changes or motion routines through the keypoint detection, description and the collaborative matching of the target and the consecutive frames for orientation in the scene, through geometric transformations with continuous references of previous frames.

For future work, we intend to design an algorithm for the robust landing of UAVs in objectives that move in the floor, only with the feedback of the camera on board, and able to recover movements of pushes or disturbances that move away from the correct landing route.

References

1. Limnaios, G.: Current usage of unmanned aircraft systems (UAS) and future challenges: a mission oriented simulator for UAS as a tool for design and performance evaluation. J. Comput. Model 4(1), 167–188 (2014)
2. Achille, C., et al.: UAV-based photogrammetry and integrated technologies for architectural applications—methodological strategies for the after-quake survey of vertical structures in Mantua (Italy). Sensors 15(7), 15520–15539 (2015)

3. Hassanalian, M., Abdelkefi, A.: Classifications, applications, and design challenges of drones: a review. Prog. Aerosp. Sci. **91**, 99–131 (2017)
4. Aguilar, W.G., Salcedo, V.S., Sandoval, D.S., Cobeña, B.: Developing of a video-based model for UAV autonomous navigation. In: Barone, D.A.C., Teles, E.O., Brackmann, C. P. (eds.) LAWCN 2017. CCIS, vol. 720, pp. 94–105. Springer, Cham (2017). https://doi.org/10.1007/978-3-319-71011-2_8
5. Duffy, J.P., et al.: Location, location, location: considerations when using lightweight drones in challenging environments. Remote Sens. Ecol. Conserv. 1–13 (2017)
6. Aguilar, W.G., et al.: Cascade classifiers and saliency maps based people detection. In: De Paolis, L.T., Bourdot, P., Mongelli, A. (eds.) AVR 2017. LNCS, vol. 10325, pp. 501–510. Springer, Cham (2017). https://doi.org/10.1007/978-3-319-60928-7_42
7. Aguilar, W.G., Angulo, C.: Real-time model-based video stabilization for microaerial vehicles. Neural Process. Lett. **43**(2), 459–477 (2016)
8. Aguilar, W.G., et al.: Pedestrian detection for UAVs using cascade classifiers and saliency maps. In: Rojas, I., Joya, G., Catala, A. (eds.) IWANN 2017. LNCS, vol. 10306, pp. 563–574. Springer, Cham (2017). https://doi.org/10.1007/978-3-319-59147-6_48
9. Tribukait, A., Bergsten, E., Eiken, O.: Pitch-plane angular displacement perception during helicopter flight and gondola centrifugation. Aerosp. Med. Hum. Perform. **87**(10), 852–861 (2016)
10. Márquez Pardo, I.: Visual control of a mobile robot by means of an overhead view (Bachelor's thesis) (2016)
11. Arróspide, J., Salgado, L.: Video based vehicle detection and tracking for driver assistance systems. Securitas Vialis **7**(1–3), 41–49 (2015)
12. Urzua, S., Munguía, R., Grau, A.: Vision-based SLAM system for MAVs in GPS-denied environments. Int. J. Micro Air Veh. **9**, 283–296 (2017)
13. Revollo Sarmiento, N., Delrieux, C., Perillo, G.M.: Software de visión por computador en sistemas de monitoreo ambiental. In: XIV Workshop de Investigadores en Ciencias de la Computación (2012)
14. Rituerto, A.: Modeling the environment with egocentric vision systems. ELCVIA Electron. Lett. Comput. Vis. Image Anal. **14**(3), 49–51 (2015)
15. Rituerto, A., Puig, L., Guerrero, J.J.: Comparison of omnidirectional and conventional monocular systems for visual slam. In: 10th OMNIVIS with RSS (2010)
16. Grenzdörffer, G.J., Niemeyer, F.: UAV based BRDF-measurements of agricultural surfaces with PFIFFikus. Int. Arch. Photogr. Remote Sens. Spat. Inf. Sci. **38**(1/C22), 229–234 (2011)
17. Remondino, F., Barazzetti, L., Nex, F., Scaioni, M., Sarazzi, D.: UAV photogrammetry for mapping and 3D modeling–current status and future perspectives. Int. Arch. Photogr. Remote Sens. Spat. Inf. Sci. **38**(1), C22 (2011)
18. Guzmán, D.A.I., Alarcón, J.R.C., Torres, A.A., Bárcenas, M.A.M.: Design of an artificial neural network to detect obstacles on highways through the flight of an UAV. Res. Comput. Sci. **105**, 31–40 (2015)
19. Paillard, A.C., Quarck, G., Denise, P.: Sensorial countermeasures for vestibular spatial disorientation. Aviat. Space environ. Med. **85**(5), 563–567 (2014)
20. Clarke, R.: Understanding the drone epidemic. Comput. Law Secur. Rev. **30**(3), 230–246 (2014)
21. Charmette, B., Royer, E., Chausse, F.: Vision-based robot localization based on the efficient matching of planar features. Mach. Vis. Appl. **27**(4), 415–436 (2016)
22. Chmaj, G., Selvaraj, H.: Distributed processing applications for UAV/drones: a survey. In: Selvaraj, H., Zydek, D., Chmaj, G. (eds.) Progress in Systems Engineering. AISC, vol. 366, pp. 449–454. Springer, Cham (2015). https://doi.org/10.1007/978-3-319-08422-0_66

23. Derpanis, K.G.: Overview of the RANSAC algorithm. Image Rochester NY **4**(1), 2–3 (2010)
24. Kendoul, F.: Survey of advances in guidance, navigation, and control of unmanned rotorcraft systems. J. Field Robot. **29**(2), 315–378 (2012)
25. Jégou, H., Douze, M., Schmid, C., Pérez, P.: Aggregating local descriptors into a compact image representation. In: 2010 IEEE Conference on Computer Vision and Pattern Recognition (CVPR), pp. 3304–3311. IEEE (2010)
26. Awad, A.I., Hassaballah, M.: Image Feature Detectors and Descriptors: Foundations and Applications, vol. 630. Springer, Heidelberg (2016)
27. Sayem, A.S.S.: Vision-Aided Navigation for Autonomous Vehicles Using Tracked Feature Points (2016)
28. Zhang, X., Wang, X., Yuan, X., Wang, S.: An improved SIFT algorithm in the application of close-range stereo image matching. In: IOP Conference Series: Earth and Environmental Science, vol. 46, No. 1, p. 012009. IOP Publishing (2016)
29. Al-khafaji, S.L., Zhou, J., Zia, A., Liew, A.W.C.: Spectral-spatial scale invariant feature transform for hyperspectral images. IEEE Trans. Image Process. **27**, 837–850 (2017)
30. Lowe, D.: Object recognition from local scale-invariant features. In: Proceedings of IEEE International Conference on Computer Vision, vol. 2, pp. 1150–1157 (1999)
31. Aguilar, W.G., Angulo, C.: Real-time video stabilization without phantom movements for micro aerial vehicles. EURASIP J. Image Video Process. **12**(1), 46 (2014)
32. Zhu, Y., Shen, X., Chen, H.: Copy-move forgery detection based on scaled ORB. Multimed. Tools Appl. **75**(6), 3221–3233 (2016)
33. Xie, S., Zhang, W., Ying, W., Zakim, K.: Fast detecting moving objects in moving background using ORB feature matching. In: 2013 Fourth International Conference on Intelligent Control and Information Processing (ICICIP), pp. 304–309. IEEE (2013)
34. Rublee, E., Rabaud, V., Konolige, K., Bradski, G.: ORB: an efficient alternative to SIFT or SURF. In: ICCV (2011)
35. Ma, Y., Soatto, S., Kosecka, J., Sastry, S.S.: An Invitation to 3-D Vision: From Images to Geometric Models, vol. 26. Springer, Heidelberg (2012)
36. Aguilar, W.G., Casaliglla, V.P., Pólit, J.L.: Obstacle avoidance based-visual navigation for micro aerial vehicles. Electronics **6**(1), 10 (2017)
37. Aguilar, W.G., Casaliglla, V.P., Pólit, J.L., Abad, V., Ruiz, H.: Obstacle avoidance for flight safety on unmanned aerial vehicles. In: Rojas, I., Joya, G., Catala, A. (eds.) IWANN 2017. LNCS, vol. 10306, pp. 575–584. Springer, Cham (2017). https://doi.org/10.1007/978-3-319-59147-6_49
38. Engel, J., Sturm, J., Cremers, D.: Accurate figure flying with a quadrocopter using onboard visual and inertial sensing. Imu **320**, 240 (2012)
39. Engel, J., Sturm, J., Cremers, D.: Camera-based navigation of a low-cost quadrocopter. In: 2012 IEEE/RSJ International Conference on Intelligent Robots and Systems (IROS), pp. 2815–2821. IEEE (2012)
40. Papakonstantinou, A., Topouzelis, K., Pavlogeorgatos, G.: Coastline zones identification and 3D coastal mapping using UAV spatial data. ISPRS Int. J. Geo-Inf. **5**(6), 75 (2016)
41. Urzua, S., Munguía, R., Grau, A.: Vision-based SLAM system for MAVs in GPS-denied environments. Int. J. Micro Air Veh. **9**(4), 283–296 (2017)
42. Aguilar, W.G., Rodríguez, G.A., Álvarez, L., Sandoval, S., Quisaguano, F., Limaico, A.: Visual SLAM with a RGB-D camera on a quadrotor UAV using on-board processing. In: Rojas, I., Joya, G., Catala, A. (eds.) IWANN 2017. LNCS, vol. 10306, pp. 596–606. Springer, Cham (2017). https://doi.org/10.1007/978-3-319-59147-6_51

43. Aguilar, W.G., Rodríguez, G.A., Álvarez, L., Sandoval, S., Quisaguano, F., Limaico, A.: Real-time 3D modeling with a RGB-D camera and on-board processing. In: De Paolis, L.T., Bourdot, P., Mongelli, A. (eds.) AVR 2017. LNCS, vol. 10325, pp. 410–419. Springer, Cham (2017). https://doi.org/10.1007/978-3-319-60928-7_35

44. Aguilar, W.G., Rodríguez, G.A., Álvarez, L., Sandoval, S., Quisaguano, F., Limaico, A.: On-board visual SLAM on a UGV using a RGB-D camera. In: Huang, Y., Wu, H., Liu, H., Yin, Z. (eds.) ICIRA 2017. LNCS (LNAI), vol. 10464, pp. 298–308. Springer, Cham (2017). https://doi.org/10.1007/978-3-319-65298-6_28

45. Aguilar, W.G., Morales, S.G.: 3D environment mapping using the Kinect V2 and path planning based on RRT algorithms. Electronics 5(4), 70 (2016)

46. Aguilar, W.G., Morales, S., Ruiz, H., Abad, V.: RRT* GL based optimal path planning for real-time navigation of UAVs. In: Rojas, I., Joya, G., Catala, A. (eds.) IWANN 2017. LNCS, vol. 10306, pp. 585–595. Springer, Cham (2017). https://doi.org/10.1007/978-3-319-59147-6_50

47. Forster, C., Lynen, S., Kneip, L., Scaramuzza, D.: Collaborative monocular slam with multiple micro aerial vehicles. In: 2013 IEEE/RSJ International Conference on Intelligent Robots and Systems (IROS), pp. 3962–3970. IEEE, November 2013

Monocular Depth Perception on a Micro-UAV Using Convolutional Neuronal Networks

Wilbert G. Aguilar[1,2(✉)], Fernando J. Quisaguano[1],
Leandro G. Alvarez[1], Jorge A. Pardo[3], and Zahira Proaño[3]

[1] CICTE Research Center, Universidad de las Fuerzas Armadas ESPE,
Sangolquí, Ecuador
wgaguilar@espe.edu.ec
[2] GREC Research Group, Universitat Politècnica de Catalunya,
Barcelona, Spain
[3] UGT Department, Universidad de las Fuerzas Armadas ESPE,
Latacunga, Ecuador

Abstract. In this article, we present the use of depth estimation in real time using the on-board camera in a micro-UAV through convolutional neuronal networks. The experiments and results of the implementation of the system in a micro-UAV are presented to verify the unsupervised model improvement with monocular cameras and the error regarding real model.

Keywords: Monocular · MAV · Depth estimation

1 Introduction

In this last decade, the interest in UAVs and their autonomy has increased steadily [1, 2], the prevention of collisions is an important requirement for autonomous flights [3, 4]. Unmanned Autonomous vehicles have raised wide interest in recent years with various applications such as inspection, monitoring [5, 6] and mapping [7–9]. Just as the estimation of depth from images has a long history in computer vision [10]. Recently, to imitate human behavior, we have developed algorithms in learning to predict paths [11, 12] directly from an RGB image, especially with the popularity of convolutional neural networks (CNN) [13].

With individual images they were studied for the first time for the extraction of depth, using Supervised Learning by Saxena, et al [13]. However, most existing approaches treat depth prediction as a supervised regression problem and as a result, require huge quantities of corresponding ground truth depth data for training [10].

Clearly there is evidence of a remarkable superiority of this method and hence the decision of the use of it in this article. The use of this method for depth detection is essential for obstacle evacuation in drones. Because the ability to detect and avoid obstacles like birds flying in a forest is fascinating and has been the subject of much research [15]. The objective of this paper is to estimate the error that this unsupervised method offers in a Parrot Bebop drone since this will be based on the captured images of the built-in camera. So the method behaves quickly and only takes about 35 ms to predict a dense depth map for a 512×256 image on a modern GPU [10].

© Springer Nature Switzerland AG 2018
N. Boudriga et al. (Eds.): UNet 2018, LNCS 11277, pp. 392–397, 2018.
https://doi.org/10.1007/978-3-030-02849-7_35

2   System Overview

The present work is developed with Mini RUAS that are man-portable and can fly outdoors as well as in confined and indoor environments [16]. Bebop 2 mini drone from the company Parrot, is a micro-scale UAV of this classification VI. It is easy to assemble and with twenty-five minutes of autonomy in the air, it also has an integrated computer which allows you to execute flight and video stability algorithms.

To obtain images we used the autonomy_bebop driver based on the official Parrot ARDrone_SDK3 SDK. This allows the use of several functions of the drone translating in topics, services, messages and parameters as well as access to the images of the drone. One of the most important points of Bebop Parrot ARDroneSDK3 is that the quality of the video is limited to 640×368 image at 30 Hz [10].

For the process of obtaining images we need to connect ROS and OpenCV with the programming language of python or c++ by converting ROS images into OpenCV images, this process is necessary since ROS publishes the images as a type of message and if it is desired to carry out a subsequent processing it must be converted to OpenCV images and corresponds to the diagram presented in Fig. 1.

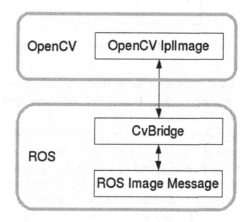

Fig. 1. Image conversion between ROS message type and OpenCV.

Finally the drone Bebop 2 can send the forward-facing camera image via WiFi to our host laptop. The laptop is equipped with GeForce GTX 1060 Q-MAX GPU for CNN prediction. There is also image transmission delay about 0.2 s.

Our contribution consists of the combined use of these current methods on UAV. To obtaining the image we must add a dependency to opencv2 and cv_bridge of ROS. Converting an image message pointer to an OpenCV message only requires a call to the function imgmsg_to_cv2(). This takes in the image message, as well as the encoding of the destination OpenCV image.

We will need an image stream. Run a camera or play a bag file to generate the image stream. Now we can run this node, remapping the image stream topic to the "image_topic" as we observed in Fig. 2.

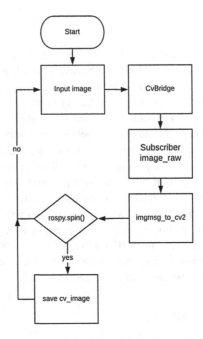

Fig. 2. Flow diagram of the process of obtaining a drone image by means of autonomy_bebop

This takes in the image message, as well as the encoding of the destination OpenCV image with imgmsg_to_cv2. Finally for the rospy.spin method to avoid leaving the program until this node is stopped.

Given a single image I at test time, our goal is to learn a function f that can predict the per-pixel scene depth, $\hat{d} = f(I)$ [17–19]. Specifically, at training time, we have access to two images I^l and I^r, corresponding to the left and right color images from a calibrated stereo pair, captured at the same moment in time. Instead of trying to directly predict the depth, we attempt to find the dense correspondence field d^r that, when applied to the left image, would enable us to reconstruct the right image. We will refer to the reconstructed image $I^l(d^r)$ as $\tilde{I}^r$. Similarly, we can also estimate the left image given the right one, $\tilde{I}^l = I^r(d^l)$. Assuming that the images are rectified [20] d corresponds to the image disparity - a scalar value per pixel that our model will learn to predict.

3   Results and Discussion

To estimate the error in the distance measured by the drone, we based on a known distance to a reference point, we calculate the error at different instances of the flying process.

We using 10 tests to have an average of them, the objects presented in Fig. 3. Given the value of the pixel of a certain coordinate of the object.

Fig. 3. The test objects in this case are cars that we reprimand with "X" and failing with "X'" for identification.

The error measured is 6.08% with respect to the distance real. This proves that our system is accurate enough to perform to the use of obstacle evasion in drones for future research.

4 Conclusions and Future Work

In this document, we propose a navigation system based on CNN applicable to various environments. But above all with methods superior to many previously shown and therefore the error of the distance obtained in a monocular image is small and could be said to improve by having objects closer to the drone.

In the future investigations, the concept obtained from convolutional neural networks will be taken but in everything to the detection of objects so that in this way an autonomous micro-UAV can be modeled and controlled.

Acknowledgement. This work is part of the project Perception and localization system for autonomous navigation of rotor micro aerial vehicle in gps-denied environments, VisualNav-Drone, 2016-PIC-024, from the Universidad de las Fuerzas Armadas ESPE, directed by Dr. Wilbert G. Aguilar.

References

1. Aguilar, W.G., Angulo, C.: Real-time model-based video stabilization for microaerial vehicles. Neural Process. Lett. **43**(2), 459–477 (2016)
2. Aguilar, W.G., Angulo, C.: Real-time video stabilization without phantom movements for micro aerial vehicles. EURASIP J. Image Video Process. **2014**(1), 46 (2014)
3. Gageik, N., Benz, P., Montenegro, S.: Obstacle detection and collision avoidance for a UAV with complementary low-cost sensors. IEEE Access **3**, 599–609 (2015)
4. Yang, S., Konam, S., Ma, C., Rosenthal, S., Veloso, M., Scherer, S.: Obstacle avoidance through deep networks based intermediate perception (2017)
5. Aguilar, W.G., et al.: Pedestrian detection for UAVs using cascade classifiers and saliency maps. In: Rojas, I., Joya, G., Catala, A. (eds.) IWANN 2017. LNCS, vol. 10306, pp. 563–574. Springer, Cham (2017). https://doi.org/10.1007/978-3-319-59147-6_48
6. Aguilar, W.G., et al.: Cascade classifiers and saliency maps based people detection. In: De Paolis, L.T., Bourdot, P., Mongelli, A. (eds.) AVR 2017. LNCS, vol. 10325, pp. 501–510. Springer, Cham (2017). https://doi.org/10.1007/978-3-319-60928-7_42
7. Aguilar, W.G., Rodríguez, G.A., Álvarez, L., Sandoval, S., Quisaguano, F., Limaico, A.: Visual SLAM with a RGB-D camera on a quadrotor UAV using on-board processing. In: Rojas, I., Joya, G., Catala, A. (eds.) IWANN 2017. LNCS, vol. 10306, pp. 596–606. Springer, Cham (2017). https://doi.org/10.1007/978-3-319-59147-6_51
8. Aguilar, W.G., Rodríguez, G.A., Álvarez, L., Sandoval, S., Quisaguano, F., Limaico, A.: Real-iime 3D modeling with a RGB-D camera and on-board processing. In: De Paolis, L.T., Bourdot, P., Mongelli, A. (eds.) AVR 2017. LNCS, vol. 10325, pp. 410–419. Springer, Cham (2017). https://doi.org/10.1007/978-3-319-60928-7_35
9. Aguilar, W.G., Rodríguez, G.A., Álvarez, L., Sandoval, S., Quisaguano, F., Limaico, A.: On-board visual SLAM on a UGV using a RGB-D camera. In: Huang, Y., Wu, H., Liu, H., Yin, Z. (eds.) ICIRA 2017. LNCS (LNAI), vol. 10464, pp. 298–308. Springer, Cham (2017). https://doi.org/10.1007/978-3-319-65298-6_28
10. Godard, C., Mac Aodha, O., Brostow, G.J.: Unsupervised monocular depth estimation with left-right consistency (2016)
11. Aguilar, W.G., Morales, S.G.: 3D environment mapping using the Kinect V2 and path planning based on RRT algorithms. Electronics **5**(4), 70 (2016)
12. Aguilar, W.G., Morales, S., Ruiz, H., Abad, V.: RRT* GL based optimal path planning for real-time navigation of UAVs. In: Rojas, I., Joya, G., Catala, A. (eds.) IWANN 2017. LNCS, vol. 10306, pp. 585–595. Springer, Cham (2017). https://doi.org/10.1007/978-3-319-59147-6_50
13. Giusti, A., et al.: A machine learning approach to visual perception of forest trails for mobile robots. IEEE Robot. Autom. Lett. **1**(2), 661–667 (2016)
14. Saxena, A., Chung, S.H., Ng, A.Y.: Learning depth from single monocular images. In: Advances in Neural Information Processing Systems, vol. 18, pp. 1161–1168 (2006)
15. Mori, T., Scherer, S.: The First results in detecting and avoiding frontal obstacle from monocular camera for micro unmanned aerial vehicles. In: 2013 IEEE International Conference on Robotics and Automation (ICRA), vol. 53, no. 9, pp. 1689–1699 (2013)
16. Montgomery, J., Roumeliotis, S.I., Johnson, A., Matthies, L.: The jet propulsion laboratory autonomous helicopter testbed: a platform for planetary exploration technology research and development. J. Feild Robot. **23**(2), 245–267 (2006)

17. Aguilar, W.G., Salcedo, V.S., Sandoval, D.S., Cobeña, B.: Developing of a video-based model for UAV autonomous navigation. In: Barone, D.A.C., Teles, E.O., Brackmann, C. P. (eds.) LAWCN 2017. CCIS, vol. 720, pp. 94–105. Springer, Cham (2017). https://doi.org/ 10.1007/978-3-319-71011-2_8
18. Aguilar, W.G., Casaliglla, V.P., Pólit, J.L.: Obstacle avoidance based-visual navigation for micro aerial vehicles. Electronics 6(1), 10 (2017)
19. Aguilar, W.G., Casaliglla, V.P., Pólit, J.L., Abad, V., Ruiz, H.: Obstacle avoidance for flight safety on unmanned aerial vehicles. In: Rojas, I., Joya, G., Catala, A. (eds.) IWANN 2017. LNCS, vol. 10306, pp. 575–584. Springer, Cham (2017). https://doi.org/10.1007/978-3-319-59147-6_49
20. Hartley, R., Zisserman, A.: Multiple view geometry, vol. 53, no. 9 (2003)

Author Index